The Handbook of Infant, Child, and Adolescent Psychotherapy

The Handbook of Infant, Child, and Adolescent Psychotherapy
A Guide to Diagnosis and Treatment

Reiss-Davis Child Study Center
Volume 1

edited by

Bonnie S. Mark, Ph.D.
and James A. Incorvaia, Ph.D.

JASON ARONSON INC.
Northvale, New Jersey
London

This book was set in 10 point Garamond by TechType of Upper Saddle River, New Jersey, and printed and bound by Book-mart Press of North Bergen, NJ.

Library of Congress Cataloging-in-Publication Data

The handbook of infant, child, and adolescent psychotherapy / edited by Bonnie S. Mark and James Incorvaia.
    p. cm.
  Includes bibliographical references and index.
  Partial Contents: v. 1. A guide to diagnosis and treatment.
  ISBN 1-56821-444-8 (v. 1)
    1. Child psychotherapy. 2. Infant psychotherapy. 3. Adolescent psychotherapy. I. Mark, Bonnie S. II. Incorvaia, James.
  [DNLM: 1. Mental Disorders—in infancy & childhood. 2. Mental Disorders—in adolescence. 3. Disabled—psychology.
4. Psychotherapy—in infancy & childhood. 5. Psychotherapy—in adolescence. WS 350.2 H2356 1995]
RJ504.H3614 1995
618.92'8914—dc20
DNLM/DLC
for Library of Congress   94–44248

Manufactured in the United States of America. Jason Aronson Inc. offers books and cassettes. For information and catalog write to Jason Aronson Inc., 230 Livingston Street, Northvale, New Jersey 07647.

Contents

PART V:

SELF-INHIBITING AND SELF-DESTRUCTIVE BEHAVIOR: REEXAMINING MIND, BODY, AND PSYCHOSOMATIC DISORDERS

PART VI:

ISSUES OF TRANSFERENCE AND COUNTERTRANSFERENCE IN PSYCHOTHERAPY

Preface

As the Reiss-Davis Child Study Center approaches a half-century of service to children, adolescents, and families in the greater Los Angeles area, the staff, consultants, and alumni felt it was an appropriate time to develop a series of books containing articles that reflect the dynamic philosophy underpinning all the curricular and clinical work done at the center.

The Reiss-Davis Child Study Center was the dream of Oscar Reiss, a Los Angeles pediatrician who, in the 1940s, wanted to develop a center for children that would offer both diagnostic and psychotherapeutic services on a sliding scale. Through the effort of his family and friends, and the hard work and dedicated commitment of one of his young colleagues, David Davis, his dream came to fruition in 1950 with the opening of a storefront mental health clinic called the Oscar Reiss Clinic for Child

Guidance, with Davis becoming the Center's first board president.

To honor the contributions made by the founders, the Center was first renamed the Reiss-Davis Child Guidance Clinic. In 1965 it was given the name by which it is now widely recognized, the Reiss-Davis Child Study Center.

Since its inception, Reiss-Davis has not only served the mental health needs of young people in Los Angeles but has also graduated many professionals from its postgraduate and postdoctoral training programs in the fields of psychiatry, psychology, clinical social work, and educational psychology. Fellows have come to the Center from more than twenty-five states across the United States, and from other countries, including Argentina, Australia, Brazil, Canada, China, England, Ecuador, France, Iceland, Israel, and Japan. Thanks to the dreams of Oscar Reiss, realized in our fellowship program—and through our fellows—the Reiss-Davis Child Study Center helps to meet the mental health needs of children around the globe.

Reiss-Davis has also become internationally known and respected in the field of children's mental health through the psychoanalytically oriented writings of some of its illustrious staff members over the years, including Rocco Motto (director of Reiss-Davis from 1953 until his retirement in 1977, and the person most responsible for actualizing and expanding on Reiss's dream), Rudolf Ekstein, Seymour Friedman, Chris Heinicke, the late Mortimer Meyer, and many others.

Over the years Reiss-Davis has been especially known for offering among its services, when indicated, long-term, intensive psychoanalytically oriented psychotherapy to children. While dedicated to a psychodynamic understanding of children, the Reiss-Davis Child Study Center has not, however, limited its services to only one mode of treatment and/or intervention. Its affiliation with and move to the grounds of Vista del Mar Child and Family Services in 1977 has allowed the Center to expand its services to the psychotherapeutic intervention of residentially placed children and adolescents, diagnostic services to children in Vista's foster placement and adoptions program, as well as intra-agency referrals to the other affiliates of Julia Ann Singer Center and Home-SAFE.

The Center has also attempted to meet the multifaceted needs of the diverse population of patients it serves in the Los Angeles community by offering many other programs and services for assessment and remediation, including the Learning Disabilities Clinic (PEDS) for children, adolescents, and young adults who are having problems learning; the Children of Divorce/ Stepfamily Resource Clinic for parents and their children who need help around the problems and realities of marital dissolution and/or blending families; the ADHD Clinic for children and adolescents suspected of having attention deficit disorder with or without hyperactivity; the Mother-Infant-Toddler Program for mothers who are having difficulties bonding effectively with their newborns and toddlers; and the Bridges to Understanding Project, a school-based service for middle-school children to help young teens deal more effectively with issues of prejudice and intolerance in the schools and in the community.

Additionally, the Center offers community outreach through its speakers bureau, school consultation service, continuing education programs, and its school-based mental heath services to South Central and East Los Angeles and Watts through contracts with the State Department of Mental Health in the Primary Intervention Program (PIP), and the state department of education in the Healthy Start Program.

Finally, the Center is involved in researching aspects of children's mental health in the following areas: the study of the effectiveness of outcomes of psychotherapy using multiple Rorschach testing throughout the course of therapy; the study of clinic-based child mental health care in conjunction with UCLA and the National Institute for Mental Health as part of a study by Dr. John Weisz; the effects of maternal bonding on a young child's self-esteem; the effects of in-school counseling intervention groups in the area of prejudice on students' attitudes toward other ethnic and racial groups and on their self-esteem; and the effects of differential diagnostics on the intervention strategies of ADD/ADHD children and adolescents.

These programs and services, offered to address the needs of children and their families in the Los Angeles area, fulfill the fourfold mission established by Oscar Reiss almost 50 years ago when he mandated that the Center would first, offer emotionally disturbed children, adolescents, and their families a mental health facility that would include quality diagnostic and therapeutic services on a sliding scale; second, offer graduates in the fields of psychiatry, psychology, and clinical social work specialized advanced training in working with the mental health needs of children, adolescents, and their families; third, offer mental health research in the area of childhood emotional disturbance; and fourth, offer community education and outreach to mental health professionals, educators, and the lay community in the greater Los Angeles area.

This series of books represents another example of the Center's commitment to mental health education and outreach as it endeavors to offer those in the field of mental health a compilation of articles by professionals who have been affiliated with or have had a significant influence on the staff and fellows of the Reiss-Davis Child Study Center.

Volume 1 of the *Handbook of Infant, Child, and Adolescent Psychotherapy* represents a collection of the professional writings of child and family specialists in the areas of psychiatry, psychology, clinical social work, education, and child development who have been in some way associated with the Reiss-Davis Child Study Center. The authors include clinicians from throughout the United States, England, and Switzerland with theoretical orientations ranging from self psychology and object relations to cognitive, relational, and developmental schools of thought. The articles they contribute to this volume offer the clinician a comprehensive look at numerous issues in the assessment and treatment of mental health problems in working with infants, children, adolescents, and their families.

This first volume is divided into eight parts: Part I focuses on issues of infant development and includes chapters by internationally known researchers and analysts Bertrand Cramer, Daniel Stern, and James Grotstein; Part II focuses on new directions in assessment of children and families and includes chapters by Robert Moradi on treatment planning through the family therapy evaluation, Van Dyke De Golia on an integrated model for parent and child work, and James Incorvaia on the use of inquiry in doing psychological diagnostic assessments; Part III focuses on issues of treating children and adolescents with learning and physical disabilities and includes chapters by Joseph Palombo on treating nonspecific learning disabilities, Donald Tessmer and Janet Ciriello on a long-term psychoeducational child–parent treatment case, and Renee Cohen on working with visually impaired infants and their families; Part IV focuses on issues of physical and emotional abuse and trauma and includes chapters by Morton Shane on trauma uncovered in the analysis of an adolescent, Idell Natterson on issues of sexual abuse in the treatment of children, Esther Fine on the psychodynamic issues of child abuse, and Bonnie Mark on the psychotherapeutic uncovering of the trauma of family dysfunction in a patient's attempt to understand his childhood and adolescence; Part V focuses on issues of mind–body and psychosomatic dysfunction, and includes chapters by Rita Lynn on treating an eating disordered adolescent, Shelley Alhanati on a psychoanalytic approach to mind–body issues, and Carl Hoppe on the use of short-term techniques in working with a young inhibited, traumatized child. Part VI focuses on issues of transference and countertransference and includes chapters by Carol Francis on transference and countertransference issues in play therapy, Estelle Shane on a self-psychological view of impasses in therapy, and Irene Pierce Stiver and Jean Baker Miller on aspects of healing in psychotherapy; Part VII focuses on the specialized use of metaphor and fairy tales in psychotherapy and includes chapters by Joan Lang on what the metaphors of fairy tales signify for female patients, and Rudolf and Jean Ekstein on the use of rewriting fairy tales in working with children and adolescents; and Part VIII focuses on a dialogue between Rudolf Ekstein and Bruno Bettelheim, two psychoanalysts who were on staff at Reiss-Davis and pioneers in the use of fairy tales in therapeutic work with children.

It is the hope of all of us at the Center that the readers of this series of books will be stimulated by its many offerings and find it a useful tool in their attempts to meet the mental health needs of their young clients.

James A. Incorvaia, Ph.D.
Executive Director
Reiss-Davis Child Study Center

Acknowledgments

We wish first of all to thank all the authors of Volume 1 of this *Handbook* for their willingness to share with us their contributions to this book and for their acceptance of suggestions for modifications of the material. This book represents their collective energy and efforts.

Many others have contributed to completing this book. We offer thanks and appreciation to all of the administrative and support staff at Reiss-Davis with particular thanks to Jill Loew for her patience and perseverance, and to Mildred Smoodin for her very thorough proofreading of many of the chapters in this first volume. A special thank you to Donald Tessmer for many hours of assistance including organizing, reading, and suggesting revisions to numerous drafts of the chapters in this book. We want to thank Marion Solomon for introducing the concept of writing a collective text and for her consistent encouragement and inspiration as a clinician and writer. We are also grateful to Jonathan Judaken for his editorial expertise and constant search for clarity and to Lee Freehling, Reiss-Davis librarian, for her encouragement throughout this project. A most special thank you to Ariel Mark, still young, but always inspiring his mother to question and to learn.

We want to acknowledge the tremendous support and encouragement offered by the staff, alumni, and fellows at the Reiss-Davis Child Study Center as we prepared this book for publication. We also want to thank Gerald Zaslaw, CEO of Vista del Mar Child and Family Services, and its affiliated agencies of the Reiss-Davis Child Study Center, the Julia Ann Singer Center, and Home-SAFE, for his continued support for this book.

Finally, we want to thank Michael Moskowitz, Ruth Brody, and especially Jason Aronson at Jason Aronson Inc. for giving us the opportunity to make Volume 1 of the *Handbook of Infant, Child, and Adolescent Psychotherapy* a reality.

Bonnie S. Mark, Ph.D.
James A. Incorvaia, Ph.D.

Contributors

Shelley Alhanati, Ph.D.
Consultant and Supervisor, Reiss-Davis Child Study Center.

Janet Ciriello, Ed.D.
Chairperson, Psychology Service and Leader of the Postdoctoral Training Program in Psychodynamic Child and Adolescent Psychotherapy and Psychodiagnosis, Reiss-Davis Child Study Center

Renee A. Cohen, Ph.D.
Psychologist in private practice, West Los Angeles, California.

Bertrand Cramer, M.D.
Vice President, World Association for Infant Mental Health.

Van Dyke De Golia, M.D.
Medical Director, Reiss-Davis Child Study Center
Assistant Clinical Professor of Psychiatry, UCLA School of Medicine.

Jean Ekstein, M.S.
Elementary school teacher, Los Angeles Unified School District.

Rudolf Ekstein, Ph.D.
Clinical Professor of Medical Psychology, UCLA
Training Analyst, Los Angeles Psychoanalytic Society/Institute and Southern California Psychoanalytic Institute.

Esther Fine, L.C.S.W.
Child psychologist, Reiss-Davis Child Study Center.

Carol A. Francis, Psy.D.
Clinical psychologist in private practice, Torrance, California.

James S. Grotstein, M.D.
Clinical Professor of Psychiatry, UCLA School of Medicine
Training and Supervising Analyst, Los Angeles Psychoanalytic Society/Institute and Psychoanalytic Center of California, Los Angeles.

Carl Hoppe, Ph.D.
Psychologist in private practice, West Los Angeles, California.

James A. Incorvaia, Ph.D.
Executive Director, Reiss-Davis Child Study Center

Joan A. Lang, M.D.
Professor of Psychiatry, University of Texas Medical Branch, Galveston.

Rita Lynn
Group analyst and supervisor in private practice, West Los Angeles, California.

Bonnie S. Mark, Ph.D.
Senior Staff Consultant, Reiss-Davis Child Study Center
Director, Center for Psychological Services
Psychologist in private practice, West Los Angeles, California.

Jean Baker Miller, M.D.
Clinical Professor of Psychiatry, Boston University School of
Medicine
Director of Education, Stone Center, Wellesley College.

Robert Moradi, M.D.
Assistant Clinical Professor of Psychiatry, UCLA School of
Medicine.

Idell Natterson, Ph.D.
Clinical Social Worker and Educational Psychologist in private practice, Beverly Hills, California.

Joseph Palombo, L.C.S.W.
Founding Dean, Institute for Clinical Social Work, Chicago
Faculty Member, Child and Adolescent Psychotherapy Pro-
gram, Chicago Institute for Psychoanalysis
Research Associate, Department of Pediatrics, Rush-Presby-
terian-St. Luke's Medical Center.

Estelle Shane, Ph.D.
Training and Supervising Analyst, The Institute of Contemporary Psychoanalysis.

Morton Shane, M.D.
Clinical Professor of Psychiatry, UCLA
Training and Supervising Analyst, The Institute of Contempo-
rary Psychoanalysis.

Daniel Stern, M.D.
Professor of Psychiatry and Human Development, Brown
University and University of Geneva, Switzerland
Director of Research, Butler Hospital, Providence, Rhode
Island.

Irene Pierce Stiver, Ph.D.
Senior Consultant, Women's Treatment Program, McLean Hospital, Belmont, Massachusetts
Lecturer on Psychology, Department of Psychiatry, Harvard Medical School.

Donald Tessmer, Ph.D.
Director, Learning Disabilities Clinic and Co-Director, Attention Deficit Disorder Clinic, Reiss-Davis Child Study Center.

PART I

New Directions in Infant Research and Treatment

INTRODUCTION TO PART I

Some of the most important contributions to understanding the emotional problems of children and adolescents have come from the fields of infant psychiatry and child development. It is within the early roots of development that the complexities of child and adolescent psychopathology can best be understood.

Reiss-Davis's approach to understanding the emotional problems of the young people it serves begins with the developmental lines of Anna Freud. Postgraduate fellows are offered training in child development, child/adolescent psychopathology, and infant observation. In fact, one of the key figures in setting up the Child Development Training Program and encouraging the Mother–Infant-Toddler Program was the late Ruth

Pierce, one of the pioneers in this field and someone whose work influenced generations of Los Angeles clinicians.

The three analysts who have contributed to this section of the *Handbook* are well known in Los Angeles, but their work is international in scope. Their chapters examine the beginnings of a child's life, exploring predispositions and behavioral characteristics that forge individual temperament and contribute to the psychic life of the infant. All three contributors reexamine the current psychoanalytic models of infant development, based on their extensive research.

Chapter 1, by Bertrand Cramer, "The Beginnings of Psychic Life," reassesses the significance of the reconstruction of early psychic events and discusses a wide range of contemporary psychoanalytic approaches to the problem by focusing on the mother–child interaction as it affects the infant's psychic experience. Exemplifying Cramer's theoretical perspective are two detailed case illustrations: the first deals with an eating inhibition transmitted from mother to child, the second with a mother who experienced her child's behavior as rough and aggressive.

In Chapter 2, "One Way to Build a Clinically Relevant Child," Daniel Stern extends his innovative work on the infant's representation of his or her own experiences. Stern's seminal 1985 book, *The Interpersonal World of the Infant,* introduced the term *RIGS* (the representation of an interaction that has been generalized). Here he presents an analogous new concept, *schema-of-way-of-being-with,* explaining that this new term is conceptualized from the assumed "subjective" point of view of the infant involved in the interaction. Stern highlights behavior that is enacted or experienced by the infant as goal-directed or motivated conduct that results in what he calls an "emergent moment." Many of these moments form a network of schemas that he argues represent the infant's lived experience. Six schematic formats, drawn from the clinical examples of an infant with a depressed mother, are discussed.

In Chapter 3, James Grotstein continues to probe the arena of early development by exploring the nebulous yet undeniable existence of the infant's psychic life. "The Infantile Neurosis Reassessed" reviews infant psychic phenomena as evidenced by developmental research and clinical observation. Grotstein incorporates the conclusions of researchers and clinicians, addresses apparent contradictions and disparities in their investigations, and proposes his working model of the infant's psychic life by synthesizing findings from researchers' "labs" and analysts' "couches." He raises several questions concerning the developmental stages of the infant's unconscious, including the role of neurosis and psychosis in this development, as well as a consideration of whether the infant's intrapsychic world corresponds with that of the adult's regressive memory.

1

The Beginnings of Psychic Life

Bertrand Cramer, M.D.

THE SEARCH FOR THE ORIGINS OF PSYCHIC LIFE

How do we pinpoint the earliest manifestations of psychic activity? Does it take place in the fetus or in the newborn, or only later, when the child develops the capacity for language? Or, as work done with parents and babies suggests, have the future baby's psychic contents already germinated before conception as a result of the parents' combined fantasied projections?

Various "families" of psychoanalytic theorists view this controversial question very differently. The Kleinian perspective is the most radical in assigning a rich fantasy life to babies. But for many French psychoanalysts, fantasies are elaborated through deferred action (which translates the German Freudian concept of *Nachträgigkeit* or the French concept of *après-coup*) and are shaped by many revisions that take place long after the incipient stages of life. It is thus fruitless to look for authentic, pure, archaic contents, and infant observation is useless in illuminating unconscious processes. Ego psychologists, on the other hand, have fostered the method of infant observation with the precise aim of identifying early manifestations of fantasies and conflicts.

Generally, the genetic point of view and the search for a reconstruction of early psychic events has lost credibility in many quarters, and is no longer considered—in its pure form—as the major paradigm in psychoanalysis. Infancy is viewed less as a real state and more as a metaphor that needs to be rediscovered in analysis. This relative decline of the genetic point of view is due in great part to a change in theory: actual reconstruction of what *really* happened in infancy appears to be as impossible a task as finding an answer to a poorly formulated question. Construction, however, appears to take the leading role, especially if we take into account two factors: first, the analysand can produce versions of his or her past that have been reorganized according to the logic of later stages, and second, the contribution of the analyst's theory about the past plays a crucial role in interpreting the final product.

MOTHERS ARE PART OF THE BABY'S PSYCHIC LIFE

So then why continue to work with young infants?

My contention is that the analyst working in the field of infancy who follows the lead of Winnicott, who considered that "there is no such thing as an infant"—that is, where we find an infant, we find maternal care (Khan 1975)—*can* study how the mother contributes to shape the infant's inner world and how the infant reacts to this influence. In a setting of mother–infant conjoint psychotherapy, the mother consults on behalf of her symptomatic infant and, in so doing, reveals how she views the infant in terms of mental representations based on her own storehouse of memories, fantasies, and unconscious conflicts. The advantage (aside from comfort) to the therapist over *direct* infant observation is the ability to interpret the mother's projective identifications onto the child in terms of her own unconscious conflicts as she reveals them to the therapist.[1]

The objection could be raised that in this method we are dealing with the mother's psychic functioning and not the infant's. But, in fact, as we will see in detail later, the baby is immersed in the mother's psychic functioning, which becomes one of the founding blocks of the baby's own inner life. The reality of the mother's penetration of the baby through her projective identifications, and the baby's need to cope with this "foreign body," is my basic hypothesis. Babies, because they need to cathect their mothers' thoughts, feelings, and attitudes, are either forced to *introject* or *eject* these maternal projections. More often, they compose with them, taking them into account in their own economy of pleasures and pains, of fantasies and values.

I thus suggest that a conjoint psychotherapeutic setting allows us to study how mothers and babies deal with their respective needs, desires, and prohibitions; how they communicate these issues to each other; and how together they enact the issues behaviorally.[2] While psychoanalysis has taught us to consider the infant as the creator of its fantasy world, I am trying here to tease out themes and styles that are internalized by the infant from the store of maternal unconscious contents and are complementary to what the infant creates on its own.

MOTHER–BABY INTERACTION

In each mother–infant dyad we observe a characteristic form of interaction—with original, mutual creations by child and

---

[1]For a detailed study of technique in mother–infant psychotherapy, see Cramer and Palacio-Espasa (1993).

[2]For a scientific study of interactions in joint psychotherapy, see Cramer and Stern (1988).

mother—around all the basic issues of the self and relationships: feeding, sleeping, approach and withdrawal, greeting and separating, excitement and restraint, the diminishing of arousal, and so on. Soon a set of conventions is created, determining in fairly rigid ways how each step of the day is negotiated. Shared meanings are created, defining what is pleasurable and what is frightening, what is idealized and what is despised, what being a boy or a girl requires. Zones or personal boundaries are created, defining what can be shared and what must remain secret, what can be explored and what remains out of bounds. In essence, this mutual creation of the meanings of experience develops into a philosophy of life. Through this process family traditions are transmitted, and babies enter into a specific cultural milieu. If we believe that such a powerful sharing of meanings is at work in the complex and repeated structure of early interactions, we are tempted to say—as does the title of this chapter—that we are witnessing the beginnings of psychic structure, and that these beginnings contribute to ego formation, to the construction of identifications, to the selection of preferred modes of defense and drive discharge. We might even postulate that the forerunners of ethics, aesthetics, and talents are embedded in these earliest interactions.

SYMPTOMATIC INTERACTIVE SEQUENCES

In conjoint psychotherapy we are often able to distinguish a clear correspondence between a core conflict in the mother—revealed by her own account of her problems with the infant—and the enactment of this core conflict in repeated interactions. I call this dynamic *symptomatic interactive sequences*. These interactions are surprisingly precise, revealing through the details of gestures, approach and withdrawal, voice intonations, and mimicry simultaneously the mother's focal conflict with her child and the resulting compromises created by both mother and baby. Rhythm, sequential order, and intensity are all crucial ingredients of this behavioral vocabulary.

A Case of Eating Inhibition

Jane, a 12-month-old baby, was referred because of feeding negativism. She would refuse what her mother offered by turning her head away. The mother, Ann, was upset because she "loves to prepare food and hates to have to throw it away." Ann announced that she is a gourmet and loves to eat, just like all the other members of her family, for whom eating is a main attraction. But this love of eating, which was almost an addiction, was conflictual on several accounts. First, Ann feels obese and ugly because of overeating. Second, eating for her is highly sexualized by haunting memories of hysterical vomiting in childhood after witnessing parental oral intercourse. Moreover, eating was her main filiation with her father, who was a baker, for whom she entertained conscious incestuous fantasies. Presently, she has two concerns: that her husband will seduce their infant daughter, and that Jane might start overeating, just as Ann herself has done.

Two issues were evident at the beginning of this mother–infant psychotherapy:

1. The mother confused overeating with unchecked sexual impulse.
2. The mother unconsciously planned to curb her infant's potential impulsiveness by teaching her elementary discipline. She wanted to introduce ascetic controls aimed at curbing a wayward sexuality, enforcing rigid control over the child's overeating propensities. She had succeeded so well in this project that she had inadvertently induced a form of anorexia in her daughter.

In what follows, I illustrate how such a form of superego intrapsychic conflict is enacted at the interpersonal level with the child, who now represents the mother's unbridled impulsive self.

The Symptomatic Interactive Sequence between Ann and Jane

This therapy was recorded on video, which makes a convincing demonstration of symptomatic interaction. I will try to capture this sequence through words.

Ann begins by explaining that her struggle against overeating is a daily concern, that she berates herself constantly, muttering to herself: "You fat slob, stop gorging yourself with this disgusting junk." She is despondent as she relates this fact about herself. At the same time, Jane, who is sitting on Ann's lap, turns to a large bag that Ann carries with her; Jane opens the cover and digs into the bag, out of which she pulls a chocolate bar. While Ann continues to talk to me, she notices Jane's gesture and says to her: "You're going to dirty yourself all over the place," while trying to pull away the chocolate.

This interdiction was the first of six similar prohibitions given over a 10-minute period, and spoken in a low voice, almost automatically, while Ann kept talking to me about her own problems. The verbal prohibitions were accompanied by gestures such as pulling the chocolate away, closing the paper wrapping, and so on. On one occasion, there was a real struggle: Ann pulled the chocolate bar away and Jane kept reaching for it, grunting in a show of irritation. On two occasions, Ann broke a piece of chocolate and put it in her own mouth! Once, Ann emitted a disgusted grunt as Jane put the chocolate in her mouth.

Several features of this sequence are remarkable. Ann was extremely persistent and unbending in her prohibitions. This censorship role seemed to function automatically, as if it were part of a well-established routine, probably not quite conscious, for Ann. There was also an amazing temporal and thematic coincidence. It was while Ann was talking about her inability to control her own oral impulses that Jane enacted the conflict by asserting her right to fulfill *her* oral impulses, which caused the struggle around the chocolate bar. It was as if mother and child had prearranged to perform a psychodrama of Ann's most pressing conflict. Clearly, this interactive sequence was symptomatic: it linked both the mother's and the infant's symptoms (overeating and anorexia). The mother–infant interaction was used as a stage on which intrapsychic conflict was played out: Jane represented unchecked oral impulses, and Ann kept in check her daughter's impulses where *she* failed in controlling her own. An intrapsychic conflict had now moved to the interpersonal level, and Jane was used as a prop to enact the conflict.

When I questioned Ann on the meaning of her strict behavior in this sequence, she explained that she knew that she could not control her "alimentary orgies" and that overeating is "a delicious but piggish vice." The sexualization of eating is obvious, and she explained that most of all she wanted to prevent Jane from one day feeling like she does. She revealed that she "hated the round shapes that attract men's attention." Her ideal was to be an anorectic girl or even a boy with no shape.

It was important to interpret Ann's unconscious wish to turn Jane into a sexless being to prevent Jane's submitting to impulses she could no more control than could her mother. In this case, the mother was trying to induce her baby girl into becoming her ideal, *the opposite of herself*. Experiencing herself as fat, ugly, and sexual, she wanted her daughter to be like a boy, thin and ascetic in her relationship to her drives. It was this ego ideal that organized all aspects of her interactions around feeding her daughter. Disciplining her daughter's alimentary initiative was a *must* for Ann, as it allowed her the illusion that, through her daughter, she would create her longed-for ego ideal of total mastery over her body and denial of her feminine seductiveness.

The therapy had two main effects: the child resumed eating, but more important, the mother discovered that her child was different from her, that she would not necessarily turn into an "obese, oversexed slob."

The Infant's Subjective Experience

Now let's ponder the infant's experience. I would postulate that the infant daughter developed fairly strong concepts in the following areas:

1. To be loved by her mother, she had to restrain any impulsive need to eat, which she managed well by creating anorectic behavior. (This shows the extreme efforts infants will make in order to submit to their mothers' ego ideals, *which become an integral part of their own systems*).
2. She should extend this ascetic trend to other domains, thus heralding her own attitude toward other drives.
3. Her opposition to feeding might be an equivalent to her mother's defenses against intrusion into her bodily sphere, probably originating in sexual fears.

4. She might have been structuring her ego ideal around a central theme of delaying gratification and therefore possibly developing a pleasure in frustration.

These are all hypotheses, the content of which we cannot prove or disprove, but three points are clear:

1. The mother's conflict over drive control, and her confusion between sexuality and feeding, profoundly influenced her interactions with her daughter, induced her daughter into creating anorectic behavior, and affected her daughter's acquired meanings about food and drive discharge.
2. Mother and infant created together a symptomatic interactive sequence, which became a preferential mode of relating and a vehicle for mutual communication. This collusion centered on the area of impulse control and denial of gratification.
3. The psychotherapeutic resolution of the mother's own conflict altered the interaction *and* the child's attitude. The anorexia was cured. This change brought with it correlated changes in the child's subjective experience and in several aspects of her psychic functioning.

If the mother no longer needs to exert her control vicariously, through the infant, we may hope that an ego-ideal of ascetic control becomes less compulsory in the child, as the lifting of the anorexia seems to indicate.

A Case of Infant Aggression

Let us turn to another case of a mother, Mary, who was sent to me because her daughter's pediatrician was concerned about the mother's sense of helplessness with Sarah, her baby girl (13 months old).[3] The mother complained that Sarah was rough and aggressive with her, which surprised me, because Sarah seemed quite inoffensive, even passive.

---

[3]This case is described in detail, with a particular emphasis on transgenerational transmission over three generations in Cramer (1992).

The Symptomatic Interaction Sequences between Sarah and Mary

While Mary is complaining at length that Sarah hits and scratches her, little Sarah is quite subdued, sitting on her mother's knees and pulling at a ribbon attached to her mother's sweater. At one point, she brings her hand to her mother's lower lip and starts fingering it; Mary stops talking immediately and becomes hyper-alert, looking at Sarah. After a few seconds, she whispers, "You scratch . . . don't scratch . . . give me a hug." Sarah stops and drops her shoe on the ground. Mary asks, "Do you want to go down?" and she proceeds to put Sarah on the floor, facing away from her, toward me. Within ten seconds, Sarah rotates back toward her mother and reaches for Mary's shoe, but Mary withdraws her foot immediately.

I commented on Mary's expectation that contact with Sarah would be painful. I noted that Mary had positioned Sarah away from her body, as if she wanted to avoid any physical contact. Mary acknowledged that she always expects pain in their contacts, adding, "I wish she would show tenderness. She never does."

Here, the symptomatic interactive sequence enacted the mother's projection of aggression and her punishment of distancing. It was also repetitive, as was demonstrated in subsequent sessions. The compulsive nature of this scenario and the rigidity of Mary's accusations against her young daughter suggested that she was "externalizing" an inner conflict onto the interactive sphere.

In the psychotherapy we learned that this mother had had a sadomasochistic relationship with her mother. An intensely charged screen memory came back to her in the first session. At the age of 14 she slapped her mother in the face and saw her leave for work with the marks of her fingers on her cheek. This reawakened powerful guilt feelings: How could a child hit her own mother? It was simple then to show her how she was atoning now for the past guilt by suffering from the scratches that she let her daughter inflict on her face. We came to understand that she needed to project her aggression onto Sarah and to get her to act out the aggression, aiming precisely at her face.

The Infant's Subjective Experience

If we now try to imagine what the child's experience of this aggressively tinted relationship might be, we could propose that:

1. Sarah has to remain tame and passive, with little initiated body contact with mother, lest she be accused and pushed away. Yet, at the same time, she has to fulfill the terms of the contract her mother imposes on her. She has to be aggressive toward her mother in order to help her mother externalize her guilt. Thus she is caught in a double bind.
2. It is probable that for Sarah it will be difficult to disentangle affective solicitations from aggressive ones, due to her mother's confusion between the two.
3. One may assume that body contact will be fraught with anxiety and expectations of rejection in the child.

Interestingly, individual psychotherapy became necessary when Sarah was 4 years old and, in response to her mother's pregnancy, became aggressive and hyperactive. In our first session, she drew a spider "who wants to bite [her] hand." The therapist asked what Sarah's hand had done. Sarah answered, "Sarah's hand hits and bites, like the spider. At night, the spider scratched my face!" We were amazed to hear this reference to scratching the face, which three years earlier had been the main object of accusation on the mother's part. We were also impressed to note that the theme of violence to the body remained central, as if Sarah had organized her own aggression against the pregnant mother according to scenarios that had become in their own way precious, shared meanings between mother and child.

HOW MOTHERS SHAPE THEIR INFANTS' FANTASIES

This and other cases encouraged us to imagine that early interactions do indeed create furrows or trails that co-determine the shape and content of fantasies, privileged forms of relating, and, possibly, character traits in infants. Mental creations of later ages utilize imaging, values, and preferences that were co-determined early by mothers and babies as they designed together the shape of their shared experience. Needless to say, I do not believe that reconstruction in psychoanalysis locates the exact shape of these early configurations. But one *can* often discover how hidden areas of mental contents or functions were, in fact, internalized in response to the parents' own particular psychic functioning. Certain choices in life, the development of talents, the fixation on certain images are often discovered to be linked with a hidden aspect of the patient's parent's history.

CONCLUSION

Attempts to uncover this prehistorical layer of a patient's psychic functioning in conjoint psychotherapy reveal meanings shared between mothers and babies. I have suggested that we follow a reverse path to the one we usually take in thinking about the infant's creation of her psychic structure. Usually we reconstruct, or construct, what we imagine the baby's experience to be according to *her* construction of maternal representations, according to *her* drives and archaic fantasies. Here I am suggesting a complementary point of view: to examine how maternal conflicts are enacted with the baby, which, in turn, partly defines the baby's preferred modes of defense, gratification, and ego and ego–ideal contents. These shared experiences give shape to the infant's fantasies, leaving an everlasting imprint that contributes to the form and content of her psychic life.

In classical psychoanalysis, construction or reconstruction of the earliest form of psychic functioning has mainly considered the infant to be the omnipotent creator of his objects and relationships. Data on transgenerational transmission brings complementary evidence, however. Data gathered in mother–infant psychotherapies encourage us to consider that, in all aspects of functioning and of psychopathology, we would gain much by identifying how parents have oriented, focused, biased, and shaped the form and content of their infants' psychic lives.

This domain of psychic filiation is much easier to grasp when observing mothers and babies together. However, some adult patients in analysis, mostly through transference and provocation of countertransference, can provide clues that help the analyst to reformulate his or her interpretations, taking into account the parental projective identifications and imagined models of early interactions. This will not revolutionize psychoanalytic theory, but it will provide a broader interpretative imagination.

Paradoxically, I do not think that we will ever locate and describe the beginnings of psychic life, because the first traces of psychic life are shadows of the parents' own psychic contents. What appear as early forms are, in fact, already the continuation of earlier events in the parents' histories. The best metaphor for conceptualizing psychic time is the snake that bites its tail. Infants become human because of what parents lend them as humanness.

REFERENCES

Cramer, B. (1992). *The Importance of Being a Baby.* Reading, MA: Addison-Wesley.

Cramer, B., and Palacio-Espasa, F. (1993). *La pratique des psychothérapies mères–bébés.* Paris: PUF.

Cramer, B., and Stern, D. N. (1988). Evaluation of changes in mother–infant brief psychotherapy: a single case study. *Infant Mental Health Journal* 9:20–45.

Khan, M. R. (1975). Introduction. In *Through Paediatrics to Psychoanalysis,* by D. W. Winnicott. The International Psychoanalytical Library. London: Hogarth.

2

One Way to Build a Clinically Relevant Child[1]

Daniel N. Stern, M.D.

INTRODUCTION

The object-related representational world of the infant—
made up of the baby's subjective experience of participating in

[1] An earlier version of this text is to appear in the *Journal de la psychanalyse de l'enfant*.

The ideas in this article have been presented at several occasions to a work group on "Psychoanalysis and Artificial Intelligence" assembled by André Haynal and consisting of him, Guy Céllerier, Marc Archinard, Jean-Jacques Ducret, Michel Heller, Olivier Réal, Richard Vuagniaux, and me. I wish to thank the members of this group for the suggestions, criticisms, and many ideas they have contributed.

interpersonal events—holds the greatest clinical interest for us. But, we wonder, what might a representation of an object-related subjective experience be like? This is the question we will explore in this chapter.

What we need is something like an object-related, interpersonal-experience schema; a schema that includes, all together, the feelings, actions, thoughts, perceptions, motivations, and so on that are lived during an interpersonal event; a schema that captures what it is like to "be-with-another-in-a-certain-way"; and a schema that well represents the affective components of experience. Are such schemas available to us, conceptually speaking?

Psychoanalysis and much of developmental psychology traditionally considered that representations had to be in the basic form of perceptual schemas (e.g., images) or of conceptual schemas (e.g., symbols). Piaget, of course, added sensorimotor schemas as another basic form of representation. Nelson and Greundel (1981), Nelson (1986), Mandler (1979, 1983, 1988), Shank and Abelson (1977), and Shank (1982) have added another basic form of human representation available to children, namely, a sequence of events that is represented as a script, or scenario, or event representation. So we have at least four different kinds of basic representational formats to work with in creating something like a whole-experience schema: percepts, concepts, sensorimotor operations, and event sequences.

Any one of these formats alone is inadequate to our task, and even all of them taken together are not sufficient and would not produce much of clinical interest. They are sufficient for explaining motor acts, event knowledge, and so on—good for explaining what they were created to explain. But as concerns object-related subjective experience, we need at least two other forms of representation. These are a basic format for representing affects and motivation, and a format for representing the whole experience.

With regard to the first, it has proven difficult to conceptualize how affects are represented. On the one hand, many clinicians have insisted that because of the phenomenon of "free-floating" affect, that is, affect that appears to be unattached or detached from thoughts, motives, or perceptions, we need a way of representing affect that is independent from cognition, perception, and motor action. We have a tendency to view affect as linked to other mental events in its representations, to cognition or event knowledge (Bretherton 1984), or to motivation and adaptive goals (Trevarthen 1993). In any case, we rarely specify what the nature of such representations might be.

I suggest that affects are represented multiply in several forms. The one that will interest us most is what I call the *temporal feeling shape*, the temporal contour of feeling that unfolds during a moment in which a motive is in play. The motive can be of almost any kind: wanting and waiting to be fed, trying to capture Mother's attention, or trying to disengage from an interaction with her. The temporal feeling shape combines into a single subjective experience that shifts in activation/arousal, hedonic tone, intensity of affect, strength of the activated motivation, and quality of affect, all in the course of a lived moment. The temporal feature—the time contour of these shifts—is the structural backbone of the feeling experience. Subjectively speaking, all of these co-occurring shifts are experienced and represented as one feeling shape, much as a phrase of polyphonic music would be. The experience is one of being "in time" and that the time is being contoured subjectively. It is called a temporal feeling shape, or *feeling shape* for short, for reasons to be fully explained below. I tentatively propose the feeling shape as a basic format that infants might use for representing the affective experience that accompanies the physical or mental enactment of a motive.

The second needed addition to our notions of representational formats is some kind of representation of the whole experience of being-with-another-in-a-certain-way. The whole experience includes some (or all) of the experiences in each of the basic representational formats (sensorimotor, perceptual, conceptual, scripts, feeling shapes). Each of these separate schemas—as a fundamental representational format—is processed independently and in parallel with the others. But this raises the question of how the whole experience, as represented, can be re-evoked and relived from its diverse, separate component schemas. One solution—compatible with and inspired by recent developments in cognitive science—is to suppose that the subjective phenomena of a whole experience are an emergent property of the activation of the network of schemas. This is conceptually possible, but still seems somewhat magical without the guidance of preexisting formats that provide a general structure for the emergent property. A whole-experience schema is just such a format.

I suggest that a narrative-like format, or *protonarrative enve-lope,* is the fundamental representational format that coordinates the separate basic schemas into a single, subjective, emergent whole experience. The basic assumption here is that the enactment of a motive, during a moment, is naturally parsed as a narrative-like structure. Accordingly, all moments of being-with-another-in-a-certain-way are also represented as proto-narrative envelopes. Finally, we have six different parallel schemas: perceptual, conceptual, sensorimotor, scripts, feeling shapes, and the more holistic proto-narrative envelope. To-gether, they form a network of schemas, or *schema-of-being-with.* It is a composite unit, capable of yielding emergent properties and intuitively appealing from a clinical point of view. But before examining these suggestions further, I will give an extended example of what I mean clinically by a schema-of-being-with.

CLINICAL EXAMPLES OF SCHEMAS-OF-BEING-WITH: AN INFANT WITH A DEPRESSED MOTHER

This clinical situation has been chosen as illustrative for the following reason. While we cannot know the nature of the infant's subjective experience, we can observe the interpersonal events that transpire between an infant and a depressed mother. We can also know how adults who as infants had depressed mothers reconstruct their early experience. For the former perspective, I will rely on my own clinical experience, and, even more, on the many excellent observational reports on infants with depressed mothers, which are largely in agreement (Emde

1983a, Field 1987, Lewis and Miller 1990, Murray 1988, 1992, Osofsky et al. 1990).

For the report on how adults in psychoanalysis reconstruct their early experience with a depressed mother, I will rely on A. Green's account of the "dead mother complex," by which he means a mother who is physically present but psychically absent (Green 1986).

These two different perspectives, observational and reconstructive, while not identical, are remarkably convergent. This convergence encourages me, using both, to postulate the nature of the infant's experiences of being-with-a-depressed-mother (I will comment in passing on some of the differences between these two viewpoints).

When mothers get depressed, there is not quite the "brutal change" and "love lost at one blow" that adult patients may describe as a single, clear, traumatic event as reconstructed. Rather, there is a progressive process of usually partial disengagement. Instead of one traumatic subjective experience, there are at least four different subjective experiences—leading to four separate schemas-of-being-with—that together start to make up part of the infant's representational world from the beginning of the mother's psychic "disappearance" in the context of her physical presence. I will only give summarized accounts of the schemas involved. These are:

An Experience of Repeated Microdepression

Compared with the infant's expectations and wishes, the depressed mother's face is flat and expressionless. She breaks eye contact and does not seek to reestablish it. Her contingent responsiveness is less. There is a disappearance of her animation, tonicity, and so on. Resonant invariants are evoked in the infant: the flight of his animation, a deflation of his posture, a fall in positive affect and facial expressivity, a decrease in activation. The experience is descriptively one of a microdepression.

What gives these moments their special character is that they are triggered by a desire/motive to be with the mother. After the infant's attempts to invite and solicit the mother—to come to life, to be there emotionally, to play—have failed, the infant, it appears, tries to be with her by way of identification and imitation. (It is becoming more clear that the infant's microdepressions are the result not only of lack of responsive stimulation from the mother, which is nonspecific, but also the result of imitative and/or contagious processes, which are highly specific.) The two phenomena, trying to be with via identificatory/ imitative means and the experience of depression, become linked together in a single "moment" of subjective experience with a characteristic temporal feeling shape. This combination of the two phenomena is a recurrent way-of-being-with-Mother, which is identifiable and becomes represented as a regular part of the infant's subjective experience. Many schemas parallel to it form, and the network of these schemas makes up a schema-of-being-with. Clinical evidence that corroborates these descriptions has been observed by Osofsky (personal communication).

Certain adult patients often exhibit abrupt and usually short-lived plunges in positive affect that do not have an obvious external trigger. Clinical inquiry reveals that the moment of abrupt hedonic fall correlates with the memory, phantasy, or a current attempt to identify with someone.

One way to think about such a situation clinically is to realize that microdepressions and desires or attempts to identify are associated—this could imply that the two parts being associated come from different "places" originally, and the dynamic reason behind the association may be clinically interesting. However, from the point of view of schemas-of-being-with, the desire to identify and microdepressive states have not been "associated" in the usual sense; they belong together—from the beginning—in the same protonarrative envelope because they were components of a single coherent unit of interpersonal experience, that is, of repeated lived, subjective experiences-of-being-with, that became represented. In this case we seek not the reasons for the association but more about the original events that fused the two components into one subjective experience. In some cases the two approaches will arrive at the same endpoint in the same amount of time, in other cases they will not.

The Infant's Experience as Reanimator

Faced with a resonant microdepression, the infant invariably tries to get Mother to come back to life, at this stage, a coping mechanism, not a defense. It turns to face her and establish mutual eye contact. It raises its eyebrows and opens wide its eyes and mouth in an invitation to interaction. It vocalizes, smiles, gestures, and is often very creative with humor and invention. When all this doesn't work, it turns its head away for a moment and then turns back to try again. This pattern of trying to recapture and reanimate Mother (and self) is regularly seen with maternal depression and also in the experimental situation called the "still face," which was developed exactly to study what infants do under these conditions (Tronick et al. 1978).

The important point about this envelope of infant behaviors is that it sometimes works and the mother is reanimated, even though depressed. It works because maternal depression is not all or none and not constant. Mothers differ in their availability to be reanimated from day to day or from hour to hour. Most depressed mothers are very distressed by their relative unavailability for their infant and often fight harder against that than against any other feature of their depression, and with variable success. It is reasonable to think that if the infant's attempts at reanimation are rarely successful, it will gradually extinguish its efforts. And, indeed, some infants do—with their mothers at least. But many do not. (Variable, infrequent reinforcement is a good way to maintain a behavior, not to extinguish it.) And for those who do not, the experience as potential reanimator continues to be a second way-of-being-with-Mother under these conditions. It makes up a different network of schemas.

This way-of-being-with can be readily seen as one root for later developments in the direction of becoming a "charmer" or "life of the party." Part of the schema will include the gratification of having succeeded in the task of reanimation. The infant receives the rewards of having succeeded as well as the secondary benefits of success. The situation is (to exaggerate) almost addictive. It is little wonder that if such a schema becomes more important, it may play a not insignificant role in object choice. Only people in need of frequently reapplied efforts of reanimation in life are workable candidates as partners.

The Experience of Mother as a Background Context in Seeking Stimulation Elsewhere

After repeated failures at reanimation, the infant turns away to seek a more appropriate level of stimulation. Here, the invariants are the solo search for stimulation, a certain level of autoregulated vigilance and activation, an amplification of curiosity, and so on, all occurring in the invariant physical presence of Mother, but where she is an element of the background. That is, the external search for stimulation implies the mother's presence somewhere in the background. This is yet a third way-of-being-with-Mother.

It is a paradoxical way-of-being-with-another in that it makes it possible for solo acts of curiosity and searching for external stimulation to also serve as acts of attachment, to the extent that the presence of another (even though in the background) is invariably invoked by such seemingly unsocial activities.

The Experience of an Inauthentic Mother and Self

Depressed mothers often try very hard. They know only too well that they are insufficiently there for their children and insufficiently stimulating. They tend to overcompensate in bursts. They make a huge effort, reaching into their repertoire and going through the right steps, but without the feeling. The result is—for stretches of time—a certain inauthenticity revealed in failures of fine tuning and minor discrepancies of behavioral coordination. I believe that infants can discriminate a forced interactive flow from an easy flow, but they are so eager for a more enlivened interaction that they accept the minor violations and adjust their own behavior accordingly. The result—to overstate the case—is a false interaction between a false mother and a false self. The behavior is forced, the feeling is off, but the desire is very real. And it is better than nothing. This is a fourth way-of-being-with-Mother, providing a fourth network of schemas-of-being-with.

These four networks of schemas-of-being-with are likely to be present in all such cases. However, they do not exhaust the possibilities. For example, another very likely one—seen clinically—concerns a feeling of imminent but unpredictable disaster (loss/abandonment) (i.e., will the mother be psychically available—this time?). Such a schema-of-being-with could evolve, with developmental elaborations, into a variety of anxiety phenomena. Other case-specific schemas are to be expected.

The interaction with the depressed mother shuttles back and forth between these four or more schemas-of-being-with for months, that is, usually for the duration of the acute phase of the depression. Which of the four will have relative predominance is variable. Some mothers, for instance, cannot love well, but can get themselves up to stimulate the infant. These infants have less need for autostimulation or stimulation elsewhere, but the acceptable (but not optimal) stimulation they receive is without a sufficient dose of loving. Other mothers can continue to love their infants—perhaps the only persons they can still love—and it shows. But they cannot get themselves up to adequate levels of stimulation. In this case the split between exciting sensations and love tilts the other way. Or, some mothers can be reanimated (enough of the time) by their infants. This favors the infants' becoming more "antidepressant," creative signal readers and performers.

What is remarkable is that the reconstruction from adult patients in Green's account includes most of the same elements that appear in the observational-prospective account. (It adds others, of course. The prospective account can say little about reconstructions after the fact.) Where the two accounts mainly differ is in which initial conditions are assumed to be pathogenic. The reconstructed account posits a single "abrupt" traumatic event that focuses on the mother's withdrawal of cathexis. The other elements then get added later on in the course of progressive reconstructions and defensive elaborations that fill out the evolution of the clinical picture.

The observational-prospective account posits an initial condition consisting of four or more different related ways-of-being-with-Mother that are represented in four different networks of schemas. These are not conceived of as reconstructions or defensive elaborations; rather, they are four parallel subjective experiences that make up the original pathogenic terrain. All four are the starting conditions on which later reconstructions will be based. In this view, the initial conditions are richer and more elaborated. The trauma has been somewhat demystified and transformed into the ordinary. This perspective requires less reconstructive work after the fact, since there is more to start with, to build on.

These two complementary perspectives are each potentially enriching to the other—and together provide the triangulation necessary to understand better the nature of the evolution of constructions as well as of development. It is in this sense that the notion of the schema-of-being-with can be of clinical utility in a specific case. Hypothesizing these representational units permits us to identify and conceptualize early experiences that may be the origins of later elaborated pathology and may thus inform the reconstructive process.

The infant's ways-of-being-with a depressed mother have been used as our main example. We could have used other examples, such as different patterns of attachment, or moments of anxiety, anger, or threat. Almost any repeating experience that characterizes what happens when the infant is with someone can qualify as a way-of-being-with that may have clinical pertinence.

AN OUTLINE OF THE MODEL

The Key Role of Motivated, Goal-Oriented Behavior

The model presented here presupposes the centrality of goal-directed motivation in understanding clinically relevant (or any) human behavior, especially its subjective aspects, a centrality pervasive in the theories that inform us. Goal-directedness is at the core of Freud's notions of drive, unconscious fantasy, and purposive ideas. It is interesting in this regard that in his notebooks Darwin muses that motives are the basic unit of the universe in that they are the functional units of evolution.[3] From a different perspective, students of event knowledge and narrative structure have found motives and goal orientation indispensable aspects (see below). Similarly, students of affect (Scherer 1986, Steimer-Krause 1992), of motor action (von Cranach et al. 1982), of cybernetics (Céllerier 1976), of earliest language production (Bloom 1973, Brown 1973), of ethology, and others all place goal-directedness at the core of their explanatory concepts.

The range of motives and goals that may serve a central role is largely that developed by Sandler (1985), Emde (1988), Emde et al. (1991), Lichtenberg (1989), and Sandler and Sandler (1992). It includes external and internal states of object-relatedness, affect states, states of self-esteem and safety, as well as physiological need satisfaction and consummatory acts. Also, attempts to reestablish a perturbed state of equilibrium must be added to this list.

There are large, long-acting motives, and within these, smaller, short-acting motives can be nested. We are most interested here in motives that arise in interpersonal situations, particularly those that are easily seen as the many and different ways-of-being-with-another, that is, of a size appropriate for everyday folk psychology (Bruner 1990).

The enactment (behaviorally or mentally) of a motive and the subjective experience of this enactment result in four phenomena: the emergent moment; temporal feeling shapes; protonarrative envelopes; and schemas-of-being-with. All four are the consequences of motives being put into play.

The Emergent Moment as the Referent Event for Representation

Representations are about something; they have a referent. The referent we are interested in is defined and bounded by a motive put in play in an interpersonal situation. It is thus a

---

[3]I am indebted to Colwyn Trevarthen for calling my attention to this reference to Darwin.

subjective experience involving affects, thoughts, perceptions, actions, motives, persons, and so on, all at the same time, such as trying to identify with or reanimate a depressed mother. In other words, the referent is a lived moment of a whole experience. Accordingly, I will propose a basic subjective unit of interpersonal experience lived in the here and now, which will be called a "moment." The moment is a subjective chunk of experience constructed by the mind as the experience is being lived. One experiences oneself as being "in" a moment. It organizes the diverse simultaneous happenings that are registered during a motivated event. In this sense, the moment is an emergent property of mind and will be called an emergent moment. It is the referent event for representation (as well as the product of existing representations).

The cognitive sciences have conceived of emergent properties of mind as a way of describing how the mind makes sense of or renders coherent an experience made up of many simultaneously occurring independent parts (e.g., Céllerier 1992, Churchland 1984, Dennett 1991, Edelman 1990, Maturana and Varela 1979, Rummelhart et al. 1986). In this view, the mind appears to process in parallel and in partial independence a large number of simultaneous mental happenings that occur during any interpersonal interaction; motivational shifts, visual images, affect shifts, sensations, motor actions, ideas, states of arousal, language, place and space, time, and so on are all processed simultaneously in parallel throughout all "centers" in the mind as well as in specialized ones devoted to processing each (parallel distributed processing, or PDP). The parallel processing of each element is carried out with lower-level, local mental operations that are never translatable into subjective experience; they are operationally unconscious. The resulting mental pandemonium is the normal state of things. And from the interplay, coordination, integration of these lower-level processes, a more global mental event emerges: an emergent property of the mind, which has coherence and sense in the context in which it emerges. That is, the diverse events and feelings are tied together as necessary elements of a single unified happening. The emergent moment is just such an emergent property of mind that accomplishes this integration of ongoing experience.

(Its dependence on already existing schemas will be mentioned below.)

The emergent moment, however, does not arise from the ongoing and unfolding mental pandemonium in one stroke. It emerges as a movement toward coherence in successive (often transient) stages of multiple drafts that need not reach a final state of fixity of coherence but only a workable current draft (or two). There is revision during the experience itself, as well as after the fact. There need not be one crystallizing instant, but rather the progression of multiple drafts of fragments in competition. (Much of what is taken to be "thoughts" are these fragments of drafts in the process of emergence.)

(Imagine the infant trying to identify with and imitate its depressed mother to get closer to her, and becoming more depressed as this happens.)

What provides the subjective sense of organization, coherence, and boundary to these "moments," thereby giving them the status of subjective units? Along with Trevarthen (1993) and Emde (1983b, Emde et al. 1991) we will assume that motives and affects play a major role in the subjective structuring of emergent moments and other experiences. This is so because the moment is a goal-directed unit of experience. Moving toward a motivated goal involves the unfolding of an affective contour and the illusion of a narrative-like structure. We will take these up in order.

Temporal Feeling Shapes as a Representational Format for Affect

When a motive is enacted (e.g., trying to reanimate Mother), there is necessarily a shift in affect, hedonics, arousal, and level of motivation/goal achievement that accompanies that enactment. A combination of separate experiences (i.e., affect, arousal, motivation) subjectively drawn from past interactions unfold in the present through temporal contours, which seem to be subjectively experienced as a single complex feeling. A combination (an emergent property) of the temporal contours of all of these is the feeling shape. It includes the particular quality of feeling that gets temporally contoured, which depends on the affects and motivations involved.

The notion of a feeling shape and how it is derived is confluent with the ideas of many affect researchers and theorists such as Tompkins (1962, 1963) and Scherer (1984). Feeling shapes and affects are both finally seen as emergent properties of several other separate processes. (Vitality affects, which I have previously described to examine affect attunement, are now seen as a subcategory of feeling shapes (Stern et al. 1984, Stern 1985). The temporal feeling shape is not only a subjective event that occurs in real time, it also occurs *in* time. One is "inside of" the experience. The feeling shape subjectively structures the experience of time, much as music does.

We tend to forget or underestimate the temporal aspects of experience. For so many phenomena, we act as if they had no temporal extension, or that the temporal aspect were adequately covered by the sequencing of events, even though the events, in themselves, are not considered in temporal terms. Actual subjective experience, however, occurs very much in the flow of time, which gives it an important part of its structure and felt quality.

This relative neglect is surprising in light of the ample evidence that exquisite timing abilities are in place from very early in life. There are now many experimental studies that suggest, explicitly or implicitly, that infants are sensitive to the temporal features of both speech and nonspeech sounds (Bertoncini et al. 1987, 1988, Clarkson et al. 1989, 1991, Kaye 1992, Spence 1992, Swain 1992, Zelazo et al. 1984). It is also suggested that infants by 3 months of age can imitate, in their own vocalizations, musical elements of what they hear (Papoušek and Papoušek 1981). Even simple games played by mothers and young infants demand a precise evaluation of short periods of time on the infant's part (Stern 1977). Recent work and reviews by Lewkowicz document the experimental evidence supporting the notion of the infant as having precocious and often exquisite abilities to discriminate different features of time (e.g., duration, rhythm, etc.) (Lewkowicz 1989, 1992).

The identification, then, of a unit such as a feeling shape seems to be within the infant's capabilities. It offers the infant a way of temporally structuring an emergent moment. (It is worth mentioning how early and relatively easily most children learn and remember melodies and lyrics tied to melodies.) The temporal feeling shape can thus be viewed as a plausible representational format for schematizing affective experience.

The Protonarrative Envelope as the Form of Representing the Whole, Lived Experience

When enacted in an interpersonal situation, motive (desire) creates, subjectively, a narrative-like structure. As the motivated events move in time toward their goal, they generate a dramatic line of tension (Labov 1972) as well as the other main element of a narrative-like structure, namely, a protoplot, with an agent, an action, an instrumentality, a goal, and a context (Burke 1945). In brief, goal-directed movement leaves in its immediate wake—so to speak—the tendency to experience events in terms of dramatic lines and plots. These provide coherence and boundary features to the moment. Bruner (1990) points out that this narrative unit is a basic unit for comprehending human behavior in most folk psychologies and for children. Narrative-like structures can be seen as the inevitable counterparts of motivated, goal-directed behavior, and their comprehension should appear long before the ability to verbally produce these structures.

The dramatic line of tension is invariably synchronous with the feeling shape. This is natural since the motive–goal tension is played out in terms of temporal shifts in affect, arousal, motivational strength, and goal attainment.

To the extent that the infant can sense and identify the feeling shape as described above, it has mastered the form with which to sense the dramatic line of tension that accompanies the trajectory of an enacted motive. It is in this way that the temporal contour is very much the structural backbone of an emergent moment. It is in this sense that affect—in the form of feeling shapes—plays a special role in coordinating and organizing memory and experience, as long suggested by others (e.g., Emde 1983b, Emde et al. 1991).

Concerning the elements of a protoplot, when might the infant be able to sense them and experience them appropriately distributed in and as part of the feeling contour?

I will begin with the elements of the plot. By 3–4 months of age, if not before, the infant has sufficient capacities to differentiate self from other. Part of this differentiation rests on its ability to recognize its own "agency," its being the author of intended actions (see Stern [1985] for detailed argumentation). At the same time, it starts to have an appreciation of primitive forms of "causality," and its behavior is clearly goal oriented. We even speak of "instrumental crying" at 3 months to get something, as well as other "instrumental" behaviors, for example, smiling. In a sense, then, well before the first half of the first year, the infant has a primitive sense of agent, object, goal, and instrumentality.

Context, the where and when of the plot, remains to be discussed. Here the work of Rovee-Collier and Fagen (1981) shows that infants, by at least 3 months, have a great sensitivity to spatial surroundings (the where). Less work on the when in infancy is available (see Nelson on autobiographical memory, 1988 and 1989).

Trevarthen has long held that infants beginning in the first months of life share with the mother "primary motives" that imply an abbreviated protoplot (1980, 1982). These are evident in what he calls protoconversation (Trevarthen 1989). These ideas are compatible with the point of view being developed here, and have at various points stimulated and inspired it.

The protoplot is subjectively experienced as unfolding in or along with the temporal feeling shape. These two aspects merge to form a subjective structure, the proto-narrative envelope, the form in which the whole experience is represented as a single global unit.

Schemas-of-Being-With and the Problem of Memories, Fantasies, and Autobiographical Narratives

After repeated experiences of many "moments" of the general class of being-with-another-in-a-certain-way (e.g., reanimating

Mother), each of the basic schema formats of that class of moments will form, that is, sensorimotor, perceptual, and conceptual schemas; feeling shapes; scripts; and the global proto-narrative envelope. In this account, the term *schema-of-being-with* refers to the entire network of schemas that represent the different aspects and levels of a repeated interpersonal experience.

The network of schemas, then, *is* the form in which the lived experience is represented. That is, different components of the lived experience are represented in different basic formats. And many components are represented multiply and simultaneously in different formats. For instance, in order to render event sequences, an experience must be divided into discrete units, and these units ordered in time. In order to render the affect, the same experience must be represented in an analog form to preserve the temporal feeling shape. Thus, the network of schemas-of-being-with is rich and diverse, with multiple codings.

We assume that each of the separate, parallel schemas making up the network forms in the manner now well described, that is, by the identification of invariant elements, and the construction of prototypes and categories on the basis of constellations of invariant elements (Rosch and Floyd 1978, Strauss 1979; see also Stern 1985 for such prototypes involving interpersonal interactions. The schema-of-a-way-of-being-with is analogous to what I have previously called a RIG—the representation of an interaction that has become generalized [Stern 1985]. The difference between the two is that the schema-of-being-with is conceptualized from an assumed subjective point of view of the infant being in the interaction, while the RIG is identified from the adult's objective point of view observing the interaction from the outside.)

We can now proceed to the question of where phantasies, certain memories, and autobiographical narratives come from, that is, what serves as their reference material.

We assume that the network of schemas-of-ways-of-being-with is, in fact, the only reference for elaborating fantasies, memories, narratives, and "present moments" (Where else could they come from?) To accomplish that role, the network of schemas must be of a flexible and general form from which diverse mental phenomena can be constructed. The multiple system of schematization described above provides just such a flexible system. We now need a process (descriptively) that can use this flexible system. I call this process *refiguration,* borrowing the term proposed by Ricoeur (1983, 1984, 1985) for the process of going from history to narration, from fixed serial order to arranged reorderings, from one pattern of emphasis and stress to a new pattern, from "objective" events in real time to imaginary events in virtual time.

Refiguration is the process whereby attention can move back and forth freely between the multiple schematic formats. The patterns of shifting attention create virtual sequences or virtual overlaps, or virtual co-occurrences, or various combinations thereof. Attention can also be directed to two formats at the same time—one held in "central attention" and the other in "peripheral attention"—creating a foreground–background relationship, which can be reversed. The possibilities for montage are almost unlimited.

An example familiar to all of us is illustrative. Imagine fantasizing your favorite sexual event. The mind can wander over the network of schemas of the event. It can visit each part at whatever speed (lingering time) it wishes. It can revisit certain parts. It can start over. It can rush to the end and then fill in the middle. It can hold the high point in the foreground and replay another portion at the same time in the background, and so on. In short, it can create the montage that is most satisfying or functional. The fantasy, then, is one possible virtual experience that results from refiguring the network of schemas.

The exact form of the fantasy is mostly determined by the present context. The context would include, at least, the reason (motive) for evoking the fantasy, as well as the functional use to which the fantasy will be put. The present context may account for much more. What is the basic difference between a fantasy, a generalized memory, and the script that emerges in preparing a narrative? Are they not all refigurings of lived experience as represented in the network of schemas? The "decision" about whether the refiguring should best take the form of fantasy, memory, or narrative is also determined by the total present context that provokes the refiguring process. The basic difference between these three mental phenomena may only be the function required of the refiguration by the demands of the immediate context, each function having a different format.

This is a different viewpoint, as it sees memories, fantasies, and narrations as all coming from the same source material but emerging (being refigured) under different demand conditions.

THE NATURAL SELECTION OF SCHEMAS AND NETWORKS

Edelman (1987) suggests that the neural networks formed within each individual brain compete with one another, resulting in a survival of the most functional networks on an ontogenetic scale. Céllerier (1992) has offered a similar proposal, but the units vying for natural selection within the individual are schemes—the more adaptive ones being selected and given more active time and control over behavior. Thelen (1990) provides a concrete illustration of this in the evolution of infant's schemes of reaching. When infants first start to reach, there is great variability between them as well as a wide range of reaching patterns (i.e., reaching schemes) seen within each child. Over the next months, a competition between reaching schemes and resultant motor patterns takes place within each child, with the most functional winning out.

In a similar fashion, several schemas-of-ways-of-being-with are probably constructed for the same repeating experiences. And these are subject to natural selection during each infant's development. This point is important to emphasize for several reasons. How does the infant know what invariants to use in chunking the flow of experiences into "moments," or which to privilege in constructing its schemas? How does it know which portions of the emergent moment to select to become part of the schema? How does it know how many different parallel and multiple forms of encoding make up the most useful network of schemas? It doesn't. It is an empirical question decided by trial and error and progressive approximation to a form that is most

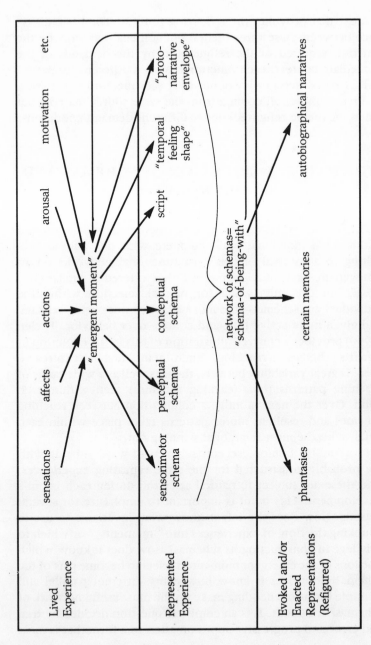

Figure 2–1. Features of the Infant's Object-Related Subjective Experience

functional for guiding the construction and conduct of emergent moments, that is, for being most preadapted to ongoing events; and for permitting the refiguration of the network of schemas to produce fantasies, memories, and (later) narratives, each with their own functional values for adaptation.

· In summary, a sketch has been presented of some of the features necessary in thinking about the infant's object-related subjective experience and its representation. These have been schematized as shown in Figure 2–1.

These notions are put forward as steps toward conceptualizing how the infant forms and uses an object-related representational world in a fashion that advances clinical thinking and research.

REFERENCES

Bertoncini, J., Bijeljac-Babic, R., Blumstein, S., and Mehler, J. (1987). Discrimination in neonates of very short CVs. *Journal of the Acoustical Society of America* 82:31–37.

Bertoncini, J., Bijeljac-Babic, R., Jusczyk, P. W., et al. (1988). An investigation of young infants' perceptual representations of speech sounds. *Journal of Experimental Psychology: General* 117:21–33.

Bloom, L. (1973). *One Word at a Time: The Use of Single Word Utterances before Syntax*. The Hague: Mouton.

Bretherton, I. (1984). Representing the social world. In *Symbolic Play: The Development of Social Understanding*, ed. I. Bretherton, pp. 1–41. New York: Academic.

Brown, R. (1973). *A First Language: The Early Stages*. Cambridge, MA: Harvard University Press.

Bruner, J. (1990). *Acts of Meaning*. Cambridge, MA: Harvard University Press.

Burke, K. (1945). *Grammar of Motives*. New York: Prentice Hall.

Céllerier, G. (1976). La genèse historique de la cybernétique ou la téléonomie est-elle une catégorie de l'entendement? *Revue européenne des sciences sociales* 14:273–290.

_____ (1992). Le constructivisme génétique aujourd'hui. In *Le Cheminement des Découvertes de l'Enfant*, ed. B. Inhelder and G. Céllerier. Lausanne: Delachaux et Niestlé.

Churchland, P. M. (1984). *Matter and Consciousness*. Cambridge, MA: MIT Press.

Clarkson, M. G., Clifton, R. K., Swain, I. U., and Perris, E. E. (1989). Stimulus duration and repetition rate influence newborn's head orientation toward sound. *Developmental Psychobiology* 22:683–705.

Clarkson, M. G., Swain, I. U., Clifton, R. K., and Cohen, K. (1991). Newborn's head orientation toward trains of brief sounds. *Journal of the Acoustical Society of America* 89:2411–2420.

The controversial discussions, 1943–1944. (1967). *Bulletin of the British Psychoanalytical Society* 10.

Dennett, D. (1991). *Consciousness Explained*. Boston: Little, Brown.

Edelman, G. M. (1987). *Neural Darwinism*. New York: Basic Books.

_____ (1990). *The Remembered Present: A Biological Theory of Consciousness*. New York: Basic Books.

Emde, R. N., ed. (1983a). *René A. Spitz: Dialogics from Infancy: Selected Papers*. New York: International Universities Press.

_____ (1983b). The pre-representational self and its affective core. *Psychoanalytic Study of the Child* 38:165–192. New Haven: Yale University Press.

_____ (1988). Development terminable and interminable: 1. Innate and motivational factors from infancy. *International Journal of Psycho-Analysis* 69:23–42.

Emde, R. N., Biringen, Z., Clyman, R. B. and Oppenheim, D. (1991). The moral self of infancy: affective core and procedural knowledge. *Developmental Review* 11:251–270.

Field, T. (1987). Affective and interactive disturbances in infants. In *Handbook of Infant Development*, ed. J. D. Osofsky, chapter 19, pp. 972–1005. New York: Wiley.

Green, A. (1986). *On Private Madness*. London: Hogarth.

Kaye, K. L. (1992). *Nonsense syllable list learning in newborns*. Poster presented at the International Conference on Infant Studies (ICIS), Miami, FL, May.

Labov, W. (1972). *Language in the Inner City*. Philadelphia: University of Pennsylvania Press.

Laplanche, J., and Pontalis, J. B. (1967). *Vocabulaire de la psychanalyse*. Paris: Presses Universitaires de France.

Lewis, M., and Miller, S. M., eds. (1990). *Handbook of Developmental Psychopathology*. New York: Plenum.

Lewkowicz, D. J. (1989). The role of temporal factors in infant behavior and development. In *Time and Human Cognition: A Life-Span Perspective*, ed. I. Levin and D. Zakay, pp. 9–62. Amsterdam: North Holland.

_____ (1992). The development of temporally based intersensory perception in human infants. In *Time, Action, and Cognition: Towards Bridging the Gap*, ed. F. Macar, V. Pouthas, and W. J. Friedman, pp. 35–43. Dordrecht: Kluwer Academic.

Lichtenberg, J. (1989). *Psychoanalysis and Motivation*. Hillsdale, NJ: Analytic.

Mandler, J. M. (1979). Categorical and schematic organization in memory. In *Memory Organization and Structure*, ed. C. R. Puff, pp. 259–299. New York: Academic.

Mandler, J. M. (1983). Representation. In *Cognitive development*, ed. J. H. Flavell and E. M. Markman, vol. 3 of *Handbook of Child Psychology*, ed. P. Mussen, 4th ed., pp. 420–494. New York: Wiley.

_____ (1988). How to build a baby: on the development of an accessible representational system. *Cognitive Development* 3:113–136.

Maturana, H. R., and Varela, F. J. (1979). *Autopoiesis and Cognition: The Realization of the Living*. Dordrecht: Reidel.

Murray, L. (1988). Effects of post-natal depression on infant development. Direct studies of early mother–infant interaction. In *Motherhood and Mental Illness*, ed. I. Brockington and R. Kumer, vol. 2, pp. 235–257. Bristol: John Wright.

_____ (1992). Impact of post-natal depression on infant development. *Journal of Child Psychology and Psychiatry* 33:543–561.

Nelson, K. (1986). *Event Knowledge: Structure and Function in Development*. Hillsdale, NJ: Erlbaum.

_____ (1988). The ontogeny of memory for real events. In

Remembering Reconsidered: Ecological and Traditional Approaches to the Study of Memory, ed. M. Neisser and W. Winograd. New York: Cambridge University Press.

―――― (1989). Remembering: a functional developmental perspective. In *Memory: Interdisciplinary Approaches*, ed. G. G. P. Soloman, C. Kelley, and B. Stephens, pp. 127–150. New York: Springer.

Nelson, K., and Greundel, J. M. (1981). Generalized event representation: basic building blocks of cognitive development. In *Advances in Developmental Psychology*, vol. 1, ed. M. E. Lamb and A. L. Brown. Hillsdale, NJ: Erlbaum.

Osofsky, J. D., Hann, D., Biringen, Z., Emde, R. N., et al. (1990). Emotional availability: strengths and vulnerabilities in development. In *Abstracts of papers presented at the Seventh International Conference on Infant Studies*, ed. C. Rovee-Collier, p. 64. Montreal: Ablex.

Papousêk, M., and Papousêk, H. (1981). Musical elements in the infant's vocalization: their significance for communication, cognition, and creativity. In *Advances in Infancy Research*, ed. L. P. Lipsitt. Norwood, NJ: Ablex.

Ricoeur, P. (1983) (1984) (1985). *Temps et récit*, Vol. 1–3. Paris: Editions du Seuil.

Rosch, E., and Floyd, B. B., eds. (1978). *Cognition and Categorization*. Hillsdale, NJ: Erlbaum.

Rovee-Collier, K., and Fagen, J. W. (1981). The retrieval of memory in early infancy. In *Advances in Infancy Research*, vol. 1, ed. L. P. Lipsitt. Norwood, NJ: Ablex.

Rumelhart, D. D., McClelland, J. L., and the PDP Research Group (1986). *Parallel Distributed Processing: Explorations in the Microstructure of Cognition*. Cambridge, MA: Bradford/MIT Press.

Sandler, J. (1985). Towards a reconsideration of the psychoanalytic theory of motivation. *Bulletin of the Anna Freud Center* 8:223–243.

Sandler, J., and Sandler, A. M. (1992). *Internal Objects Revisited*. Unpublished manuscript.

Scherer, K. R. (1984). On the nature and function of emotion: a component process approach. In *Approaches to Emotion*, ed. K. R. Scherer and P. Ekman. Hillsdale, NJ: Erlbaum.

_____ (1986). Vocal affect expression. *Psychological Bulletin* 99:143–165.

Shank, R. C., and Abelson, R. (1977). *Scripts, Plans, Goals and Understanding*. Hillsdale, NJ: Erlbaum.

_____ (1982). *Dynamic Memory: A Theory of Reminding and Learning in Computers and People*. New York: Cambridge University Press.

Spence, M. J. (1992). *Infant's discrimination of novel and repeatedly experienced speech passages*. Poster presented at the International Conference on Infant Studies (ICIS). Miami, FL, May.

Steimer-Krause, E. (1992). *Transference and non-verbal behaviors*. Presentation at the International Psychoanalytic Association, Standing Committee on Psychoanalytic Research, London, March.

Stern, D. N. (1977). *The First Relationship: Infant and Mother*. Cambridge, MA. Harvard University Press.

_____ (1985) *The Interpersonal World of the Infant: A View from Psychoanalysis and Developmental Psychology*. New York: Basic Books.

Stern, D. N., Hofer, L., Haft, W., and Dore, J. (1984). Affect attunement: the sharing of feeling states between mother and infant by means of intermodal fluency. In *Social Perception in Infants,* ed. T. Field and N. Fox, pp. 249–268 Norwood, NJ: Ablex.

Strauss, M. S. (1979). Abstraction of prototypical information by adults and ten-month-old infants. *Journal of Experimental Psychology: Human Learning and Memory* 5:618–632.

Swain, I. U. (1992). *Newborn response to auditory stimulus complexity*. Paper presented at the International Conference on Infant Studies (ICIS), Miami, FL, May.

Thelen, E. (1990). Dynamical systems and the generation of individual differences. In *Individual Differences in Infancy: Reliability, Stability and Prediction*, ed. J. Colombo and J. W. Fagen. Hillsdale, NJ: Erlbaum.

Timmons, C. R. (1992). Evidence for a memory network in infancy. *Infant Behavior and Development*. 15:211. Abstracts of papers presented at the Eighth International Conference on Infant Studies (ICIS), Miami, FL, May.

Tomkins, S. S. (1962). *Affect, Imagery, Consciousness: vol. 1. The Positive Affects*. New York: Springer.

_____ (1963). *Affect, Imagery Consciousness: vol. 2. The Negative Affects*. New York: Springer.

Trevarthen, C. (1980). The foundations of intersubjectivity: development of interpersonal and cooperative understanding in infants. In *The Social Foundations of Language and Thought: Essays in honor of J. S. Bruner*, ed. D. Olsen, pp. 316–342. New York: W. W. Norton.

_____ (1982). The primary motives for cooperative understanding. In *Social cognition: studies on the development of understanding,* ed. G. Butterworth and P. Light, pp. 77–109. Brighton: Harvesters Press.

_____ (1989). Signs before speech. In *The Semiotic Web*, ed. T. A. Sebeok and J. Umiker-Sebeok. Berlin: Mouton de Gruyter.

_____ (1993). The function of emotions in early infant communication and development. In *New Perspectives in Early Communicative Development*, ed. J. Nadel and L. Camaioni. London: Routledge.

Tronick, E., Als, H., Adamson, L., et al. (1978). The infant's response to entrapment between contradictory messages in face-to-face interaction. *Journal of the American Academy of Child Psychiatry* 17:1–13.

Von Cranach, M., Kalbermatten, U., Indermühle, K., and Gugler, B. (1982). *Goal-Directed Action*. New York: Academic Press.

Zelazo, P. R., Brody, L. B., and Chaika, H. (1984). Neonatal habituation and dishabituation of headturning to rattle sounds. *Infant Behavior and Development* 7:311–321.

3

The Infantile Neurosis
Reassessed

James S. Grotstein, M.D.

The child knows its mother by the smile in her eyes.

Virgil

"THIS HOUSE AGAINST THIS HOUSE"

Any attempt to integrate and realign the concept of the infantile neurosis with recent infant research findings entails integrating some of the disparate schools within psychoanalysis itself, each of which has relevant and cogent contributions to make to the subject of the infantile neurosis and to infant development. Little integrative work has been done, for example, even within the multifarious British schools, so that Fairbairn's and Winnicott's contributions—to say nothing of so many others—have not yet found their way into Kleinian theory (Grotstein 1991a,b,c, Hughes 1989, 1994a,b, Rayner 1991, Sutherland 1980). I refer, for instance, to the failure to integrate Fairbairn's (1952) concept of "schizoid" with Tustin's (1972) concept of "autistic."

American mental health workers know of the concept of object relations but have learned of it largely through Kernberg's efforts to edit and cannibalize the British version(s) and then graft the remainder onto the American school's (principally Jacobson's, 1964, 1967) concepts of object representations and (principally Mahler's, 1968) of infant development. Americans do not realize, for instance, that the Kleinians are not included under the rubric of "object relations," that their concept of "internal object relations" is at variance with that of the independent school (the true "object relations school"), and, furthermore, that both their conceptions of "internal objects" differ significantly from the American concept of "object representations."[1,2]

TOWARD A REDEFINITION OF THE INFANTILE NEUROSIS—AND PSYCHOSIS

With the above in mind I should now like to broaden the redefinition of the infantile neurosis to include not only Balint's (1968) "basic fault" but also Winnicott's (1951, 1960a,b, 1969, 1971c,d) conceptions of transitional objects and space, the holding environment, object usage, and true and false selves. Briefly, after formulating the pathology of the true and false

---

[1]The only major exceptions to this generalization are from the school of Anna Freud (1936, 1965), mainly including Sandler and Rosenblatt's (1962) contributions to the theory of the object representational world.

[2]Even the usage of the concept of projective identification is at variance in the United States with the understanding of Kleinians in England and the rest of the world; e.g., (a) to the latter projection and projective identification are identical and inseparable (there can be no projection without identification), and (b) the "identification" aspect of the concept *always* refers to the subject who projects, *not* to the object who *counterprojectively* or really *introjectively* identifies with the infant's (patient's) projection (Grotstein 1981, 1994e,f,h).

selves, Winnicott traced them and their objects back to their normal counterparts, the "being self" and the "active self," respectively. The former was related to (but without communication because no communication is necessary) by an environmental object or holding environment, whereas the active self actively engages the object of need and must communicate with it. The former is the private self, always to be looked for but never found; the latter is always present and assertive. Lacan (1966) must have had the former in mind when he formulated the pre-mirror, nonalienated self.

Winnicott's concept of object usage has been recently brilliantly expanded by Hopkins (1989) and Hamilton (1991). The sum of substance of this elusive, religious, and yet clinically cogent concept, one that complements Klein, is to the effect that the infant must "use" Mother (really, the invisible effigy of Mother) in a way that it uses its transitional object—roughly, cruelly, destructively. While doing so, the infant cannot yet tell the difference between its real mother and the subjective mother it autopoietically creates in projective identificatory illusion in the potential space between them. The more the mother, particularly her temperament, survives the destructive attacks, the easier it is for the infant to differentiate its subjective mother from its real mother—and thus acquire a sense of its own thinking space separate from the world of external persons.[3] *The creation of this space is one of the tasks of the infantile neurosis.*

This concept of the subjective mother and her normally passing into oblivion issues from a larger principle—that the psychoanalytic infant must be disburdened of omnipotent, autopoietic fantasies and preconceptions in order to make room for realistic images. Under the concept of subjective objects one would include not only those imaginatively *created* by the infant but also those already there as *inherent preconceptions*

---

[3]Object usage is another area in which the infant (according to Klein but expressed in different language) experiences its innocence to be jeopardized— believing that it may have destroyed the breast. Whereas Klein (1940) assigns this belief to the infant's inherent capacity for destructiveness, Fairbairn (1952) suggests that the infant is originally afraid, depending on mother's reception of it, that its very *love* is bad.

(Bion's [1975] "memoirs of the future"; Jung's [1934] *arche-types*), which are *released* to find their anticipated counterparts in reality. Thus, the psychoanalytic infant must *unlearn* what it is overpredisposed to find in the world of reality—amplified by its feelings, fantasies, and preconceptions—in dramatic contrast to the developmental infant, whose tabula rasa is starving for data to *learn* anew in the external world.

To add to the mélange, Americans in particular, except for those who have been trained in the discipline of critical studies, are virtually unaware of the new school of semiotics, particularly that espoused by Lacan and his followers, to say nothing of the post-Lacanian French feminists (Kristeva, Cixous, Irrigary) and their new concepts of development as well as, in particular, Lacan's radical concept of the dissociation (de-centering) of the subject "I." For instance, Lacan (1966) believed that the infant experiences being somatically and psychically unintegrated until its image is captured in the mirror during the mirror stage of development. Following this, an integration does take place, but it is an alienating one—the infant has identified itself in the mirror of the Other and is forever identified as a self, alienated from the pre-mirror self.

Lacan also stated that mental and somatic fragmentation dreams in later life, including images of mutilation, are derived from this pre-mirror stage of nonintegration. Kristeva (1982), on the other hand, has helped us understand the role of the mother and infant as "le sémiotique," a language of physical signs implicit between mother and infant before the dawn of verbal language.

In summary, one of the tasks of the infantile neurosis is rehearsing for the future; another is the creation of space and boundaries (internal and external) so that family relationships are protected and also that a mental space is created where logical laws are followed so that one can plan and think ("trial [or suspended] action"). Yet another is to develop the distinction and integrity of one's different selves ("alter egos"). Thus Freud's id should be rethought as an alter ego that originates language, whereas the ego proper originates speech (Lacan). The ego ideal is the "priest-self," one who sacrificed his or her rights for a sensuous life in order to bear the lost and then sublimated omnipotence for the ego (self) as a standard for its once and future excellence (Freud 1914, Grotstein 1994c,d).

As one scans over the breadth of developmental findings, it seems that the more that is being unearthed about the early infant's *empirical* abilities, the less is being ascribed to the unconscious (both primary and secondary), and along with that omission, there emerges the conclusion that the infant has little or no capacity for fantasy (conscious or unconscious) prior to the development of the capacity for symbolization. Stern (1985), for instance, states that the early infant can perceive reality, possess cross-modal sensuality, and can recognize its mother but can*not* engage in fantasy, particularly unconscious fantasy, because of this inability to use symbols, by which he means verbal. I would contest this and would state further that Stern confuses *imagination* (image formation from the senses as a primitive "language") with *symbolization*. The former belongs to an older and more basic communicative register than verbalization and symbolization. It belongs to the language of the senses and of personification (projective identification).

The problem seems to be that of the current understanding—or, may I say, "misunderstanding"—of the concept of the unconscious itself and therefore of the nature of the internal world. In this regard, Subbotsky (1992), a cognitive psychologist who speaks from a background in the works of Piaget and Vigotsky, has recently convincingly demonstrated that infants achieve the capacity for phantasmal transformations of their experiences from very early on. His researches are in direct contradiction to Stern's (1985) assertions.

The tension arc between infant development and psychoanalysis is matched by two other tension arcs, those between different developmentalists themselves and those correspondingly between different analytic schools. It appears from the outset, for instance, that infant development research (particularly in this country) generally supports the analytic philosophy of self psychology, while British and continental developmentalists seem to lean toward Winnicott mainly and Fairbairn to a lesser degree. Some, indeed, respect Klein as well.

I shall also argue that some of the psychoanalytic conclusions emanating from infant development depend in no small measure on the geopolitics of psychoanalytic training; for example, a developmentalist trained in the American school of ego psychology[4] will—and has—come to conclusions that will be at variance with those trained, for instance, in London, Paris, or Rome. Trevarthen (1980, 1983) and Murray (1964), who are *British* trained and influenced, seem to believe that the infant is never without organization.

Thus Trevarthen, for instance, believes that the infant enters into a primary intersubjective field with its mother around 2 months of age, in contrast to the views of Stern, who disagrees with Trevarthen's concept of "primary intersubjectivity" and suggests that the infant enters this area at 9 months. Moreover, British and continental developmentalists are more at home with Klein and the British independent school of analysis (object relations) than are many Americans, yet the contributions of Sander and Demos are exceptions to my generalization since they are American-trained yet demonstrate a familiarity with the concepts of the British schools.

It is likewise true that the theater of infant development research was "dark" during the rise of psychoanalysis, and so it must be admitted, consequently, that many traditional psychoanalytic concepts from both sides of the Atlantic have remained unchallenged for too long. Infant development research has supplied so much rich data that it behooves us to reassess and, if need be, realign our ideas in light of them. The concepts of the primacy of infantile sexuality, autoerotism, the instinctual drives, primary narcissism, and, more lately, the normal autistic and symbiotic stages of development are all probable candidates for revision. All the above are subsumed in a broader concept of the infantile neurosis; thus, the aim of this contribution is to dignify infant development research by realignment with it.

Infantile Neurosis

In the course of developing my conception of the infantile neurosis and its interface with infant development research, I

---

[4]Lacan (1966) more specifically and appropriately refers to it as "the New York School."

should also like to link the classical concept of primary narcissism with a similar but less often mentioned idea, that of primary identification (Freud 1913 [1912–1913])—and also that of primary object choice (Balint 1965),[5] and then align them all with the implications about the mental status of the infant at birth (according to infant developmentalists)—and then integrate the preceding ideas with the conceptions of Klein, Winnicott, Bowlby, Hofer, Lacan, and others. In other words, a comparison between psychoanalytic development theory and infant research findings must first be redefined and refined within its own discipline. Then assessments must be made as to *which* psychoanalytic school's theory and *which* developmentalist's findings and conclusions can be used.

The Oedipus Complex

The very primacy, let alone nature, of the Oedipus complex, which is the nucleus of the infantile neurosis, is itself a candidate for revision, although, curiously, little mention is made of this in the development literature—and for a reason; classically it has a later developmental arrival than is accorded infancy.

Furthermore, infant development research is not the only new consideration for comparison with psychoanalytic theories of development. Parallel to it are notable contributions from neurobiology, neuropsychology, personality disorder research, and child abuse research, to mention but a few new cogent perspectives that need to be integrated into psychoanalytic theory and practice. To these may also be added the work on personality trait development by Chess and Thomas (1986), particularly their contributions on "goodness of fit" and cumulative trauma."[6] The "red thread" running through these perspectives is the factor of heritable and/or early acquired threshold and neurocognitive disabilities that confer on the infant liabilities that can have far-reaching consequences in

---

[5]Thus, the infant of primary narcissism, of primary identification, and of primary object choice are coeval "alter egos," each of which defines the other(s) (Grotstein 1994g).

[6]This concept was originally formulated by Khan (1964).

development and adjustment (DeMause 1974, Palombo 1993, Stone 1988).

Palombo's contributions are to the issue. In his discussion of infantile autism in a recent publication, he called attention to (1) the pathomorphic emphasis that psychoanalytic theory imparts to normal development, and (2) the isomorphic nature of the infant being considered. His point was (1) that development proceeds independent of pathology, and (2) that each infant brings more far-ranging individual differences than we could ever have imagined. Each infant has its own private experience of the personal events in its life and encodes them with personal meaning. Depending on its own inborn neuropsychological (perceptual-cognitive) capacity to give personal meaning to these experiences, the infant is then able (or unable) to communicate these personal meanings as *shared meanings* with another caring person in order to achieve mutuality and an intersubjective moment.

To these conceptualizations of inherited or acquired personality trait and neurocognitive disorders must be added heritable and acquired threshold state vulnerabilities. Stone (1988) and Grotstein (1980, 1987, 1993), for example, describe *hyperirritability* as the "red thread" running through a variety of primitive mental disorders, particularly the borderline, whose psychodynamics must be augmented by concepts such as *self-regulation* (Grotstein 1991a,b,c, 1993, Krystal 1981, 1982, 1983, 1990, Taylor 1984, 1987a,b, 1992, 1993).

The phenomenon of self- and interactional regulation is an important area that has been uncovered by infant development research. Reich (1960) and then Kohut (1971, 1977, 1978a,b, 1984), independent of that research, applied this concept to the vicissitudes of self-esteem. Lately, it has been applied to the regulation of the experience of shame (Schore 1991).

The Infantile Neurosis of Traditional Classical Analysis

The infantile neurosis is a composite concept that has traditionally embraced the oedipal phase of development and its regressive elaborations but employs the Oedipus complex of the phallic stage as the principal organizer of the latter. This traditional and classical use of the concept has seemingly kept it out of developmental considerations since the former ("pregenital") deals mainly with the first 2 years of life.

Yet, since other schools have different ideas about the time of arrival of the Oedipus complex—and even classical contributors have allowed for an earlier onset in trace form (Brody and Axelrad 1966, 1970, Loewald 1979, Rangell 1955)—I believe that the infantile neurosis, if the very name is to be taken literally, deserves to be compared with developmental findings. It is interesting that the term is seldom seen in the British psychoanalytic literature despite the fact that their conception of the infant allows for a more truly infantile onset of mental life.

BACKGROUND: THE CLASSICAL CONCEPTION

Classical formulations about early mental life followed conceptualizations that depended on the notion of infantile sexuality, which was subserved in turn by such concepts as primary narcissism, autoerotism, pregenitality, identification, and anaclitic object choice. Abraham (1924) made the first major thrust in deepening and broadening our ideas about developmental stages by his explorations of the passive and active aspects of the oral and anal pregenital stages and by relating them to distinct phases of object-relatedness. Yet he never challenged Freud's contention that there was such a phase as primary narcissism, one that is a state of primary identification with the object (primary undifferentiation) where mental life could not occur.

The term *infantile* was used by Freud in numerous ways. He frequently employed it to connote the genetic hypotheses (e.g., infantile sexuality, infantile amnesia, etc.). He originally employed the term *neurosis* to designate the first symptomatic manifestations of a psychic conflict between a traumatic reality and the censorship by consciousness (Breuer and Freud 1893–1895). Later it came to designate the symptomatic manifestations of a psychic conflict between an instinctual drive and the defenses of the ego (Freud 1897).

The concept of the infantile neurosis per se emerged from Freud's (1909) "Analysis of a Phobia in a Five-Year-Old Boy," but he went into greater detail in his subsequent analysis of the case of the Wolf Man (1918 [1914]), the origin of whose obsessional neurosis was found to have originated in the infantile phase of development (18 months of age). He accidentally witnessed the primal scene between his parents and became fixated to that event. It was followed by sexual seduction by his sister and by a view from the rear of a maid washing a floor on her hands and knees, a pattern that also fixated itself on him for erotic object choice in his future. In Freud's analysis of the case unconscious incestuous strivings for his mother were stimulated, but his father's having preempted him—and Mother's having submitted to his father—aroused not only jealousy of his father but castration anxiety vis-à-vis the idea of his mother's not having a penis, a traumatic reminder to him of what could befall him if he did not surrender his oedipal desires. Thus, the primal scene and castration anxiety became organizers for the development of a neurosis in which an infantile claim had to be abandoned.

As a "neurosis" it came to mean that all children undergo a paradoxically normal phase of psychopathology that has a prodromal or incubational phase followed by an irruption of fantasies into overt behavioral manifestations (ego dystonic). These then fall back into the unconscious, leaving traces behind to commemorate their appearance. The infantile neurosis is destined to rise again in the child's future adulthood, in which case it becomes an abnormal event of psychopathology known as a "neurosis."

The idea of an infantile neurosis thus became a signifier for a paradox but in two separate ways: (1) as a signifier for the oedipal phase of development, it conveys an oxymoron: "normal psychopathology"; (2) as "infantile," it signified the earliest phases of development (the Wolf Man's neurosis went back to 18 months of age, but today we would hardly call that infantile—maybe "toddler").

Today, we would question the time-appropriateness of infantile as a constant conjunction with the oedipal phase—except for the fact that classical analysts understand the preoedipal (pregenital) phases of development to be characterized by fixations whose clinical importance lies largely in their being regressively elaborated from defensive maneuvers that arise primarily in oedipal anxiety.

Nagera (1963, 1966, 1969) believes that the infantile neurosis is characteristic of the phallic-oedipal level of development and is an attempt to organize all the previous neurotic conflicts and developmental shortcomings into a single organization. He subscribes to a later developmental sequence theory but does not question the word *infantile*.

Mahler (1968) seeks to integrate the conception of the infantile neurosis with her discoveries of the object relations phases of the infant–mother interaction, known as the autistic, symbiotic, and separation-individuation phases. She believes that the oedipal conflict that characterizes the infantile neurosis can be greatly shaped by these pre-oedipal relationships. In particular, she states that there are three principal anxieties of childhood that converge in the rapprochement period and that may continue past the second year of life. These are (1) the fear of object loss, compensated for by the introjection of an ambivalent object in which there is (2) fear of losing the object's love with (3) the development of subsequent vulnerability.

Tolpin (1970, 1971) calls attention to Freud's using the concept of the infantile neurosis as an underlying motive force but believes that he also blurred the clarity of this metapsychological concept by referring to clinically manifest disorders associated with the oedipal stage. She believes

> that the infantile neurosis is not a clinically manifest entity, e.g., phobic or obsessional neurosis, accessible by observation of symptomatology. . . . The term infantile neurosis should be reserved for the metapsychological concept that designates the repressed, potentially pathogenic oedipal conflict (associated with the phallic-oedipal phase) which is central in the pathology of the transference neurosis. [1970, p. 278]

Klein's Conception of the Infantile Neurosis

Klein's (1928, 1945) conception of the early onset of the Oedipus complex in the late oral stage, combined with her concept of infant rivalry (envy) with the breast as an antecedent to the tripartite rivalry-jealousy of the phallic oedipal stage, opened the way for an earlier and more extensive understanding of the Oedipus complex than was true of the classical. Moreover, her discovery of persecutory anxiety in infants at 3 weeks of age and of depressive anxiety at 3 to 4 months of age inaugurated her formulation of a yet more basic sequence of anxieties, the persecutory anxiety of the paranoid-schizoid position and depressive anxiety of the depressive position.

Isaacs (1952), also speaking from the Kleinian perspective, proposes the "principle of genetic continuity" allows for significant primitive happenings as events in their own right, events that do not need later oedipal validation.

Klein was so loyal to Freud that she appeared to be hesitant to change any of his ideas, let alone his terminology. As a result, her discovery of an infantile mental life that existed before the onset of Freud's phallic oedipal complex was termed by her, presumably out of deference to him, the infantile neurosis. Yet, if one reads between the lines, one can clearly see that she was describing what she oftentimes referred to as "psychotic anxieties." She never employed the term *the infantile psychosis,* however. I do believe, out of deference to her and her monumental work, we should now apply the term *infantile psychosis* to Klein's conception of the paranoid-schizoid and early depressive positions, the latter of which is interposed by the later arrival of the Oedipus complex. In other words, the infantile psychosis has to do with the mother–infant dyad, whereas the infantile neurosis has to do with the oedipal triad.

Fairbairn's Conception of the Infantile Neurosis

Likewise, Fairbairn (1952), who was really both a Freudian and a Kleinian revisionist, proffered the schizoid and depressive positions, followed by the transitional stage, which in turn was followed by mature dependency. He, like Klein, eschewed infantile sexuality in favor of infantile dependency. His own view of the Oedipus complex was unique. While suspended between Klein and the classical view as to its time of onset, he gave its structure and significance a unique twist: he believed that the Oedipus complex represents a condensation of four split object relationships into two in a tripartite situation.

In other words, the "acceptable object" and the "unacceptable object," which, according to him, become internalized and modified to become the "rejecting object" and the "exciting object," constitute the internal objects of endopsychic structure. They are related to by split-off ego structures, the antilibidinal ego and the libidinal ego, respectively. Whereas the rejecting object and the antilibidinal object indirectly repress the exciting object and the libidinal ego, the central ego and its ideal object directly repress all four entities (comprising two endopsychic structures). Thus the exciting object is the incestuously desired one, and the libidinal ego experiences the incestuous desire. This incestuous couple is attacked and indirectly repressed by the rejecting object and antilibidinal ego, both constituting a primitive superego.

Fairbairn's endopsychic structure constitutes a picture of the hysterical patient's unconscious object relationships. Yet they are derived from a series of two earlier dyadic relationships: an acceptable and an unacceptable mother (with separate egos attached) and an acceptable and unacceptable father (also with separate egos attached). In the oedipal phase the acceptable mother and acceptable father are condensed (not united) into a single exciting object, and the unacceptable mother and unacceptable father condense into a rejecting object.

THE INFANTILE NEUROSIS (AND "PSYCHOSIS") REDEFINED

Thus, for Freud and his followers the infantile neurosis conveyed and still conveys the idea of a universal and invariant "illness" that all children (infants?) must suffer as they undergo maturation. It is predicated on the basis of the interdiction by castration anxiety of normal impulses whose phantasies, thoughts, and behavioral expression are forbidden. It constitutes the termination of infantile sexuality (omnipotence) carried forward to the phallic stage and, as such, represents the culmination of weaning—that is, the surrender of the infant's— and child's—rights and entitlement to Mother's body to Father. It is characterized by the experience of unconscious primal scene preoccupation and by castration anxiety.

It has become apparent that there is a discrepancy in the classical conception of the infantile neurosis. The chronological constraints imposed on it (phallic stage) predicate a "childhood neurosis," not an infantile one. It allows for infantile moments of experience as maturational arrests (fixations) whose option is picked up as regressive elaborations (defenses) against phallic-oedipal anxiety. Moreover, not only does the infantile neurosis become the "childhood neurosis" of the phallic-oedipal period, but it also deepens in time since infancy is also *non-time-bound* as the "once and forever infant" within us.

I postulate that the infantile neurosis is better redefined in terms of Klein's—and Fairbairn's—"psychotic" positions (not stages). Positions carry with them the possibility of synchronic (depth and permanence) as well as diachronic (chronologically sequential and linear) dimensions. Bion (1962, 1963) also suggested that the two positions are dialectical.

In other words, one never truly leaves the paranoid-schizoid position nor completely occupies the depressive position. There is always a tension arc between them. Having given the nod to *positions* over *stages*, I should now like to place them dialectically together in a dual track ("Siamese twinship"), where the former occupied the synchronic axis of development (depth and timelessness) and the other the diachronic (linear, sequential) (Grotstein 1988, 1994g). Klein and Fairbairn do seem to agree with the orthodox/classical view of the infantile neurosis in terms of pathomorphism, however, that is, in the universality and ineluctability of *suffering* in the infantile stages.

By virtue of the fact of my redefinition of the infantile neurosis in terms of archaic positions, I should suggest that the basic cluster of persecutory anxieties that Klein ascribed to the paranoid-schizoid position should now be termed the *infantile psychosis*. Further, this infantile psychosis extends into the early part of the depressive position during which the infant is dealing with clinical depressive anxieties. The *infantile neurosis proper* begins to develop during the transitional stage (Fairbairn 1952) once whole objects replace part objects. Yet it must be remembered that the infantile neurosis is both extensive from the infantile psychosis in sequential time and parallel synchronically at the same time with and dialectical to the infantile psychosis.

THE FACTOR OF "SUFFERING" IN THE INFANTILE NEUROSIS: THE INTERGENERATIONAL AND TRANSGENERATIONAL NEUROSIS/PSYCHOSIS

In another contribution I attempted to link this idea of universal developmental suffering with the myth of the Crucifixion and the images of the Pietà and the Stabat Mater, and these in turn with the concept of innocence, blessedness, and curse (Grotstein 1994c,d). Insofar as the infantile neurosis presupposes a developmental phase of ineluctable suffering, I link this idea with the myth of the Crucifixion and of its correlate, the universal occurrence of human sacrifice—generally the sacrifice of the innocent infant or child.

I suggest, consequently, that the infantile neurosis/psychosis is in a synchronic dimension that integrates stages and positions (separate and inseparable from) the transgenerational (ancestral) and intergenerational (parents and grandparents) infantile neuroses/psychoses with which they are in dialectical relationship. This formulation suggests, among other things, as alluded to earlier, that the infantile neurosis, like infant development itself, is part of a dual track (Grotstein 1988, 1994g), a parallel partnership. The infant with an infantile neurosis/psychosis confronts a mother, father, and siblings, each of whom has his or her own infantile neurosis/psychosis. Perhaps we should call it the "infantile neurosis/psychosis complex" or "interaction."

Thus, the infant's infantile neurosis/psychosis may be a

painful condensation of its own natural one *and* that of each or both of its parents projected into it. The infant is destined to wish (unconsciously) to attack the union of the parental couple, yet the father may also wish to attack the infant's union with Mother's breast, and Mother herself may, out of envy and hatred, begrudge her own infant's superior entitlement to the care she herself felt denied in her own infancy, and so on. Thus, the infant, like Oedipus himself, may experience a *curse* rather than a blessing (or both ambivalently) and may come to believe that its very existence is a threat to the parental couple's union—and therefore that it must sacrifice its own welfare for them, a belief that may be part of "folie à trois."

The concept of the necessity for human sacrifice was alluded to by Freud (1913 [1912–13]) when he discussed the primal horde and their ritual sacrificing of the primal father. Klein and Winnicott alluded to the mother as a sacrifice to the infant's omnipotent neediness. *It is my contention that the sacrifice of the innocent infant is the profoundest level of the Oedipus complex and of the infantile neurosis and characterizes, furthermore, the infantile neurosis of all cultures.*

The pain the infant universally suffers in this redefined infantile neurosis is first and foremost the experience of separation from the primal object and its consequences. Freud (1923) seemed to be in agreement with this idea when he stated, "anxiety of separation becomes anxiety of castration by displacement of the cathexis from the object to the organ which insures reunion with the object."

Klein (1932, 1945, 1948, 1950, 1952a,b,c) has dealt with the consequences as the evocation of persecutory anxiety due to the release of bad objects formed by the infant's own death instinct. Fairbairn (1952) also spoke of the release of bad objects but meant the repressed realistic badness of the needed object that is released during separation and in neurotic and psychotic illness. Winnicott (1952a, 1958, 1962, 1963a,b,c) described this phenomenon as "unthinkable anxiety" and "the failure to go on being." Bion (1962, 1963) referred to it as "infantile catastrophe" and "nameless dread." Mahler (1952, 1958, 1968, 1972) has spoken of annihilation anxiety. All agree that the infant suffers a severe reaction if the caretaker is absent too long.

Winnicott (1952a,b, 1958, 1960a) additionally described two separate abandonment–impingement scenarios, one of *privation* and another of *deprivation*.

The infantile neurosis must also be conceived in terms of its counterpart, that is, whether or not the infant's mother and father projectively identify their blessing on the infant or curse it with the projective identification of *their* own unresolved infantile neuroses (Apprey 1987a,b, Apprey and Stein 1991, Cramer 1975, 1982a,b, 1984, 1986).

Child abuse is in no small measure due to the envy by one or another parent of the infant or child he or she abuses because of the latter's superior claim to the entitlements of innocence and grace. Cramer and Apprey have done significant work in this area. Mention must also be made of Bollas's (1987, 1993) concept of "extractive introjection," the robbing of a child of his or her identity prerogatives by concretely presuming ("pre-assuming") attributes of the infant or child away from the latter's sense of self and arrogating these attributes for themselves. "Upstaging" or "preempting" are milder words for this subtle but profound form of personality abuse. Here one must consider the "*Medea* complex" and also the panoply of intergenerational factors.

"INNOCENCE," "BLESSING," AND "CURSE"

Further, I should like to borrow a concept from both Scripture and William Blake (1789–1794), that of innocence (to which I have just alluded), and apply its relevance to development theory and to the infantile neurosis. What I have in mind here is the age-old religious conflict between the infant's sense of innocence and of its sense of original sin. There is something to be said in favor of believing that the infant believes in its innocence when that is reinforced by its caretakers—and that this is experienced as a sense of being "blessed."

Infants who experience less fortunate circumstances may feel unblessed or even cursed. They may demand to have their imagined entitlements restored—or may sink into the dark

oblivion of surrender or even foreclosure as existential vaga-
bonds—the "walking dead." Infants who are properly engaged
and attuned feel innocence and also its lack when frustration
mobilizes their dark, hidden phylogenetic inventory. Generally,
this is "RIG"-ed out (to use Stern's [1985] term [Representations
of Interactions that have been Generalized]. When it is not
RIG-ed out, the infant—or child—may default into the "Black
Hole," that is, may surrender its soul by forfeiting its bodily
existence—in order to avoid pain—and thus fall victim to what
I have come to call the "death instinct" mode (Grotstein 1982,
1990a,b,c,d, 1994i), which Fairbairn (1952) interpreted as
"Evil, be thou my good!" Shame and hopelessness are their
companions; cynical, defiant oppositionality their behavior.

Finally, I suggest that there is an epigenesis to the experience
of innocence: primal innocence, a challenge to it when the child
enters the "Forest of Experience" and encounters "Error," and,
transcending that, "higher innocence," the acceptance of the
world as it is and oneself as one is—that is, freeing the external
world and objects from one's personal claims of entitlement.

THE SKIN, SENSUALITY, AND THE QUESTION OF NORMAL AUTISM

In a recent contribution Ogden (1989a) called attention to a
quantum change in analytic theory occasioned by the neo-
Kleinian contributions of Bick (1968, 1986), Meltzer (1975),
Tustin (1972, 1981, 1984, 1986), and of other contributors,
each of whom has investigated what he has termed "the primitive edge of experience." Specifically Ogden (1989a) and Marcelli (1983) even earlier, have attempted to integrate Bick's
(1968, 1986) "second skin," Meltzer's (1975) "adhesive identification" (which he has renamed "adhesive identity,") and
Tustin's (1972, 1981, 1984, 1986, 1987, 1990a,b, 1991, 1993)
"autosensualism" into a broader concept of an "autistic contig-
uous position" that is more primitive even than Klein's (1940)
"paranoid-schizoid position" but that is in a dialectical tension
arc with it as well as with her "depressive position."

To the above must be added the contributions of Anzieu (1989), especially his "skin ego" and "skin envelope," and Grotstein's (1980, 1993) concept of the skin boundary frontier. The ever-moving cursor of psychoanalysis has shifted from infantile sexuality, autoerotism, and the Oedipus complex through infantile dependency and attachment-bonding theory to the importance of perception (infant development research) and skin autosensualism (newer psychoanalytic theory). In this regard, the work of M. F. A. Montague (1971) on the importance of *touching* is to be included, as well as the subsequent wealth of literature on this subject.

I should like now to expand on my reference to Tustin. She has devoted her life to the psychoanalytic treatment of autistic children and has come up with some important conclusions. Her first formulations were that infants fated to become autistic suffered from a premature abruption of primary oneness and felt exiled precipitously into a precocious two-ness with an abnormally high sense of anxiety about the "me"/"not-me" interface. They become either encapsulated or entanglement (confusional) types.

Further, I agree with Lacan (1953, 1966, 1975) that the bright lights of empirical enlightenment may have also bleached out the unconscious itself by making the "ego" the administrative seat of perception because of its facility for adaptation—and *speech*, which has been confused with *language*. This is perhaps my major theme: infant development research has expanded our knowledge of the infant, but at what cost? I suggest that the *Unbewußt* (the "unknown," literally; the "unconscious," conventionally) itself might be in danger. Insofar as the infantile neurosis is the organizer (can we say "strange attractor"?) of its autoerotic predecessors (which Stern [1985] disavows), what I am asking at this point is what will be the fate of the concept of one's mythic inheritance, not only the unconscious itself, because it is merely the container, but of what it contains? In this regard, empirical research now informs us of the existence of "unconscious perception" (Dixon and Henley 1991).

Infants bring with them at birth a vast array of inherent "hardware" and "software." The content of primal repression—or, put otherwise, of the unrepressed unconscious—

consists of countless capacities and "programs," even narrative scripts or mythic themes that anticipate the infant's future. Infants learn not only by "taking in" the ingredients of their perceived reality (after first skillfully encoding this reality both objectively and subjectively) but also by selecting from their inherent warehouse of possibilities those that apply to the situation perceived at the moment. Thus, *un*learning becomes as important as learning. We know that this principle is true in psychoanalytic treatment generally.

IDENTIFICATION

Moreover, it is possible—maybe even probable—that infants and children do *not* learn from identification but from individually sorting out their own experiences. In identification, the "shadow of the object falls on the ego" (Freud 1914); thus the ego obligatorily becomes the object—and not itself! The role of objects and selfobjects in rearing probably has more to do with shepherding and protecting the infant so that its optimum capacities are selectively chosen from the vast reservoir of inherent possibilities.

CONTRIBUTIONS FROM INFANT DEVELOPMENT

The contributions of infant development research are vast, extensive, and evocative. Some of the current pioneers in this area are Louis Sander (1980, 1987), Colwyn Trevarthen (1980, 1983), and Virginia Demos (1988). The origins of this pursuit go back to the ancient days of psychoanalysis, that is, to Hug-Helmuth (1920), Melanie Klein (1928, 1932, 1940, 1945, 1948, 1950, 1952a,b,c), Anna Freud (1936, 1965), Bergman and Escalona (1949), and others, but the current thrust owes its beginnings to Bowlby (1958, 1960, 1969, 1973, 1980) and Spitz (1959) and their many descendants. It is unfortunate that Esther

Bick (1968, 1986), the Kleinian infant observer, published only two short contributions from the wealth of her clinical experience. I am certain that her intuitive observations would be—as they have been if oral testimony is correct—at considerable odds with those advanced by infant observers in this country—and similarly the French and the Italian observers, whose backgrounds seem to afford greater generosity to the probability that the infant is born with an unconscious and has a rich phantasmal mental life from the beginning.

It is almost impossible to list the significant contributions made in this field. Lichtenberg (1983), Greenspan and Greenspan (1985), and Stern (1985, 1989) have attempted to do so, and thus most of my references are to them, particularly the latter, and through them to others. While demonstrating the unusually early onset of the interpersonal capacities of the infant, Stern in particular emphasizes that he and others are at the same time elaborating the infant's subjective experiences. It is in this latter area that the most controversy would lie. What constitutes interpersonal capacities and what constitutes subjective experiences?

Stern (1985) states:

> It is a basic assumption . . . that some senses of the self do exist long prior to self-awareness and language. These include the sense of agency, of physical cohesion, of continuity in time, of having intentions in mind, and other such experiences. . . . Self reflection and language come to work upon these preverbal existential senses of the self and, in so doing, not only reveal their ongoing existence but transform them into new experiences. [p. 6]

Stern then goes on to ponder that some preverbal senses of self may begin at birth (or even before), while others must await their own individual maturational turn. Following this he lists the senses of self he believes are important: agency, physical cohesion, continuity, affectivity (the principal organizing sense), subjective self, creating organization, and transmuting meaning.

After describing some of the quantum shifts in the infant's developmental life, Stern asks the question:

Does the advent of new infant behaviors such as focal eye contact and smiling make the parent attribute a new persona to the infant whose subjective experience has not as yet changed at all? In fact, any change in the infant may come about partly by virtue of the adult interpreting the infant differently and acting accordingly. (The adult would be working within the infant's proximal zone of development, that is, in an area appropriate to infant capacities not yet present but very soon to emerge.) Most probably, it works both ways. [p. 9]

The first series of observations and conclusions seem to affirm that the infant has a separate and actively developing sense of self from the beginning. Though Stern is careful to avoid the word, he seems to be describing the sense of a developing self as a conventional ego. Stern is Cartesian insofar as he seems to be saying, "The infant strives to make sense of its perceptions; therefore it is!" It did not occur to Stern to ask, as Lacan did: Where is the origin of language, not speech? Is the observer the self—the only self? In fairness to Stern, however, he is ably conveying fascinating new empirical data that effectively seems to put to rest the question of infant *consciousness* of being a self, an inchoate self that is separate but not readily individuated.

Since the issue of the infantile neurosis seems to center on the primal scene, the Oedipus complex, and castration anxiety rather than (classically) earlier phenomena, it has not seemed to have been discussed in terms of infant observation research. The subject is not listed in either Lichtenberg's or Stern's indices. Observers from the Kleinian ranks, knowing that Klein posited an oral Oedipus complex anterior to the phallic one, and one timed during the depressive position, would have certainly made comparisons. The comparisons made by developmental-ists, however, have to do with whether or not the infant is in a stage of fusion known as primary narcissism, which was later translated by Mahler (1952, 1958, 1968, 1972) into the autistic and symbiotic developmental stages.

In his later statement about the cooperative act between mother and infant in creating the sense of a developing self, Stern becomes admirably poetic and transcends his empirical shackles. One is reminded of Winnicott's famous dictum, "There is no such thing as an infant; there is only an infant and its mother." But the larger issue is that of the intersubjective approach in understanding the emergence of the maturational unfolding of the infant's mental life. The term *intersubjective* has come to convey different meanings to different workers. Trevarthen seems to understand it as a sense that the infant is aware of its mother's subjectivity as a self as she is of the infant's. To Brandchaft and Stolorow (1990) it seems to have the meaning of a sense of respect for the subjectivity of the infant/patient by its caretaker *and* a vulnerability on the part of the caretaker's own subjectivity as to its consequences on the infant/patient.

Perhaps Winnicott (1951, 1969, 1971a,b,c,d) formulated it best when he conceived of potential space, of illusion, and of the transitional object—that the infant is to discover it at the same time that it is offered by Mother so that the question of where it started or from whom is not to be asked. In other words, the infant develops through *mutual imagination*.

I should like to summarize my own impressions and conclusions about the developmental/clinical interface:

1. There are two infants at birth; there is the one described by the developmentalists and the one described by the clinicians. There is a conscious perceptual-cognitive infant (who is the author of speech), and there is an unconscious one (the author of language, dreams, and phantasies). The latter is the sponsor of the infantile neurosis. The figure of "Siamese twinship" describes their unique existences; they may either be fused, symbiotic, or separate—at the same time or alternately—and experience a discontinuous continuity with each other via a Möbius-strip connection.

   With this image in mind, one can conceive of the possibilities of the coexistence of primary narcissism (normal autism and symbiosis) *and* separation with individuation from the ego psychology developmental point of view; of the simultaneity of the paranoid-schizoid, depressive, and autistic-contiguous positions from the Kleinian and neo-Kleinian points of view; of the schizoid and depressive positions; and of the holding environment and object usage. These dialectics are, in turn, in dialectical opposition to the perceptual-cognitive (sensory-motor) infant of Piaget and current developmental theorists.

2. The infant is born with a dual-track capacity; that is, it is informed by two great information-processing systems, primary and secondary. The latter is what infant developmentalists have been studying; the former is what psychoanalysts have been clinically intuiting from reconstructions.

3. One of the most important findings of infant development research for psychoanalysis is the nature and complexity of the *intersubjective field*, one of whose components is *attunement*. The latter has come to have far-reaching importance for psychoanalytic theory and technique and helps to bypass the issue of the so-called demonic infant, the classical and Kleinian infant who is born, as it were, from the "original sins" of its drive endowment. The emphasis has shifted from the infant to the couple as the irreducible unit of study, thanks to Winnicott and Bowlby, and now to developmental findings.

   Yet here again a dual-track consideration is necessary clinically. Although attunement is vital, infants/patients allegedly accept —and must accept—responsibility for their feelings (and suffering) because of their *belief* that they are the origin of all causality. This belief is necessary in order to have a sense of agency, but its omnipotence must be tempered by reality later.

4. The primary (information) processing system operates via projective identification and splitting (as well as by idealization and magic omnipotent denial). It also has phylogenetically honed "information" at its disposal. The universality of the Oedipus complex (the regulator of rivalry and interpersonal boundaries) is but one; the awareness of prey–predator anxiety—and the adaptive strategies with which to cope with it—is another.

5. Phantasy is the language of sensual imagery (from the skin's sense organs) and is admixed with affects and drives to become the fundamental language of our lives.

Dreams are its clearest expression. The infant probably dreams. It is the basic language, and may even be related to the "ground language" referred to by Schreber (Freud 1911).

6. Infants are born into what appears to be randomness, but actually is chaos (Winnicott's [1988] "non-integration") until it becomes organized. They organize this chaos around their projective assignments of personal meaning. In other words, they seek to personalize the data of their experience by creating it before they can allow it to be created—much like the infant God of Genesis. It is only in the depressive position that "God" can admit that he or she did not create him- or herself or his or her parents, Adam and Eve, but was, instead, created by their intercourse. *This is the infantile neurosis/psychosis!*

7. As a consequence, infants *believe* that they, for instance, harbor an active death instinct when they see Mother angry, because of their need to account for it and to control it.

8. Thus, the infant is autopoietic, autochthonous, and solipsistic in the organization of its inner and outer world and is so because it needs a system of hermeneutics in order to be unified around a theory of personal causality. ("I create the world before I can allow it to impact me!")

9. The infant is "sexual" in the classical autoerotic sense (as well as in the pathologically defensive sense) and yet is also not sexual ("alter egos"). The latter constitutes the "innocent self." The early infant probably goes through an early latency period before sexuality (curiosity) takes over.

10. *The developmental infant is the "alter ego" to the infant of the infantile neurosis/psychosis (primal scene). They are both there from the beginning. The primal scene represents all the factors that interfere with the infant's blissful union with the primal object and may include atavistic prey–predator anxiety, chaos, stranger anxiety, "bad" mother, father, siblings, and so on—and all the demons of which imagination can conceive—via projective identification.*

11. The concept of the Siamese twinship (dual track) accounts for and reconciles all the disparate theories of infant development epigenesis. The discrepancies between them can now be understood as coeval with one another. Thus, Winnicott's (1988) and Lacan's (1953, 1966, 1975) nonintegrated stage can be thought of as existing side by side with an emerging sense of self and, later, of a core self. At the same time the infant can have an unconscious estimation of itself as an "other self" regarded as an "object" by itself as "subject" ("I").

A critical point is that of 3 to 4 months of age when the core self develops. This is the time when Klein believes that the depressive position appears, when Mahler believes in the beginning of "hatching," Spitz the "social smile," Parens (1979) normal assertiveness, Winnicott the transitional object, Trevarthen primary intersubjectivity, the phenomenon of the "imaginary companion," Lumsden and Wilson (1981, 1983) altruism. Biologically it is the beginning of myelination of the corpus callosum, the great cerebral hemispheric bridge.

Stranger anxiety (Spitz 1959) makes its appearance around 9 months of age, and a large portion of the neurons begin to disappear around 18 months (Schore 1994). These clusters of discontinuous peaks of biological substrates seem to indicate that the infant begins to crystallize or organize a coherent sense of "selves" under the integrative organization of what is beginning more and more to be a unitary self.

REFERENCES

Abraham, K. (1924). A short study of the development of the libido. In *Selected Papers on Psycho-Analysis*, pp. 418–501. London: Hogarth, 1948.

Anzieu, D. (1989). *The Skin Ego*. Trans. C. Turner. New Haven: Yale University Press.

Apprey, M. (1987a). Projective identification and maternal misconception in disturbed mothers. *British Journal of Psychotherapy* 4 (1):5–22.

_____ (1987b). "When one dies another lives": the invariant unconscious fantasy in response to a destructive maternal projective identification. *Journal of the Melanie Klein Society* 5(2):18–53.

Apprey, M., & Stein, H. F. (1993). *Intersubjectivity, Projective Identification, and Otherness*. Pittsburg: Duquesne University Press.

Balint, M. (1965). *Primary Love and Psycho-Analytic Technique*. London: Tavistock.

Bergman, P., & Escalona, S. (1949). Unusual sensitivities in very young children. *Psychoanalytic Study of the Child* 3/4:333–352. New York: International Universities Press.

Bick, E. (1968). The experience of the skin in early object relations. *International Journal of Psycho-Analysis* 49:484–486.

_____ (1986). Further considerations on the function of the skin in early object relations. *British Journal of Psychotherapy* 2:292–299.

Bion, W. R. (1962). *Learning from Experience*. London: Heinemann.

_____ (1963). *Elements of Psycho-analysis*. London: Heinemann.

_____ (1975). *A Memoir of the Future, Book 1: The Dream*. Rio de Janeiro, Brazil: Imago.

Blake, W. (1789–1794). *Songs of Innocence and Experience*. Oxford: Oxford University Press, 1967.

Bollas, C. (1987). *The Shadow of the Object: Psychoanalysis of the Unthought Known*. New York: International Universities Press.

_____ (1993). *Being a Character: Psychoanalysis and Self Experience*. London: Routledge.

Bower, T. G. R. (1978). The infant's discovery of objects and mother. In *Origins of the Infant's Social Responsiveness*, ed., E. B. Thoman. Hillsdale, NJ: Erlbaum.

_____ (1982). *Development in Infancy*. San Francisco: W. H. Freeman.

Bowlby, J. (1958). The nature of the child's tie to his mother.

International Journal of Psycho-Analysis 39:350–373.

_____ (1960). Separation anxiety. *International Journal of Psycho-Analysis* 41:80–113.

_____ (1969). *Attachment and Loss*, vol. 1, *Attachment*. New York: Basic Books.

_____ (1973). *Attachment and Loss*, vol. 2, *Separation: Anxiety and Anger*. New York: Basic Books.

_____ (1980). *Attachment and Loss*, vol. 3, *Loss: Sadness and Depression*. New York: Jason Aronson.

Brandchaft, B., and Stolorow, R. (1990). Varieties of therapeutic alliance. *The Annual of Psychoanalysis* 18:99–114. Hillsdale, NJ: Analytic Press.

Brody, S., & Axelrad, S. (1966). Anxiety, socialization, and ego-formation in infancy. *International Journal of Psycho-Analysis*, 47:218–229.

_____ (1970). *Anxiety and Ego Formation*. New York: International Universities Press.

Chess, S., & Thomas, A., eds. (1986). *Temperament in Clinical Practice*. New York: Guilford.

Cramer, B. (1975). Outstanding developmental progression in three boys: a longitudinal study. *Psychoanalytic Study of the Child* 30:15–48. New Haven: Yale University Press.

_____ (1982a). Interaction réelle, interaction fantasmatique: réflexions au sujet des thérapies et des observations de nourrissons. *Psychothérapies* 1: 39–47.

_____ (1982b). La psychiatrie du bébé: une introduction. In *La Dynamique du nourrisson*, ed. M. Soulé, pp. 28–83. Paris: Editions Sociales Françaises.

_____ (1984). *Modèles psychoanalytiques, modèles interactifs: recoupement possible?* Paper presented at the International Symposium on Psychiatry and Psychoanalysis, Montreal, Canada, September.

_____ (1986). Assessment of parent–infant relationship. In *Affective Development in Infancy*, ed. T. B. Brazelton and M. W. Yogman, pp. 27–38. Norwood, NJ: Ablex.

DeMause, L. (1974). The evolution of childhood. In *The History of Childhood*, pp. 1–73. New York: Psychohistory.

Demos, V. (1988). Affect and the development of the self. In *Frontiers in Self Psychology: Progress in Self Psychology*, vol.

3, ed. A. Goldberg, pp. 27–53. Hillsdale, NJ: Analytic.

Fairbairn, W. R. D. (1952). *Psychoanalytic Studies of the Personality*. London: Routledge and Kegan Paul.

Freud, A. (1936). *The Ego and the Mechanisms of Defence*. New York: International Universities Press.

_____ *Normality and Pathology in Childhood*. New York: International Universities Press.

Freud, S. (1909). Analysis of a phobia in a five-year-old boy. *Standard Edition* 10:3–47.

_____ (1913[1912–1913]). Totem and taboo. *Standard Edition* 13:1–64.

_____ (1914). On narcissism: an introduction. *Standard Edition* 14:67–104.

_____ (1918[1914]). From the history of an infantile neurosis. *Standard Edition* 17:3–122.

_____ (1923). The ego and the id. *Standard Edition* 19:3–59.

Greenspan, S., and Greenspan, N. T. (1985). *First Feelings: Milestones in the Emotional Development of Your Baby and Child from Birth to Age Four*. New York: Viking.

Grotstein, J. (1980). A proposed revision of the psychoanalytic concept of primitive mental states. 1. An introduction to a newer psychoanalytic metapsychology. *Contemporary Psychoanalysis* 16 (4):479–546.

_____ (1981). *Splitting and Projective Identification*. New York: Jason Aronson.

_____ (1982). Newer perspectives in object relations theory. *Contemporary Psychoanalysis, A Memorial Issue in Honor of Dr. Max Deutscher* 18:43–91.

_____ (1987). Borderline as a disorder of self-regulation. In *The Borderline Patient: Emerging Concepts in Diagnosis, Psychodynamics, and Treatment*, vol. 1, ed. J. Grotstein, M. Solomon, and J. Langs, pp. 347–383. Hillsdale, NJ: Analytic.

_____ (1988). The "Siamese twinship" of the cerebral hemispheres and of the brain-mind continuum: toward a "psychology" for the corpus callosum. *Hemispheric Specialization, Affect, and Creativity*, for *Psychiatric Clinics of North America* 11(3):399–412.

_____ (1990a). The "Black Hole" as the basic psychotic experience: some newer psychoanalytic and neuroscience perspectives on psychosis. *Journal of the American Academy of Psychoanalysis* 18(1):29–46.

_____ (1990b). Nothingness, meaninglessness, chaos, and the "Black Hole": Part 1. The importance of nothingness, meaninglessness, and chaos in psychoanalysis. *Contemporary Psychoanalysis* 26(2):257–290.

_____ (1990c). Nothingness, meaninglessness, chaos, and the "Black Hole": Part 2. *Contemporary Psychoanalysis* 26(3):377–407.

_____ (1990d). Nothingness, meaninglessness, chaos, and the "Black Hole": Part 3. Self-interactional regulation and the background presence of primary identification. *Contemporary Psychoanalysis* 27(1):1–13.

_____ (1991a). An American view of the British psychoanalytic experience: psychoanalysis in counterpoint. Part 1. Introduction: the Americanization of psychoanalysis. *Journal of Melanie Klein and Object Relations* 9(2):1–15.

_____ (1991b). An American view of the British psychoanalytic experience: psychoanalysis in counterpoint. Part 2. The Kleinian school. *Journal of Melanie Klein and Object Relations* 9(2):16–33.

_____ (1991c). An American view of the British psychoanalytic experience: psychoanalysis in counterpoint. Part 3. The contributions of the British object relations school. *Journal of Melanie Klein and Object Relations* 9 (2):34–62.

_____ (1993). Boundary difficulties in borderline patients. In *Master Clinicians on Treating the Regressed Patient, vol 2*, ed. L. B. Boyer and P. Giovacchini, pp. 107–142. Northvale, NJ: Jason Aronson.

_____ (1994a). Notes on Fairbairn's metapsychology. In *Fairbairn and the Origins of Object Relations*, ed. D. Rinsley and J. Grotstein, pp. 112–148. NY: Guilford.

_____ (1994b). Endopsychic structures and the cartography of the internal world: six endopsychic characters in search of an author. In *Fairbairn and the Origins of Object Relations*, ed. D. Rinsley and J. Grotstein, pp. 174–194. NY: Guilford.

_____ (1994c). Why Oedipus and not Christ? The importance of "innocence," "original sin," and human sacrifice in psychoanalytic theory and practice. 1. The crucifixion and the pieta, and the transference/countertransference neurosis/psychosis. Manuscript in preparation.

———— (1994d). Why Oedipus and not Christ? The importance of "innocence," "original sin," and human sacrifice in psychoanalytic theory and practice. 2. A selective rereading of the myth of Oedipus and of the synoptic gospels. Manuscript in preparation.

———— (1994e). Projective identification reappraised: projective identification, introjective identification, the transference/countertransference neurosis/psychosis, and their consummate expression in the crucifixion, the pieta, and "therapeutic exorcism" Part 1. Projective identification. *Contemporary Psychoanalysis*. In press.

———— (1994f). Projective identification reappraised: Projective identification, introjective identification, the transference/countertransference neurosis/psychosis, and their consummate expression in the crucifixion, the pieta, and "therapeutic exorcism." Part 2. The countertransference complex. *Contemporary Psychoanalysis*. In press.

———— (1994g). The dual-track theorem and the "Siamese-twinship" paradigm for psychoanalytic concepts. Manuscript accepted for publication in *Contemporary Psychoanalysis*.

———— (1994h). *Projective Identification, Introjective Identification, and Countertransference*. Book in preparation.

———— (1994i). *"And at the Same Time and on Another Level . ."*: *A Textbook on Psychoanalytic Technique*. Book in preparation.

———— (1994j). Object relations theory. In *Textbook of Psychoanalysis*, ed. E. Nersessian and R. Kopff. American Psychiatric Press. In press.

Hamilton, V. (1991). Use or misuse: the analyst as object. A clinical illustration of Winnicott's concept of "object usage." Unpublished manuscript.

Heinicke, C. M., and Westheimer, I. J. (1965). *Brief Separation*. New York: International Universities Press.

Hopkins, B. (1989). Jesus in object-use: a Winnicottian account of the resurrection myth. *International Review of Psycho-Analysis* 16:93–100.

Hug-Helmuth, H. V. (1920). Child psychology and education.

74   James S. Grotstein, M.D.

International Journal of Psycho-Analysis 1:316–323.

Hughes, J. M. (1989). *Reshaping the Psychoanalytic Domain: The Work of Melanie Klein, W. R. D. Fairbairn, and D. W. Winnicott*. Berkeley and Los Angeles: University of California Press.

Isaacs, S. (1952). The nature and function of phantasy. In *Developments in Psycho-Analysis*, ed. J. Riviere, pp. 67–121. London: Hogarth.

Jacobson, E. (1964). *The Self and the Object World*. New York: International Universities Press.

Jung, C. G. (1934). *Archetypes and the Collective Unconscious*: *Collected Works*. Trans. R. F. C. Hull. New York: Bollinger Series 20, 1959.

Khan, M. (1964). The concept of cumulative trauma. In *The British School of Psychoanalysis: The Independent Tradition*, ed. G. Kohon, pp. 101–116. London: Free Association Books.

Klein, M. (1928). Early stages of the Oedipus conflict. In *Contributions to Psycho-Analysis, 1921–1945*, pp. 202–214. London: Hogarth, 1950.

_____ (1932). The effect of early anxiety situations on the sexual development of the girl. In *The Psychoanalysis of Children*, pp. 268–325. New York: Humanities, 1969.

_____ (1940). Mourning and its relation to manic-depressive states. In *Contributions to Psycho-Analysis, 1921–1945*, pp. 311–338. London: Hogarth, 1950.

_____ (1945). The Oedipus complex in the light of early anxieties. In *Contributions to Psycho-Analysis, 1921–1945*, pp. 339–390. London: Hogarth, 1950.

_____ (1948). On the theory of anxiety and guilt. In *Envy and Gratitude and Other Works, 1946–1963*, pp. 1–24. New York: Delacorte, 1975.

_____ (1950). *Contributions to Psycho-Analysis, 1921–1945*. London: Hogarth.

_____ (1952a). *Developments in Psycho-Analysis* ed. M. Klein, P. Heinemann, S. Isaacs, and J. Riviere. London: Hogarth.

_____ (1952b). Some theoretical conclusions regarding the emotional life of the infant. In *Developments in Psycho-Analysis*, ed. M. Klein, P. Heinemann, S. Isaacs, and J. Riviere, pp.

198–236. London: Hogarth.

_____ (1952c). Notes on some schizoid mechanisms. In *Developments in Psycho-Analysis*, ed. M. Klein, P. Heinemann, S. Isaacs, and J. Riviere, pp. 292–320. London: Hogarth.

Kohut, H. (1971). *The Analysis of the Self: A Systematic Approach to the Psychoanalytic Treatment of Narcissistic Personality Disorders*. New York: International Universities Press.

_____ (1977). *The Restoration of the Self*. New York: International Universities Press.

_____ (1978a). *The Search for the Self*, vol. 1, ed. P. Ornstein. New York: International Universities Press.

_____ (1978b). *The Search for the Self*, vol. 2. ed. P. Ornstein. New York: International Universities Press.

_____ (1984). *How Does Analysis Cure?* ed. A. Goldberg, with collaboration of P. E. Stepansky. Chicago: University of Chicago Press.

Kristeva, J. (1982). *Powers of Horror: An Essay on Abjection*. Trans. L. S. Roudiez. New York: Columbia University Press.

Krystal, H. (1981). The hedonic element in affectivity. *The Annual of Psychoanalysis* 9:93–115. New York: International Universities Press.

_____ (1982). Alexithymia and the affectiveness of psychoanalytic treatment. *International Journal of Psychoanalytic Psychotherapy* 9:353–378.

_____ (1983). The activating aspects of emotions. *Psychoanalysis and Contemporary Thought* 5:605– 642.

_____ (1990). An information processing view of object relations. *Psychoanalytic Inquiry* 10 (2) :221–251.

Lacan, J. (1966). The function and field of speech and language in psychoanalysis. In *Ecrits*, pp. 30–113. Paris: Seuil.

_____ (1975). *Le Séminaire 20 (1972–1973)*. Paris: Seuil.

Lichtenberg, J. D. (1983). *Psychoanalysis and Infant Research*. Hillsdale, NJ: Analytic.

Lichtenstein, H. (1961). Identity and sexuality. *Journal of the American Psychoanalytic Association* 9:179–260.

_____ (1964). The role of narcissism in the emergence and maintenance of a primary identity. *International Journal of Psycho-Analysis* 45:49–56.

———— (1983). *The Dilemma of Human Identity*. New York: Jason Aronson.

Loewald, H. W. (1979). The waning of the Oedipus complex. *Journal of the American Psychoanalytic Association* 27:751–776.

Lumsden, C. J., and Wilson, E. O. (1981). *Genes, Mind, and Culture: The Co-Evolutionary Process*. Cambridge, MA: Harvard University Press.

———— (1983). *Promethean Fire: Reflections on the Origin of Mind*. Cambridge, MA: Harvard University Press.

Mahler, M. S. (1968). *On Human Symbiosis and the Vicissitudes of Individuation*. New York: International Universities Press.

Mahler, M. S., Pine, F., and Bergman, A. (1975). *The Psychological Birth of the Human Infant*. New York: Basic Books.

Marcelli, D. (1983). La position autistique. Hypothèses psychopathologiques et ontogénétiques. *Psychiatrie enfant* 24(1):5–55.

Meltzer, D. W. (1975). Adhesive identification. *Contemporary Psychoanalysis* 11: 289–310.

Meltzer, D. W., Bremner, J., Hoxter, S., et al. (1975). *Explorations in Autism*. Strath Tay, Perthshire, Scotland: Clunie.

Montague, A. (1971). *Touching, the Human Significance of the Skin*. New York: Columbia University Press.

Murray, J. (1964). Narcissism and the ego ideal. *Journal of the American Psychoanalytic Association* 12:477–511.

Murray, L. (1991). *A prospective study of the impact of maternal depression on infant development*. Paper and videotape presented at "The Psychic Life of the Infant: Origins of Human Identity," conferences sponsored by the University of Massachusetts at Amherst, June.

Nagera, H. (1963). The developmental profile: notes on some practical considerations regarding its use. *Psychoanalytic Study of the Child* 18:511–540. New York: International Universities Press.

———— (1966). *Early Childhood Disturbances, the Infantile Neurosis, and the Adulthood Disturbances*. New York: International Universities Press.

———— (1969). The imaginary companion: its significance for ego development and conflict solution. *Psychoanalytic Study of the Child* 24:165–196. New York: International Universities Press.

Ogden, T. (1989a). *The Primitive Edge of Experience*. Northvale, NJ: Jason Aronson.

Palombo, J. (1993). Neurocognitive deficits, developmental distortions, and incoherent narratives. In *Fear of Fusion*, ed. J. S. Grotstein. *Psychoanalytic Inquiry* 13(1):85–102.

Parens, H. (1979). *The Development of Aggression in Early Childhood*. New York: Jason Aronson.

Rangell, L. (1955). The role of the parent in the Oedipus complex. *Bulletin of the Menninger Clinic* 19:9–15.

Rayner, E. (1991). *The Independent Mind in British Psychoanalysis*. Northvale: Jason Aronson.

Reich, A. (1960). Pathological forms of self-esteem regulation. In *Psychoanalytic Contributions*, pp. 238–311. New York: International Universities Press, 1973.

Sander, L. (1980). New knowledge about the infant from current research: implications for psychoanalysis. *Journal of the American Psychoanalytic Association* 28(1):181–198.

––––– (1987). Awareness of inner experience. *Child Abuse and Neglect* 2:339–346.

Schore, A. (1991). Early superego development: the emergence of shame and narcissistic affect regulation in the practicing period. *Psychoanalysis and Contemporary Thought* 14(2):187–250.

––––– (1994). *Affect Regulation and the Origin of the Self: The Neurobiology of Emotional Development*. Hillsdale, NJ: Erlbaum.

Spitz, R. (1959). *A Genetic Field Theory of Ego Formation: Its Implications for Pathology*. New York: International Universities Press.

Stanfield, B. B. (1984). Postnatal reorganization of cortical projections: the role of collateral elimination. *TINS* 7:37–41.

Stern, D. (1985). *The Interpersonal World of the Infant*. New York: Basic Books.

––––– (1989). The representation of rational patterns: developmental considerations. In *Relation Disturbances and Early Childhood: A Developmental Approach*, ed. A. J. Sameroff and R. N. Emde, pp. 52–69. New York: Basic Books.

Stone, M. H. (1988). Toward a psychobiological theory on borderline personality disorder: Is irritability the red thread that runs through borderline conditions? *Dissociations* 1(2):2–15.

Subbotsky, E. V. (1992). *Foundations of Mind: Children's Understanding of Reality*. Cambridge, MA: Harvard University Press.

Sutherland, J. (1980). The British object relations theorists: Balint, Winnicott, Fairbairn, Guntrip. *Journal of the American Psychoanalytic Association* 28:829–860.

Taylor, G. J. (1984). Alexithymia: concept, measurement and implications for treatment. *American Journal of Psychiatry* 141(6) :725–732.

_____ (1987a). *Psychosomatic Medicine in Contemporary Psychoanalysis*. Madison, CT: International Universities Press.

_____ (1987b). Alexithymia: history and validation of the concept. *Transcultural Psychiatric Research Review* 24:85–95.

_____ (1992). Psychoanalysis and psychosomatics: a new synthesis. *Journal of the American Academy of Psychoanalysis* 20(2) :251–275.

_____ (1993). Clinical application of a dysregulation model of illness and disease: a case of spasmodic torticollis. *International Journal of Psycho-Analysis* 74:581–596.

Tolpin, M. (1970). The infantile neurosis: a metapsychological concept and a paradigmatic case history. *Psychoanalytic Study of the Child* 25:273–305. New York: International Universities Press.

_____ (1971). On the beginning of a cohesive self: an application of the concept of transmuting internalization to the study of the transitional object and signal anxiety. *Psychoanalytic Study of the Child* 26:316–352. New Haven, CT: Yale University Press.

Trevarthen, C. (1980). The foundations of intersubjectivity: development of interpersonal and cooperative understanding in infants. In *The Social Foundations of Language and Thought: Essays in Honor of J. S. Bruner*, ed. D. Olson, pp. 316–342. New York: W. W. Norton,

_____ (1983). Development of the cerebral mechanisms of language. In *Neuropsychology of Language, Reading, and Spell-*

ing, ed. U. Kirk, pp. 45–80. New York: Academic.

Tustin, F. (1972). *Autism and Childhood Psychosis*. London: Hogarth.

_____ (1981). *Autistic States in Children*. London: Routledge and Kegan Paul.

_____ (1984). Autistic shapes. *International Review of Psycho-Analysis* 11:279–290.

_____ (1986). *Autistic Barriers in Neurotic Patients*. New Haven, CT: Yale University Press.

_____ (1987). The rhythm of safety. *Winnicott Studies. The Journal of the Squiggle Foundation* 2:19–31.

_____ (1990a). Autistic encapsulation in neurotic patients. In *Master Clinicians: On Treating the Regressed Patient*, eds. L. B. Boyer and P. L. Giovacchini, pp. 117–138. Northvale, NJ: Jason Aronson.

_____ (1990b). *The Protective Shell in Children and Adults*. London: Karnac Books.

_____ (1991). Revised understandings of psychogenic autism. *International Journal of Psycho-Analysis* 72(4):585–591.

_____ (1993). On psychogenic autism. In *Fear of Fusion*, ed. J. S. Grotstein. *Psychoanalytic Inquiry* 13(1):34–41.

Winnicott, D. W. (1951). Transitional objects and transitional phenomena. In *Collected Papers: Through Paediatrics to Psycho-Analysis*, pp. 229–242. New York: Basic Books, 1958.

_____ (1952a). Anxiety associated with insecurity. In *Collected Papers: Through Paediatrics to Psycho-Analysis*, pp. 97–100. New York: Basic Books, 1958.

_____ (1952b). Psychoses and child care. In *Collected Papers: Through Paediatrics to Psycho-Analysis*, pp. 219–228. New York: Basic Book, 1958.

_____ (1958). The capacity to be alone. In *The Maturational Processes and the Facilitating Environment*, pp. 29–36. New York: International Universities Press, 1965.

_____ (1960a). The theory of the parent–infant relationship. *The Maturational Processes and the Facilitating Environment: Studies in the Theory of Emotional Development*, pp. 37–55. New York: International Universities Press, 1965.

_____ (1960b). Ego distortion in terms of true and false self. In *The Maturational Processes and the Facilitating Environ-*

ment: *Studies in the Theory of Emotional Development*, pp. 140–152. New York: International Universities Press, 1965.

_____ (1962). Ego integration in child development. In *The Maturational Processes and the Facilitating Environment. Studies in the Theory of Emotional Development*, pp. 56–63. New York: International Universities Press, 1965.

_____ (1963a). Communicating and not communicating leading to a study of certain opposites. In *The Maturational Processes and the Facilitating Environment: Studies in the Theory of Emotional Development*, pp. 179–192. New York: International Universities Press, 1965.

_____ (1963b). The mentally ill in your case load. In *The Maturational Processes and the Facilitating Environment: Studies in the Theory of Emotional Development*, pp. 217–229. New York: International Universities Press, 1965.

_____ (1969). The use of an object and relating through identification. In *Playing and Reality*, pp. 86–94. London: Tavistock, 1971.

_____ (1971a). Playing: a theoretical statement. In *Playing and Reality*, pp. 38–52. London: Tavistock.

_____ (1971b). Playing: creative activity and the search for the self. In *Playing and Reality*, pp. 53–64. London: Tavistock.

_____ (1971c). Mirror-role of mother and family in child development. In *Playing and Reality*, pp. 11–118. London: Tavistock.

_____ (1971d). Interrelating apart from instinctual drive and in terms of cross-identification. In *Playing and Reality*, pp. 119–137. London: Tavistock.

PART II

Reexamining Assessment and Treatment of Children and Families

INTRODUCTION TO PART II

Assessment has long been recognized as central to under-standing the emotional problems of children and adolescents. The use of diagnostic teams and a multidisciplinary approach to diagnostic assessment allows the most appropriate individual-ized treatment plan to be generated for each child. Reiss-Davis has always made the diagnostic process a vital part of its program at the Center and has developed new, more innovative methods of assessment to help identify unique characteristics in children's behavior as well as unusual family patterns to com-plement the more traditional assessment approaches it has always embraced. A few of these more innovative methods of assessment are explored in the following three chapters written by members of the Reiss-Davis staff.

Chapter 4, by Dr. Van Dyke De Golia, medical director at the Reiss-Davis Child Study Center, describes an alternative model of evaluation and intervention. "An Integrative Model for Child and Parent Assessment" combines views from psychodynamic psychiatry and a family-systems approach. De Golia illustrates the integration of these models through a comprehensive case description of the assessment and long-term treatment of a 6-year-old boy manifesting behavior problems at school, whose depression and suicidal ideation at home mirror his mother's similar struggle with her own depression and suicidal thoughts.

In "Family Therapy Evaluation and Treatment Planning" (Chapter 5), Robert Moradi, who teaches in and supervises the Family Therapy Program at the center, suggests new means of assessment using initial contacts between patient and therapist. He explores the use of the therapist's conscious and unconscious fantasies, daydreams, and free associations coupled with the family's intersubjective interactions as tools in the evaluation. Moradi's innovative integration of information derived from initial contacts between the therapist and family members, including the first phone call, setting appointments, clarifying of fees and fee collection, cancellation policies, and other issues present in the early stages of assessment, are explored in this chapter.

Chapter 6—"Inquiry and the Difference It Makes in Diagnostic Psychological Testing"—by James Incorvaia, Executive Director of the Reiss-Davis Child Study Center, illustrates how methods of inquiry across the gamut of psychological diagnostic testing can yield much richer results by uncovering more of the uniqueness of the child's personality, including many unconscious processes. Incorvaia offers techniques and illustrates different approaches for specific diagnostic tests that will enhance the diagnostician's results.

4

An Integrative Model for Child and Parent Assessment

Van Dyke De Golia, M.D.

As in all areas of medicine, the assessment of a presenting complaint determines the type of therapeutic intervention or treatment. In psychiatry, this principle is equally important and closely followed. However, the presenting complaint is often complicated by multiple factors, none of which is easily isolated or dismissed as more or less significant. As a result, the problem can be examined from a variety of vantage points—biological, interpersonal, family systems, intrapsychic, cognitive, and behavioral. Entertaining so many points of view simultaneously is a Herculean task, and often the clinician settles on the view he or she feels most comfortable with. The assessment and corresponding intervention then reflect this bias.

Although limiting one's field of vision can be argued as appropriate assessing and treating adult psychopathology, in child psychiatry it can be misleading and even harmful. Children and their presenting complaints often cannot be separated from their social, family, or educational contexts. Likewise, the biological substratum and intrapsychic dynamics, as they are set forth in the early years of life, provide the building blocks with which development takes place and outer experience forms. To focus on any one aspect of a child's experience to the exclusion of other aspects without first making a thorough assessment would result in not fully understanding the presenting problem. With children this is particularly important because what is normal to one child at a certain age is not necessarily normal at a later age, and what is normal to one child raised in a certain family and cultural setting may be abnormal for a child from an entirely different family and cultural experience.

Historically, within child psychiatry, many of these points of view of a clinical problem have been antagonistic and divergent. Two notable ones are those of psychodynamic psychiatry and the family systems approach. In many respects, the divergence of these approaches speaks directly to the significance that inner and outer forces (often seen as opposing) have on influencing a child and his or her behavior. In its infancy, child psychiatry was powerfully influenced by the view of psychodynamic theory. Now, the pendulum seems to have swung in the other direction and more emphasis seems to be placed on the outer forces, the effects of parents and siblings, and how their interactional patterns may produce clinical symptoms in children. However, choosing either way of assessing a clinical problem to the exclusion of the other, no matter how correct it may be in and of itself, limits one's understanding and has a direct effect on the intervention offered.

In this chapter, I present an alternative, integrative model of intervention. My focus will be especially on integrating the views of individual psychodynamic psychiatry and family dynamics. I hope to show that maintaining both points of view can enhance and enrich our understanding of a clinical problem and effect a more favorable outcome. To illustrate this model, I will present an ongoing case of a latency-aged child after one year of treatment and then discuss the implications that I believe this case suggests for treatment. This case was seen as part of a psychotherapy research study so that a comprehensive assessment, including individual, family, educational and psychological evaluations, as well as behavioral ratings by school and parents were all obtained prior to starting treatment.

CASE PRESENTATION

Chris was a 6-year-old Hispanic boy who was referred for evaluation by his kindergarten teacher because of severe behavior problems. Chris and his mother met with a social worker in an extensive diagnostic evaluation that took place over ten to twelve sessions. I was then referred the case for long-term individual psychotherapy. I treated the first few sessions as an opportunity to gather information and make my own assessment of the presenting problems. I met with Chris and his mother on the first visit at the mother's request. For the following sessions, I met the mother alone and then Chris alone. At the fourth session, I met with the father and mother together. Chris's mother had been very reluctant to involve her husband because he reportedly did not believe that Chris needed psychiatric attention and felt that the problem was with his wife worrying too much. The mother was very sensitive to her husband's criticism and felt that she could not talk openly about her concerns if he was present.

During the first session, Chris was initially very restless and immediately wanted to play a game of Candyland. As we played, he told me that he beat his previous doctor many times at the game. I then asked a few questions in order to get to know him and learn about his past experience in therapy. Chris sat patiently and played with toys as I talked with his mother. His mother related that Chris had had severe behavior problems at school and at home. According to the mother, his kindergarten teacher had described Chris as being impulsive, hyperactive, oppositional, and aggressive, especially toward his peers. In class he had much difficulty "controlling himself." Often he would mimic the teacher or other children, run around the classroom, refuse to sit in his seat, or refuse to talk when he was confronted about his behavior. On the playground, Chris's behavior was even more disorganized; in particular, he had difficulty keeping his hands to himself. Other children seemed to feel bothered by Chris and didn't like to play with him. Chris complained that other children often teased him, which made him feel bad. Because of these behavior problems, his school performance was poor, and his teacher was considering recommending that he be held back a year so that his behavior could be better controlled before proceeding into the first grade.

Chris's mother acknowledged that he was a "handful" at home too. She noted that Chris was very active, always on the go, was often extremely demanding of her attention, and complained incessantly about having to do any activity she initiated (even if he seemed to enjoy the activity). The mother was especially disturbed by his constant fighting with and jealousy of his two brothers, Michael, 10 years old, and Mark, 3 years old. As a result, she felt exhausted and frustrated in her attempts to manage Chris. She tried desperately to talk with him in hopes of finding out what was making him act up. However, when she did, he would often clam up and be very stubborn. Only at bedtime did he talk freely. But then he would usually ask her repeatedly about subjects she felt uncomfortable talking about. These subjects included his father's frequent absences and heavy work schedule, his maternal grandmother's death the previous year, the loss of a young friend's leg in a car accident 6 months ago, the death of his baby chickens, fears about his mother dying, and recurrent nightmares of being attacked and having his head cut off.

The mother admitted that over the last 6 months Chris had come to dislike school and often complained about having to go. This surprised her, because in the past Chris seemed to enjoy school and usually looked forward to going. However, at that time he got along well with the other children and did not present any behavior problems. Chris maintained that the difference was that in preschool he could play more and do as he wished, whereas in kindergarten he had to follow rules and do schoolwork. His mother noted that since he had been doing progressively worse in school (he was suspended twice for behavior problems), he was often coming home feeling sad, sometimes tearful, and even talked about wishing he was dead. At times he would withdraw to his room, play by himself, and show little interest in playing with the neighborhood children. She commented that over the last several months Chris seemed much more irritable, and his moods would swing from happy and energetic to suddenly angry and sad without any provocation. These fluctuations were always short-lived, often occurred every few hours, never lasted for longer than a day, and were unpredictable. When he was asked about these mood and behavior changes, Chris often maintained that a bug in his head told him to act a certain way. The mother denied that he suffered from any appetite or sleep disturbance.

In her individual session, Chris's mother related that these mood swings and suicidal ideations were difficult for her because over the two previous years she, too, had struggled with feelings of depression and suicidal thoughts. Her depression had gotten so severe three months earlier that she was begun on a trial of an antidepressant medication. However, she stopped taking the medication after one week because of intolerable side effects. Fortunately, the depression abated. The onset of her depression was unclear but seemed related to the loss of her mother, the reemergence of longstanding feelings of low self-esteem following her mother's death (she always viewed herself as the less attractive, more troublesome daughter, especially in relation to her twin sister), and the intensification of feelings of disappointment and dissatisfaction in her relationship with her husband. She had seen a social worker in individual psychotherapy for over two years to help her deal with these feelings. The social worker had attempted to see both parents in marital therapy to help resolve their differences when the marital difficulties seemed to block further individual work. But after a few sessions Chris's father refused to continue with treatment because he felt unjustly blamed. This refusal left Chris's mother feeling angry and even more depressed. On initiating Chris's treatment with me, she had decided that she would continue to live together with her husband for financial reasons and for the sake of the children. She intended to structure her own life so that she and her husband would rarely see each other. She chose not to initiate divorce proceedings, but was not opposed to them if the father wanted a divorce. She acknowledged that she felt no feelings of love or intimacy for her husband, even though she cared about him a great deal. Since she felt that Chris's father seemed to be content with a more distant relationship and was more self-involved, she would be the same.

The mother stated that Chris's developmental history was essentially unremarkable. He was the product of a planned, uncomplicated pregnancy, which terminated in an expected Cesarean section. Chris's birth weight was 8 pounds, 6 ounces. His apgar scores were unknown. There were no complications following the delivery, and Chris went home with his mother after a few days. Chris was described as a cuddly, affectionate infant who was calm and rarely cried. Excessive motor activity, impulsivity, and distractibility were not noted during infancy. He met all of his developmental milestones at the expected times. Early in his infancy, Chris's mother took him to work with her. Later, from 9 months to 4 years old, the family used five or six different live-in Spanish-speaking babysitters to care for him during the day. The mother denied any history of enuresis, encopresis, fire setting, cruelty to animals, or psychotic symptoms.

Chris's medical history was significant for two hospitalizations. At 1½ years old he was hospitalized for a week in Mexico City for typhoid fever. Reportedly he received blood transfusions with his mother's blood and was treated with antibiotics. At the age of 3½, Chris was hospitalized again, this time for acute appendicitis. However, he refused to cooperate with the doctors and was mute about his symptoms. He was treated with antibiotics but then was discharged after a few days. A few months later he was readmitted because of an exacerbation of his condition, and he underwent an appendectomy. On entering the hospital for the operation, Chris did not allow anyone to get near him. His mother reported that he would start screaming and jump up and down on his bed and tell the doctors, "You're going to kill me." At one point, he removed the IV from his arm.

For the next session, I met with Chris's mother and father. During this session I was able to observe the parents' interactions and obtain further history. Throughout most of the session, the mother dominated the discussion and the father sat quietly until he was directly addressed.

The father, 36, and the mother, 32, were born and raised in northern Mexico. Both are now naturalized United States citizens. The father had lived in the United States since he was a young adolescent, whereas the mother had not settled here until she was 19 years old. Both came from very large families (each greater than six siblings) and had most of their extended family still living in Mexico. However, the father seemed to have some family living in California with whom they maintained close contact. In fact, this created problems at times for the mother because she often felt criticized by her in-laws for not being a better mother. Interestingly, each parent was raised in a family where the father was relatively passive and uninvolved. Their mothers (Chris's grandmothers) were said to be strong, dominant figures. Neither parent had a particularly difficult childhood. Only the mother remembered having a difficult relationship with a parent, her mother. She described herself as being stubborn and rebellious, always trying to defy her mother. She felt that as a consequence her mother labeled her as the "bad child" in the family. This was in direct contrast to her twin sister, whom she felt was the family favorite. The only significant family history for psychiatric problems was in the area of substance abuse. Each parent had a sibling who had had problems with alcohol. There was no history of depression, legal problems, or learning disabilities. Chris's older brother, Michael, seemed to have some difficulties with poor school performance, social withdrawal, low self-esteem, mild depression, and excessively passive behavior. But he was not aggressive and troublesome and so had not been evaluated by a psychiatrist or mental health worker.

Chris's parents had been married for over 10 years. This was the first and only marriage for both of them. Neither had been responsible for children other than their own three. The mother worked as a housekeeper. The father carried three jobs after having been without work for several months. He worked as a cook for a wealthy Los Angeles family during the day (a job his wife secured) and then spent the night house-sitting at a large estate. On a part-time basis, he ran a catering service with a few friends. The mother often would assist him with this work.

Both parents seemed to value hard work highly and hoped to provide their children with a life much different from their own early experience. However, the mother admitted that she no longer felt the desire to work so hard and earn money. She wanted to use her time developing herself, perhaps go back to school and earn a college degree, as well as have more time with her children. She complained that her husband tended to worry too much about money and did not share the responsibilities of taking care of the children. Nevertheless, although he did not understand why his wife would want to earn a college degree, the father seemed to support her wish to work toward one. He did feel that she was unrealistic about wanting him to quit his overnight house-sitting job when she wanted to quit her own job and still be able to afford a comfortable middle-class life style.

During this couples session, the parents showed very little physical affection toward each other. They sat far apart and had little eye contact. When they spoke to one another, the mother often seemed tense and the father appeared frustrated. The father related that he had mixed feelings about Chris coming for treatment. He did not feel that Chris suffered from problems or difficulties that were "out of the ordinary" and would not eventually resolve on their own. He indicated that at least part of the problem was his wife's difficulty in disciplining the children, Chris in particular. The children were never defiant and oppositional with him—it was only with their mother that they acted up. He did admit that Chris was more stubborn and defiant than his brothers. He further noted that it was not easy to get Chris to do things, but he felt that this was just the way Chris was and wasn't sure it needed to be changed or even could be changed.

The father stated that he felt that he had as good a relationship with Chris as he had with the other two boys. But he and Chris rarely talked alone, and Chris never told him about his worries and his concerns as he did his mother. It seemed that the time Chris and his father spent together was usually when Chris was with his brothers. They often would watch television together or all go to a movie during the afternoon. The mother had Chris involved in soccer and baseball teams, but the father never attended these activities. The father also tended to prefer not to get involved in setting limits at home and insisting that his children participate in various activities. He did not understand why, for example, his wife forced Chris to play on the soccer and baseball teams when Chris complained about having to go to the games. As a child, the father was never involved in such activities, so he did not understand why his sons should have to be. He admitted that since Mark was still a toddler, when he spent the afternoon with his boys, most of his attention would be focused on Mark. Although he seemed to enjoy all three sons, he was clearly quite taken by Mark. Clearly, he disagreed with his wife about how to raise the children, but he chose to avoid arguing with her because he felt that it would only exacerbate the home situation and their relationship.

As part of a comprehensive diagnostic evaluation, Chris was given separate educational and psychological assessments. He was also rated on a Beitchman Self Rating Scale by his treating psychiatrist and on an Achenbach Child Behavior Checklist for ages 4–16 by his parents and teacher. In addition, he was given a Children's Global Assessment Scale score (CGAS).

The educational assessment was administered by an educational psychologist. The tests used included the Peabody Picture Vocabulary Test, the Wide Range Achievement Test-Revised (WRAT-R), and the Peabody Individual Achievement Test (PIAT). On the vocabulary test, Chris had a standard score equivalent of 100 and age equivalent of 6 years, 4 months. His scores on the PIAT ranged from 110 (2.2 grade equivalent) in general information to 97 (1.1) in reading recognition. On the WRAT-R he scored from 89 (pre-first-grade equivalent) in spelling production to 85 (pre-first) in mathematic fundamentals. A Biery Visual Motor Integration test was given because he demonstrated some difficulty with visual-motor production. On this test he was given a standard score of 10 or an age-equivalent score of 6 years, 5 months. The overall testing concluded that Chris was functioning cognitively within the average range of ability. Some increased motor activity was noted when he was administered the WRAT-R and PIAT, but it did not seem consistent with behavior usually associated with an attention deficit disorder. He appeared to be ready academically to begin first-grade work.

The psychological assessment was performed by two different clinical psychologists. Each administered different tests that produced similar results but offered contrasting conclusions. The tests used included the Weschsler Intelligence Scale for Children-Revised (WISC-R), the Family Relations Test (FRT), the Bender-Gestalt Test of Visual Motor Integration, the House-Tree-Person Drawing, the Thematic Apperception Test (TAT), the Michigan Pictures, a Rorschach, Sentence Completion, and Draw-a-Person. Both psychologists found Chris to be very anxious, fidgety, and somewhat oppositional. In particular, he seemed to have difficulty maintaining his attention to tasks for any more than 2 to 3 minutes at a time. On the WISC-R, he obtained an overall IQ of 104 with a performance IQ of 106 and a verbal IQ of 102. The testing results indicated that he was quite emotionally troubled. The Bender was very disorganized, with constant perseveration, merging and meshing of drawings, and lack of integration. The FRT indicated that Chris struggled with feelings of anger toward his mother and fears of abandonment by his father and, to a lesser extent, his mother. It also revealed that he felt his father was more involved with his siblings, but that he felt protective of his family and tended to deny his negative feelings about them. The other tests showed that he was mistrustful of others, had a low frustration tolerance, and poor impulse control. In addition, his responses suggested that he had a preoccupation with death and sadness, and had a high level of anxiety that seemed to interfere with his thinking and objective perception of reality. Chris appeared particularly troubled by his inability to control his aggressive impulses and feared resultant physical punishment. Serious difficulty relating to both adults and peers seemed to result from his preoccupation with himself. Although severe anxiety and poorly controlled aggression, along with family relationship difficulties, appeared to be the dominant themes uncovered in both testing assessments, one psychologist felt Chris suffered from an attention deficit disorder, and the other felt he had an impulse disorder. Both agreed that the family instability significantly aggravated his condition.

The Achenbach Child Behavior Checklists, one filled out by Chris's parents and one by his teacher, were fairly consistent with each other. Troublesome behaviors included arguing, obsessional thinking, demanding attention, nightmares, cruelty or meanness to others, and intrusiveness. His teacher noted that once Chris was able to stay put in his seat he was a hard worker and a conscientious student. His work was neat and carefully done. He had most difficulty reading out loud in class. On the CGAS Chris was given a score of 60, indicating that he had variable functioning with sporadic difficulties or symptoms in several but not all social areas.

TREATMENT

After the initial assessment it was apparent that Chris was having great difficulty managing his aggressive impulses, but the cause of this difficulty was not clear. Early traumatic experiences, parental discord, Mother's depression, the arrival of a new sibling, Father's disengagement from the family, and an underlying affective disturbance or an attention deficit disorder with hyperactivity all seemed to be possible factors in his behavior problems. Instead of making a definitive diagnosis, I chose to continue to meet with Chris and his parents on a regular basis to further assess his behavior as well as to assess his interactions with me as they evolved in a therapeutic setting. I began meeting with Chris once a week and with his parents once or twice a month. Initially I hoped to meet with his parents together as a couple. But when this was done, both seemed restrained in talking about their concerns about Chris and their feelings about each other. Thus, I decided to see them separately in order to give each of them an opportunity to talk more openly and for each to develop a working relationship with me.

In my next session with Chris he immediately wanted to play a game of Candyland. As we played he was very focused on the game and rarely responded to any of my questions. When he won the game, he was very excited and delighted with himself. As a result he insisted on playing a second time. Again he won and seemed to feel quite good.

Later in the session he turned to my dollhouse and a black Lego sports car. When he noticed the car, he oohed and aahed and commented on what a "neat" car it was. He then began constructing a scene where he arranged all the beds in the dollhouse in one room and placed the mother, father, two children, and dog figures on them. He noted that the whole family was asleep, and as they slept, he shoved several small toy guns underneath their beds. He then took the black car and had it fly around the house until it landed on a nearby object on my table. He stated that the car was a "spaceship" equipped with "laser guns." He pretended that the car/spaceship fired laser bullets at other objects or toys and then had the objects blow up. Eventually the car landed safely on a toy cannister, which he identified as "the moon." At the end of the session Chris again commented how much he liked my black car and asked if he could take it home with him to play with. I said I was sorry but that the car would be here to play with at our next session. As he left my office, he eagerly showed his mother my car and said he wished she would buy him one just like mine.

In the next session a week later, Chris proceeded to re-create a similar scene. He went to the dollhouse and arranged all the beds in one room. He again placed the family figures on the beds and the guns underneath them. He showed a particular interest in the toy guns and examined them closely. He noted that the guns were needed to be used for protection against anybody who might try to break in the house. He then identified two twin G.I. Joe dolls as the "aliens." Soon these aliens were immersed in battle against the car/spaceship. One battle was fought after another. As the spaceship tried to shoot lasers at the aliens, the aliens threw bombs and explosives at the spaceship. After several minutes, without either side clearly winning, Chris had the spaceship run the aliens off the table; they fell onto my rug, which he described as a vast "ocean filled with killer sharks and man-eating whales." After struggling in the ocean for a few minutes, the aliens somehow escaped at the time the session ended. Throughout this session, as he had during the previous session, Chris did not involve me in his play. For the most part I watched and followed the play as it unfolded. When I did comment, he rarely responded.

At the beginning of the next session Chris appeared eager and happy to see me. First he wanted to play a board game and then immediately re-created the scene of the family sleeping while the aliens and spaceship fought. This time, however, he identified two toy Lego figures as representing himself and me. His Lego figure was dressed in a white spacesuit, and my figure was dressed in jeans and a sweater. He placed the two of us in the car/spaceship and had us operate the spaceship as it fought the aliens in repeated battles.

Gradually, over the next 4 months, these recurrent scenes were further elaborated on. Chris built a "family" of "robots," both little and big, out of the Lego set and included them in his play. The robots joined forces with the aliens and tried to destroy the spaceship. The big robots were used to protect the little ones during the battles. The aliens were then stationed on one of my shelves. A rubber band and small toy pulley allowed the aliens to swing down onto the "moon" and attack the car/spaceship or the figures representing Chris and me. A house was constructed out of the Lego set and was placed on the "moon." Repeatedly, the aliens would desperately try to break into the house as we hid on a bed inside. Sometimes we would be lucky and sneak out a back window and then trap the aliens inside. Occasionally Chris would excitedly smash the house to pieces with either us or the aliens inside.

Once, as the house broke in two while being attacked by the aliens, it accidentally fell off the table and was just caught on my chair, avoiding hitting the ground and smashing into pieces. Chris was excited by how close the house came to being destroyed and yet was saved. I noted how it was nice to be with someone else—namely, me—when the house was in such danger and almost destroyed. Later that session he had the family dog paired with us in one of our battles against the aliens. At the end of the session he had the dog eat up the aliens and, for the first time, indicated that the aliens could be at least momentarily conquered.

After the dog consumed the aliens, Chris mentioned to me that his own baby German shepherd, Princess, had run away 3 to 4 weeks earlier. His mother had told me about how preoccupied he was with having lost Princess. At bedtime he often would talk and wonder what had become of Princess. As a result, he would sometimes have difficulty falling asleep. But, he never spoke about the dog to me. As he now began to talk about Princess, I encouraged him to talk about his feelings, but he quickly closed up and became quiet as the session ended.

In a later session the toy dog was named Ruff, and he became a regular companion in the battles against the aliens. Gradually the focus of the ensuing sessions shifted from the aliens trying to break into the Lego house, as the dog, Chris, and I tried to hide inside, to the three of us being caught in the turbulent, stormy ocean filled with killer sharks and man-eating whales. The house would be rocked and smashed by the powerful waves. Eventually we would escape from the house, fight off the sharks and whales, and swim to safe, dry land. Often at the end or even during these sessions, he would have the aliens locked in the dollhouse garage and closely watched over by Ruff, the dog.

It is interesting to note that as this play emerged, Chris had noted in his talk about Princess that he especially missed the protection he felt she had given him against the bedtime noises he heard and the strangers he imagined to be outside his bedroom window. In the past when he became frightened, he would either get in bed with one of his brothers or his parents, or he would call out to his mother to come comfort him. But at this time his younger brother had been having difficulty, wetting his bed at night, and Chris was afraid that if he went to his parents' or brothers' beds, he would find them wet. He was left with nowhere to go. His mother, too, had indicated that she had grown tired of his demands and expected him to fall asleep alone.

After approximately 4 months of treatment, Chris began showing greater interest in drawing and especially in playing board games. His drawings were of jets shooting lasers at the other jets and incorporated many of the same themes his previous play had. Gradually, however, his interest in such fighting waned, and he insisted on playing *only* board games. Whereas at the beginning of treatment he would play one or two games at the start of each session, he now turned to spending the whole session playing various games. During the game playing he would be very intent on winning and would get impatient with me at times for going too slow when I would try to develop conversation. Rarely would he ever talk about his life outside of treatment. Instead, the focus was usually on the game playing and whatever feelings arose related to the games.

During the sessions in which his play developed and was elaborated on and those in which most of the time was spent in game playing, information about the family and Chris's life outside of treatment was provided by his parents. At the onset of treatment I had arranged for his father to bring Chris to his sessions alone without either brother. Frequently the father and I would speak for a few minutes at the end of sessions, and on occasion I would meet with him in a more extended format. The father indicated that Chris was showing slow but definite improvement at home and more dramatic changes at school. At home Chris seemed to get along better and was less provocative with his brothers, but he continued to complain a lot to his mother about virtually everything she wanted him to do. At school the teacher reported only mild difficulty with his aggressiveness and intrusiveness toward others. She especially felt that Chris was doing very well academically. The father himself said he felt more comfortable with his own life because his catering business was picking up and developing well. The earlier financial concerns were less pressing. He revealed that although Chris had little to say to him, he felt closer to Chris because of the time they spent together alone coming to the sessions each week, and he had a little better appreciation for how Chris was feeling. Nevertheless, the father would often make it clear that he felt Chris's difficulty was not rooted in some deep psychological problem. He felt more that Chris was simply a difficult, highly verbal, complaining young boy with a personality style not too different from that of Chris's mother.

During the early sessions I had with Chris's mother, she often talked about how hard it was for her to manage with Chris's worries and excessive demands. She was particularly bothered by his concern about death and dying. At bedtime, she noted that he would often have difficulty falling asleep. As she sat with him and tried to comfort him, he would perseverate about his dead grandmother, the dead baby chicks (which were accidentally stepped on and drowned), the lost puppy, the fear that his mother might die, and the possibility that it might be better if he were dead. Mostly I listened and encouraged her to talk about her feelings.

As I acknowledged these feelings, she began to talk more about the disappointment she felt in her marriage. She felt irreparably hurt by her husband's refusal to participate in couples therapy. She admitted that she was very angry with him and had given up trying to make their relationship work. Even being around the home was difficult. It seemed that she and her husband constantly saw things differently and could not agree on anything. Goals and expectations for the children, along with rules about discipline, were especially sore spots between them. After a while the mother felt so resentful that she even structured her day with work so that she and her husband would only see each other an hour per day.

As the 5- to 6-month milestone in Chris's treatment approached, these feelings became even more intense. At this time the father's catering business began to pick up and became very busy. She struggled with whether she would help her husband cater parties. In the past she felt she often ended up becoming one of the main organizers of these parties, even though it was her husband's responsibility. She acknowledged that she was tired of always taking care of everyone else and never feeling cared for herself. Despite her hard work and devotion to whatever she pursued—family, catering, and so on—no one seemed to appreciate her. She considered not helping with the catering at all but feared that might provoke her husband. Eventually she decided to help in a limited capacity.

While she struggled with these feelings, she also began to think more about her own needs and desires. She had worked as a housekeeper since coming to the United States but felt increasingly more dissatisfied with the work. She wanted to improve herself, as well as her family, even if it meant taking a risk and losing income. She felt she had devoted herself to her family but had gotten little in return for herself. Through the first few months of Chris's treatment, she had begun taking courses in child development at a local junior college. She found these courses interesting and practical in that they helped her better understand her own children, but she wanted to earn a degree so she could do some kind of work that required specialized training. After a few months she chose to quit her housekeeper work and serve as a teacher's aide at a high school, which she felt would complement the college courses.

Over the next few months Chris focused more and more on game playing. We played checkers, Chutes and Ladders, Candyland, Fish, and Uno over and over again. Chris was very intent on playing each game by the rules and was quite happy when he won. When he lost, he usually sulked and had difficulty talking about how bad it felt to lose. On occasion he would rig the card games so he was sure to win. At the end of one session he exclaimed that "Uno was [his] most favorite game in the whole world." Later, however, he mentioned that his younger brother had lost almost all of the cards at home, so he was not able to play Uno except with me.

As Chris used the sessions more for game playing, his father and mother revealed that major changes were taking place in their lives. Chris's school performance continued to improve, and his teacher remarked about Chris's strong desire to learn. On his semester report card he received several outstandings. The father explained that his work was going well, and as a result he was able to spend more time with the boys during the day and weekend. The mother disclosed that she no longer felt so angry at her husband and had decided to make a real effort to make her marriage work for the children's sake. As a consequence, the family was now taking weekend trips to the mountains, Palm Springs, and Mexico. The trips were reported to be tiring for the parents but enjoyable for the children. It seemed that, gradually, a greater sense of a family working together and caring for one another was being established.

In addition, at this time the mother noted that Chris was developing a very close friendship with a neighborhood boy who was about his age. This friend, Peter, and Chris seemed to do everything together and wanted constantly to be together. The mother expressed some concern about their closeness. She was worried that Chris was too easily influenced by Peter and too insistent on being only with him. She felt that Chris should spend time with his family and relatives in addition to wanting to be with Peter. At times Chris became oppositional and difficult when his mother tried to separate him from Peter. The mother also stated that Chris seemed to be easily hurt by Peter and sometimes angered. Evidently Peter insisted that Chris play only the games Peter wanted to play, and they had to play by his rules only. Chris submitted to these conditions in order to maintain the friendship. But at night he often talked to his mother about his feelings of frustration with Peter. Usually I reassured the mother that Chris was struggling with very normal developmental issues and encouraged her to empathize with Chris's feelings.

Gradually Chris returned to his play with the Lego house, a black sports car, and aliens. This return preceded the family's first week-long vacation at a resort in Mexico. First Chris began building a garage with strong walls out of the Lego set to protect the car. He noted that we had to be watchful of the aliens entering the front door, so he included a back door to escape through in case of an emergency. He then placed the car/ spaceship, himself, me, and the dog all in the garage, noting that we would all be safe there. As the vacation approached, Chris had a large transformer, and the three of us battled the aliens. Only the aliens were killed. But new aliens appeared to do more battle. At the end of one session, Chris aggressively crushed several hardened Play-Doh figures, which he labeled as additional aliens. He seemed to take particular delight in cutting the heads off a few of these figures.

In the next session, after returning from the family vacation, Chris insisted on playing with the plastic potato-head family. Slowly he assembled and dressed a father, a mother, and a small boy. He played with the different clothing and body parts. Interestingly, he gave the potato-head boy the father's hat and shoes. Both parents seemed to share parts belonging to the other. Although he could identify the mother and father, the parts he gave them seemed to diminish their differences. Throughout this play no talk occurred between the figures, and Chris did not mention his vacation.

A day later I met with his parents, who acknowledged that the vacation was difficult but a success. Both felt that although the boys were demanding and often fought with one another, the vacation drew the family closer together. Furthermore, they revealed that they had decided together that, since Chris had continued to do so well in school, they would buy him a dog to replace Princess. During this session the parents seemed much more affectionate and attentive to each other as they talked about their experiences and plans. As the session came to a close, I complimented them on what a nice job they had done managing three active boys for a whole week so far away from home.

During the next 2 months, as we approached the 1-year point of his treatment, Chris's play became more varied. He continued playing games but also began drawing more and using Play-Doh in the battles with the aliens. One day he insisted on playing checkers and took much pleasure in completely dominating me by gaining several kings before he actually ended the game by jumping me. During the game he noted that Peter played checkers by his own rules, with which Chris wasn't familiar, so he often lost. I remarked that he might want to use me to practice with so he could do better next time against Peter.

In other sessions he drew airplanes shooting multicolored lasers at other airplanes. Rarely did the lasers destroy the enemy planes. Instead, they seemed to pick off the wings of the other planes one by one. Eventually the weakened pilots would escape by parachute but then be killed as they were floating to safety.

In the following parents' session, both parents reported that Chris had continued to improve in school, but less so at home. The mother complained that Chris would provoke his brothers by teasing and did not care for his new dog as much as she had hoped. She acknowledged that Chris enjoyed playing with the dog but refused to clean up after him. She admitted that it hadn't really become a problem because the oldest boy had been willing to take over Chris's responsibilities. Nevertheless, the mother was concerned about teaching Chris how to accept responsibility on his own. She also wondered if Chris's continued intense friendship with Peter was not excessive.

In addition, the mother expressed concern about her other two boys. She worried that her youngest son might develop problems similar to Chris's difficulties when he entered kindergarten in the fall. She noted that the oldest boy had become increasingly more demanding and uncooperative. She also felt frustrated by his insatiable wish to have the latest and most fashionable clothes or sports equipment, regardless of expense. No matter what she seemed to do for him, it was never enough. In the end, she doubted whether she was being a good mother because she could not satisfy his every need.

Throughout this session I listened carefully to the mother's complaints and asked the father if he, too, shared similar concerns. He supported his wife's feeling about the older boy and about Chris's provocative behavior. However, he did not seem so disturbed by Chris's relationship with Peter, and I acknowledged that such friendships are normal and often important for children.

At the end of the session the mother revealed that Chris had recently become infatuated with New York City, the Statue of Liberty, and Yankee Stadium. She seemed hurt that Chris refused to speak any Spanish and often insisted that his parents do the same. I commented that Chris seemed to be struggling on some level with his identity, and his behavior should not necessarily be taken as a rejection of her or his family. Instead, I thought his interest in America was an indication of his thoughtfulness and intelligence. I suggested that they talk more with him about his feelings about America and his not wishing to speak Spanish as these feelings come up in the future. As the session closed, we agreed that it was best that I meet with both parents together once a month to discuss Chris's progress and their feelings about managing Chris as well as the other boys.

DISCUSSION

Over the year of psychotherapeutic treatment, Chris and his parents have shown significant improvements. As I indicated earlier, at the onset of treatment Chris seemed to have difficulty managing his aggressive impulses. The etiology of this difficulty was unclear, but the difficulty was severe enough to have affected Chris in most areas of his functioning. As a result, Chris seemed to have suffered from feelings of depression and a diminished sense of his own effectiveness or competence.

As his treatment evolved, his play demonstrated that Chris struggled with feelings that the world was unsafe and dangerous. No one (including himself) seemed able to provide protection against the attacks he feared from the alien invaders. The main support (that one would expect for a 6-year-old boy), the family, was experienced as passive and preoccupied as they slept soundly while the battles with the aliens ensued. This left Chris having to manage his fears alone.

I believe a major contributing factor to the feeling that his world was unsafe was his parents' inability to calm his fears. The mother herself was overwhelmed with feelings of depression. Only 1 to 2 years earlier, she had lost her own mother and did not seem to have resolved this loss. Following the loss she seemed to be experiencing a greater need herself to be loved and cared for. At first she turned to her husband and family to have this need fulfilled, but neither was able to do so. The children were contending with their own developmental issues and were hardly able to meet their mother's needs. The father was preoccupied with his own work and the need to provide monetarily for the family. (His own life experiences and emotional development may have limited his ability to engage in the degree of intimacy that would have satisfied his wife's longings at this time.) In addition, his work prevented him from sleeping at home several days a week, and his self-absorption and unavailability were thus felt more strongly.

An attempt at addressing these marital difficulties with couples therapy was made prior to beginning Chris's treatment. But the couples therapy seemed to exacerbate the situation, as the father refused to participate, leaving the mother feeling more angry and disillusioned. Then, despite the complicating demands of having a toddler at home, she gradually began to pursue her own personal goals. Unfortunately for Chris, this meant that his mother was even less available.

The result of his feeling that his parents were unavailable for him was, I believe, enormous anger and rage, which only intensified his feelings of being unsafe. At home and at school this anger was manifested in his frequent irritability and mood swings. To a greater extent these feelings were acted out in the provocative, intrusive interactions he had with his brothers and peers. In his relationship with his mother, the anger was expressed through oppositional behavior. With his father Chris seemed to keep his feelings in check, perhaps repressed, because of a fear of retaliation. In his individual sessions this anger was intensely played out over and over again as the aliens (his projected hostility) battled his constructed threesome—himself, me, and the dog (which, of course, was a kind of family).

Regardless of his apparent aggressiveness, I believe Chris was very frightened by the power of his anger and rage. This was seen a number of times in his play. Two examples were (1) when the aliens hung the Lego house (which I took to represent the family) by a rubber band and teetered it on the edge of the moon, so close to disaster, and (2) when the aliens ran the Lego house off my table with the expectation that it would hit the floor and smash into pieces. Somehow the house landed on my chair and was saved. In the two cases Chris seemed fascinated yet very anxious at how close the house had come to being destroyed. Interestingly, at home this feared destructiveness resulting from overwhelming rage was paralleled by his mother's own concern that she would destroy her husband and family if she spoke openly about the feelings of frustration and disappointment she had about her marriage.

This unresolved anger and the fear of its destructiveness ultimately led to Chris's repetitive aggressive behavior as well as to his parents' unresolvable marital conflicts. It seems to me that the child-centered treatment gave both Chris and his parents an opportunity to express these feelings through play and words. By being seen separately (the child separate from the parents and the parents separate from one another) and having the treatment focus principally on Chris (although work was done on all fronts), both Chris and his parents experienced the therapy as nonthreatening. They could then begin expressing their thoughts and feelings without the fear of being attacked or judged. This was in contrast to their experience at home and in the previous couples therapy.

Moreover, this technique allowed me to establish a stronger, individual relationship to each family member. The character of my relationship with the father was more like being partners. The father did not seem threatened by my relationship with

Chris, and we could work together to help Chris. I did not replace the father, but I could encourage him to be more active, more fatherly, with his son. In addition, I could provide other functions the father was unable to provide that would promote Chris's own growth and development.

My relationship with the mother was perhaps more complicated. In many ways she looked to me for guidance and instruction on how to raise Chris and to understand his behavior. I found listening to her concerns and then educating her on child and family development helpful. My goal was specifically to help her empathize more with Chris's feelings and experience as well as with her husband's predicament. This approach seemed to enable her to work through her own feelings of anger. In the end she was more able to give to Chris, even though she came to further her own development by pursuing personal goals.

My relationship with Chris seemed to incorporate features similar to the relationship I had established with both of his parents. I was clearly a partner with him as we fought the aliens. Through many sessions I sat, watched, and listened carefully as his play unfolded. Gradually he was able to express what was most deeply disturbing him.

Initially he was overcome with fears about the lack of safety and protection. I believe that these concerns applied to his outside life and his feelings about his parents, as well as to the nature of his transference with me. As these fears were expressed in his play and then interpreted, he was able to move into a more competitive play. In our game playing he engaged me personally as he struggled to win and was not deterred by fears of destroying me or fears that I would retaliate and harm him. It seems to me that, as the treatment progressed, Chris was able to work through many of his difficulties in the area of competitive strivings. As a result, he seemed to come to feel safe in his maleness and not feel as threatened by me. It is not surprising then that after a year of treatment he was able to establish a close, intimate relationship with another boy, began to draw phallic, multicolored pictures of airplanes, and had the more positive toy figures (the "good guys") win their battles more consistently against the aliens. I believe, too, that his newfound sense of identity as an American, big and powerful like the symbols (the Statue of Liberty, New York City, and the New York Yankees) of America that so intrigued him, was an expression of this expanded male view of himself.

One area that seemed to have been less fully worked through is the anger and rage that he felt toward his parents, particularly his mother. After a year of treatment, he continued to struggle with his mother and complain about her demands. He refused to obey her rules. At times he was still provocative and hostile toward his brothers. His play remained very aggressive, though more varied and complex. It seemed that only through aggressive play and oppositional behavior was he able to express his rage. Expressing these feelings directly in words, or even acknowledging that they existed, was still very dangerous. In the therapy and within the transference, this difficulty was clearly seen, as his activity with me was mostly nonverbal and he seemed to disregard many of my verbal interventions.

Gradually, then, as the treatment for Chris evolved, both he and his parents were able to establish strong, trusting relationships with me and begin to talk about their most guarded feelings. As these feelings were explored without repercussions, a greater sense of control and safety emerged. I believe that this sense of control and safety was a powerful factor in bringing about the changes that took place in both Chris and his parents. As they all felt more safe and could begin working through their fears, they were freed to develop more fully in their own ways and yet to also give more fully to one another. The treatment model that I used, where an overall family systems view was taken but with an understanding of individual development and a focus on individual work (at least for the initial phase of treatment), seemed to enhance and fuel this therapeutic process. The improvement in Chris's school performance, the intimate relationship with his friend Peter, the mother's pursuit of personal goals, and her renewed commitment to her family and marriage are all examples supporting the change. Chris seemed to develop an improved sense of his own effectiveness and competence along with a resolution of his feelings of depression. His excessive activity and behavior difficulties, too, while not completely resolved, greatly diminished. This change in his behavior and attention without the use of medication seemed no longer to support a diagnosis of an attention deficit disorder with hyperactivity. Instead, his difficulty managing aggressive impulses would be more consistent with a behavior or anxiety disorder.

5

Family Therapy Evaluation and Treatment Planning

Robert Moradi, M.D.

A psychodynamic family evaluation and treatment is a craft bordering on art. Descriptions frequently are not enough to portray what actually happens, like asking a painter to tell you how he or she paints. The description of how the therapist becomes one with the family requires an objectivity and distance that inevitably does an injustice to the nuances of the process.

The notion of "joining" the family has to take place at a subconscious level for the therapist; otherwise the family will not allow the intrusion of an objective observer. Let me clarify with an example.

USE OF THERAPIST'S UNCONSCIOUS
FOR DIAGNOSIS

I met with the parents of John, a 7-year-old boy, for the initial session. Their main concerns were that he yelled at his parents, occasionally hit his mother, hit his peers at school, and "could not stay by himself for a single moment." At the end of the session with the parents, I suggested a meeting with the mother and son in 2 days. During the intervening 2 days, whenever I tried to recapture what the parents' concerns about John were, my mind would go blank. John came in with his mother, open faced, pleasant, and playful. He sat on a chair away from his mother and asked if he could show me a trick he had learned about folding a piece of paper. I told him that I wanted to talk with him for the first half hour and then he could show it to me. During the half hour, he related to me comfortably and told me that he didn't have many nightmares, but sometimes he would wake up in the middle of the night because he would hear his father watching horror movies on TV. He cannot sleep with his mother when his father is in town, and his father sometimes spanks him. About his mother, he said, "She does things for me before I ask her."

Looking back at the two sessions, I realized why I had "blanked out" the parents' concerns about John. I had joined the unconscious of the system and its main focus, which was the problem between the parents. The blankness of my mind about John's problems was diagnostic of the central issues that lay elsewhere in the family system.

The pain between the parents was intense. They sat across the room from each other; they did not agree with most issues of concern about John; they addressed me in the way two opposing lawyers in a courtroom would address the judge. Father was reluctantly there and Mother was burdened with trying to keep the process in motion by watching her words.

These pictures of the parents had imprinted me with the tension in the marriage, which was more emotionally charged for them than were their worries about their son. Although they were in my office for their son, their way of relating to each other was more prominent than the concerns about John, most of which they disagreed about. I was curious about what had created this tension between them, rather than how John (whom I had not met yet) had reacted to the tension.

JOINING THE FAMILY'S INTERSUBJECTIVE SPACE

Entering into a family's intersubjective space is a challenge requiring attention to several dimensions at constant interplay. At the center of it is allowing oneself to listen to and experience the family without preconceived notions or agendas, to hear and watch with a sense of curiosity and wonderment and a sense of respect for the family, and, to be as nonintrusive as possible. The only role of the therapist during the initial meetings should be to inquire about what is not understood.

NEUTRALITY

The analogy that comes to mind is that of an audience at a play, but sitting in the scene with the actors while the play is going on. The actors are aware of the audience's presence, but if the audience remains neutral, the play will take its own natural form. And what I mean by neutral is not the concept of blank screen neutrality of a classical analytic situation. Rather, neutrality here means becoming part of—while remaining apart. In practical terms, it means asking questions only when we need clarification to be able to follow the plot, to respond to questions in simple, clear terms, in tune with the tempo of the family and free of judgments. If asked to make observations about the family, or a member of the family, it means doing so based on what has been happening in the "play" with no pretension that we know any more than any member of the family, but staying in charge of the context and parameters of the session.

Now, to return to John to clarify these points. When the first half-hour of our talk was over, I told him, "If you want, you can show me your paper trick now." He sat on the floor, using the coffee table between the chairs, and began folding a regular piece of paper from a writing pad into triangles. Mother was sitting on the couch in front of him, and I found myself gently sliding down from my chair until I was sitting on the floor, Mother on my left and John on my right side. I did not invite Mother to sit on the floor, and my own way of sliding down from my chair seemed as if it just happened without any of us noticing it, but it felt right to all of us. This form of neutrality means creating a context within which the unconscious material can surface. The context contained in it elements such as instructing him that we had to talk for one half-hour, inviting him to show me his trick (therapist in charge of the parameters of the session), going down to his level by sitting on the floor and not imposing it on the mother, who might feel awkward, but leaving room in case she wanted to join at any level. The therapist's job is similar to that of an air-traffic controller, not to be mistaken with the pilot. The ultimate control of the plane is in the hands of the cockpit crew, and we can only inform them where the plane is or is headed, and even that only if we are asked. However, we are responsible for giving them clear guidelines about when and in what order they can "take off" or "land." This is similar to my letting John know that we needed to talk during the first half-hour of the session, and although he asked two more times to "fly" before the half-hour was over, I told him how many more minutes were left, and he went along with it in an accepting, calm way. I believe he recognized that my intention was not to control him, but to get to know him.

OBSERVATION OF DYADIC INTERACTIONS

Now everything is ready for the play to start; the players are in place. The therapist at this point is a facilitator of the act, providing tools (in this instance a few sheets of paper, a pair of scissors, and a stapler).

John began folding the paper into triangles that folded onto each other (perhaps his own version of origami). As he attempted to create the triangles, the lines wouldn't line up, and he whined out of frustration. Mother bent forward at each whining sound and helped him fold the paper on the line. John went to the next triangle and whined again, Mother bent and folded it on the line for him, on and on. John used Mother's hands interchangeably with his own. He had no conscious knowledge of the other. He never asked for her to help; she just did. He never acknowledged her assistance. I saw that after John's frustration over the first couple of triangles, Mother began predicting the upcoming frustrating points for him and would intervene before he experienced the frustration.

USE OF EMERGED MATERIAL IN ESTABLISHING THERAPEUTIC GOALS

I have been trusted in the intimate space of the relationship between two people, which by its nature precludes outsiders. Although the symbiosis between the mother and son is obvious, in order for them to tell me why they have had to establish such a dysfunctional tie, I need to be respectful, nonjudgmental, and at the same time acknowledge its existence. I said to the mother, "John is taking your help for granted." John did not make any comments, as if I had just said he had two hands. For the mother it created some discomfort, but not enough for her to change her way of helping John. She continued, but this time pausing for a second or two before she actually folded the paper for him. She looked at me from time to time as if to say, "I know you are seeing it, but I can't help it." (But it also felt like she knew it was all right with me, that I was not criticizing her for it, that I had stated the obvious.) Her pauses, however, indicated to me that an intervention was made, that she had become more conscious of what she was doing. This meant we had established our first mutually agreed on goal, that is, undoing her role in the creation of John's low frustration tolerance.

The identification of a parent during the process of evaluation of the family as the creator of the child's problem is a sensitive task. It has to be presented to the parent at the appropriate moment *and must be based on observation within the session regardless of the extent of hearsay reports by family members*. It is valid only if we all *experience it together*, and we all agree on its description. Then we have a piece of truth about the family's mythology. *It has to be concrete, simple, affect laden, and in the here and now*. We then have a mutually established historical point that includes the therapist, a point of referral in the future against which changes can be measured. In this example, Mother's inability to allow John the necessary experience of frustration is viewed as her creating his impulsivity.

TIMING OF INTERPRETATIONS

Almost all interpretations made before a treatment contract is developed will be premature. For example, John's frustration in forming a triangle was perhaps a metaphor about the triangle of his relationship with his parents. It was tempting to make a "smart" interpretation about the use of triangles, but instead, I addressed his "frustration when things don't come easy" to him. Another premature interpretation would be making a connection between John's sleep problems and problems in the marriage, for example, Father watching horror movies in the middle of the night rather than being in bed with Mother.

Avoiding interpretation is important to remaining the nonintrusive audience. Using Erik Erikson's analogy of the sun's play with the waves, we have to remain as noninteractive with the family as the rays of sunshine with the shape of the waves. By mimicking the sun, the therapist is attempting not to change the forms of the family at this time, but to bring light and clarity to the already existing forms.

INSTILLING HOPE: ANOTHER GOAL OF THE ASSESSMENT PROCESS

At the next session I met with John and his father. He told us that his father spanked him (Father clarified that the last time was 2 or 3 years previously) and that he likes it better when his dad is out of town (Father had a family business in Southeast Asia and would spend 6 or 7 months out of each year overseas). He said he gets to sleep with Mom when Dad is out of town. Father became quiet. I observed out loud that "Dad had become distant," and they both acknowledged the truth of this. John had no idea why, and the father (a very reserved, shy, and antitherapy middle-aged man) was not about to tell us his feelings. So I wondered out loud "if Dad's feelings were hurt?" Father's eyes welled up, and John was completely surprised. He could not believe that what he said could affect his "strong" Dad. I further observed that "perhaps when Dad's feelings are hurt, he becomes quiet and distant." By addressing Dad's feelings, I sensed that some hope was instilled in the father's dark and lonely internal world. Perhaps we had established a bridge. He experienced me inside of his world without threatening or shaming him.

FACILITATING DIRECT COMMUNICATION

During the same session I asked Dad how his father would have reacted if Father had talked to Grandfather the way John talked to him? He responded by telling us how his parents left him at age 7 to be raised by an aunt in a different city. He experienced his aunt's husband as a father figure, harsh, distant, and authoritarian. He would have never dared to talk to him directly. John said, "That's like my brother [his 18-year-old half brother from Mother's first marriage] who locks me in the bathroom if I change the channel on the TV."

They had begun comparing notes, finding similarities in their experiences and empathizing with each other. The lines of communication were opening up. The two of them talked directly to each other for what appeared to be the longest they had ever talked. I sat quietly avoiding their gazes, in this way encouraging their talking with each other. They seemed excited by these moments of present connection between them in the safety of the session.

THERAPIST AS STABILIZER

The task of the therapist when seeing a dyad of the family is to create a stabilizing environment that serves to promote the healthy connection between the members of the dyad. The mother in the above situation would not have been able to contain her anxiety to allow the direct talks between the father and son. The therapist's task is to be a mother substitute for the members of the dyad. My avoiding their gaze encouraged the father and son to look at each other. As they felt safe with each other, I gently removed myself from the scene, allowing their interaction, and although they raised their voices at times and John periodically cried, they maintained their connection.

EMERGENCE OF HISTORICAL MATERIAL BY ADDRESSING IN-SESSION MATERIAL

At the fourth evaluation session, I met with Mother, Father, and son. John announced that he was "very hungry." Mother said that they had been planning to eat the dinner that Father had prepared after going home. John began whining to Mother that he wanted a hamburger from the fast-food restaurant. Father stayed quiet. Mother felt caught. She told me, "You see, this is what happens." I asked if she would tell me what she thought was happening. She said, "I don't care if he eats the hamburger or Dad's oriental food." Dad said, "But I've been cooking all day." It became clear that Father wished that Mother would enforce eating at home, but Mother didn't want to be the one to say no. She was caught between the two of them and her fear that any position she might take would make one of them angry with her. I addressed her no-win situation. I asked if she had thoughts about why she was in this situation. She talked about her deep-seated fear that she would be abandoned by her son if she did not do everything for him, that she already feels abandoned by her husband, that she fears that she could repeat the cycle of her own parents' abuse and neglect. She feels guilty for having left her older son at an early age because she felt she could not be a good mother. Father and son listened carefully while Mother cried and told her thoughts. When the intensity subsided, I addressed John and said, "Your Mom and Dad are different in the way they show their feelings." John responded, "Yeah, Dad never cries"; and Father said, "She does all the crying." I said, "You wish there was room for your feelings too."

We also talked about how John plays a role in the friction between Mom and Dad. This was discussed when he was whining to his mother about the dinner, which was in fact an issue between John and his father, as Mother was neutral about it.

TIMING FOR NEGOTIATION OF TREATMENT CONTRACT

By now I had witnessed the conflicts in the family, and we had experienced some events together. This *experience* gives me the license to begin the phase of negotiation of some of the treatment contract. I asked the parents to come without John to the next session for us to "plan what needs to be done." This gave them some time to think about interventions that might help.

There is no absolute number of evaluation sessions required before a treatment plan can be developed. Sometimes the treatment plan evolves out of the first or the second session, but frequently it takes five or six sessions of evaluation and, occasionally, longer. The timing of the treatment plan is critical. This is a time when enough has been touched on, there is a sense of trust and safety in the sessions, there is hope for healing the wounds, and the therapist feels the need to begin the interpretive part of the work.

Treatment Plan

The parents arrived on time as before (a good prognostic sign for their motivation about the process). I asked them how our previous meetings had been for them.

Asking the family about the experience of the first few

meetings provides me the opportunity to test my perceptions about how we have connected up to that point. They educate me about what went wrong, if the pace in the explorations was too fast or too slow, and if they felt I understood their pain; if I didn't, they can describe it again.

Mother responded by telling us that the last meeting was hard for John; he felt pressured. But when he was being picked up from school to come to the last session, he announced with bravado to his friends, "OK, I have to go to the psychiatrist now." I remarked, "I felt I put John on the hot seat last time; I hope it wasn't too disturbing to him. What do you think the pressures were for him?" Father responded by saying, "He is not used to his mother hesitating in giving him what he wants." Mother agreed and said, "If we were not here, I couldn't have said no to him when he wanted the hamburger." Father said, "I couldn't believe that he really didn't know how many of my arguments with his mother are over him." I heard a number of things:

1. The father wished his wife could be stricter with their son.
2. Mother also wished she could be stricter.
3. John is being scapegoated by Father as the main reason for the marital conflicts.
4. Father also understood that John has been oblivious to his role in the conflicts between the parents.
5. Mother felt that being in the session was what made her more assertive vis-à-vis John. My recollection was that Mother didn't assertively say no to John about the hamburger, but I didn't challenge her assessment of her own assertiveness.
6. Father had become a participant in the discussion in the meeting (unlike his aloof, skeptical position during our initial meeting).
7. Although the last session was difficult for John, he had liked coming to the meetings, based on the way he announced it to his peers.

The hard task is in deciding which of the observations to share with them, what needs to be highlighted or addressed, and what needs to be left for a more appropriate time. My rule, especially during the evaluation phase, is to start with the least controversial issue and highlight points that will further the therapeutic alliance. This is still the time of establishing and enhancing rapport with all of the members of the family, particularly the ones most resistant to the process.

So I responded only to John's hardship during the previous meeting (least controversial between the parents at that moment) and then I asked, "What do you think he liked about coming here?" This is an attempt to clarify further, gain more information about John's internal process (or the parents' own projection into his internal process), and, at the same time, focus on what has worked between John and me.

Mother responded, "Oh, he likes to talk about what bothers him. After his first meeting with you, he told me that he couldn't wait to come back and tell you all about his brother."

If this were a therapy session and not an evaluation session, and I didn't have the agenda of forging a treatment plan with them, I would have asked questions about who John complains to about his brother, how Mother feels when caught between her two sons, what Father thinks about the conflict between the boys, and so on. I filed all of these for when I have a contract with them that implies permission to enter these potentially sore spots. That will be the time family members have consented to enduring some pain as the walls of denial are chipped away, projections confronted, displacements identified, and the process of mourning the loss of fantasies and expectations begun. Up until the time that permission is authorized, entering the wounds could be experienced as an intrusion similar to the original traumata that created them. The unauthorized exploration of the fragile ego of a family in crisis would add to their defenses against humiliation and painful separations. What I mean here by timing is the therapist's sense that the family has authorized entry into selected paths in the complex fabric of the system.

THE EXTENT OF INVOLVING THE FAMILY IN FORMULATING THE TREATMENT PLAN

I asked the parents, "So what do you think John needs?" Mother responded, "My older son was in therapy for a long time and he feels it helped him a lot. . . . I'm glad he had it, especially when I could not be there to take care of him. With John, I'm going in the opposite direction; I am there even if he doesn't want me to be." Mother had chosen to leave her first marriage because she had found the care of her son an emotionally overwhelming task. I asked the father what he thought. Father replied, "I think that there's something wrong that he can't stay alone for a moment; he always has to have someone with him, even when he goes to the bathroom." I had sensed that Father's skepticism about therapy had softened. So I said, "I think John would benefit from some work on his fears and frustration." I know enough about John at this point to have formulated in my mind his need for development of an observing ego to avert his potential for growing up with lacunae in his superego and his separation anxiety, which was perhaps an internalization of the same anxiety within his parents and his older brother (Mother's fear of being abandoned by John, thus, her reaction formation taking the form of an obedient servant; Father abandoned by his parents at John's age; and older brother abandoned by Mother).

However, John's problems were not merely intrapsychic. He was clearly part of a dysfunctional system. Mother's overprotectiveness was hampering John's development of a healthy sense of ego boundaries, and interfering with his autonomy in performing his tasks competently. This hampered his self-esteem and self-confidence. The relationship with his father was almost nonexistent. The father was experienced by John mainly as a nuisance, someone to be avoided or, at best, tolerated until he leaves on his next trip. This could become a basis for his relationship with men in authority in the future, as his relationship with his mother could translate into expecting women to be his servants. I didn't feel the need to say any of this to the parents at this point. We had already agreed that John needed therapy; loading them up with the extent of John's psychopathology could be overwhelming to them and take away their hope. But I needed to address John's behavior within the family as a basis to recommend dyadic and family sessions, so I added, "But he also has some issues with the two of you." Mother said, "Yes, I think you're right that he takes me for granted. I've been noticing it much more since the day he and I were here." It was clear that Mother was open to the idea of some work together with John, but I wasn't sure about the father; he was quiet again. In my mind, I translated the father's silence as his hopelessness about his relationship with his son. So I said to him: "I think you and your son can become closer, [and that] it will be good for both of you. Do you think it could be possible?" This was an acknowledgment of the distance he feels between himself and his son, instilling hope by saying that they could be closer, validating his subconscious notion that it would be good for them and asking him to join me to make it possible. He responded, "When you spend half of the year away from your family, it's hard to stay close to them; so I'm thinking about taking my family, in a year or two, to live in the Orient with me." This was as close as he could come to expressing how powerful his desire was to get closer to his son, but also to his wife, because he said "my family."

By this time we had established John's need for individual psychotherapy, and the need for dyadic psychotherapy for John and each of his parents. In order to make it concrete, I suggested, "What if I see John by himself once a week and see him for the second session of the week with each one of you alternating, and, whenever we feel the need, the three of you together?" The parents agreed.

SUGGESTING CONJOINT THERAPY TO THE PARENTS; ENTERING DANGEROUS TERRITORY

Now it was time to introduce their need for conjoint work. So I asked, "Do you think the relationship between the two of you could have an effect on John also?" With a cold and angry tone, Mother said, "You know, Doctor, after the last meeting we had with you, I saw another therapist and he was worse."

I felt inadequate, betrayed, and abandoned. With difficulty in uttering the words, I said, "I am sorry, I must have hurt you last time." Mother said, "You made me feel like I was the cause of all his problems." This gave me more hope because she was telling me what had hurt her, so I said, "You came back to me in spite of my insensitivity toward you." Her rageful face softened, her body stooped, and she began sobbing. Her husband and I sat quietly for a few minutes until she could catch her breath. She then smiled and said in a half-joking way, "I told you that the other guy was worse than you." I felt that we had experienced a whole range of affects together. She gave me a taste of what she experiences most of the time, namely, feeling inadequate, betrayed, and abandoned. She educated me about her sensitivities. She also taught me that she responds favorably to my owning up to my mistakes and affirming her feelings. Because I felt our connection become deeper, I ventured, "What is the problem between the two of you?" She said, "We started as the most passionate lovers in Tokyo. I was a successful model and my husband was expanding his import-export business between the U.S. and the Orient. We partied every night for four years until I became pregnant with John. We decided to get married and settle down in the U.S." She was talking about all of this with great nostalgia. He was listening to her with deep curiosity. So I asked him, "What happened then?" He said, "After John was born, my business in the Orient required more of my attention." His choice of words and the way he paralleled the birth of his son with increased demands of his business were significant clues to what had happened, that is, their passionate one-to-one life was disrupted by the mother's attention to the baby. Father must have felt abandoned and, thus, "My business required more of my attention." Again, I decided that we had not yet started the therapy, so it would have been premature for me to draw their attention to the parallel between the baby and Father's business.

ON HANDLING SHAME AND BLAME DURING EVALUATION

Since I had sensed Father's softened position toward our meeting, I said to him, "You don't seem put upon the way you looked the first time I saw you." He said, "We have seen a therapist before and it didn't work." "Why?" I asked. "It was three or four years ago. We saw her only three times." Mother jumped in, "My husband didn't like it because we had to drive a distance and she was too expensive," she said sarcastically. So I asked, "What do you think was the real reason?" She responded, "The therapist told him that he couldn't hide behind his boyish naïveté and pretend that he had no role in my depression." This seemed to have been too much for him at that moment, so I decided not to go further with it; but I kept in mind that there is an iatrogenic wound in him that needs to be attended to. So, I told him, "If we decide to work together, I hope you will tell me whenever you feel that I am blaming you." The issue of blame had been highlighted so many times since my questioning them about their relationship's role in John's problems that I needed to diffuse their feelings of responsibility for their child's pain. At the same time, I had to invite them to join me in exploring what had gone wrong with the relationship. It was clear that shame could prevent the father from getting in touch with his feelings of abandonment when he lost his wife to his son. At the same time, her rage was flaring about being abandoned when she was hoping for a "settled-down" family to raise their child together. They both needed to mourn the loss of the "passionate first four years" of their togetherness, accept their anger at their son who "destroyed" the romantic dyad, accept the reality of the triangle, stop acting out, and develop a sense of self-sufficiency so the triangulations would not be experienced as betrayals. So I said to them, "You used to have something precious between you which has been lost for a while. Do you want to work on putting it back?" Father said, "We should give it a try." Tears ran down Mother's face, and I read into it that she saw some hope for her family. I said, "Your presence here speaks to the hope that you both have"; and I continued, "What if we meet in this format once a week?" They both agreed. I asked them, "How would the cost of all this be for you?" Father said, "Hard, but this is important."

STRUCTURE OF TREATMENT SESSIONS

Who is going to be in therapy with whom and the frequency of the sessions is as varied as the number of families we see. In the case of the family presented here, I saw fit to be the individual therapist for the 7-year-old child as well as the therapist for the family and the couple. I did not address the older brother's role yet because I felt we already had enough variables to juggle before adding another player. I was hoping that at some future point, as the issues with the older son surfaced, he would be included in the process. The factors that determine the structure of treatment include timing, family's resources, therapist's availability (in terms of time and emotions), the age of the child (some children need their own therapist from the beginning; some may require it after a while), and most important, the dynamics of the relationships.

SUMMARY

A number of issues need to be addressed in planning a psychodynamic family psychotherapy. This is particularly true when one member of the family, usually a child, is identified by the family as the patient. The most difficult task for the therapist is distributing the problems of the member of the family who has been the unconscious depository for the conflicts within the family system into therapeutic goals in the work with the dysfunctional dyads and triads. The family's homeostasis cannot be disrupted by an outsider. The role of the therapist is not to introduce his or her own way of living and value systems into the family. The family's pain, and timely identification of it by the therapist, creates the only motivation for change.

In his book *Dancing with the Family*, Carl A. Whitaker writes, "Therapists really don't have the power to inflict growth on a family" (p. 22).

We should remember that the parents bring the child in with a deep sense of shame. Those of us who have worked with shame know the delicacy of working through this most painful of human experiences. The shift from the identified patient to the family as patient has in its core the potential for humiliation. This shift can only be fueled by the trust of the parents in the therapist. Their antenna for detecting the therapist's prejudices is extremely sensitive, so much so that at times we become the object of their projective identification, that is, they see in us the intolerable judgments they have against themselves.

Finally, I have to reemphasize that this approach to setting the stage for a psychodynamic family therapy is what I have found to be useful in a private practice model. This is the situation where the therapist has to, or wants to, create a "holding environment" for the whole family system without the support of other therapists or an institution. This is usually the initiation phase for a long-term treatment for both intrapsychic and interpersonal conflicts. This open-ended, "non-history-taking" approach to the evaluation sets the stage for the long-term goal for the family to live and grow to its potential. Inherent within this potential is for each member to individuate and grow as the intrapsychic wounds and the wounds between the members of the dyads and triads begin to heal. Like a good parent, the therapist's task is to help the family discover its own meaning rather than imposing one from the outside. This meaning will vary for each member of a healthy family, while certain basic elements are agreed on by all members.

REFERENCE

Whitaker, C. and Bumberry, W. (1988). *Dancing with the Family*. New York: Brunner/Mazel.

6

Inquiry and the Difference It Makes in Diagnostic Psychological Testing

James A. Incorvaia, Ph.D.

Throughout the years many have argued that the diagnostic process is unnecessary in psychiatric work (Beck et al. 1962, Duncan et al. 1992, Eron 1966, Foulds 1955, Friedman and Fanger 1991, Gauron and Dickinson 1966, Persons 1993, Pinkster 1967, Schmidt and Fonda 1956, Szasz 1961). This same argument has also existed in the psychoanalytic community (Fine 1971, Fordham 1972, A. Freud 1965, Menninger 1959, Sharpe 1978).

Although many psychodynamic clinicians have questioned the need for diagnostic work, McWilliams (1994) suggests six interrelational advantages of doing a diagnostic evaluation especially within a psychoanalytic framework: (1) utility in treatment planning; (2) implicit information about prognosis; (3) help protecting the consumer of mental health services; (4) help enabling the therapist to communicate empathy; (5) reduction of the probability that certain easily frightened people will flee from therapy; and (6) help in facilitating therapy. Her ideas are consistent with the viewpoint of the Reiss-Davis Child Study Center over the years (Motto and Friedman 1967, Pruyser 1976) that the diagnostic process plays a very important part in the entire clinical program.

As for the role psychological diagnostic testing plays in the overall diagnostic evaluation process, once again the literature indicates that the criticism other professionals have lodged against testing ranges from its being superfluous to its being useless and even, in some cases, dangerous (Greenspoon and Gersten, 1977, Groth-Marnat 1990, Holt 1967, Rogers 1954). Fortunately, many others feel that psychological diagnostic testing can and does make a significant contribution to the diagnostic process (Allison et al. 1968, Appelbaum 1976, Holt 1967, Kernberg 1975, Miller 1987, Pope and Scott 1967, Smith 1977, Woody and Woody 1972).

Some authors, while favoring testing, warn against the possible problems and pitfalls of poor diagnostic psychological testing. For example, Allison and colleagues (1968) argue that psychologists who treat psychological diagnostic testing from a psychometric orientation do the whole field of testing a disservice:

> When clinical psychological testing consists of procedures such as the administration of a questionnaire by a clerk or a psychometrician who may or may not be present and whose interest is limited to seeing that the test form is correctly completed, test scores are the sole source of data. In such an approach, there is no cognizance of the individual's style of responding and his behavioral reactions to specific test items or the test situation generally. Moreover, the processes that enter into the decision to respond one way or another or the effects of a previous question upon a subsequent one are ignored [in] . . . a mechanical approach to psychological testing through a concentration on test scores [p. 4].

Tallent (1976) agrees:

> The early days of clinical psychology in psychiatric settings again saw "mental testers" very much concerned with scores and

proficiency levels. The orientation was essentially that of a technician, where the data were delivered to a clinician for interpretation. Such an orientation frequently leads to incomplete interpretation of data—an entirely unacceptable procedure in personality evaluations, at least according to our point of view. However, many psychologists have carried over from early psychometric procedures to projective techniques the propensity to talk about tests rather than about people. [p. 64]

Astin (1969) suggests another pitfall of diagnostic testing—the inherent potential for being judgmental in the testing situation.

What we need to be effective, says Groth-Marnat (1990), is to be "able to integrate the test data into a relevant description of the person. . . . Yet, the end goal is not merely to describe the person, but rather to develop relevant answers to specific questions, aid in problem solving and facilitate decision making" (p. 5). In order to achieve these goals, Smith (1977) suggests that one must learn to analyze the data the patient gives:

> Freud wanted to show how the latent content is derived from the manifest content. In a real sense the psychological tester has the same task in making inferences from his data. We can approach this task in part through an analysis of the patient's verbalizations. . . . These data always occupy an important place in the understanding of the patient. . . . And the inferences one draws from these data can extend in all directions—dynamic, genetic, adaptive. [pp. 170–171]

Although few would argue with Smith's suggestion of how to use test data, many would complain that they are often unable to elicit this material from their patients. This seems especially true of those who work with children. Miller (1987) notes: "Tests cannot match interviews as opportunities to learn directly from patients just what they consciously and clearly formulate in the areas of self-concept, self-esteem, values, and conceptualizations about such matters as the impact of the past on the present or the meaning of symptoms or attitudes toward treatment" (p. 518).

The solution to the problem posed by Miller is the proper use of inquiry—a solution I've developed as a result of over 30 years of testing and supervising graduate and postdoctoral students in psychology, education, and other related fields in the area of diagnostic-psychological testing and projective technique. During that time, the single most frequent complaint about doing psychological diagnostic testing was that the paucity of material one is able to cull from protocols results in a lack of richness in diagnostic conclusions. This has been most evident in the use of the Rorschach test, where many supervisees complain that the only determinant they are able to score from their patients' protocols is form (F), a determinant that does not permit them to assess the richness of each patient's ideational and affective life, or to assess depth of personality.

In testing, the term *inquiry* has most often been associated with the Rorschach inkblot test, but it should be a vital part of all diagnostic psychological testing. Inquiry can, for example, be useful in exploring the nuances of responses on the Wechsler tests, in further understanding the meaning of stories given in the Thematic Apperception Test (TAT) and/or Children's Apperception Test (CAT); and in pursuing responses to the Sentence Completion test—allowing it to become an informal interview. In fact, I have found no projective testing and few standardized cognitive/achievement testing situations where inquiry could not effectively be used. The remainder of this chapter will explore how clinical and educational psychologists can reap the many benefits and avoid the pitfalls of missed opportunities for inquiry in administering diagnostic tests commonly found in batteries given to patients.

Because inquiry is most associated with the Rorschach inkblot test, I would like to begin by exploring its use in administering this very valuable clinical tool. Though I received training first under Maggie Hertz and later from Sam Beck, Bruno Klopfer, and Zygmunt Piotrowski, I have since the mid-1970s advocated, taught, and used in my own clinical work John Exner's *Rorschach: A Comprehensive System* (1993). My suggestions for inquiry on the Rorschach are intended to complement Exner's procedure for inquiry.

To understand the purpose of the inquiry phase in Exner's method of administering and scoring the Rorschach, I will briefly review its place in the comprehensive system. First, a patient is given the free-association phase, in which he or she is asked to respond to the simple question, "What might this be?" As Exner warns, it is very important insofar as possible not to deviate from these directions. After administering the ten cards in sequential order, the patient then begins the second phase of the test, the inquiry phase, by going through each response on each card with the examiner questioning him or her about those responses in order to determine where the patient saw the response and what determined it. Exner (1993) suggests, and I want to emphasize, that successful questioning depends on how the inquiry phase is presented to the patient.

Why is it so important for patients to understand the purpose of the inquiry phase before they begin to do it? Recall what it was like as a child in school being asked to repeat a test or assignment. This usually meant either that the work had been done incorrectly or in a way other than how the teacher wanted it to be done. Transferential feelings from those kinds of experiences can easily be projected onto the inquiry phase of the Rorschach, as the tester asks patients to go over their responses again.

I suggest telling patients they did a fine job in responding to the free-association phase of the test, but in order for the test to be properly scored, you will need to make sure that you thoroughly understand the responses given. For that reason you are going to briefly go through each of the responses, which you have recorded verbatim, asking the patients only two general categories of questions: where the particular response occurred on the blot, and what about the blot made it look like the response given. With these two questions and some latitude in their presentation, you should be able then to begin the inquiry phase. It is also important to make it clear that this is not a different part of the association phase of the test; the new-information-gathering part of the test is over, and no further responses are being sought. This phase is needed only to score the test more accurately. It is especially important to make this point because, if the patient feels that you are just being kind but really want better responses, this particular phase of the test will be met with great resistance.

Once proper understanding of the inquiry has occurred, the

next consideration centers on deciding what to inquire about in each patient's responses. Making that decision can be complicated by the perception that responses to Rorschachs are form based, without any elaboration.

Some resolution of this frustration might be suggested by grammatical structure. Form-based responses (the subject/object of the content) on the Rorschach tend to be given primarily as nouns, and the nouns given tend to be solely based on the form features of the blot. It is in the modifiers—adjectives, adverbs, and other grammatical forms that modify the noun—where lurk those other determinants often missed by the neophyte Rorschachian. Thus, it is the modifiers that need to be investigated.

I suggest beginning the process of exploring a response in a reverse-order format, starting with the noun and then moving to adjectives, adverbs, and so on—unlike the way most people seem naturally to go about doing the inquiry. For example, if a patient gives the following response to card 6, using the whole blot—"It looks like a dirty, old, rough bearskin rug"—I have found that most examiners will repeat the entire response, ending with the noun *rug*. Not surprisingly, they will only get the form features of the response back from the patient, such as "It has feet, a head, a body," or even more simply, "It is the shape of a rug." Frustrated by the paucity of material, examiners often just move on to the next response.

If, however, one assumes that the rug (noun) is not just any rug but (based on modifiers) a bearskin rug; and that this bearskin rug is not any old bearskin rug, but a rough (modifier) bearskin rug; and that this rough bearskin rug is not just a rough bearskin rug, but an old (modifier), rough bearskin rug; and finally that it is a dirty (modifier), old, rough bearskin rug; then it is important to explore each of these modifiers in the response in the inverse order of its presentation. That is, if one just repeats the entire response, the last thing the patient hears is "rug." Rug, being a noun, can only be explained in terms of its form-based aspects; as a result, the examiner will usually only get form as a determinant.

In this example, after reading the whole response to the patient, I suggest that the following be said: "Well, on this response you said, 'It's a dirty, old, rough bearskin rug. What about it makes it look like a *rug*?'' If the patient responds with form features, one can reply, "But what about it makes it look like a *bearskin* rug?'' By so doing, other possible determinants, such as a chromatic color, shading, or texture, may be revealed. Moving backward to the next question—"But what makes it look like a *rough* bearskin rug?''—one almost invariably will find the patient attempting in some way to describe the tactile aspects of the blot through textural representation. And when pursuing the modifier *old* by saying, "But you said it was an *old*, rough bearskin rug?'' the patient will frequently give a response that suggests morbidity or damage to the rug, thus adding another score to this response (Morbid). Finally, "But you said it was a *dirty*, old, rough bearskin rug?'' will most probably elicit some suggestion of achromatic color as the basis of that aspect of the response.

Some may consider using this technique to be leading the patient, something that needs to be avoided on the Rorschach. I don't feel there is any danger of leading in this technique; for whenever someone gives a response with modifiers, those modifiers are based on features of the blot that usually represent determinants (i.e., the features that determined the response or word used) and/or other scores to which the patient is responding, or he or she would not have given the response in that manner. It should also be noted that these responses may not be given as clearly as I've just presented them in the above example. Rather, the modifiers may be imbedded in other parts of a response. It will, therefore, be necessary to pursue these modifiers, wherever they may be, in as matter-of-fact and diligent a manner as possible in order to be able to understand the nuances of the patient's behavior as reflected on the Rorschach.

Inquiry is not limited only to the Rorschach but can be used in any diagnostic test in a battery. For example, another form of projective test for which inquiry can be useful is the thematic or story-telling type of test such as the TAT or the CAT. On this type of test the diagnostic material is not limited only to the story the patient spontaneously gives to a card; one should feel free, after the initial story is presented, to explore any aspect of that story and/or any deviations from the directions to clarify any confusion in its presentation. For example, if, after being told that a response should have a beginning, middle, and end, a patient tells a story without an antecedent or cause for the behavior described to have occurred, one might inquire, "What led up to that?" "How did that happen?" Likewise, if a patient tells a story without any resolution or conclusion, one can say, "And then what happens?"

Frequently, young people give stories with a very short time frame (though it's possible to find this in older patients as well). It is thus often important and revealing to inquire about what happens later in the character's life. For example, if on card 1 of the TAT a patient tells a story about the trials and tribulations of a boy playing a violin and leaves it at that level, it is beneficial to inquire what happened later in the boy's life. Similarly, if a character seems magically to learn to play the violin, one may want to explore what happened that allowed him or her to play, as well as who might have been responsible for the change.

Exploring the ego functions of the patient through the use of thematic tests like the TAT can also be useful in understanding the patient's strengths and weaknesses. Some of the ego functions that can be investigated are reality testing, where, for example, one can note the reaction to the normal pull of the card (i.e., the usual card pull versus the story the patient tells); the focus of the patient's attention on minor characters, and unusual and/or usually undetected aspects of the card rather than the usual and popularly responded-to areas; and how accurately the patient perceives the card as it is. For example, does the patient see the violin on card 1 of the TAT or does he or she see a ham sandwich, a piece of cake, or something else that seems very unrelated to the usual pull of the card and/or to the reality aspects of the card? Reality-testing aspects of ego functioning can also be seen in the story the patient tells to the card. Is the story realistic, or is it an unfathomable or unrealistic type of story?

Another ego function that can be inquired into on the thematic tests is object relations, where one can begin to see the types of relationships the patient identifies with, especially in terms of the main character in the story. Inquiring about those relationships; wondering with the patient who particular people in the card are, if they are not mentioned in terms of relationships; and noticing any lack of relationships in a story are an important part of understanding this important ego function. For example, one might question the relationship of those who help the main character or others on a particular task or allow a certain resolution or goal to occur.

Though there are a number of other ego functions that could be explored using inquiry on the thematic tests, the limitations of this chapter do not permit their being individually explored. The above examples, however, should be seen as an illustration of how one might explore any of the other ego functions relevant for a given patient.

Another type of test that works well in terms of inquiring about personality factors in a patient is the Incomplete Sentence Blank-type of test. This type of test is administered by reading to or letting the patient read the stem of standardized material and having the patient respond either verbally or in writing by finishing the sentence with the first thing that comes to mind related to his or her life. I do not particularly like to ask patients to read and write out the answers by themselves but prefer to read the stem to the patients and have them respond with whatever comes to mind. For the most part, patients will give responses readily to the sentence stems, finding the test relatively easy; but I frequently find that the responses patients give on the Incomplete Sentence Blank test do not fully help me to understand how they perceive things, nor do they easily allow me to uncover unconscious motivation. For this reason, here, too, I find inquiry an important technique to enrich my understanding in these areas. After I have written down all of the patient's responses to the stems originally read to him or her, I then go back to explore any of the answers that either I don't understand or that I wish to have expanded. In this way the test lends itself to being a type of informal interview that can be easier for the patient to respond to than the more typical clinical interview because it's based on something the patient has already given as an answer as well as being based in part on his or her own world experiences.

One of the stems to the Incomplete Sentence Blank test that is frequently used for children and adolescents at Reiss-Davis is "I think of myself as." This particular stem is very rich for types of responses that are spontaneously given by patients, but the responses often create many other questions, allowing the clinician to explore these nuances. It is especially important to use inquiry to explore questions on the Incomplete Sentence Blank test that center on self, important primary objects in patients' experience, and other aspects that need to be dealt with in their everyday interactions. Using the inquiry technique with the Incomplete Sentence Blank test thus permits diagnosticians to uncover a wealth of data to better understand patients, especially at their conscious level of functioning.

The human figure type of drawing tests is also frequently given as part of a battery for children, adolescents, and adults, and with these tests, too, the use of inquiry is helpful. One method of exploration is to use some of the postdrawing questions that Hammer (1963) and Buck (1966) have used in the House-Tree-Person Projective Drawing Technique. I have, however, found that, even using these questions in a standardized fashion, it is still very useful to inquire further about certain responses given to those questions or to material not covered in the questions.

In administering the House-Tree-Person Projective Drawing Technique, I follow the customary format of first presenting the paper on the desk with the longer margin perpendicular to the patient and asking him or her to draw a house. It can be any house, but the best house he or she can draw. After a patient has completed the house, I present another piece of paper, this time with the longer margin parallel to the patient, and ask him or her to draw a tree, again, any tree, but the best he or she can draw. After removing the drawing of the tree, I place another piece of paper in front of the patient, the same way I did for the tree, and ask the patient to draw a person, a whole person but not a stick drawing. I also ask him or her not just to sketch it, but to draw the best figure he or she can. Once that drawing is completed, I turn the paper over and ask the patient to draw me someone of the opposite sex. I specifically use that term because there are times when I am not sure of the sex of the person in the drawing that was first done. If I hazard a guess and it is incorrect, the patient can become upset, which can influence the second drawing and can also have an effect on the rest of the testing that session.

After I have the two person drawings, I then ask the patient to give me a name and age for each, assuring hesitant patients that these are their creations, they can be any name and age the patient desires. I ask patients to choose one of the drawings, to create a story about what the figure is doing in the drawing, what led up to that, and how it will end. After patients complete the story for the first figure, I give the same directions for the second figure. If these directions sound familiar, it is because they are the directions also given for doing the Thematic Apperception Test (TAT).

It is, in fact, not by chance that I present the House-Tree-Person test before giving the TAT. For I have found that it helps to cut down considerably on complaints about going through the TAT cards when that test is introduced with, "Now we have some pictures that have already been drawn so you will not have to draw any more. Just tell me stories about what is happening in the picture, what led up to it, and how it will end." Psychologically, it seems to patients that the task has been made easier by not having to draw the figures, and so they are much more motivated to go through the TAT cards without complaint. While information can be derived from the story about each figure the patient has drawn, the story can be inquired into further for missing parts, further clarification, and understanding and motivation of the figures, very much as discussed above in the section on the Thematic Apperception Test.

The other tests given in the typical battery at Reiss-Davis Child Study Center are a Wechsler test (WPPSI-R, WISC-III, WAIS-R) and the Bender-Gestalt test. These tests do not obviously appear to lend themselves to the inquiry process. But it is possible, as suggested by Hutt (1977) and a number of other psychodynamically oriented diagnosticians, in the association phase of the Bender-Gestalt test to have patients associate to their elaborated figures and the standard figures of the test, seeing what comes to mind. This technique allows for some projection from the patient, which can then be explored further through inquiry. It should be noted, though, that this test is the most limited test in the test battery in terms of using inquiry, because it does not require a verbal response or creativity—it is basically a visual-motor task.

The final test in the battery, the Wechsler test, is a standardized test, and, therefore, the inquiry technique must be used with care. This does not, however, mean that one cannot do inquiry on the Wechsler once the test is completed. As to how specific subtests lend themselves to inquiry, an example is the Picture Arrangement subtest. Because it deals with social issues, this is a very rich subtest for projective content. After the test is completed, you can go back and set the cards up as the patient responded to them in the earlier administration of the subtest, choosing those that were not correctly answered or were given in an unusual manner, and asking the patient to explain the responses in order. Except for the problem of memory, patients are usually able to explain their reasons for ordering the cards the way they did. This can be useful in helping to clarify what caused an error during the administration of the test, if an error was made, or an unusual way of responding to the item. An example of the latter might be where the patient laughed or exhibited some type of response to the particular item different from responses to the rest of the items.

Inquiry on the Picture Completion subtest is helpful in looking at the patient's cognitive functioning, especially the area of word finding and the use of nonspecific language. For instance, when a child, adolescent, or adult uses *thing* to describe a missing part while pointing to the right area, one gives credit for the response but can inquire, "What is that called?" to see if the patient has the correct word available to him or her.

Subtests that specifically call for a verbal response, such as Vocabulary, Information, and Comprehension, are ripe for projective content, and thus for inquiry. When patients give an unusual response to one of these subtest items, it is important to inquire what they mean by the response and/or to ask for further clarification about the response for the purpose of scoring, if for nothing else. But idiosyncratic answers are also often ripe with projective material, and inquiring more fully into those areas can uncover dynamic possibilities. This is especially true of the Comprehension subtest items, where unusual responses can *only* be understood more fully through inquiry.

The remaining Wechsler subtests don't lend themselves as easily to inquiry. However, after the entire test is completed, the examiner should always review any items (even performance items) that appeared to be difficult, confusing, or unusually executed, by asking patients, for example, if they can explain the method or plan used to figure the problem out. This can also be done on the Arithmetic subtest to explore an unusual answer or to understand the math procedure used when different than expected.

Thus inquiry is no longer limited to the Rorschach, but should be used across the many tests given in a test battery to better understand the patient. In this way, psychological diagnostic testing material will be far more relevant to the diagnostic process, as it will more accurately reflect how patients see their world. And examiners can explore the consciously experienced feelings and ideas of patients, as well as their more unconscious motivations. These findings will not only aid in making the diagnostic evaluation more comprehensive but will allow psychological testers to feel they have made a major contribution to the diagnostic process and, even more important, to patients and their treatment plans. Following some of the suggestions made in this chapter will help evaluators to appreciate inquiry and the difference it makes in the process of diagnostic psychological testing.

REFERENCES

Allison, J., Blatt, S., and Zimet, C. (1968). *Interpretation of Psychological Tests*. New York: Harper & Row.

Appelbaum, S. (1976). Introduction to *The Only Dance There Is*, by R. Dass. New York: Jason Aronson.

Astin, A. (1969). Folklore and selectivity. *Saturday Review*, December 20, pp. 57–58.

Beck, A., Ward, C., Mendelson, M., et al. (1962). Reliability of psychiatric diagnosis, 2. *American Journal of Psychiatry* 119:351–357.

Buck, J. (1966) *The House, Tree, Person Technique, Revised Manual*. Beverly Hills: Western Psychological Services, 1966.

Duncan, B., Solovey, A., and Rusk, G. (1992). *Changing the Rules*. New York: Guilford.

Eron, L. (1966). *Classification of Behavior Disorders*. Chicago: Aldine.

Exner, J. (1993). *Rorschach: A Comprehensive System*, vol. 1, 3rd ed. New York: Wiley.

Fine, R. (1971). *Healing of the Mind*. New York: David McKay.

Fordham, M. (1972). "Theory of maturation." In *Handbook of Child Psychoanalysis*, ed. B. Wolman, pp. 461–500. New York: Van Nostrand Reinhold.

Foulds, G. (1955). The reliability of psychiatric and the validity of psychological diagnoses. *Journal of Mental Science* 101:851–862.

Friedman, S., and Fanger, M. (1991). *Expanding Psychotherapeutic Possibilities*. New York: Free Press.

Freud, A. (1965). *Normality and Pathology in Childhood*. New York: International Universities Press.

Gauron, E., and Dickinson, J. (1966). Diagnostic decision-making in psychiatry. *Archives of General Psychiatry* 14:233–237.

Greenspoon, J., and Gersten, C. (1977). A new look at psychological testing: psychological testing from the standpoint of a behaviorist. *American Psychologist* 22:848–853.

Groth-Marnat, G. (1990). *Handbook of Psychological Assessment*, 2nd ed. New York: Wiley.

Hammer, E., ed. (1963). *Clinical Application of Projective Drawings*. Springfield: Thomas.

Holt, R. (1967). Diagnostic testing. *Journal of Nervous and Mental Disease* 144:444–465.

Hutt, M. (1977). *The Hutt Adaptation of the Bender-Gestalt Test*, 3rd ed. New York: Grune and Stratton.

Kernberg, O. (1975). *Borderline Conditions and Pathological Narcissism*. New York: Jason Aronson.

Levy, L. (1963). *Psychological Interpretation*. New York: Holt,

Rinehart and Winston.

McWilliams, N. (1994). *Psychoanalytic Diagnosis*. New York: Guilford.

Mahrer, A., ed. (1970). *New Approaches to Personality Classification*. New York: Columbia University Press.

Menninger, K. (1959). *A Psychiatrist's World*. New York: Viking.

Miller, S. (1987). A comparison of methods of inquiry. *Bulletin of the Menninger Clinic* 51:505–518.

Motto, R., and Friedman, S. (1967). The Team function in the diagnostic process. *Reiss-Davis Clinic Bulletin* 4:68–76.

Persons, J. (1993). Case conceptualization in cognitive behavior therapy. In *Cognitive Therapies in Action*, ed. K. Kuehlwein and H. Rosen. San Francisco: Jossey-Bass.

Pinkster, H. (1967). *The irrelevancy of psychiatric diagnosis*. Paper read at the American Psychiatric Association meeting, May.

Pope, B., and Scott, W. (1967). *Psychological Diagnosis in Clinical Practice*. New York: Oxford University Press.

Pruyser, P. W. (1976). Diagnosis and the difference it makes. *Bulletin of the Menninger Clinic* 40:411–602.

Rogers, C. (1954). An overview of research and some questions for the future. In *Psychotherapy and Personality Change*, ed. C. Rogers and R. Dymond, pp. 413–434. Chicago: University of Chicago Press.

Schmidt, H., and Fonda, C. (1956). The reliability of psychiatric prognosis: a new look. *Journal of Abnormal and Social Psychology*, 52:262–267.

Sharpe, E. (1978). *Collected Papers on Psychoanalysis*. New York: Brunner/Mazel.

Shore, M. (1972). Psychological testing. In *Clinical Assessment in Counseling and Psychotherapy*, ed. R. Woody and J. Woody, pp. 187–225. Englewood Cliffs, NJ: Prentice Hall.

Smith, S. (1977). Psychological testing and the mind of the tester. In *Diagnosis and the Difference It Makes*, ed. P. Pruyser, pp. 167–174. New York: Jason Aronson.

Szasz, T. (1961). *Myth of Mental Illness*. New York: Hoeber-Harper.

Tallent, N. (1976). *Psychological Report Writing*. Englewood Cliffs, NJ: Prentice Hall.

Woody, R., and Woody, J. (1972). *Clinical Assessment in Counseling and Psychotherapy*. Englewood Cliffs, NJ: Prentice Hall.

PART III

Issues of Education, Learning Difficulties, and Physically Challenged Children

INTRODUCTION TO PART III

We cannot minimize the importance of academic functioning in assessing and working therapeutically with children and adolescents. Learning and other disabilities can play a significant role in their emotional problems and can severely affect their self-esteem.

Since the late 1970s Reiss-Davis has offered learning disability assessment and remediation services, as well as research and training programs in the area of learning disabilities, to address these important aspects in working with children. Most recently, an Attention Deficit Disorder Clinic was developed in conjunction with the Learning Disabilities Clinic to assess and remediate this special area of dysfunction that occurs in numerous children, adolescents, and young adults—affecting not only their academic but also their emotional development.

In this section three chapters examine the obstacles that may circumscribe the limits of individual growth and development, and offer techniques for fostering successful adjustment and realizing potential capabilities in these children.

Chapter 7, "Psychodynamic and Relational Problems of Children with Nonverbal Learning Disabilities," by Joseph Palombo, reviews the major theories of nonverbal learning disabilities and looks specifically at the psychodynamics and social misperceptions associated with these right-hemispheric dysfunctions. Drawing on a clinical perspective based on Palombo's self-psychological orientation, this chapter is directed toward the child who has cognitive and affective deficits present in a number of arenas, including visual-spatial processing, arithmetic skills, affect processing, and related academic and social-emotional problems.

In Chapter 8, Donald Tessmer, director of the Learning Disabilities Clinic, and Janet Ciriello, director of psychology and the Postgraduate Fellowship Training Program at the Reiss-Davis Child Study Center, join together to present their collaborative parent–child treatment of a case spanning 14 years at the Center. This case involves a learning-disabled, depressed, anxious older adolescent and his mother, who was emotionally injured in her childhood at the same age her son's symptoms began to appear. "The Game Ain't Over 'til It's Over: A Long-Term Psychoeducational Child and Parent Treatment Case" examines the parallels in both the child's and the parent's experiences of trauma. Ciriello's work with the parent helped to foster a sense of emotional stability and external well-being for the mother and for her son. Tessmer's treatment of the boy blends psychotherapy and educational support. The chapter illustrates how, over time, through the use of baseball as a metaphor, the treatment foundation was strengthened, allowing the development of hope, the setting of goals, and the pursuit of vocational and educational direction.

In "Working with Visually Impaired Infants and Their Families: Implications for Other Physically Challenged Patients" (Chapter 9), Renee Cohen addresses the importance of understanding an entire family's needs when a physically disabled infant is born. Parental and sibling reactions to this unique situation are presented. As Cohen explores the phases parents go through on learning that their child is physically challenged, she discusses interventions that will prove helpful on a number of levels to the clinician working with this type of family stress.

7

Psychodynamic and Relational Problems of Children with Nonverbal Learning Disabilities

Joseph Palombo, L.C.S.W.[1]

INTRODUCTION

Learning disabilities are conditions presumed to be of neurological origin that occur in children or adults of at least average intelligence. These conditions are not the result of trauma or medically diagnosed neurological abnormalities (Abrams 1987, Hammil et al. 1987, National Joint Committee on Learning Disabilities 1987). The conditions affect one or more of a broad range of cognitive functions, and the severity of the deficits is

[1] I wish to acknowledge the contributions to this work made by my colleagues of the interdisciplinary NVLD/SLD study group: Meryl Lipton, Karen Pierce, Walter Raine, Pearl Reiger, and Warren Rosen. Without their assistance this chapter would not have been possible.

highly variable. In addition, some children are affected in a single area, while others are affected in several areas (Bryan and Bryan 1975, Johnson and Mykelbust 1967, Lerner 1971, Rourke et al. 1983, Silver 1979). Because different areas are affected in different children, it is impossible to make general statements about the impact of these difficulties on a child's psychological development or the psychopathology that is likely to result. Delineation of the subtypes of learning disabilities may help provide a better understanding of their psychological sequelae.

There is no unanimity among the experts about the number of subtypes of learning disabilities (Coplin and Morgan 1988, Morrison and Segal 1991). A consensus exists, however, that a simple demarcation can be made between two different subtypes: verbal learning disabilities and nonverbal learning disabilities. Verbal learning disabilities include the dyslexias, auditory processing difficulties, and other disorders that affect the reception, expression, and processing of verbal and written language. Nonverbal learning disabilities include the disabilities related to visual-spatial processing of information and disorders associated with the reception, expression, and processing of affective communications. Some researchers, such as Pennington (1991), prefer to categorize learning disorders differently and do not consider the two subtypes to encompass the entire range of learning disabilities. They suggest that nonverbal learning disabilities are divisible into disabilities related to visual-spatial cognition difficulties and social cognition disorders.[2]

Regardless of which view is taken, it is possible to make two generalizations about the impact of learning disabilities on a child's behavior and personality development. First, if the area affected is not critical for most day-to-day functioning; the child may initially be unaffected by the deficit. As the child matures, if the social context does not place great value on the particular skill in which the child is deficient, the child may not experience the deficit as particularly handicapping. The effects of the deficit may be that the child feels him- or herself to be different from other children. The child then develops self-esteem problems.

---

[2]See Badian 1986, 1992, Benowitz et al. 1990, Denkla 1983, Duane 1989, Johnson 1987, Pennington 1991, Rourke 1989, and Rourke and Fuerst 1991.

If the area affected is more critical to the child's functioning, then the effects are more devastating. The child experiences the world differently from the way the world is experienced by others. Information critical for the child's assessment of situations is not available, or if the information is available to the child, it is processed in a highly idiosyncratic way. The child's responses are markedly different from those of most of the child's peers. Adults and caregivers find themselves puzzled by the child's responses or interpret those responses as hostile, negativistic, or confusing. They then respond to the child's responses as intentional, or bewildering. In turn, the child views those responses through his or her clouded perceptions and experiences them as injurious. A pattern of relating emerges that fuels the child's confusion; the dialogue between the child and others in the environment becomes derailed; the child's responses are viewed as pathological and as indicative of serious disturbances. These problems are usually compounded by serious self-esteem problems.[3]

Unless diagnosticians consider the learning disability to be part of the etiology of the emotional problems, the child's problem will be misdiagnosed. Children with learning disabilities are often correctly diagnosed by those unfamiliar with learning disabilities as either suffering from severe narcissistic or borderline personality disorders. However, a variety of dynamics, unrelated to the learning disability, are postulated as causing the disturbance. Dynamics often mentioned are failure to resolve the rapprochement phase of development, splitting of the good-self and object representations, failures in parental empathy. Obviously, these dynamics miss the mark since they do not take into account an important piece of evidence in formulating the diagnosis (Fairchild and Keith 1981, Garber 1988). Therapists who base their treatment on such faulty or incomplete understanding often face serious difficulties. Some highly intuitive therapists may manage to establish a dialogue with the child

---

[3]See Beres 1971, Brumback and Staton 1983, Christman 1984, Gardner 1979, Glosser and Koppell 1987, Greenspan 1989, Palombo 1979, 1985b, 1987, 1991, 1993a, 1994, Rosenberger 1988, Rothstein et al. 1988, Shane 1984, Silver 1974, 1989, Vigilante 1983, Weil 1970, 1973, 1978, 1985.

and may eventually help the child achieve a modicum of improvement. Other therapists, however, give up hope of ever being able to understand the child and find the treatment to be stalemated by their own discouragement and the child's despair.

In this chapter I will discuss some of the psychodynamics children with nonverbal learning disabilities (NVLD) present, and delineate the impact of these deficits on the relationships they form. I begin with a consideration of some current theories of NVLD; I then present a phenomenological description of the child with a nonverbal learning disability from two perspectives: a diachronic, or developmental, perspective, and a synchronic perspective, that is, a perspective of the clinical presentation the child makes at the time of an evaluation. Finally, I discuss the psychodynamics associated with these problems, and the relational problems that result.

My thesis is as follows: Children with NVLD, because of their deficits, are unable to decode a range of nonverbal communications. Their understanding of social contexts is incomplete. They construe a unique set of personal meanings from their experiences. These personal meanings are integrated into a self-narrative that includes a view of reality that appears coherent to the child. However, this self-narrative and view of reality may not make sense to others in the child's context. When the child's self-narrative and view of reality are not concordant with those of others, the dialogue between the child and others is derailed. This derailment interferes with the child's ability to draw sustenance from his or her caregivers or to use selfobject functions caregivers can provide. The child develops disorders of the self, and relational problems. The disorders reflect selfobject deficits that lead to narcissistic vulnerability. A variety of defenses is brought into play to deal with the anxiety and rage that are generated. Symptomatic behaviors, sometimes quite pervasive, emerge. On the other hand, from a relational standpoint, the attachments the child forms are complex and often dysfunctional. The child seeks others to complement his or her cognitive and affective deficits, a desire that may or may not find a response in the caregivers. Problems arise regardless of the caregivers' responses, and relational problems follow. In turn, these relational problems have serious consequences for the child's sense of self.

NVLD: SYNDROME, SUBTYPE, OR SYMPTOM?

The model for understanding children with NVLD's symptoms was initially derived from neurology. The discovery, late in the nineteenth century, that the aphasias were related to left brain dysfunctions led neurologists to speculate that dyslexia was related to similar brain dysfunctions. A broader hypothesis was developed of a direct relationship between brain function and behavior. Hiscock and Kinsbourne state that "among the most popular neural models of learning disability are those that invoke an abnormality of cerebral hemisphere specialization" (1987, p. 130).

Studies of hemispheric specialization led researchers to hypothesize that the right and left hemispheres process information differently. For Goldberg and Costa, "the right hemisphere has a greater ability to perform intermodal integration and to process novel stimuli; the left hemisphere is more capable of unimodal and motor processing as well as the storage of compact codes" (1981, p. 144). The left hemisphere has greater facility for utilizing information previously learned, while the right hemisphere tends to approach every task as a novel experience. The left hemisphere is better equipped to process verbal language, which is a representational system shared by the cultural context in which the child is raised. But the right hemisphere is better equipped to process nonverbal languages, which are differently structured from the linear sequential verbal mode of communication.

Studies indicate that the right hemisphere, in addition to being more specialized in intermodal integration of stimuli and in processing novel stimuli, is more proficient than the left hemisphere at processing visual-spatial information, such as visual-spatial relationships, and in the performance of visual-motor tasks. It is better equipped than the left hemisphere to recognize and process a wide range of nonverbal cues, including vocal intonations, affective expressions, and gestures. Furthermore, it is involved in processing and modulating affects, and is implicated in the development of social skills (Semrud-Clikeman and Hynd 1990).

A comparison of adults and children who suffered right hemisphere strokes or injuries revealed problems in the areas of nonverbal communication to be common to both groups. This led Weintraub and Mesulam to propose the hypothesis that "there is a syndrome of early right-hemisphere dysfunction that may be genetically determined and that is associated with introversion, poor social perception, chronic emotional difficulties, inability to display affect, and impairment in visuospatial representation" (1983, p. 468). In neuropsychological terms, such a syndrome would be identified as a nonverbal learning disability.

Neuropsychological theories explain the relationship between brain and behavior through the concepts of *brain systems* and *hemispheric specialization.* A variety of brain systems operate within each of the hemispheres, and are correlated with syndromes, or with behavioral manifestations. Within the neuropsychological paradigm, learning disabilities are considered to be caused by limitations or deficits in cognitive capacities that are related to neurological variations in endowment. And although the children do not manifest any medically diagnosed neurological abnormalities, they often exhibit a significant number of soft neurological signs (Coplin and Morgan 1988). "Explanatory constructs within this paradigm involve reference to the degree of intactness and organization of various systems in the brain that are purportedly involved in specific kinds of intellectual performance. . . . [S]ince these systems are often assigned to specific locations in the brain, deficient performance on intellectual tasks is frequently explained in terms of damage or malfunctioning of certain areas of the brain" (Torgesen 1986, p. 401).

Historically, the concept of nonverbal language deficits was introduced in 1967 by Johnson and Myklebust in their book on learning disabilities. Later Johnson (1987) and Myklebust (1975) each separately elaborated on the description of children with

NVLD. Two other exponents of the neuropsychological paradigm are Pennington (1991) and Rourke (1985, 1989, 1993, Rourke and Fuerst 1991). Both of these authors suggest that learning disabilities may best be classified into subtypes. Subtype classification is based on the phenomenological categorization of a cluster of symptoms presumed to be related to each other, but not due to any identifiable etiological factor. A subtype becomes a syndrome when the cluster of symptoms is identified as having a common etiology.

Pennington developed a typology of five different subtypes of learning disabilities. They are: (1) phonological processing difficulties, which lead to the dyslexias; (2) executive function disorders, connected with Attention Deficit Disorders; (3) problems with spatial cognition, which manifest as difficulties in the visual-motor areas—arithmetic and handwriting difficulties are examples; (4) problems in social cognition, which include the group of children within the autistic spectrum (from autistic to children with Asperger's syndrome); and (5) long-term memory disorders, such as those of people who suffer from amnesias resulting from brain injuries. (See Table 7–1.)

Of the five subtypes of learning disabilities described by Pennington, the ones we are interested in are those of *spatial cognition* and *social cognition*. For Pennington, spatial cognition disorders constitute nonverbal learning disabilities. These are right hemisphere dysfunctions that involve the visual and spatial systems. He considers these two systems to be distin-

TABLE 7–1. Modular Brain Functions and Learning Disorders

Function	Localization	Disorder
Phonological processing	Left presylvian	Dyslexia
Executive functions	Prefrontal	Attention deficit disorder
Spatial cognition	Posterior right hemisphere	Specific math/handwriting
Social cognition	Limbic, orbital, right hemisphere	Autism spectrum disorder
Long-term memory	Hippocampus, amygdala	Amnesia

From Pennington 1991. Copyright © 1991 by Guilford Press and used by permission.

guishable in their functions because some spatial tasks require no visual input, while some visual tasks, such as reading, require no spatial input. The functions included in these systems are object localization and identification, short-and long-term visual or spatial memory, deployment of attention to extrapersonal space, mental rotation and displacements, spatial imagery, and spatial construction. The primary presenting symptoms of children with this subtype of right hemisphere learning disorder are specific problems in mathematics and in handwriting. Correlated to these are problems in social cognition, attention, and conceptual skills.

Pennington takes exception with those who classify social learning disabilities as right hemisphere dysfunctions. He considers this classification to be misleading because social and cognitive processes are not localized exclusively in the right hemisphere. Emotional and social cognition appear to be "subserved by the limbic system and by portions of the frontal lobe" (p. 12). He places problems in social cognition within the autistic spectrum, which includes Asperger's syndrome. Children with social cognition problems present with difficulties in making social contact and understanding social contexts. Secondary problems for these children are pragmatic language problems, echolalia, stereotypies, and deficits in symbolic play.

Rourke's (1989, 1993) approach is to classify children based on the discrepancy between their performance and verbal IQs. He describes three subtypes: (1) The R-S-A subtype includes children with reading, spelling, and arithmetic problems. These children usually perform poorly in all three areas. Although their verbal IQ is higher than their performance IQ, the differential is not as high as in children in the other groups. (2) The R-S subtype includes children with reading and spelling problems. Their performance IQ is higher than their verbal IQ. And (3) the A subtype includes children with arithmetic difficulties. Their performance IQ is lower than their verbal IQ. (See Table 7–2.)

Rourke defines the children in the group A subtype as children with "nonverbal disabilities." In contrast to Pennington, Rourke believes that the children's socioemotional and adaptational difficulties are related to the primary visual-spatial-organization output deficits (also called by Rourke Nonverbal Perceptual-Organization-Output Disorder, or NPOOD). These

TABLE 7–2.   Rourke's subtype classification

Subtype	Relation of VIQ to PIQ	Relation of PIQ to VIQ	Symptom
R-S-A Group	Both low, but VIQ higher	Both low, but PIQ lower	Performance on reading, spelling, and arithmetic is low
S-A Group	VIQ lower	PIQ higher.	Performance on reading and spelling is low
A Group	VIQ higher	PIQ lower	Performance on arithmetic is low

difficulties lead to problems in identifying and recognizing faces, expressing emotions, and other problems in nonverbal communication. Rourke does not find these children's emotional difficulties to be as extreme as the children Pennington identifies as having social cognition difficulties.

Both Pennington and Rourke note that verbal language is an area of strength for children with NVLD. The children develop skills at communicating verbally that are beyond those expected for their years. However, their capacity to deal with abstract concepts is not on a par with their verbal competencies.

From this brief review of the literature, we are left with the question of whether there is a right hemisphere *syndrome* associated with a set of markers (i.e., behaviors, modes of processing information, and the like) that might be called nonverbal learning disabilities. Or, whether this set of markers constitutes a *subtype* of learning disabilities, related to a set of brain systems. Or, whether the markers simply consist of a set of *symptoms* whose etiology is currently unknown.

If such a right hemisphere syndrome exists, it would encompass a range of dysfunctions, including visuospatial difficulties; gross motor dysfunctions; difficulties in verbal comprehension, in arithmetic computation, in affect processing, in recognition of nonverbal cues, and in social skills. Controversy surrounds the inclusion of arithmetic problems in this syndrome. Most investigators include arithmetic problems in their descriptions of the syndrome (Semrud-Clikeman and Hynd 1990), and Rourke insists that arithmetic difficulties are the clear markers for the subtype. Yet clinically we see children with visuospatial problems who do not have arithmetic difficulties. We also see children with affect-processing problems who do not have visuospatial or arithmetic problems.

A second question centers on the issue of whether social learning disabilities are distinct from NVLD or are part of a different subtype. Some problems are clearly due to dysfunctions in cognition, some to difficulties in affect processing. Yet the relationship between cognition and affectivity remains controversial, if not obscure. If affective communication is central to the formation of attachments and social relationships, then it may be that this group of disorders should be considered separate from the group of dysfunctions related to visual-spatial-perceptual problems. Pennington's proposal would have merit were it not for the fact that clinically we see a group of children who have social relationship difficulties, and who would not be diagnosable as suffering from disorders classifiable within the autistic spectrum.

Finally, it is not clear whether the broad set of symptoms described should be categorized together as constituting a single entity called nonverbal learning disabilities. Clinical experience, based on anecdotal accounts, does not seem to support the view of a clearly delineated syndrome, or a clearly demarcated subtype. We see very few children who manifest all these difficulties and who do not have other problems that confound their presentation. Some suffer from Pervasive Developmental Disorders; some are suspected of suffering from Asperger's syndrome; others are thought to be high-functioning autistic children. But a large group of these children present quite differently, with disorders not of the severity associated with the autistic spectrum.

Answers to these questions are of critical importance to therapists who treat these children. Diagnostic judgment must be made of the emotional problems from which a child suffers. Differences in how a disturbance is understood lead to different formulations of the psychodynamics and relational problems attributed to the child. Unless a correct assessment is made the proper treatment cannot be provided.

In the meantime, since most research supports the hypothesis of an entity, whether a syndrome or a subtype, in this chapter I will restrict the definition of a nonverbal learning disability to the subtypes identified by Pennington as Spatial Cognition, and by Rourke as nonverbal learning disability. I will not consider the Autistic Spectrum disorders as included in this entity.

PHENOMENOLOGICAL DESCRIPTION OF THE CHILD WITH NVLD

I now turn to a phenomenological description of the major components of this entity. What follows is a composite profile of children with NVLD. It is not meant to be a comprehensive picture. It is one culled from a review of the literature, and from my and my colleagues' clinical experiences.[4]

The profile is organized under two different headings: a diachronic or developmental perspective, and a synchronic perspective—that is, the perspective of the child's clinical presentation. The latter includes a description of the status of the child's functioning from a social and emotional perspective. Obviously, since these are arbitrary categorizations, considerable overlap exists between them.

The Diachronic Perspective: A Developmental Profile

No direct observations have been made of these children's early development; what is available is reconstructed from their histories. Caregivers report that as infants they are passive, fail to engage in exploratory play, and do not respond as expected. Many cannot use toddler toys or enjoy coloring or drawing. They are unable to put puzzles together (Johnson 1987).

When the children start to walk, their visual-spatial-motor

---

[4]See Badian 1986, 1992, Heath and Kush 1991, Hiscock and Kinsbourne 1987, Johnson 1987, Johnson and Mykelbust 1967, Mykelbust 1975, Nass, Petersen, and Koch 1989, Pearl et al. 1986, Pennington 1991, Rourke 1989, Rourke and Fuerst 1991, Semrud-Clikeman and Hynd 1990, 1991, Voeller 1986, Weintraub and Mesulam 1983.

problems emerge. They appear clumsy and ill coordinated—caregivers must watch them closely because they bump into furniture, are unsteady on their feet, break toys, and endanger themselves. Slow to learn from their caregivers' limits and instructions, they appear unable to understand causal relationships, and caregivers must intervene and correct them constantly. In turn the children respond with frustration and anger. Often, their frustration escalates, so that by the age of 2 temper tantrums emerge that are much more intense than the ones that normally occur at this age.

Their self-help skills do not develop comparably to those of other children their age. They are slow to learn to feed and dress themselves. They do not master tasks such as hand washing or grooming, and must be helped and reminded to complete these tasks well into latency, when other children already perform them independently.

By the age of 3, they go through an initial stage when their speech is difficult to understand because of articulation problems. These problems dissipate, and they then become quite adept at verbal communication. This channel becomes reinforced by caregivers, who then become overreliant on it to relate to the children.

In groups, difficulties interacting with other children become evident. They seem not to know how to play with others, clinging to the caregivers who accompany them, seeming to have difficulties separating. If this strategy is unsuccessful, they isolate themselves.

By the time they reach kindergarten or first grade, other problems become evident. Although by this age they appear to be quite bright and have excellent verbal abilities, they have major problems in the area of peer relationships. They are unable to form friendships or to sustain being with other children even for brief periods of time without erupting. Academically, they start out having difficulty decoding letters and words, but once they discover the rules they become good readers. Their writing, however, is illegible, complicated by their small motor problems and visuospatial difficulties. Arithmetic difficulties emerge once simple computation is introduced.

If the caregivers have had other children, from the very beginning they sense that the child is different, although they are hard put to pinpoint what it is they feel. They find themselves frustrated in their efforts to understand the child. Unable to decode the child's cues, they find the child to be socially unresponsive. Caregivers feel placed in the position of constantly having to correct, limit, or punish the child, who in turn responds with fury at what he or she experiences as unfair treatment. The family ends up feeling controlled by the child in all its activities. Often caregivers feel guilty, blaming themselves for their failure to parent properly. This frustration may initiate a cycle in which the caregivers feel rejected by the child and in turn distance themselves emotionally from him or her. Some caregivers are intuitively able to read the child's messages and soon find themselves being the only ones who can communicate effectively with the child. If that does not occur, the difficulties are compounded by the child's increasing demands on the caregiver and the child's inability to cope.

Sometimes caregivers unwittingly contribute to the confusion because of their own personality difficulties. Some caregivers themselves have NVLD. The household then appears like that of a family in which each member speaks a different language. While a measure of communication occurs, large areas are fraught with misunderstandings. The level of frustration, the anger resulting from constant injury, the lack of gratification in having such a difficult child, all contribute to the ensuing chaos.

By the time the child is 7 or 8, the full-fledged syndrome manifests itself. It is often at this point that children are referred for therapy.

The Synchronic Perspective: Clinical Presentation

Children with NVLD are generally referred for a variety of problems. Boys are often referred because of behavioral problems whereas girls may be referred because of their social isolation. Both boys and girls often present with clinical signs of severe anxiety, depression, attentional problems, obsessional preoccupations, and low self-esteem. They perform poorly in some academic areas, but not in all. They are good readers, but have great difficulty with tasks involving writing or arithmetic. Neuropsychological testing reveals their cognitive deficits, while their histories and the clinical impression from diagnostic interviews disclose their social and emotional distress.

The Neurocognitive Profile

Visual-spatial-motor area: Rourke (1989, 1993) provides a detailed catalog of these children's assets and deficits. He proposes that areas of primary deficits are tactile perception, such as finger agnosia—that is, the failure to identify which finger is touched in the absence of a visual cue; visual perception, such as discriminating and recognizing visual details, and organizing visual stimuli; complex psychomotor tasks that require cross-modal integration of visual perception and motor output, such as putting puzzles together or solving mazes; and dealing with novel materials and adjusting to new situations. The children also have problems with attention, exploratory behavior, tactile and visual memory, concept formation, and problem solving. Concomitant with these difficulties are speech problems and problems in prosody that lead to speaking in a monotone or with a singsong voice.

Related academic problems are poor handwriting and deficient skill in arithmetic. While they are good readers, their reading comprehension is not on a par with their verbal skills. Art classes are the bane of these children. Many behavior problems emerge in that setting because the tasks require the capacity for visual-spatial-perceptual organization the children do not possess.

Verbal language area: The children are either average or above average in verbal language skills. They have good syntax and good pragmatics. Reversal of pronouns is common at an early age and clears up with maturation. Most of them have good memories and manifest rote memory verbalizations that makes them look much smarter than they actually are. What seems characteristic is that their concepts lack precision. Although they appear sophisticated, there is a shallowness to the content of their expressions. A child may talk a lot and use a vocabulary that seems advanced for his or her age, but the communications are not always well connected, and the content appears superficial. The problem with concept formation limits their capacity to reason, analyze, and synthesize materials.

Later on, as the child moves to higher grades, reading comprehension drops. Complex material becomes much harder to grasp, and the concepts related to it are harder to understand. They cannot organize a narrative to pick out the main points from supporting details, the relevant from the irrelevant. They also have difficulty reading between the lines, making inferences, and understanding the double meaning of expressions. Their capacity to give a narrative account of an event is limited. They grasp an aspect of the total picture and miss the broader gestalt. Asked to report on an event, they give an account that appears disconnected and devoid of feeling. It becomes very difficult to reconstruct what has happened from their reports.

The Social-Emotional Profile

Lai states: "The concept of 'social skills' is a multi-faceted one, consisting of the integration of several capacities, including the interpretation of nonverbal cues in the environment, the ability to experience a range of emotions in differing contextual circumstances, and the development of a flexible repertoire of behaviors to meet the needs of a particular, complex social interaction, among others" (1990, p. 2).

The area of affective communication is problematic for children with NVLD. This area may be discussed from three points of view: the reception, expression, and processing of affective information.

Receptively, the children appear unable to decode prosodic or vocal intonations, although their hearing is unimpaired. If their caregiver's voice sounds serious, they may misunderstand the tone of voice as conveying anger. They also have difficulty reading facial expressions and bodily gestures, as though they suffer from a "nonverbal dyslexia" (Badian 1986).

In the expressive area we see the counterpart of these problems. The children do not use body gestures in speaking, and so

seem wooden and constricted. They do not use vocal intonations, speaking either in a flat monotone or with a singsong
voice. It is difficult to read their mood from their facial expressions.

We know very little about the ways in which they process
affective information. It is not clear whether their problem lies
in the area of decoding affective states, or in the area of visual
processing. They respond to affect-laden situations with anxiety, withdrawal, or sadness, and appear to have problems
modulating certain affects. When frustrated, they lose control
and have temper tantrums. Their response to most feelings is
one of generalized excitement that is unfocused and lacking in
content. To adults these children appear to have no compassion
or empathy for others. They appear not to have the same
feelings about events and people that their peers are capable of
having.

Their functioning in social situations is often puzzling. They
interact quite well with adults, but not as well with peers. This
may be because adults are more predictable in their responses
and can be engaged verbally, while their peers respond more
nonverbally and are more erratic in their responses. Since they
are unable to decode social cues involved in "reading" other
people's body language, facial expression, and vocal intonations, they are inept in social situations. They seldom make solid
eye contact, which may be due to their inability to organize the
face of the person they are looking at. Grasping the subtle
nuances of a social situation is difficult: they lack a sense of
humor; they do not know when they are being teased; they
interpret concretely colloquialisms or metaphorical expressions.

Sometimes they are taken to be rude, although they are not
consciously being disrespectful. They will start a conversation
with a stranger as though they were old friends, and will ask
personal questions and share personal facts too quickly. They do
not respect the privacy that we presume others to need. Nor
does their sense of body in space allow them to respect the usual
social distances, such as a culturally determined conversational
distance.

In contrast to children with Asperger's syndrome, these children appear to crave social contact and to be capable of relating to others. They try reaching out to other people, but their attempts are inept and are often misread. The children then pull back defensively and isolate themselves or become belligerent, though they do not give up the effort to connect. Unlike the "self-involvement" of autistic children, the withdrawal of children with NVLD is reactive rather than primary.

With peers their play is disruptive; they appear unable to negotiate social interchanges with other kids. Often a caregiver will say, "He just wants to play the way he wants to play. He doesn't want to share in the play." It is as though they have their own program. Negotiating and interacting with others is difficult.

The children also exhibit a number of psychiatric symptoms related to the experience of their deficit. At a young age, their frustration with confusing social situations often leads them to become emotionally overwhelmed and to fragment. This frustration lends itself in younger children to motor output such as hand flapping, jumping up and down excitedly, or extreme temper tantrums. They are then mistaken for children who suffer from Asperger's syndrome or mild autism. They generally suffer from high levels of anxiety, and severe self-esteem problems. They also suffer from depression, obsessive compulsive symptoms, or attentional problems that lead them to be misdiagnosed as having ADD.

PSYCHODYNAMICS AND RELATIONAL PROBLEMS OF CHILDREN WITH NVLD

Current psychoanalytic developmental theories, such as those proposed by Stern (1989) and Lichtenberg (1989), do not take into account the effects of neurocognitive differences and consequently do not explain their impact on children's personality development. They emphasize trauma and environmental over constitutional and neurocognitive factors. Only Weil (1970, 1973, 1978, 1985) and Greenspan (1989) attempt an integration of the concept of differences in endowment into their theories.

But even their theories do not speak directly of learning disabilities. Rothstein and her associates (1988) have written about learning disorders, of which learning disabilities are a subset. Their broader focus fails to conceptualize the specific effects of neurocognitive differences. In earlier publications (Palombo 1979, 1985a,b, 1987) I proposed that a relationship may exist between borderline personality disorders in children and severe learning disabilities. More recently I presented a conceptual scheme integrating the effects of neurocognitive differences on the development of children with learning disabilities (Palombo 1991, 1993a, 1994).

Rourke (Rourke and Fuerst 1991) reviewed and summarized the literature, from 1980 to the time of publication of his work, on the relationship of socioemotional problems to learning disabilities. He states that no single personality pattern or psychopathological outcome could be found to be common to all children with learning disabilities. Children with NVLD have a tendency "to develop an internalized form of socio/emotional disturbance" (p. 85). He made no attempt to explain the relational problems or the psychodynamics of these children.

In what follows I partially address the task of developing a theory through which to understand these children's psychological problems. I present a model for understanding some of their complex psychodynamics, and some of the relational problems they present. I do not believe we are yet in a position to give a good account of the course of their development.

The Self-Narratives of Children with Learning Disabilities

To gain a better understanding of the psychodynamics behind the symptoms and the relational problems children with NVLD present, I turn to a discussion of the motifs or themes that organize these children's self-narratives. Like the "invariant organizing principles" discussed by Stolorow and Atwood (1992), these motifs reflect the set of patterns that are shaped by the child's integration of the meanings of his or her experiences.

From the perspective of self psychology, to be a self or to be a person is to be a member of a community of others who function as selfobjects (Kohut 1971, 1977, 1981). Meanings emerge within a dialogue with others, who are members of the community in which the child is raised and who provide the context from within which meanings are created for and by the child (Palombo 1991). Furthermore, to be a self is to have a self-narrative that organizes the child's personal and shared meanings into a coherent whole, reflecting the child's view of reality. The self-narrative is the story the child configures from the personal and the shared meanings derived from self experiences. Shared meanings represent the area of overlap between what the child understands and what others intend him or her to understand through their communications. In a sense the area of shared meanings represents "reality." "Reality" is the area of agreement within a community. Agreement is reached through the use of shared meanings as to what the world is about. However, when the child's cognitive competencies are impaired, the scripts construed from experience will have idiosyncratic features and will encode meanings that are different from the meanings others attach to similar experiences. The child attaches personal meanings to those experiences. For example, a child with a problem in visual-spatial relationships who has difficulties "reading" facial expressions, "misperceives" the facial contours and the physiognomic expression of the caregiver. He or she cannot decode the meaning of the expression. Even if the caregiver matches the child's feeling state, the child cannot consistently associate the caregiver's facial expression with the affective response. The child is left to guess at the meaning of the interaction, often misses the mark, and attaches a personal meaning to the interaction that is different from the meaning the caregiver intended to convey. The child does not share in the meaning but construes his or her own personal meaning. The child may then develop patterns of expectations that lead to the belief that caregivers are uncaring and unresponsive. These patterns become motifs that shape future interactions and are a source of disorders of the self.

Psychodynamics of Children with NVLD

The psychodynamics of children with NVLD are difficult to ascertain not only because the data are often not available but also because of the complexity of sorting out what is primary and what is secondary in these dynamics. What follows is, therefore, speculative. What is clear is that for the child with NVLD all interactions are fraught with anxiety. This anxiety leads to defenses that in turn lead to symptomatic behaviors. It is possible to conjecture that some of the disorders of the self encountered in these children are related to the uniqueness of their experiences of those who attempt to provide selfobject functions for them.

As we have seen, these children's clinical presentation is complex and difficult to characterize. We can infer from the transferences they form that these children cannot experience the mirroring, soothing, and comforting that are essential for a healthy sense of self to develop. Rather, they interpret their transactions with others as having a different meaning than those intended by the caregivers. Their cognitive and affective deficits seem to interfere with the use of selfobject functions caregivers are ready to provide. They experience the interchanges as a failure in empathy. The resulting deficits impose severe limits on the range and depth of connectedness between child and caregiver.

Similar difficulties may be reconstructed as lying in the path to the acquisition of idealizing or alter ego functions. Since most selfobject functions are performed nonverbally, they occur in a domain that is difficult for these children to decode. Such experiences as those of being safely held by a protective caregiver, or of feeling reassured by the modulating influence of a caregiver's regulatory interventions, or of feeling pride in, and admiration of, a caregiver were construed as having a different meaning for these children than such experiences have for other children. The affects conveyed by the caregivers were either not perceived or misread. The gestures were misinterpreted. The result is that the child drew personal meanings that at best only partially reflects what occurred.

But these children suffer most from an absence of alter ego experiences, which are meant to provide a linkage with others whose humanity we share. Keenly aware of the differences between themselves and other children, children with NVLD cannot point to specific features to help them understand the dissimilarities between themselves and others or why others reject them, and they then feel injured and respond with rage or withdrawal.

A variety of disorders of the self emerge as a result of these selfobject deficits, not all of which are distinctive to children with NVLD. Most common are the pervasive self-esteem problems, since their deficits expose these children to constant narcissistic injuries from which they cannot escape. For the child with NVLD faced with the inability to decode nonverbal communications, who must deal with the fear generated by novel situations, who must struggle with the limitations imposed by the inaccessibility of feelings, a secondary set of deficits develops in addition to the primary cognitive and affective deficits. These are selfobject deficits that generate their own set of narcissistic vulnerabilities and symptoms.

Characteristic of these vulnerabilities are a propensity for rage attacks and pervasive anxieties. Children with NVLD are prone to express rage as a result of the constant frustration produced by failed communications, or to withdrawal into silent despair at never being fully appreciated and understood. The injuries they experience do not lead to the flagrantly grandiose behaviors that are common to children with problems of a different etiology. Instead, the fantasies of children with NVLD are filled with the wish for recognition, fame, and power. In addition, because the children's efforts at communication are met with obfuscation, they often become engulfed by a sense of helplessness that leads to pervasive anxiety. This intolerable anxiety leads to a variety of defenses, which in turn lead to symptomatic responses and/or behaviors. But since the meaning of the danger to the child motivates the response and the choice of defenses, no specific set of symptoms can be associated with this anxiety. What is often the case is that the anxiety is alleviated the moment the deficit is filled by someone providing the missing selfobject or complementary functions.

Finally, more disturbed children present with a different set of dynamics. For those children the meanings of the experiences are not integrated into the self-narrative, and incoherences creep into the story. The psychopathology that emerges is therefore the result of the child's incomplete integration of the personal and shared meanings of his or her experiences (Palombo 1991, 1992, 1993a,b). Such children present with "borderline" pathology. Their responses are chaotic and reflect the absence of an internal sense of cohesion. It is difficult to sort out whether the level of pathology is related to the severity of the deficits, to the unresponsiveness of the environment, or to a combination of these. The picture is often clouded because there is also evidence of other neurological or psychiatric problems.

The Relational Problems of Children with NVLD

Two types of sequelae of NVLD emerge in these children's relationships to others: one is related to the child's different perception of the world from that of others, the other results from the tangled dependence on others. The first type of difficulty is more specific to children with NVLD, while the second may be found more generally in most children with learning disabilities. Both types lead to relational problems with caregivers, other adults, and peers. These relational problems arise because of the mismatches between a child's expectations and those of significant others in the child's context.

Different views of "reality"

Embedded in the child's self-narrative is a motif, or an invariant organizing principle, that dictates how the child will interpret what occurs. This motif will vary from child to child depending on the factors that contributed to its organization. For children with NVLD the motifs are drawn from the personal meanings of their experiences, meanings that did not include dimensions of the communications with others that are highly significant. However, when the self-narrative includes both shared and personal meanings, the reality of the child with NVLD is not so radically different from that of others. The differences are subtle and elusive, and emerge in the nuances of communicative interchanges. But their emergence is not consciously noticed, so that when the dialogue becomes derailed there is a feeling of frustration and puzzlement as to what occurred. To the extent a child's self-narrative and construction of reality is concordant with that of others, the dialogue is maintained and no relational problems arise. The child feels the self-narrative is coherent story, and feels a sense of self cohesion, intactness, and well-being. But when the self-narrative is not concordant with that of others, a variety of problems arise.

An example of the type of relational problems that result from a discordant self-narrative comes from the experience of a 10-year-old boy enrolled in a summer camp he was attending for the first time. He had been in two other summer camps from which he was sent home early because his behavior was found to be intolerable. The hope was that in the more supportive atmosphere of a camp with personnel that had been informed of his learning disabilities, he could have a more successful experience.

The first two days of camp, he was accompanied by his counselor everywhere he went. The counselor verbally mediated all situations. Andy appeared to be making a good adjustment. However, on the third day, the group was left alone for a brief period of time. Some of the children in his cabin, who had been to camp together before, began playing a game that was unfamiliar to Andy. Wishing to include him, they quickly explained the rules to him and began the game. Andy participated and soon found himself being called "out" because he had violated one of the rules. He responded with fury. He insisted that the rules were wrong, that the other kids were being unfair and wanted to exclude him from their group. He became verbally abusive, and when one of the children approached him to try to calm him down, he assaulted the child. By the time the counselor returned to the group, chaos had broken out. In reconstructing what happened, the counselor found that Andy not only had misunderstood the rules but insisted that his version of the rules was the correct one, even though this was a game he had never played before.

Several factors entered into Andy's response to this situation. Some had to do with the novelty of the situation, some to his fear of rejection by the group. The point this vignette illustrates is that Andy developed patterns of interpreting social situations that were idiosyncratic for him. He attached his own personal meanings to occurrences and responded as though those were the only correct interpretations that could be made of the circumstances. Everyone else was wrong. Unfortunately, these patterns were so persistent that Andy got sent home from this camp also after 3 days.

Compensatory and complementary functions:

A different type of relational difficulty results from the inability of children with NVLD to compensate for their deficits. Such children develop a reliance on others to complement their deficits.

The brain's plasticity and its capacity to take over functions other areas are incapable of performing is well known. The phenomenon of compensation for physical handicaps is also well documented. When it comes to compensations for neuro-cognitive deficits, similar phenomena may be observed, although these are less well documented in the literature. Clearly, not all children compensate for their deficits (Miller 1991, 1992). Since verbal expressive capacities are an area of strength for children with NVLD, these children can learn to verbally mediate nonverbal tasks. They achieve the goal of completing a task by talking their way through the nonverbal steps. Some children learn that strategy for themselves, while others can gain from being taught the strategy. The limitations of the strategy lie in the children's shortcomings in dealing with abstract conceptual material. Since this capacity is not as well developed as are their verbal expressive capacities, children may be able to verbalize their understanding of what is required but not be able to perform the expected tasks.

The compensatory strategies children can develop are limited only by their creativity. Some children develop strategies other than those of verbal mediation. Some learn to structure their environment to minimize the reliance on visual cues. Others, with help, learn to rehearse verbally what is to occur in anticipation of an encounter with a new situation. When a child is capable of using such compensatory strategies, the negative impact of the disability is attenuated, as are the relational problems and psychopathology. However, for reasons that are not clear, some children do not acquire compensatory functions. These children learn to rely on others to complement their deficient functioning.

The notion of complementarity is related to that of compensation. A simple way to distinguish between them is to say that compensation consists of strategies a child uses to achieve the desired goal without the mediating intervention of another person, while complementarity consists in the use of others to help achieve the goal. At its simplest level the concept of selfobject provides a mode of thinking about one form of complementarity, delineating the ways in which others provide psychological functions to help a person maintain a sense of self cohesion (Kohut 1971, 1977, 1981). A related group of phenomena is the group I define as *complementary functions*. A complementary function is a function performed by another person to fill in an affective, cognitive, social, or functional deficit. The person performing the function augments the competencies of the person requiring the function. In ego psychological terms some of these functions were called *auxiliary ego functions*. My definition extends the concept to encompass the entire range of competencies and functions (Palombo 1991).

While all children require the complementarity of their caregivers because of their immaturity, children with NVLD tend to draw from caregivers additional functions that serve to complement their deficient competencies. What is different about these children is that the areas that require complementarity are not those that are usually identified as part of the caregiving process. Caregivers confront the problem of identifying the child's deficits before they can provide the requisite function. Since caregivers are often totally in the dark about what the child requires, they must respond intuitively. Through their empathic capacities they may be able to perform tasks for the child the child cannot perform, and therefore fill in the child's deficits. These caregivers often recognize that their child's difference compels them to respond as they do. If they do not, they cause the child serious distress.

Other caregivers either cannot or do not complement the child's deficits, and the child is then left to fend for him- or herself. Some caregivers simply cannot decode the child's cues, and their frustration is intensified by the repeated failures to understand the child's needs. Others believe that "giving in" to the child would encourage regressive trends and withhold responding to the child, interpreting the behavior as infantile or negativistic.

Relational problems emerge whether or not a caregiver complements the child's deficits, and each set of responses produces its own set of relational difficulties. If a caregiver devotes her- or himself to complementing a child's deficits, a complex relationship evolves that presents the caregivers with difficult dilemmas. On the one hand, the child may become extremely dependent on the caregiver so that it is impossible for the caregiver to distinguish between what the child can or cannot do. The caregiver will feel that the psychological survival of the child is in the balance. If the caregivers yields to every one of the child's demands, the relationship becomes a symbiotic one. At best, if the caregiver does not accede to all the demands, the dependence is less extreme, but the child will appear to suffer from separation anxiety. This dependence is further complicated by the anxiety and uncertainty the caregiver feels about how to proceed.

On the other hand, if the caregiver is unable to complement the function, or refrains from responding, the child's coping capacities are taxed maximally. The child develops serious behavioral problems; withdraws, feeling defeated by the environment; or simply fragments. The caregivers are then experienced as unempathic, negligent, or uncaring.

These problems appear to be unavoidable. The choices are between the better of two bad alternatives. A way out of these dilemmas may be available if caregivers have an understanding of the dynamics that drive the interaction. In the first instance, when a symbiotic tie or severe separation anxiety develops, it is the child's survival needs and not necessarily unconscious destructive needs in the caregivers to maintain the child's helpless state that stimulate the caregivers' responses. In the second instance, the caregivers' inability to decode the child's communications, or their frustration at having such a difficult child, may drive the interaction. The only way out of these dilemmas is to have a good understanding, at the earliest stages of development, of the nature of the child's deficits. Since that is not possible before the ages of 3 or 4, clinical judgment must be exercised about how best to proceed. My clinical experience leads me to recommend that the better alternative to follow is to allow a symbiosis to form, minimizing the child's distress. After the child matures sufficiently to cope with the environment, the attachment can be resolved.

REFERENCES

Abrams, J. C. (1987). The National Joint Committee on Learning Disabilities: history, mission, process. *Journal of Learning Disabilities* 20(2):102–108.

Badian, N. A. (1986). Nonverbal disorders of learning: the reverse of dyslexia? *Annals of Dyslexia* 36: 253–269.

_____ (1992). Nonverbal learning disability, school behavior, and dyslexia. *Annals of Dyslexia* 42:159–178.

Benowitz, L. I., Moya, K. L., and Levine, D. N. (1990). Impaired verbal reasoning and constructional apraxia in subjects with right hemisphere damage. *Neuropsychologia* 38:231–241.

Beres, D. (1971). Ego autonomy and ego pathology. *Psychoanalytic Study of the Child* 26:3–24. New Haven, CT: Yale University Press.

Brumback, R. A., and Staton, R. D. (1983). Learning disability and childhood depression. *Journal of American Orthopsychiatry* 20:269–281.

Bryan, T. H., and Bryan, J. H. (1975). *Understanding Learning Disabilities*. New York: Alfred.

Christman, D. M. (1984). Notes on learning disabilities and the borderline personality. *Clinical Social Work Journal* 12(1):18–30.

Coplin, J. W., and Morgan, S. B. (1988). Learning disabilities: a multidimensional perspective. *Journal of Learning Disabilities* 21(10):614–622.

Denkla, M. B. (1983). The neuropsychology of social-emotional learning disabilities. *Archives of Neurology* 40:461–462.

Duane, D. D. (1989). Neurobiological correlates of learning disorders. *Journal of the American Academy of Child and*

Adolescent Psychiatry 28:314–318.

Fairchild, M., and Keith, C. (1981). Issues of autonomy in the psychotherapy of children with learning problems. *Clinical Social Work Journal* 9(2):134–142.

Garber, B. (1988). The emotional implications of learning disabilities: a theoretical integration. *The Annual of Psychoanalysis,* vol. 16, pp. 111–128. Madison, CT: International Universities Press.

Gardner, R. A. (1979). Psychogenic difficulties secondary to minimal brain dysfunction. In *Basic Handbook of Child Psychiatry*, ed. J. D. Noshpitz, chap. 28, pp. 614–628. New York: Basic Books.

Glosser, G., and Koppell, S. (1987). Emotional-behavioral patterns in children with learning disabilities: lateralized hemispheric differences. *Journal of Learning Disabilities* 20(6):365–368.

Goldberg, E., and Costa, L. D. (1981). Hemisphere differences in the acquisition and use of descriptive systems. *Brain and Language* 14:144–173.

Greenspan, S. I. (1989). *The Development of the Ego: Implications for Personality Theory, Psychopathology, and the Psychotherapeutic Process*. Madison, CT: International Universities Press.

Hammill, D. D., Leigh, J. E., McNutt, G., and Larsen, S. C. (1987). A new definition of learning. *Journal of Learning Disabilities* 20(2):109–113.

Heath, C. P., and Kush, J. C. (1991). Use of discrepancy formulas in the assessment of learning disabilities. *Neuropsychological Foundations of Learning Disabilities*, ed. J. S. Obrzut and G. W. Hynd, pp. 287–307. San Diego: Academic.

Hiscock, M., and Kinsbourne, M. (1987). Specialization of the cerebral hemispheres: implications for learning. *Journal of Learning Disabilities* 20(3):130–143.

Johnson, D. J. (1987). Nonverbal learning disabilities. *Pediatric Annals* 16:133–141.

Johnson, D. J., and Myklebust, H. R. (1967). *Learning Disabilities: Educational Principles and Practices*. New York: Grune and Stratton.

Kohut, H. (1971). *The Analysis of the Self*. New York: International Universities Press.

_____ (1977). *The Restoration of the Self*. New York: International Universities Press.

_____ (1981). *How Does Analysis Cure?* Chicago: University of Chicago Press.

Lai, Z. C. (1990). A proposed neural circuitry underlying the processing of emotional cues derived from a syndrome of social skill impairment: a functional evolutionary architectonic perspective. Special Area paper.ˈ Clinical Psychology Program, University of Minnesota, unpublished.

Lerner, J. W. (1971). *Children with Learning Disabilities*, 2nd ed., pt. I, pp. 2–71. Boston: Houghton Mifflin.

Lichtenberg, J. D. (1989). *Psychoanalysis and Motivation*. Hillsdale, NJ: Analytic.

Miller, L. (1991). Psychotherapy of the brain-injured patient: principles and practices. *Cognitive Rehabilitation*, pp. 24–30. March/April.

_____ (1992). The primitive personality and the organic personality: a neuropsychodynamic model for evaluation and treatment. *Psychoanalytic Psychology* 9(1):93–109.

Morrison, S. R., and Siegel, L. S. (1991). Learning disabilities: a critical review of definitional and assessment issues. In *Neuropsychological Foundations of Learning Disabilities*, ed. J. S. Obrzut and G. W. Hynd, pp. 79–97. San Diego: Academic.

Myklebust, H. R. (1975). Nonverbal learning disabilities: assessment and intervention. In *Progress in Learning Disabilities,* vol. 3, pp. 85–121. New York: Grune & Stratton.

Nass, R., Petersen, H. D., and Koch, D. (1989). Differential effects of congenital left and right brain injury on intelligence. *Brain and Cognition* 9:258–266.

National Joint Committee on Learning Disabilities (1987). 1. Learning disabilities: issues on definition. *Journal of Learning Disabilities* 20(2):107–113.

Palombo, J. (1979). Perceptual deficits and self-esteem in adolescence. *Clinical Social Work Journal* 7(1):34–61.

_____ (1985a). The treatment of borderline neurocognitively impaired children: a perspective from self psychology. *Clinical Social Work Journal* 13(2):117–128.

_____ (1985b). Self psychology and countertransference in the treatment of children. *Child and Adolescent Social Work Journal* 2(1)36–48.

—— (1987). Selfobject transferences in the treatment of borderline neurocognitively impaired children. In *The Borderline Patient: Emerging Concepts in Diagnosis, Psychodynamics, and Treatment*, ed. J. S. Grotstein, M. Solomon, and J. A. Langs. Hillsdale, NJ: Analytic.

—— (1991). Neurocognitive differences, self-cohesion, and incoherent self-narratives. *Child and Adolescent Social Work Journal* 8:449–472.

—— (1993a). Neurocognitive differences, developmental distortions, and incoherent narratives. *Psychoanalytic Inquiry 1992*, vol. 3, pp. 63–84.

—— (1993b). Learning disabilities in children: developmental, diagnostic, and treatment considerations. From the *Proceedings: National Academies of Practice, Fourth National Health Policy Forum, Healthy Children 2000: Obstacles and Opportunities.* April 24–25, 1992.

—— (1994). Incoherent self-narratives and disorders of the self in children with learning disabilities. *Smith College Studies in Social Work* 64(2):129–152.

Palombo, J., and Feigon, J. (1984). Borderline personality in childhood and its relationship to neurocognitive deficits. *Child and Adolescent Social Work Journal* 1:18–33.

Pearl, R., Donahue, M., and Bryan, T. (1986). Social relationships of learning-disabled children. In *Psychological and Educational Perspectives on Learning Disabilities*, ed. J. K. Torgesen and B. Y. Wong. San Diego: Academic.

Pennington, B. F. (1991). *Diagnosing Learning Disorders: A Neuropsychological Framework*. New York: Guilford.

Rosenberger, J. (1988). Self psychology as a theoretical base for understanding the impact of learning disabilities. *Child and Adolescent Social Work Journal* 5:269–280.

Rothstein, A., Benjamin, L., Crosby, M., and Eisenstadt, K. (1988). *Learning Disorders: An Integration of Neuropsychological and Psychoanalytic Considerations*. Madison, CT: International Universities Press.

Rourke, B. P., ed. (1985). *Neuropsychology of Learning Disabilities: Essentials of Subtype Analysis*. New York: Guilford.

_____ (1989). *Nonverbal Learning Disabilities: The Syndrome and the Model*. New York: Guilford.

_____ (1993). Arithmetic disabilities, specific and otherwise: a neuropsychological perspective. *Journal of Learning Disabilities* 26(4):214–226.

Rourke, B. P., Bakker, D. J., Fisk, J. L., and Strang, J. D. (1983). *Child Neuropsychology: An Introduction to Theory, Research and Clinical Practice*. New York: Guilford.

Rourke, B. P., and Fuerst, D. R. (1991). *Learning Disabilities and Psychosocial Functioning: A Neuropsychological Perspective*. New York: Guilford.

Semrud-Clikeman, M., and Hynd, G. W. (1990). Right hemisphere dysfunction in nonverbal learning disabilities: social, academic, and adaptive functioning in adults and children. *Psychological Bulletin* 107:196–209.

_____ (1991). Specific nonverbal and social-skills deficits in children with learning disabilities. In *Neuropsychological Foundations of Learning Disabilities: A Handbook of Issues, Methods, and Practices*, ed. J. E. Obrzut and G. W. Hyde, pp. 603–629. San Diego: Academic.

Shane, E. (1984). Self psychology: A new conceptualization for the understanding of learning-disabled children. In *Kohut's Legacy: Contributions to Self Psychology*, ed. P. E. Stepansky and A. Goldberg, pp. 191–202. Hillsdale, NJ: Analytic.

Silver, L. B. (1974). Emotional and social problems of children with developmental disabilities. *Handbook on Learning Disabilities*, ed. R. E. Webber. Englewood Cliffs, NJ: Prentice-Hall.

_____ (1979). Children with perceptual and other learning problems. In *The Handbook of Child Psychiatry*, vol. 3, ed. J. D. Noshpitz, pp. 605–614. New York: Basic Books.

_____ (1989). Psychological and family problems associated with learning disabilities: assessment and intervention. *Journal of the American Academy of Child and Adolescent Psychiatry* 28:319–325.

Stern, D. N. (1985). *The Interpersonal World of the Infant*. New York: Basic Books.

_____ (1989). The representation of relational patterns: developmental considerations. In *Relationship Disturbances in Early*

Childhood, ed. A. J. Sameroff and R. N. Emde. New York: Basic Books.

Stolorow, R. D., and Atwood, G. E. (1992). *Contexts of Being: The Intersubjective Foundations of Psychological Life.* Hillsdale, NJ: Analytic.

Torgesen, J. K. (1986). Learning disabilities theory: its current state and future prospects. *Journal of Learning Disabilities* 19(7):399–407.

Vigilante, F. W. (1983). *Working with Families of Learning Disabled children*, pp. 429–436. New York: Child Welfare League of America.

Voeller, K. K. S. (1986). Right-hemisphere deficit syndrome in children. *American Journal of Psychiatry* 148(8):1004–1009.

Weil, A. P. (1970). The basic core. *Psychoanalytic Study of the Child* 25:442–460. New York: International Universities Press.

_____ (1973). Children with minimal brain dysfunction: diagnostic and therapeutic considerations. In *Children with Learning Problems*, ed. S. G. Sapir and A. C. Nitzburg, pp. 551–568. New York: Brunner/Mazel.

_____ (1978). Maturational variations and genetic-dynamic issues. *Journal of the American Psychoanalytic Association*, 26(3):461–492.

_____ (1985). Thoughts about early pathology. *Journal of the American Psychoanalytic Association* 33:335–352.

Weintraub, S., and Mesulam, M. M. (1983). Developmental learning disabilities of the right hemisphere: emotional, interpersonal, and cognitive components. *Archives of Neurology* 40:463–468.

8

The Game Ain't Over 'til It's Over: A Long-Term Psychoeducational Child and Parent Treatment Case

Donald Tessmer, Ph.D.
Janet Ciriello, Ed.D.

This chapter offers a unique approach for the treatment of patients who do not fit into traditional therapeutic modes. The model grew out of our experience at the Reiss-Davis Child Study Center working with individuals whose neurocognitive anomalies are intertwined with emotional problems. We realized that while a psychodynamic approach yields insight into patients' inner lives, we needed therapeutic techniques to accommodate the differences in how these particular patients perceive, process, integrate, and communicate information back to the world. Patients with neurocognitive problems are seen at Reiss-Davis with enough frequency that it has caused us to examine the role of the therapist and the goals of therapy. One patient's 14-year treatment journey from boyhood to manhood and the treatment of his mother are described in this chapter to illustrate the unique approach of psychoeducational therapy.

Psychoeducational treatment requires that every patient be given an approach uniquely designed for that particular patient and his or her specific needs. It is clear from this perspective that we must develop a treatment to fit the patient instead of having the patient fit the model as in the legend of the infamous procrustean bed. The following case is of a boy, whom I will call Hank, who experienced four clinicians with different treatment models during the course of his therapy at Reiss-Davis. As his story unfolds, it will become clear how we eventually connected and used the metaphor of baseball within the psychoeducational treatment model. Hank evolved from a rather low-functioning adolescent to a young adult who completed his education, held a job, and surpassed many of the expectations of the psychometric assessment results and predictions of school counselors. The overall clinical insights, though, presented more hope. One without the other is often insufficient. Since school is the "work" of the child, a treatment model that did not incorporate this essential aspect of Hank's life would have caused a missed opportunity to enter his world that was available to the therapist.

Psychoeducational criteria to determine candidates for this type of treatment require a full diagnostic assessment of cognitive, educational, and emotional functioning of the individual's issues, including the overlap in each of these areas that interferes in overall functioning. Individuals with learning disabilities are all unique in their cognitive strengths and weaknesses, while many share a pattern of associated emotional and social adjustment issues.

An extensive history will be given because of the many signs of learning problems and emotional indicators present throughout Hank's life before coming to Reiss-Davis.

Hank was 10 years old when his mother sought an evaluation because his pediatrician felt that he was "very close to having a peptic ulcer." Mother was obtaining a second opinion of her son's physical condition at the University of California at Los Angeles, and she wanted Reiss-Davis to evaluate his emotional state. She also stated that Hank was "eating himself alive," that he had collapsed 2 months earlier with severe stomach pain, and had subsequently been in perpetual pain. Hank obtained some relief through medication and by maintaining an "ulcer diet," but he was mostly irritable, hostile, and involved in continual arguments at home. Mother described Hank earlier in life as a shy, docile, obedient child who seldom spoke. As an infant, he was also very quiet and clung to her. Articulation problems, including stuttering, had accompanied the onset of speech, causing Hank to continue in speech classes up to the time of his intake at Reiss-Davis.

Hank was very close to his mother but was able to separate and gain relative self-assurance after a successful nursery school experience at age 3. His small stature and general immaturity had always been of concern to Mother and also to Hank. Mother thought this accounted for his habit of bed-wetting and his obsessive hold on a favorite pillow, which he had kept for years and fingered for hours at a time. His reliance on this transitional object was very frustrating to his mother. She expressed guilt for Hank's persistent hold on the object by associating it with an early weaning and the fact that she had never permitted him a pacifier. Hank's school experience was challenging from the beginning, though Mother described him as wiry, strong, and well coordinated. He became an excellent athlete in his younger years, and he was sought after by peers and made friends. He was described by Mother as fiercely competitive, and he drove himself very hard to achieve athletic success. But, he and his father were never able to share any of these activities since Hank always felt criticized by him. At about age 9, with improved speech and self-confidence, along with athletic recognition, Hank became more rebellious at school, and temper outbursts increased at home. This development accompanied heightened parental tension, and his parents' marriage was subsequently open to angry conflicts that Hank tried to quell by pleading with his parents to stop, but to no avail.

When Hank was 9 years old, his mother was hospitalized for a saline abortion. During discussions with her doctor, she acknowledged a great deal of unhappiness with her husband and reported being pushed into the procedure by him against her will. She told of severe and physically violent arguments with her husband after the procedure, the content of these fights being predominantly about her dissatisfaction with him. Hank would frequently awake from sleep, witness these episodes, try to intervene, and be sent back to bed by his mother. Hank never recalled being told about the abortion, nor was he told that his mother was going to be hospitalized until the last moment, when vague reasons were given. He was unprepared for the abandonment, fear, and confusion he experienced.

At the time of the intake, Hank had primary enuresis with accompanying shame for bed-wetting and was 2 years behind in physical development; yet his parents had, until this point, felt little need to investigate his psychological functioning. His mother was quick to state that although no one could understand what he said when he was younger, "he could catch a football on the run when he was 4 years old." She reflected that after her abortion and the escalating tension at home, she sensed some change in Hank. He was reported to be somewhat rude and unruly in class. "Nothing really violent," she said, "but he definitely grew more aggressive." He reportedly "told the teacher off," but at first Mother attributed these changes to a new school and a strict math teacher. In addition, Hank started fighting with his older sister, both verbally and physically, with greater vigor and intent than ever before. The critical moment leading Mother to become most concerned began when Hank was 10 years old, as he was participating in Junior Olympics and his frequent stomach pains became more severe. His mother stated that he would double over, sometimes couldn't stand, but would get himself together enough to run, jump, throw, whatever was needed, and finished fifth in overall competition. A full medical workup was subsequently completed by his pediatrician, who referred him to a gastroenterologist who diagnosed him as having peptic ulceration. Donnatol, a composite of barbiturate and belladonna, which works against gastric activity, was prescribed for relief of symptoms with some success. The medication made Hank groggy but led to relief of symptoms. Hank began to demand medication more and more frequently. The sleepiness disappeared, and it seemed that he would request medication at times when he felt disturbed regardless of pain in his stomach. The giving of medication itself became an issue of conflict between mother and son. Hank found it hard to accept when the doctor, fearing dependency, would not refill a prescription. Hank's somatic complaints blossomed into leg pains and headaches, and he became tantrumatic, obstinate, and threatening, and accused his mother of withholding medication to cause him pain. He would throw objects and destroy his own things. Hank would calm down if put in his own room, but throughout this period he was not able to sustain any of his own responsibilities, such as homework.

Initial testing shortly after intake at Reiss-Davis, when Hank was 10 ½ years of age, indicated that he was a highly constricted child who experienced tremendous demands for achievement from his parents and others, and that at the same time he did not feel adequately nurtured by them. Test scores on the WISC-R found him functioning at the borderline level of intelligence, with a full-scale IQ of 79. However, there were indications that his true potential was higher. Hank's IQ scores were probably influenced by his anxiety as well as his great difficulty in visual-spatial skills, and retesting 2 years later continued to indicate visual-spatial difficulty. Ongoing academic testing showed that he applied a great deal of effort to learning and that he could retain information that had been taught. Hank's difficulty conceptualizing what he had learned, and subsequent difficulty applying information to new situations, led to tremendous confusion when problems called for any type of creative or inferential thinking. Additionally, he had limited receptive and expressive language. Regardless of these findings, the parents did not choose to apply for any special education assistance through the public school.

In Hank's first 9 months of treatment at Reiss-Davis with his original, dynamically oriented therapist, he was described as inhibited, guarded, and somewhat withdrawn. As he began to become familiar with the therapist, who understood learning disabilities, he became a bit more spontaneous, and through constant subtle encouragement, he was able to speak more fluently. Most of the material during this period centered on some physical complaints Hank had with his gastrointestinal difficulties, as well as his feelings about his new school program. During the end of this treatment period, he was beginning to express certain negative feelings toward a few of the teachers with whom he felt less comfortable. This beginning to express feelings was very difficult for Hank but was something he began tentatively to explore.

During this phase of treatment, Hank came to have some control of his enuresis, which was accomplished through behavioral use of alarm clocks that awakened him early in the morning so he could use the bathroom. He began to explore the possibility of some emotional base of his upset on the nights when he was enuretic, and began to see some correlations. His therapist was very concerned about Hank's learning disabilities throughout this treatment period and spoke with Hank about his academics. Treatment could be summarized as psychodynamic in overall approach, yet somewhat more directive. This initial therapy phase ended after 9 months of twice-weekly sessions because of a change in the therapist's schedule at the clinic. The parents felt it was no longer convenient for them to bring Hank to Reiss-Davis to continue with this therapist at different times, and it was speculated that Mother's jealousy of the relationship between the therapist and Hank might have influenced her decision to request reassignment.

For the next 2 years, Hank's twelfth to fourteenth, there was a shift in modality to a psychoanalytic model of treatment. During most of the sessions with his new therapist, Hank was described as sitting quietly without uttering a word. Most attempts to make contact with him were met with "resistance and failure." (It should be noted that "resistance" was the word used by this therapist, although I would understand it as closely related to Hank's learning disabilities.) Hank was described as sitting in a constricted and bent-over fashion. The therapist stated that the only instance where Hank displayed any animation was when he brought his baseball cards into one particular session—his way of attempting to connect, though unsuccessfully. There was no follow-up on this by the therapist. The sessions were described as becoming increasingly silent, with only a few words actually interchanged between Hank and the clinician during a session. Hank's progress toward the achievement of treatment goals was at best very slow. His presenting symptoms continued. Bed-wetting was still a problem, he was prone to temper tantrums, and stuttering difficulties remained problematic. It seemed that the psychoanalytic treatment approach with Hank led to regression from the few initial gains made by the first therapist and to much frustration on the part of patient and family, therapist, supervisor, and clinic. The match between the patient's needs and the therapeutic approach was not a helpful one. This phase of treatment was terminated after 2 years when the therapist left the clinic.

At this point, the case management team at Reiss-Davis suggested that the focus of treatment be shifted to educational therapy three times a week. Educational testing at that time again revealed difficulties with expressive and receptive language, reading comprehension, and arithmetic. The ensuing 2-year course of educational therapy consisted mostly of helping Hank with homework and remedial academic work. Hank was seen as a student with learning disabilities in the areas of visual-spatial skills, and verbal and nonverbal deficits in abstract thinking. He was described as having a rigid and extremely concrete approach to learning and likely neurological difficulties that made independence of functioning difficult for him. Hank could memorize rote material and understand very structured learning, but he had great difficulty functioning when academics involved higher-level verbal abstractions, which probably contributed to his difficulty in the analytic treatment. A definite shift occurred during this time, and Hank was described as very conscientious with his schoolwork and involved with the educational therapy. Concrete educational techniques and materials were used with Hank. Homework assistance helped with assignments in high-school courses, reading comprehension exercises emphasized generalizations and inferential thinking, and vocabulary development was emphasized to expand Hank's limited understanding of words. After 2 years, when Hank was about to begin his senior year of high school, the person with whom he had begun to establish a relationship left Reiss-Davis. It was at this point that the case management team recommended that Hank be seen by a clinician able to provide a four-session-per-week psychoeducational therapy model. This was determined since it would meet the dual needs of the pronounced educational and learning obstacles Hank manifested to be treated concurrently with the psychological issues interfering with his social and emotional development. The psychoeducational treatment model goals established for Hank included working on academic courses, remedial educational work, coping with family issues, improving poor social skills, vocational counseling and planning for post-high-school life, and addressing the anxiety and depression this adolescent felt. Hank had given up athletics when he was 12 because he felt that his small stature did not allow him to compete against the bigger boys. The social skills necessary for adolescence, which might have been fostered through athletic interaction, Hank had never developed, and his self-esteem plummeted. His reading was poor, as were his overall language skills. He was an anxious and depressed teenager with many avoidant kinds of features, had no real friends, and presented as very shy, with great difficulty engaging others, partly due to his stuttering. These symptoms were severe enough to cause us to occasionally consider whether Hank might have schizoid qualities.

Psychoeducational treatment allowed Hank to communicate in the only manner possible for him at the time, which was around remedial and supportive educational work. Originally Hank used me as an object in that I served a function: I helped him, and he needed that help. Over time, a relationship began to be established through which Hank could risk trusting another person. This developed into Hank's tendency toward dependency, an issue actively addressed in therapy. He often regressed to a very dependent style of wanting me to do everything for him and to take care of him. During this initial treatment phase, Hank restricted the work to an educational mode, both because he could remain safe and avoid the disturbing emotional issues and because he was so anxious about not having his schoolwork done, or not knowing how to do it, that he could not focus on anything else. If I attempted interactions other than educational work or attempted to talk about other issues with him, he would roll his head, stare off, and seem to self-stimulate as a way of keeping away my words. Hank would sometimes pick at a part of his body and shake his head from side to side when he could not tolerate my statements.

It should be remembered that at this point I was his fourth

therapist. His first therapist, a male, engaged him through a somewhat more directive, dynamic approach to treatment, and Hank experienced a loss when treatment abruptly ended. His second male therapist, using a strict psychoanalytic model, did not actively engage him, and Hank reportedly spent 2 years in near silence. The female educational therapist who saw Hank for the 2 years previous to me did educational work, and she reported that "we can't talk to each other."

Hank's overall treatment at Reiss-Davis, now in its sixth year, and the first of 8 years to follow with me, was beginning to seek the integration of psychotherapy and educational intervention. The psychoeducational model worked toward balancing these issues through building a relationship and alleviating anxiety around the learning disabilities. While Hank made it clear to me that the educational work was primary for him, some interpretation of his emotional life was begun to help him make connections between his thoughts, feelings, and behavior. Although our work initially focused on educational material, this allowed the opportunity for treatment around the anxiety school and Hank's learning disabilities produced. We discussed his dependent ways of interacting with me and others, and I offered much encouragement about looking at other parts of his life beyond schoolwork. Over time, I was able to establish a comfortable relationship and began to introduce some fairly nonthreatening interventions, which Hank at first tolerated and then began to see the benefits of. For example:

1. Hank almost never made eye contact with me and, if he did, it was very brief and had a "scared" look. We discussed why eye contact was important, and through a nonverbal cueing, this important social response was conditioned in Hank.
2. Progressive muscle relaxation and deep breathing were introduced as interventions to help Hank get in touch with the obvious tenseness of his body, especially since he still occasionally complained of stomach problems. This served as a bridge to introduce the connection between mind and body and helped Hank to identify that his anxiety could be controlled once he recognized it.

3. Because of Hank's lags in expressive and receptive language, he had difficulty with more abstract psychological concepts. To help Hank understand his inner life, some terms from transactional analysis were used so that he could identify different ego states, especially his very dependent side and rather harsh superego. We isolated the "childlike" part of Hank that wanted to remain taken care of so he wouldn't have to think about school success, responsibilities, and so on, and we examined the ensuing "parental" guilt, anxiety, and fear. This helped to develop a common language to communicate in and further build an interactive relationship. Through our interpretive work together, Hank began to understand and identify his different ego states and to discuss situations where he could understand the resulting feelings and states of mind.

4. Rational emotive therapy (Ellis 1975) provided a system whereby we could sequence and analyze an event more concretely; its consequences, both external and internal; and the cognitions or beliefs that influenced Hank's reactions. This was especially helpful because of Hank's difficulty in applying and transferring concepts from one situation to another. The use of cognitive techniques helped Hank to sequence and analyze through a system of ordering the activating events or situations and beliefs about them as a means of understanding the consequences that occur from such a sequence. This was extended to certain specific cognitive techniques suggested by Beck (1979, 1986), which again gave Hank a frame of reference to understand himself and his interactions with others.

These simplified and modified models were the initial steps toward helping Hank begin to think about and to explore his inner life. After four therapists and our one and a half years together, it still often seemed that we were at the beginning; but these educational and psychological techniques laid a foundation, since Hank was now able to tolerate, understand, and integrate many more of my interpretations.

After Hank's first year of treatment with me, he enrolled himself in a junior college that had a program for students with learning disabilities, a big step for Hank both because he had not really overtly acknowledged this problem before and because it represented a beginning in building some foundations for relating with his peers. Hank was becoming less dependent on me and more independent about setting up his own educational support systems through the college. We continued to meet four times a week, although, as the second year of therapy progressed, less and less of the time we spent together had to do with academics, and Hank was more readily open to my interpretations and reactions to his increased spontaneous talking about his life.

During this phase, Hank brought a news article to session regarding a Los Angeles Kings hockey player's stuttering problem that described how the player had been helped by joining a stutterers' group. Hank's stuttering was not pronounced during our work together; however, Hank reported that he stuttered a great deal in other circumstances and little seemed to help. Hank decided that he wanted to go to the same stutterers' class as this Kings player, and his attendance there seemed to help with his confidence and gave him techniques to use in uncomfortable circumstances. This was a significant experience on another level as Hank, through this involvement, began to reach out to others and attempted to change something in himself. Furthermore, Hank empowered himself and proved to himself that he could achieve what he was determined to do. So often, learning-disabled individuals must prove through doing, that they are capable, just as Hank learns best through doing and not just through books.

This particular successful experience led to our discussing the entire area of sports. Hank had not previously wanted to talk about this area since he considered that part of his life to be over. He had felt for a long time that he could no longer engage in athletic activities because of his relatively small stature compared with others his age. He brought in his baseball card collection and commented that his father had one, too, though their interaction around baseball cards seemed to evoke a competition between his father and himself. I shared with him my own love for baseball—playing it, watching it, and remembering the ballplayers. Baseball was to become a metaphor for us. The language of baseball became our solid common communication ground. Many of the baseball metaphors were around anxiety and socialization. In the metaphorical sense, spring training became how to fit in with a new team and a new situation. A rookie facing major league pitching or hitting for the first time translated to what those feelings were like for Hank and how he might feel in a new social situation. How to get out of a slump (both batting and emotional) was often a topic of conversation, as well as how to be a well-rounded as opposed to a one-dimensional person/ballplayer. I would take an issue in Hank's life and find an example or a metaphor from sports that would work, thus enabling him to understand it, internalize it, relate it to our previous work, and use it in his own life circumstances. The one metaphor he seemed to connect with most, and to generalize the best to other situations, was the symbol of a nervous/anxious batter. The batter must be in the game and in the box. The batter may be afraid of striking out, and that fear and negative thinking may influence him. But, mostly, if the batter does strike out, would he rather be called out looking or go down swinging? To "take your cut" became a shorthand for addressing many fears and avoidances in Hank's life.

Hank decided during this time that he wanted to be a general manager in baseball. As we talked about this, his grandiose goals began to be narrowed down to something more possible, such as, perhaps, a baseball scout. He began to reach out to others by becoming a student manager of the basketball team at his local junior college. He started to travel with the team and to take on more responsibilities. In many ways, it became his family.

Hank had actually done fairly well in a social sense until adolescence because of his interest and skill in sports; however, he never seemed to develop the coping skills necessary, perhaps because of cognitive and perceptual lags, to adjust to adolescence. This may also have been true because of his family's internal isolation. Baseball and sports integrated Hank's childhood with adolescence and adulthood. He never actually had a strong sense of family or of "team," or of a way of expressing himself. For Hank, baseball represented connection and integration; connection with me and with others, and integration, a process that was beginning to take place, incorporating his childhood fantasies and goals with his present ones.

Through our connection with baseball metaphors, Hank began to reconnect with childhood fantasies of being involved in major league ball, a fantasy that had died in early adolescence, without expression, except for his baseball card collection. Hank then "used me" and our relationship to help him to reach out. Through extensive writing of letters, he built connections with the baseball world and extended himself to the larger world. He wrote letters to general managers and to baseball scouts. His letters were almost always answered, thus validating and reinforcing his reaching out. He was seeking information and meeting people, actually meeting scouts and going to games. This gave a tremendous boost to Hank's self-esteem and also began to reestablish an identity for him.

Three years into the psychoeducational treatment, when he was 20 years old, Hank came up with the idea of going to the national winter meetings for major league baseball. This was a tremendous move for him because of his fears of meeting people and of traveling, and the fact that he had never really been away from home. Hank made most of the arrangements on his own and experienced such success that he has continued to attend these winter meetings at different cities across the country each year. What was to occur over the next 3 years, as a result of Hank's mobilization of his skills, was that he was selected as a minor league intern, followed by three jobs as clubhouse manager with minor league baseball teams during his summertime breaks from the university.

After finishing junior college, and having worked intensively with me for three and a half years, Hank transferred to a university in northern California from which he has since graduated with a bachelor's degree. While there, Hank set up his own tutoring program. He received some help from the school, though only for the first year. He hired his own tutors, and, coincidentally, the educational therapist whom he had seen at Reiss-Davis was then living in the area and was able to help him on an ongoing basis. Hank became the student manager for the university's baseball team, once again using the team as his extended family, and, as mentioned, held summertime jobs in the minor leagues. He continued to see me while on breaks from the university, and I provided a reality check for the academic struggles, which are immense, the social progress, which is usually connected with baseball, and the future hopes, which continue to expand. For many who do not fit a traditional model of treatment, the game is not over until it's over, and for Hank it has only begun.

The uniqueness of Hank's learning and emotional difficulties really only began to be understood through a comprehensive diagnostic procedure. How he perceives, learns, and communicates differently, and how this leads to different problems emotionally and socially requires examining issues in the cognitive, emotional, and educational areas. By doing so, we were able to understand the anxiety and family pressures that further repressed Hank's neurocognitive-based learning disabilities. The syndrome of depressive and anxious states, along with social adjustment difficulties, is not uncommon to the learning-disabled population. The earlier the learning problems are identified and worked with, the less the likelihood of severe emotional reactions. Children with learning disabilities as obvious as Hank's can be missed by the school, and, certainly, students with mild learning problems are easily overlooked. The latter are usually quiet kids who do not act out but who may continue to fall farther behind each year and internalize rather than externalize their problems. We are learning more about matching patients to models of therapy instead of forcing the fit between the two, and in our endeavor to explore, develop, implement, and explain how we work with different patient populations, treatment models such as psychoeducational therapy can offer unique treatment options to individuals who seem unreachable through more traditional or less flexible approaches.

PARENT WORK WITH HANK'S MOTHER

Hank's mother had an extremely unhappy and emotionally deprived childhood. Her first recalled and significant loss occurred when she was 10 years old and her mother, Hank's maternal grandmother, died unexpectedly after a short illness. Maternal grandmother was ill for several months, but the children were deprived of information or even of visits with their mother, and secretiveness and resultant feelings of confusion are clearly recalled. Mother was told of her parent's death on the street as she walked home from school. On the heels of this loss followed a legal battle for custody of Mother and her two siblings. After two unsuccessful foster home experiences, Mother was sent alone to live in a residential center; her siblings were placed in foster homes. Maternal grandfather did not or could not visit her, possibly by court order, but that circumstance is unclear, and Mother remained in this placement for about 5 years. Maternal aunt, who had been instrumental in having the children removed from their "unfit" father, also did not visit or support Mother in any way.

From that time onward, Mother remembers her anger, her loneliness, and her feelings of being different. She also remembers her inability to form friendships with peers or to allow adults to sustain her in any way. She states that she could not grieve and would not go to therapy when it was offered. She was a behavior problem in the residential center and recalls two instances of being out of control. Once she stole some wine and became drunk, and another time she attempted to drive a staff person's car and damaged it. Mother now feels angry that she was not "made" to go to therapy in order to deal with her hurt and deeply felt loss. Mother, then and now, considers that she was "a victim of the system." The rage of this seemingly passive victim endures, and expressions of passive-dependent yearnings for rescue are pervasive themes in the parent work.

As a parent to our patient, Mother has been effective in attending to his practical needs and has been able to give him guidance about concrete matters, such as how to get along on a sports team. Nevertheless, she more often substantiated his view of himself as being inadequate and different from other boys, for instance, consistently doing his homework for him in elementary and in secondary school. Her conviction was that his learning problems made him unable to do what others could do. Hank increasingly expected to have his work done for him, or done by himself only with another person to guide him. Early in our work together, Mother resisted all efforts to stop doing his work for him.

Active in her son's behalf in some areas, Mother found it almost impossible to separate her emotions from his. While the result was that Hank could not have many experiences that allowed him a growing sense of self, Mother was able to provide him with the best of school settings. The unfortunate result was our patient's increased feeling of helplessness when he did not have mother's "help."

As a young adult, Hank continues to rely on many college tutors as well as on his therapist for help with real-world issues. He demonstrates little sense of pleasure in the developmentally appropriate experiences that only now and then seem to accompany his maturation. Mother's pleasures come from his dependence on her, without which she feels like a nonperson. For example, her job is seen only as a means of providing him with the economic resources he requires. She sees herself as a loner, a person without relationships and with little interest in people and no skill in making attachments except in a dependent fashion. Dependent longings are expressed in the form of wishes for a cure from her depression and anxiety. This longing takes the form of a wish for a pill that could be a panacea for her numerous symptoms, or some form of magical renewal delivered by her therapist that would, in particular, take care of her rages.

While Mother struggles to understand her inner life, she finds it almost impossible to conceive that her son also has his own inner being. She finds it almost intolerable to think about the possibility that what takes place inside is his own private domain. She will usually change the subject when there is the tentative exploration in therapy of thoughts and feelings that might be unique to each of them. These interruptions will occur in the form of psychomotor kinesis (excessive leg movement), excessive talking, or the repetition of certain defensive and fixed ideas.

Mother values the therapy she has, although after more than 6 years she questions whether she has a relationship with her therapist.

Hank and his mother are very much alike in their schizoid and depressive personality features. Each of them requires concrete assistance with new experiences. Unfortunately for Mother, the range of her activities and thoughts grows increasingly more circumspect. On weekends and during vacations, Mother is agoraphobic, although she is always able to go to her structured work, where she is appreciated and liked and where she is successful. Mother describes herself as a "false self," in the Winnicott sense, at work. When Mother is alone, she has temper outbursts or she fills her home with the loud sounds of her radio. Ambivalence, self-doubt, rage, magical thinking, passivity, and lack of trust all result in Mother feeling alone and dependent. At times, her sadness is so great and so defended against that her regressed wishes to have her own mother to help her are both poignant and startling. Mother's borderline characteristics are difficult for most people. There is some evidence that these features operated when she was a child and that they may have contributed to the lack of helpfulness that she experienced in relation to adult figures. Indeed, Mother more often than not groups people in terms of their helpfulness or lack of helpfulness, and this therapist is often experienced as one or the other by her.

In addition to the already stated symbiotic tie, which is pervasive and deep, there is a suggestion that genetic or inherited factors have contributed to the difficulties of both Hank and his mother. Maternal grandfather is described by Mother as "weird and irresponsible." Skewed or distorted perceptions, immature personality formation, and poor social skills are shared qualities from maternal grandfather to Mother, to Hank.

When, at age 10, Hank was initially evaluated, severe abdominal pains were among the presenting problems; indeed, Mother stated that the child was "eating himself alive." In a much less problematic way, the patient continues to have gastrointestinal symptoms, peculiarities about food consumption, and is thin and not well nourished as a young adult. Mother is anorexic and has a spastic colon, which is especially active when she is particularly anxious. Neither patient will easily follow medical recommendations concerning nutrition and food intake, and, at least in Mother's history, she perceives herself to be unworthy of nourishment.

In other ways, too, such as in her inability to buy or to wear new clothing (she was given secondhand clothing in her residential placement), Mother sees herself as "different," "unacceptable," and even as "repulsive." Mother's self-image is that of the 10-year-old emotionally abandoned child left in the care of strangers, unloved, unlovable, and filled with confused thoughts. Mother has difficulty acknowledging that her childhood feelings of rage are still finding expression in many forms into the present time. She is upset about her inability to control eruptions of rage when she is alone. For example, she frequently swears at people on the street when she is alone in her car, especially at fat people. Her rage contributes to another symptom, asthma, and also to a severe sleep disturbance. The asthma, interestingly, was first a problem when Mother had another loss, the result of an abortion.

Although Mother is of above-average intellectual ability, she is rarely able to sustain abstract thinking, at least not on her own behalf. The concreteness of her thinking is mirrored in physical ailments with symbolic dimensions of dramatic, basic, life-threatening possibilities for which she constantly seeks medical care, but for which she does not follow medical recommendations. Nonetheless, her physicians are useful to her, as they are a network of caregivers. This therapist is among Mother's network of caregivers, and also a real person who is there for her. In a sense, all of the caregivers represent Mother's early lost family. Her only daughter is seen as a caregiver, her husband is not to be depended on, and she and her son are to be cared for. The degree of dependence is extreme and pathological.

In the presence of Mother, there is the felt experience of being with a pre-latency-age child. She longs for family, connectedness, and relationships. She cannot imagine what a family is, how to deal emotionally with others, or how to build relationships. Often, she wishes for closeness with other people, but she immediately retreats from that wish. During therapy sessions, for example, Mother wears dark glasses and looks away from the therapist in an attempt not to incorporate more than the therapist's voice. After more than 6 years, eye contact is limited. Abandonment, at least the possibility of such, is exquisitely present, especially during times when the therapist is preparing for or has returned from vacations.

The material in this chapter is suggestive of the complexities of long-term parent treatment when the normal development of a child has been severely compromised by the pathology of a parent. As the child began to separate from his mother emotionally, Mother's mental health deteriorated. She sees few or no positive changes in her son. She denies Hank's accomplishments or any pleasure in him. All is grim—he is helpless and inadequate, and so is she. These are Mother's mental representations of each of them. She has been unable to foster a sense of internal integration and external well-being for her son or for herself.

At the tender age of 10, what "appeared" to be normal development took a pathological course when losses occurred and derailed development of each member of the parent–child pair. For Mother, the original loss through death of her mother and then, also, of her family was in part reexperienced when she unwillingly aborted at the time her son was 10 years old. Hank, the then youngest child, continued in the role of the unborn baby, the damaged baby. He also became the object for Mother's view of her damaging or bad influences on people—he was projectively damaged or bad.

This parent treatment began with an emphasis on an educational and supportive orientation, therapeutic techniques quickly set aside by Mother, who in her guilt about what she perceived to be the damage she had caused her child pressed for a more open-ended as well as a more intensive form of treatment. Such an intensive approach goes beyond the usual parent treatment, which is about the child, yet in this family it seemed to be required in order to help the adolescent patient move toward a life of his own.

REFERENCES

Beck, A. (1986). *Anxiety Disorders and Phobias: A Cognitive Perspective*. New York: Basic Books.

_____ (1979). *Cognitive Therapy of Depression*. New York: Guilford.

Ellis, A., and Harper, R. H. (1975). *A New Guide to Rational Living*. North Hollywood, CA: Wilshire.

9

Working with Visually Impaired Infants and Their Families: Implications for Other Physically Challenged Patients

Renee A. Cohen, Ph.D.

The emotional and psychological needs of the visually impaired infant are so entwined with that of the family that attention must be given to treating the family as a unit. Not to do so would be the equivalent of not treating the whole patient. The concept of treating the patient as a family unit is relatively new. An even more revolutionary idea of treatment is treating parents as soon as their child is diagnosed as being visually impaired. What I am proposing is that the patient is in fact plural—patients. It is what I refer to as the *patient constellation*. The "patient" in this situation includes not only the visually impaired infant but also the parents, siblings, and extended family (Goldberg 1980, Irvin et al. 1982, Kennell and Klaus 1982). The birth and diagnosis of a visually impaired infant provokes a crisis for the entire family. Expectations for a healthy, normal infant are shattered. Parents and other family members are confronted with a traumatic, often unexpected situation, upsetting the equilibrium of the family. Parents, who are the ongoing caretakers of their children, need to have a mental health professional available to them as soon as a visual impairment is suspected.

It is essential that family assistance and support begin early. With professional intervention, optimizing of the attachment process, or bonding, can begin even while the extent of the visual impairment and treatment plan are being determined. Early psychological intervention on behalf of the family will go a long way in the successful treatment and adjustment of the child. When parents are given emotional support and made to feel like the valuable team members that they are, they will be more productive in the treatment and therapy of their child.

THE BIRTH OF A CHILD

During pregnancy, expectant parents experience a normal crisis in which they wonder and worry about their unborn child. The mother experiences physical changes, and both parents experience emotional changes. The birth of a healthy baby results in stress reduction. The parents relax, knowing their baby is "perfect." However, the birth of a physically challenged infant, visually or otherwise, results in heightened anxiety and stress. The parent(s) are thrust into an unexpected crisis at a time when they are physically and emotionally drained. The mother has gone through labor, which is exhausting, or possibly surgery, and both parents are sleep deprived.

COMMON REACTIONS

The first set of parental reactions that appears to occur most consistently following the birth or diagnosis of a physically challenged infant includes shock, denial, grief, guilt and inadequacy, depression, and anger. It has been suggested that these and other reactions, such as withdrawal, bitterness, resentment, and rejection, are also experienced to one degree or another whether or not they are recognized or acknowledged (Love 1970, Pozanski 1973, Yu 1972). What becomes apparent is that love is rarely mentioned within the array of parental reactions to the birth and diagnosis of a physically challenged infant. Turbulent negative reactions appear to interfere with feelings and expressions of love and nurturing, especially when strong feelings of revulsion and/or rejection are apparent (Fraiberg 1971, Gath 1977, Pozanski 1973). With time and ongoing adjustment, other parental reactions emerge: reassessment, coping and mobilization, and self-acceptance (Tuttle 1986).

Shock

Shock is nature's way of buffering the traumatic experience. In the hospital, parents should be told together about their infant's condition. This reduces the risk of misinterpretation and gives the parents an opportunity to console each other. In the case of single parents, someone close to them should be present when they are told. If the diagnosis is not detected at the time of birth but at a later examination, the findings should be discussed with sensitivity and in terms parents can understand. Arrangements should be made to assist the parent(s) and child in getting home safely. An emotionally distraught parent is frequently left to drive home, endangering her or his safety and that of others.

Denial

Parents may deny the infant's visual impairment as a permanent loss. The denial and disbelief are especially strong if the diagnosis is not made at birth, and the parents did not expect it. Parents may hope that the child will get better, outgrow the condition, or that a cure will be found. This may be a stage in parental adjustment, or it may be a lifelong attitude. Denial may be seen as a protective device as well, prompted by self-preservation and therefore not altogether maladaptive (Shokier 1979). There may be a surge of energy that prompts parents to explore all options, get second opinions, and basically leave no stone unturned. However, when denial persists beyond the initial adjustment phase, it may interfere with good medical management and the psychological adaptation by both parents and child (Pozanski 1973, Vernon 1979).

Grief or mourning

Grief or mourning seems to be experienced universally by parents of physically challenged infants. The grief reaction is a response to loss of the perfect child, of the missing or defective part of the child, of the illusion of invulnerability, and of self-esteem (Butani 1974, Solnit and Stark 1961). Parents of infants with a genetic disorder may experience multiple grief, not only for the affected child but also for future unborn children and for themselves as defective procreators.

It is essential for parents to mourn the loss of a perfect child if they are to accept the visually impaired child. Reaching some resolution of their grief is important in order to look realistically at the infant as well as to provide appropriately for the needs of the infant, each other, and the family unit. How the parents deal with the mourning process significantly influences their relationship with the infant, patterns of family interactions within the nuclear and extended family, and patterns of social relationships outside the family unit. Parents who are experiencing intense grief or pathological reactions are emotionally unavailable to their infants. These negative reactions interfere with feelings and expressions of love and nurturing. Because the infant's emotional and physical well-being may be at risk, psychological intervention is crucial. A therapist can help the parent work through the mourning process and connect with the infant in a healthy manner.

Guilt

Parents may be subject to guilt feelings, which may take different behavioral forms, such as blaming others or themselves, denial, and rejection or overprotection of the child. Feelings of guilt can frequently lead to or accompany depression.

Depression

Depression can be experienced as deep sadness, low energy, and apathy, any of which may be present in varying degrees. It may take the form of withdrawal from the infant and others, sleeping or eating disorders, or avoiding the infant and social activities. When parents are unable to meet the infant's physical, emotional, and social needs, professional intervention is essential. Depression may also be associated with anger.

Anger

Anger is generated by feelings of helplessness and frustration. The unanswered question—Why me?—persists. In the beginning, anger is intense and touches everyone, triggered by overwhelming feelings of grief and inexplicable loss. The financial burden and time expended in seeking and obtaining services for the child, which are exhausting, can also be manifested as anger.

REASSESSMENT AND REAFFIRMATION

This is a reexamining of the meaning of life. At this point, parents begin to identify priorities. They are able to determine what is important and what is not.

COPING AND MOBILIZATION

During this process, parents of visually impaired children learn to cope with the variety of demands placed on them. They become willing to identify themselves as parents of visually handicapped children, and parent support groups are especially helpful.

ACCEPTANCE

In this phase, the parents begin to accept and feel good about themselves. They begin to see themselves as individuals beyond the parental role, with many characteristics and traits. They see their child as an individual with his or her own strengths and weaknesses.

As Ware (1981) states:

> Acceptance does not mean liking the handicap. It does not mean that the anguish and lost dreams will be forgotten. They will always be remembered but relived with less frequency and with lessening intensity. Acceptance does not mean enjoying the necessity for special programs and agencies. Instead, you learn to appreciate the existence of good programs and agencies and develop confidence in your ability to make the judgments which are best for your child. It does not mean never wishing your child can see. Of course, you would like for him to have sight! You simply abandon this as an *ever-present* wish, because you know it is a fact that he cannot see and you know you love him dearly even though he cannot see. It does not mean never crying or feeling angry and depressed. These feelings will periodically return. Their recurrence does not mean that you have not adjusted or that you are losing your ability to cope. It means you are human. [p. 46]

ADJUSTMENT PROCESS

The adjustment process is not a static process but a fluid one. Although it has been suggested that families go through a specific sequence of feelings, individual family members do not adhere to an orderly, sequential, predictable set of reactions. They may go through the stages of reactions countless times in various orders, expending different amounts of time and energy at each stage; they may skip some stages altogether. Many parents have commented to me that specific events in their children's lives, especially transitions, trigger all or parts of the cycle. The emotional responses of families are too complex to classify into absolute, rigid stages. The health professional must be sensitive to a family's current emotional state and avoid categorizing family members according to predetermined expectations. It would not be unusual to have one parent in the denial or guilt stage while the other has evolved to a stage of adjustment and acceptance. The mourning and healing process is very individualized. At all times, families need to know they can express themselves without being judged and that their feelings will be acknowledged. It is essential that the health professional relate to parents as individuals rather than as a unit. It is important as well that parents and families in crisis receive both expressive (emotional and social) and instrumental (technical and educational) support from the medical and mental health communities. The attitude of professionals and the care the parents receive will profoundly affect the reactions of the parents and the care the child receives.

IMPACT ON THE FAMILY

After the infant has been diagnosed as visually impaired, the entire family experiences disequilibrium. The impact may be greater if the baby is a firstborn, a boy, or if it is a premium baby, conceived after years of trying. If the baby is of older parents, the adjustment is often more difficult, which negatively affects the support system. The extended family and friends feel awkward and uncertain about how to respond. It is not unusual to have a visitor comment on the "lovely nursery" and not mention the visually impaired infant lying in the crib. After the initial shock, grandparents, especially the maternal grandmother, have been found to be particularly supportive (Walker et al. 1971). The impact of the initial crisis and gradual adjustment on the marriage and sibling(s) are of special concern.

A supportive relationship is a source of strength for both parents during the crisis of the infant's diagnosis. This crisis does have the potential for some positive things, such as bringing the parents closer together, providing mutual support and communication. However, having a visually impaired infant can also be a source of stress and has the potential for negative effects, including pulling the family apart. The mental maturity and general mental health of the parents are vitally important, as are prior coping abilities and attitudes about visual impairment.

The ability of siblings to accept the infant is greatly influenced by and perhaps a reflection of the parents' reactions. Parents need to openly discuss the newborn's problems with siblings. The age of siblings should guide the parents. They have to be able to explain what is wrong with the baby and answer as many questions as they can at an age-appropriate level. Siblings need to be repeatedly assured that they are not to blame for the baby's problems, especially if they didn't want the baby. If siblings are not given adequate information, there will be limited opportunities for them to discuss their feelings about the visually impaired infant; and if they do not understand what has happened, they will often supply their own answers based on fantasy. Siblings should be encouraged to talk openly about their feelings and should be observed for possible adverse reactions. If siblings appear to be suffering, psychotherapy may be indicated to help them adjust and deal more effectively with their feelings. Physical complaints and behavioral changes are common signals that siblings are feeling left out, ignored, and/or need attention (it is not unusual for a fully sighted child to awaken "blind" one morning). While it is possible to prevent or alleviate some of the feelings of being left out by including siblings in the treatment plan, they should always be given the option, not be required, to participate. It is also important when working with single parents to help them balance their attention and time with the other children in the family.

Parents' reactions affect not only the siblings and extended family but the visually impaired infant as well. Relative to emotional problems arising from an infant's loss of vision, we observe that it is not the infant who has emotional problems, but rather the infant's parents, who may be having trouble accepting and adjusting to the visual loss. It is important to remember that visually impaired infants do not know what full vision is and, therefore, have not lost anything. The way they feel about themselves in the early years is directly related to the way their families feel about them. This changes as these children get older and compare themselves with peers. How they handle this will be greatly influenced by their self-concept and self-confidence, which has its formation in the early years.

BONDING

It is essential for the parents to mourn the loss of a perfect child if they are to accept the visually impaired infant. Reaching some resolution of their grief is important in order to look realistically at the infant and provide appropriately for his or her needs. It is also important in providing for each other's needs and for those of the family unit. A parent's attachment, or bonding, with his or her infant is frequently delayed during the crisis period. This delay may be due to external factors such as medical interventions or internal factors such as the parent's emotional reaction. Characteristics of the visually impaired infant will influence how readily the parents will engage and bond with him or her. Some of these traits include:

The infant's appearance: How normal the infant looks. Can the parent identify with the infant?

The infant's ability to respond to and interact with the parents.

The extent to which the defect can be corrected via surgery, prosthesis, and/or visual aids.

The infant's personality and behavior.

The love bond between parent and child is generally established during the first 18 months (Fraiberg 1971). The literature generally agrees that any prolonged parent–infant separation for medical reasons, or otherwise, delays or inhibits the attachment process. Early separation, however, need not damage the development of an optimal attachment between a parent and infant. It is important that parents know that it is not an all-or-nothing situation.

Communication is essential to the parent–infant attachment. The parents' inability to perceive the infant's needs leads to their feeling isolated and incompetent. Parents must learn how to interact with their infant and interpret his or her behaviors. Visually impaired infants are not unresponsive, but they communicate in different ways from fully sighted infants.

A visually impaired infant is a classic example of an infant who is unable to respond and initiate contact in a normal interactive pattern. The smiles of parents are reinforced when their fully sighted infants smile in return; parents interpret those smiles as, "I love you." When the parent of a visually impaired infant smiles without speaking, the baby does not respond and communication breaks down. Denied the eye contact that reinforces their nurturing and caretaking behavior, parents (and their visually impaired infants) need to find a tactile and vocal dialogue. Although the infant will not respond to a smile with a smile, he or she will smile and respond to a touch, a kiss, and the sound of the parent's voice, dialogue crucial to the child's development and to the bonding process as well. Parents of blind children are often amazed to find that a blind infant smiles in response to a parent's voice at the same time developmentally as a fully sighted infant responds to a parent's face. In fact, when a mother and her blind infant communicate with tactile and vocal dialogue, all the milestones for human object relations are met without significant differences between the blind infant and the fully sighted infant (Fraiberg 1971). The hand becomes the substitute for vision and thus becomes the bridge between the body ego and the objective world. Without this bridge, the personality may remain frozen on the level of body-centeredness and nondifferentiation of self and not self.

STRESSFUL EXPERIENCES

We all experience stress during the course of our lives and as our children grow up. Some developmentally stressful times that all families face will take on new meaning when an infant is visually impaired.

When the child enters school: The need for special classes, visual aids, mainstreaming, child's acceptance by peers, parents' awareness of the discrepancy between their child and fully sighted children.

When the child reaches puberty: Wanting the child to be independent but fearing for his or her safety. Child's feeling of being different from peers, not being able to get a driver's license, dating, and so on.

Vocational planning: Concern if the child will be able to get a job, be self-supporting.

Children going out on their own: Concerns about the future, marriage, and so on.

These areas cause stress in any family but take on more significance when a child is visually impaired because the standard resolutions are not available. Unless the parents are also visually impaired, they do not have the same experiences in their repertoire. Professionals need to be aware of these critical periods in the life of a family and respond appropriately.

Professionals have the responsibility of providing information clearly and in lay terms to parents so they understand the visual impairment and can effectively participate in the treatment plan. The support and understanding the family receives are often the crux of succesful treatment. Therefore, parents need to receive information that relates to the specific needs of their children. Don't make assumptions. Encourage parents to ask questions. I tell my parents, "The only stupid questions are the ones that aren't asked." Treat the parents and the child with respect and caring. Have good referral sources and make them appropriate as far as needs, distance, and cost. Remember that parent support groups and networking are very important. When support and consistent services are available for the parents, they are in a better position to utilize their strength and energy toward their child's growth and development.

REFERENCES

Butani, P. (1974). Reactions of mothers to the birth of an anomalous infant: a review of the literature. *Maternal–Child Nursing Journal* 3(1):59–76.

Fraiberg, S. (1971). Intervention in infancy: a program for blind infants. *Journal of the American Academy of Child Psychiatry* 10(3):381–405.

Gath, A. (1977). The impact of an abnormal child upon the parents. *British Journal of Psychiatry* 130:405–410.

Goldberg, H. K. (1980). Hearing impairment: a family crisis. *Social Work in Health Care* 5(1):33–40.

Irvin, N. A., Kennell, J. H., and Klaus, M. H. (1982). Caring for parents of an infant with a congenital malfunction. In *Parent–Infant Bonding*, ed. M. H. Klaus and J. H. Kennell, pp. 227–258. St. Louis: Mosby.

Kennell, J. H., and Klaus, M. H. (1982). Caring for the parents of premature or sick infants. In *Parent–Infant Bonding*, pp. 151–226. St. Louis: Mosby.

Love, H. D. (1970). *Parental Attitudes toward Exceptional Children*. Springfield, IL: Thomas.

Pozanski, E. A. (1973). Emotional issues in raising handicapped children. *Rehabilitation Literature* 34:322–326.

Shokier, M. H. K. (1979). Managing the family of the abnormal newborn. *Birth defects* 15(5C):199–222.

Solnit, A. J., and Stark, M. H. (1961). Mourning and the birth of a defective child. *Psychoanalytic Study of the Child* 16:523–537. New York: International Universities Press.

Tuttle, D. W. (1986). Family members responding to a visual impairment. *Education of the Visually Handicapped* 23:107–116.

Vernon, M. (1979). Parental reactions to birth-defective children. *Postgraduate Medicine* 65(2):183–189.

Walker, J. H., Thomas, M., and Russell, I. T. (1971). Spina bifida and the parents. *Developmental Medicine and Child Neurology* 13:462–476.

Ware, B. A. (1981). Shattered prebirth dreams and the parental impact of the socio-emotional development of the infant. *Proceedings of the International Symposium on Visually Handicapped Infants and Young Children*, pp. 43–52. Shefayim, Israel, June 14–19.

Yu, M. (1972). *The causes for stresses to families with deaf-blind children*. Paper presented at the Southwest Regional Meeting of the American Orthopsychiatric Association, Galveston, Texas.

PART IV

Issues of Family Trauma: Physical, Emotional, and Sexual Abuse

INTRODUCTION TO PART IV

When working with children's and adolescents' mental health needs, we must be responsive to emergencies, traumas, and abusive situations. At the Reiss-Davis Child Study Center, physical and sexual abuse as well as other traumatic family incidents are responded to by the Quick Response Program, which allows the resources of the Center to be immediately available to the child and his or her family in crisis. In addition to work with abused children and abusive parents, we offer, through the Children of Divorce/Stepfamily Resource Clinic, services to deal with the trauma associated with dissolving and blending families. In situations where physical, emotional, or sexual abuse and family trauma have occurred, the normal path of child development is usually disrupted. This section focuses on uncovering and overcoming the responses to trauma that include shame, guilt, self-loathing, anger, and the burden of misplaced responsibility. The chapters in this section illuminate these concerns and create the possibility of restoring the child's derailed developmental path as the therapeutic experience leads toward health, positive self-image, and mutually enhancing relationships.

In "The Sources of Psychological Pain in a Female Adolescent" (Chapter 10), Morton and Estelle Shane address the examination of a patient whose psychological history includes a prior psychoanalytic treatment experience laden with misunderstandings and misattunements so pronounced that the additional pain this caused complicated and interfered with Shane's treatment. He describes a reparative approach through which he helped the adolescent to overcome her previous failed analysis. He further describes the patient's recovery from childhood neglect and incest through an exploration of her anger at her mother's inability to protect her, caused by her mother's unconscious repetition of her own incestual abuse.

In Chapter 11, Idell Natterson discusses the multileveled aspects of sexual trauma and incest and describes her work with two abused female patients. "Sexual Abuse in Adolescence: Its Long-Term Effects" addresses the primary impact of sexual molestation and the consequential loss of trust in caregivers and the people close to the victims. Natterson emphasizes the importance of establishing trust through the therapeutic treatment, which is described as crucial in repairing sexual trauma in adolescents, and she offers useful techniques for achieving this goal.

"The Psychodynamics of Child Abuse" by Esther Fine (Chapter 12) examines clinical material from four cases in order to exemplify the damaging effects of parent brutality on children. Fine includes descriptions of pivotal points of transformation and aspects of treatment in a series of abused children. She explores how the results of the early repression of rageful fantasies in children can lead to breakdown of repressive mechanisms, causing children to turn their rage inward and forcing them to distort and invert their feelings, as, for example, when fantasies of killing parents turn into fears of parents dying.

Finally, Fine focuses on the key moments of understanding between the patient and the therapist that lead to healing.

Chapter 13, "Patterns of Tragedy, Threads of Hope: A Young Man's Struggle to Heal the Wounds of Physical and Emotional Abuse" by Bonnie Mark examines the trauma of family dysfunction through the eyes of a young adult male as he attempts to piece together his childhood and adolescence. This article reviews the reworking of tragedy for this young man, whose early childhood was experienced as unsafe and was punctuated by abuse, volatility, and instability. His struggle to overcome behavioral characteristics that he considered genetically binding, such as anger, his own anguish, and relational instability, are discussed.

10

The Sources of Psychological Pain in a Female Adolescent

Morton Shane, M.D.
Estelle Shane, Ph.D.

My focus in this chapter is on the contributions of self psychology to an understanding of the sources of psychological pain. I will start with the observation that my dictionary (1992) makes no distinction between the physical and the mental aspects of this phenomenon, defining it as "an unpleasant sensation occurring in varying degrees of severity as a consequence of injury, disease, or emotional disorder." Pain is thus a big subject, occupying a whole industry. Pain from organic sources often has a large psychological overlay, and specialists in its management know that providing a secure base and a definitive program for the sufferer can by itself be meliorative of pain that is ostensibly physical. The corollary of this is important for those of us who work in the psychological realm; by not providing such a secure base for our patients, in an atmosphere of mutual trust, pain, regardless of its *original* source, can be intensified. In this chapter, then, I will address both the pain that finds its source in the developmental histories of our patients, and the pain that is intensified for them iatrogenically through misunderstanding and misattunement in the clinical situation.

I want to begin, however, with a review of how psychoanalysis, while understanding and appreciating the clinical importance of psychological pain, has done so in terms that are often confused, confusing, and misleading. This may be illustrated by the fact that when I attempted to look up pain in several different psychiatric and psychoanalytic dictionaries I found that there was no entry for pain in any of them. I kept coming across the word *paranoia*, a concept amply noted and detailed in all of them. It occurred to me that perhaps the reason for the absence of the concept of pain in the important psychoanalytic lexicons has to do with the exclusively and exquisitely subjective nature of the experience it describes; whereas paranoia is observed and judged to be such by the *outside* observer, pain is felt and judged to be such by the *subject*. This seems relevant because contemporary dynamic approaches are increasingly attuned to the subjective experience of the patient, and while objective judgments may be made, they are made much more cautiously, and ordinarily in collaborative negotiation with the patient. (e.g., Schwaber 1990). This approach can be contrasted with the more classical analytic attitude, wherein the patient's subjective report is judged more or less warily, with an alertness to signs from the patient's hidden unconscious (Shane and Shane 1992). Before I turn to the self-psychological understanding of the sources of psychological pain, then, I would like to review briefly the general, overall psychoanalytic approach to the concept, wherein the original search for the source of subjective psychological pain had been translated into the more theoretical and objectified concept of unpleasure, or anxiety.

Freud speculated that the brain, and then, as he became more strictly psychological, the mind or psyche, was disrupted, that is, pained, by *any* sensation or excitation. Freud termed this overstimulated state unpleasure (1911). Concomitantly, he viewed the absence of such sensation or excitation as pleasure.

In Freud's original theory, then, the most pleasurable experience of all should be that which follows a grand mal seizure, with its total evacuation and discharge of bladder, bowel, and higher brain functioning. His actual model and prototype for all pleasure, or absence of pain, was the postorgasmic state, with his death instinct construct (1920) being but a logical extension, coming later in his thinking. Pain, then, in earlier Freudian terms, was a buildup of tension or excitation, with all such tension being conceptualized originally and exclusively as libidinal energy. Whenever libido was repressed, that is, not discharged because of conflict or for other reasons, the libido was chemically transformed into anxiety, like wine into vinegar. Thus, in this first Freudian model, *anxiety* becomes the essence and source of all psychological pain.

Toward the end of his life, at the age of 70, Freud (1926) revised this first theory of anxiety, reconceptualizing it as a signal of the danger of impending psychological pain. Freud then identified a hierarchy of such pain-threatening dangers that unfolds in a developmental sequence over the course of infancy and childhood, beginning in the young child with fear of the loss of the mother. Then, as development proceeds, a new danger is added, the fear of pain stemming from the loss of the *love* of the mother. The next danger in this hierarchical sequence is castration anxiety, followed by the danger of loss of the love of the superego (that is, pain induced by guilt, or superego anxiety); and finally in this developmental sequence, the individual experiences pain stemming from the fear of dangers to the self that emanate from reality. This hierarchy of potentially painful situations, of which anxiety becomes the signal, and then, unmastered, the source of pain, could all be defended against by the ego through appropriate measures taken either consciously or unconsciously.

With the invention of this second theory of anxiety, painful affects came to have a specific place in psychoanalytic theory, most practitioners still believing, along with Freud, that all experience of pain stems at its base from anxiety, with other painful affects, such as depression, conceptualized as secondary to and derivative from anxiety. This theory of the source of all pain prevailed in psychoanalysis for the next 40 plus years. Only slowly did other dysphoric affects become recognized in their own right as equally potent and important contributants to pain and suffering. We owe this more sophisticated understanding of emotional life to research psychologists such as Sylvan Tompkins (1962), who articulated a basic set of inborn affects of which anxiety, or fear, is but one, with other unpleasurable affects, such as sadness or shame, also and equally counting as sources for the psychological pain experienced by human beings over the course of their lifetimes. Tompkins introduced as well inborn affect potentials for pleasurable feelings, such as joy and pride, and also affects that cannot be categorized so simply as either pleasure- or unpleasure-related, such as surprise, or interest. Freud's elegant but overly simplistic theory had been complicated, then, made less clear and less objective, leading us away from the quantitative consideration inherent in a unitary affect theory, and, inevitably, toward a more careful monitoring of the individual's idiosyncratic, subjective, experience of mixed affect states.

If we retain the Freudian hierarchy described above, we can see that self psychology, along with all object relations theories (Modell 1988), adds to this sequence an additional warning signal against a potentially painful, indeed, shattering situation, the danger of dissolution or fragmentation of the self. Kohut (1971, 1977, 1984) was not the first to point to this archaic danger, conceptualized by others, for example, Anna Freud (1936, 1965), as annihilation anxiety, but Kohut focused an entire theory on it, constructing his self psychological framework around this very source of pain. Moreover, he connected the pain of self-fragmentation inevitably to the requirement of the self for requisite selfobject functions, functions serving to support, sustain, repair, and enhance the self. Thus, Kohut made of self psychology a theory based on the overriding significance of attachment within the vital self-selfobject bond. Attachment becomes the primary motivation, with the integrity of the self dependent on its preservation; thus, in self psychology, loss of self-integrity becomes the primary source of pain.

This is Kohut's self psychology, and most likely it remains the essence of self psychology even today, although many influenced by and building from Kohut's contributions have emphasized different aspects of this theory differently (Shane and Shane 1993). For example, Lichtenberg (1989) does not emphasize as primary the attachment motive and its potential for pain when frustrated as the source for all painful affect. Lichtenberg views attachment as but one of five motivational systems, conceptualizing the lack of selfobject satisfaction of attachment need as but one of five equally significant potential sources either for satisfaction, or, when the need goes unmet, for pain. Stolorow and his colleagues (1987) contribute to our understanding of psychic pain by emphasizing its intersubjective nature, a two-person orientation in which pain is experienced by both in the disruption of the vitally important selfobject tie. My own position is to view the loss of the selfobject tie as a most potent, painful situation. But I acknowledge as well that the other dangers identified in Freud's hierarchy, and the other motivations identified by Lichtenberg, can play an important role, depending on the individual and his or her experience. I also appreciate the centrality of mutuality and connection as inherent in all relationships, so that selfobject ties are not the only ties I recognize as of significance to the individual, and, therefore, as sources of pain in their disruption. Finally, I acknowledge the increasing relevance of conceptualizing the therapeutic situation as a two-person enterprise, departing from self psychology in its purest form with the latter's conceptualization of an essentially one-person psychology pertaining in the therapeutic situation.

To illustrate my view of the sources of psychological pain, I will now present a clinical example. Amanda R., at age 20, was referred to me several years ago by a colleague who had attempted to treat her analytically for a few months, but Amanda herself felt the treatment approach was unsatisfactory, causing too much distress and discomfort for her to continue. We later came to understand that this therapeutic relationship became in itself a source of pain, as Amanda felt her need for connection to another was frustrated by the ambience of this classical analytic situation. She trusted my colleague enough, however, to turn to her for another referral. She asked for someone who would be more responsive, perhaps more interactive, whereupon my colleague referred Amanda to me. But before any of this, Amanda had been in analysis with a male analyst for about 3 years. The work was helpful to her initially. She was able for the first time to reveal in depth to someone else the harrowing experiences of her childhood and adolescence. Amanda was the second of two children, her older brother having died in a swimming accident in the family swimming pool before she was born. Amanda's parents were overprivileged children of wealthy and influential people. Neither Amanda's mother nor her father had to work for monetary gain during their entire lifetimes, nor have they, though they did achieve some recognition as travel writers. Their failure as parents, however, almost defies description. Amanda remembers being in the expensive backyard of their isolated home, where the now covered swimming pool served as a stark reminder to her of danger. What apparently saved her from a complete loss or fragmentation of her self was a tie to her rather distant, disapproving paternal grandfather, a figure respected and feared by her parents as the source of their revenue, whom people said she resembled. This connection, however superficial and unsatisfactory, did serve to stabilize her. As for her parents, when she sought out either of them for food or conversation during the long days she spent alone with them at home, she was told to go away, that her mother and her father were busy with their writing. Amanda sees this response as prototypical of her childhood before age 6. The parents had lived a free and active social life with many parties, much drugs and alcohol, and a good deal of open and flagrant sexual engagement, all in disregard of Amanda's existence. She was either ignored or found to be in the way and told to go to her own room. Living in an isolated area as they did, and affecting a bohemian lifestyle, there were few servants, and none was given the direct responsibility for Amanda's care.

Since her parents were distant and indifferent to Amanda's needs, she relied on three of her four grandparents, though none of them offered or seemed to acknowledge the need for any sustained interest or protection, though they would schedule periodic rather than ongoing visits with her. When Amanda was 8, her father ran off to Europe, apparently with another woman, and dropped out of Amanda's life completely. Her mother, now free, made more overt the affair she had been having with a man who lived in the neighborhood, and who subsequently moved in. Amanda had never liked him, feeling eerie in his presence. This man and her mother openly made love in front of her, just as her parents had done with others at their parties. When her mother would look up and notice Amanda, she would either become irate and order her out of their presence, or she would affect not to observe her at all and just go on with her love making.

Amanda's unregulated life, wherein she had to find many of her own meals in the refrigerator and eat alone, was relieved only when she began attending school at age 6, and school became a source of comfort and regulation for her. But Amanda's troubles were exacerbated when she was 10 and her mother's lover began to use her sexually. He would fondle her and bring her to orgasm, and she would occasionally masturbate him, and on one occasion was forced to perform fellatio on him. This activity continued at his insistence and persistence for 6 years. Amanda felt frightened, intruded upon, humiliated for responding with orgasmic pleasure, and fearful that he might harm her physically for disobeying, refusing to participate, or telling her mother, though she was certain that her mother would only side with him anyway. When she was 15, she began a sexual relationship with a boyfriend and was able, with his help, encouragement, and protection, to tell her mother's lover, now her stepfather, to leave her alone. She never did tell her mother any of this until her mother and this man were divorced when she was 19. It was at this time, in response to Amanda's revelation, that her mother explained tearfully that she, too, had been sexually abused, by her own father.

Amanda wasn't surprised, for while she liked being with her other three grandparents, she had always felt uncomfortable around her mother's father. In terms of Amanda's revelation, her mother expressed great surprise, saying she had had no inkling of anything that went on. But Amanda told me that there were many times when the sex play between her and her stepfather should have been obvious to her mother. Once, when all three were traveling on a tour bus together in Europe, he openly left her mother's side to sit on the seat next to Amanda, spending the next several hours fondling her under a blanket, with Amanda only hoping that her mother would turn around and discover what was happening; but her mother never did.

Following the disclosure, when she was 19, of the man's abuse of her, Amanda asked to be allowed to go into treatment, and her mother agreed but soon withdrew financial support. Amanda had her own inherited money by this time and continued the payment herself. She understood her mother's refusal to pay as her continued indifference to her suffering, her mother being capable of only flickering moments of concern. The man she had sought treatment from, though initially helpful to her, was a rather strict and interpretive analyst who insisted on the use of the couch. More significantly, this analyst slowly came to focus his own attention on Amanda's contribution to the sexual activities with her mother's boyfriend. He interpreted the failure to disclose to her mother what was going on as complicity in the act designed to perpetuate the pleasure in the relationship and to secure an oedipal victory over her mother. When Amanda would protest, presenting her own conscious, subjective experience of the matter, she was told she was denying both the responsibility for and the pleasure in the relationship that she had obviously felt. When Amanda would retreat into silence, she was told she was silently shitting on the analyst.

Amanda felt both guilt and shame throughout this experience, the price she had to pay for sharing her early life and receiving some comfort thereby. It was difficult to leave this analyst because she didn't know where else to turn. This was a repetition of her entire childhood experience of being misunderstood and abused but having nowhere else to go. Her analyst had warned her that if she left she might be in danger of committing suicide or of coming to grief in some other way, for example, getting involved in destructive sexual relationships. Finally, however, she turned to her internist for help, who then referred her to my colleague. As noted, she left her very quickly, recognizing that she, too, made her feel lonely, guilty, and responsible for her experience of sexual abuse. She had somehow, through the work of her analysis, gained enough strength to refrain from again being in a relationship with an analyst who seemed to her to be so unresponsive and so lacking in understanding.

In treatment with me, Amanda at first appeared ill at ease, but she gradually became less self-conscious and less wary. The bulk of our work together has centered around alleviating her almost automatic mistrust and then clarifying and affirming her life's experiences, pointing out the difficulties she had as a child in trying to get her needs met, and noting the pervasive insecurity in which she has had to live her life. It was relatively easy to clarify as well what went wrong in her previous analysis. My main function has been as a steady presence in our ongoing relationship, remaining available to her by telephone beyond the established limits of the three, and then four times a week we ultimately set up to see one another—sitting up, I might add. Once we had reviewed her past experience and understood the current status of her relationship with her mother, Amanda and I then examined together the apparent working hypothesis of her previous analyst that the principal source of Amanda's pain was oedipal guilt, that is, guilt over having successfully won out sexually vis-à-vis her mother's lover. After extensive review of her own painful feelings in this regard—the mixture of shame, rage, guilt, hatred, humiliation, and sadness—the idea that this tragedy could be reduced to an oedipal drama seemed preposterous to both of us. What appeared much more important was the experience of lifelong parental abuse, neglect, and hyperstimulation, including her father's outright abandonment and her mother's incapacity to protect her daughter from the same incestuous abuse that she herself had suffered as a child. Amanda even wondered with me whether her mother was unconsciously repeating her own trauma via her daughter in a failed attempt at belated mastery. The achievement of this conviction that she was the victim of abuse and not the perpetrator, a new view of the situation for Amanda, generated in her something unique in her experience. She said, with great feeling and gratitude, that for the first time in her life she felt safe and protected, that someone seemed to care for her well-being more than for his or her own. I felt strongly affected as well. Staying affectively and consistently close to her experience was both vicariously and personally painful to me. Yet I also felt empowered by her response. She made me feel effective indeed, and with some justification, because, while obvious to me, to her the correction

of her previous analyst's judgment and, particularly, that analyst's blame, to which she felt painfully vulnerable, did address
a real, more current need to be absolved of responsibility for
what had happened to her.

And yet, with all of this, there was still detectable a vague but
persistent hint of mistrust in her that behind my apparent
goodwill and dependability, I might be, like other men in her
life, secretly and illicitly coveting her sexually. I could detect
this anxiety as she left each session, furtively turning her head to
catch a sidelong glance at me after she had said good-bye. I never
saw this as a wish to hang on for a moment longer; rather, it
struck me as cautiousness, self-protectiveness, even suspicious-
ness. Then something happened between us that seemed to
erase this vestige of threatened impingement coming from me.

Amanda invited me to attend the commencement exercises
conferring on her the master's degree she had been working
toward, and which attainment she saw as a direct consequence
of our relationship. After some exploration with her, I said I
would be happy to attend. She warned me to stay away from her
because she didn't want to have to explain my presence to her
family. She said she wanted someone there who was really glad
and proud to see her achieve in life, that there was no one else
but me to fill that role. So, dressed in my summer suit, I went to
what I had pictured as a small graduation from a small college,
and found myself in a crowd of over 2,000 people. There was no
chance of my even getting close to the podium, but I did get to
watch my patient cross the stage and receive her degree, and I
tried, futilely, to catch her eye from about 50 yards. When I saw
her at our next appointment, I questioned whether she had seen
me, and then, when she said no, wondered if she had had some
doubt at any time during the ceremony whether I was there at all.
She surprised me by saying that she had absolutely no doubt that
I was there, that she knew I was there, and that was that. Remarkably, the furtive looking back seemed to disappear from her
behavior soon after that experience. I was touched by the degree
of trust she had placed in me, and I remain aware of it, and of the
importance of our relationship in ameliorating the universe of
pain she has experienced in her lifetime, both with the original
parents, and, then, iatrogenically, with the accusing analyst. We

still have a long way to go, but hopefully the road will be less painful for her.

In conclusion, I want to suggest that whenever and wherever in a person's lifetime important developmental needs go unmet, pain will be experienced related to that source along with dysphoric symptomatology. The particular form the pain takes, whether depression, anxiety, shame, guilt, or humiliation, depends on myriad circumstances, but most particularly on the failure in the significant relationships of a person's life. With my patient, these failures in relationship included not just her parents and others important to her in her early childhood, but also her first analyst, whose misunderstandings and misattunements caused additional and unneeded pain.

So where does this leave Freud's original formulation, the hierarchy of dangers, renamed by Charles Brenner (1982) the calamities of childhood? Indeed, all these calamities can cause pain, including the calamity that is too often not acknowledged and that Kohut so strongly and persuasively emphasized, the calamity of the loss of self-cohesiveness attendant on the failure of needed selfobject ties. For Amanda, the stunting of her development, the loss of her mother and father, and the loss of their love, the loss, that is, of any supportive, affirming, loving relationship would seem to define the source of her psychological pain. Rather than fantasies of an oedipal conflict and attendant guilt over oedipal victory, Amanda had suffered from a lack of realistic protection that did violence to her right to a safe and secure childhood, and to an adolescence in which sexuality and affection could be allowed to unfold at their own pace.

REFERENCES

American Heritage Dictionary, 3rd ed. (1992). Boston: Houghton Mifflin.

Brenner, C. (1982). *The Mind in Conflict*. New York: International Universities Press.

Chessick, R. (1993). *A Dictionary for Psychotherapists*. Northvale, NJ: Jason Aronson.

Freud, A. (1936). *The Ego and the Mechanisms of Defence*. New York: International Universities Press.

_____ (1965). *Normality and Pathology in Childhood*. London: Hogarth.

Freud, S. (1911). Formulations on the two principles of mental functioning. *Standard Edition* 12:218–226.

_____ (1920). Beyond the pleasure principle. *Standard Edition* 18:3–64.

_____ (1926). Inhibitions, symptoms and anxiety. *Standard Edition* 20:75–175.

Kohut, H. (1971). *The Analysis of the Self*. New York: International Universities Press.

_____ (1977). *The Restoration of the Self*. New York: International Universities Press.

_____ (1984). *How Does Analysis Cure?* Chicago: University of Chicago Press.

Laplanche, J., and Pontalis, J. (1973). *The Language of Psychoanalysis*. New York: W. W. Norton.

Lichtenberg, J. (1989). *Psychoanalysis and Motivation*. Hillsdale, NJ: Analytic Press.

Modell, A. (1988). The centrality of the psychoanalytic setting and the changing aims of treatment. *Psychoanalytic Quarterly* 57:577–596.

Moore, B., and Fine, B. (1990). *Psychoanalytic Terms and Concepts*. New Haven, CT: American Psychoanalytic Association and Yale University Press.

Schwaber, E. (1990). The psychoanalyst's methodological stance. *International Journal of Psychoanalysis*, 71:31–36.

Shane, E., and Shane, M. (1992). Mahler, Kohut, and classical analysis: theoretical clinical considerations. In *Beyond the Symbiotic Orbit*, ed. S. Akhtar and H. Parens. Hillsdale, NJ: Analytic.

Shane, M., and Shane, E. (1993). Self psychology after Kohut: One theory or many? *Journal of the American Psychoanalytic Association* 41:777–797.

Stolorow, R. D., Brandchaft, B., and Atwood, G. E. (1987). *Psychoanalytic Treatment: An Intersubjective Approach*. Hillsdale, NJ: Analytic Press.

Tomkins, S. (1962). *Affect, Imagery, Consciousness*, vols. 1 and 2. New York: Springer.

11

Sexual Abuse in Adolescence: Its Long-Term Effects

Idell Natterson, Ph.D.

The experience of abuse at any age is traumatic. Although the effects of early physical abuse, sexual abuse, and neglect on the psychological and emotional development of children have received considerable attention, abuse during adolescence can also have implications for development and for the personality disorders of adulthood. Just as traumatic events of infancy and childhood may result in subsequent developmental arrest, so may rape, incest, or other forms of abuse during adolescence become the focus of self-destructive, defensive personality structures.

No one really knows how much sexual abuse occurs in the United States because most of it is kept a secret within families. In the past several years, however, reports of abuse from patients, therapists, child protective agencies, clinics, and governmental sources have increased. Sometimes the abuse reported was inflicted years, even decades earlier.

Van de Kolk (1987) gives an elegant and simple answer to the question of when events are traumatic. He states that when the individual experiences an event as traumatic, it is traumatic both theoretically and practically, regardless of the nature of trauma. Whether it is sexual or physical abuse, gross neglect, or emotional abuse, Van de Kolk assumes that the central nervous system does not distinguish the sources of trauma and deals with all traumas similarly. Thus, for such diverse trauma as rape, incest, concentration-camp experience, molestation, or witnessing a horrible crime, the human response is the same.

Differences arise because some individuals are better able than others to integrate trauma into their life experiences. According to Van de Kolk, six factors determine how well or poorly trauma is integrated: (1) duration of trauma, (2) prior traumatization, (3) preexisting personality and genetic disposition, (4) the developmental phase at the time of the trauma (the earlier, the more severe the result), (5) the severity of the stressor, and (6) the social support system of the victim during or following the trauma. In the two cases I present here, both involving sexual trauma, I emphasize this last factor, social support and empathy.

When trauma is inflicted by a person close to the victim, such as a caregiver, the primary psychological result is the loss of faith and trust in the caregiver and fear for one's physical and psychological safety (Bowlby 1984). Such a severe breach of trust by an important emotional figure hampers growth and normal development of a child and distorts the perspective of an adult. When an important figure supposed to be the main source of protection instead becomes the source of danger, the child or the adult must achieve a change in consciousness through psychological maneuvering to ensure his or her place in the family. In order to accommodate to the fear engendered by an abusing parent or spouse, the victim typically withdraws emotionally and physically from the relationship, attenuating or breaking the attachment. Bowlby discussed the long-term effects of severing the attachment, noting that the avoidance of the dangerous parent competes with the child's desire for proximity and care. Just at a time when the child needs emotional support most, the child victim gives up that support in the service of safety. The stressed child or adult has an increased need for attachment and protection, but there is no caregiver who can be trusted.

Additionally, trauma can adversely affect thinking. Abused young children experience a number of delays in their social, cognitive, and linguistic development. Piaget (1962) has pointed out that affective and cognitive development are complementary and simultaneous. Bowlby (1984) also demonstrated that sexually or physically abused children lag behind nontraumatized children intellectually and emotionally. When memory of the trauma is repressed, other learning requiring memory may also be compromised.

These are but some of the consequences of abuse. Van de Kolk suggests that many trauma victims who appear to be functioning well are in fact suffering from limited emotional and social involvement. The two women whose cases I present, both high functioning, did not experience trauma in early childhood. Thus their cognitive and verbal abilities were already established and the question of disruption or arrest was not at issue. Nevertheless, nonintegration of their traumatic experience resulted in long-term inhibition, personality disorders, and social isolation. In both cases, the patients were able to recall their traumas, but because they were not integrated, there were damaging social and psychological consequences.

Both women had good jobs, dressed well, appeared to function capably but were in chronic pain and burdened by their past. They suffered from emotional constriction and a sense of victimization in relationships, especially with men. Beth's trauma was the incest that she suffered at age 12, which led to personality constriction and guilt. Stephanie, who became pregnant from a rape that occurred when she was 15, led a life filled with shame and humiliation lasting decades.

BETH

Beth, age 40, is the divorced mother of three children, one girl and two boys. I saw her once a week for 6 months. This prim, tall, blond "preppy" woman was an only child. After her mother died of cancer when she was 1 year old, her father quickly remarried, and she was raised by her father and stepmother. During one of her parents' many stormy times together, her stepmother, a would-be "Flamenco dancer, dabbler in the arts," a fiery Latin "with men friends," left to study dance in Spain, leaving Beth and her father for 6 months. Beth, then age 12, without her stepmother, reexperienced old terrors—monsters in the closet and a fear of the dark. She accepted her father's invitation to sleep in his bed, where she felt much safer. Her father, a remote, colorless person, whom she described as a "typical Wasp" who in the past rarely spoke to her or paid attention to her and had never taken an interest in her feelings before, now seemed genuinely interested in helping. Beth felt flattered as he began to touch and fondle her in bed, but she became bewildered when he sought genital contact, and she panicked when he attempted to penetrate her. She fled from the bed. She promised her father that she would never disclose the incident. When her stepmother returned from Europe, Beth kept her secret. She feared her stepmother would again abandon her to her father, or she might blame Beth. She also speculated that her stepmother might even accept molestation as normal.

Throughout her adolescence, Beth remained withdrawn from her father and kept a distance from him. She was socially constricted, but she did well academically in high school and college.

Beth became a lawyer. Throughout law school she daydreamed of suing her father, but maintained her silence. She married and divorced twice, each time to a remote, distant, and ineffectual man like her father.

Beth's sexual trauma had several long-term effects. She maintained an ambivalence toward women stemming from distrust of her stepmother in whom she never confided, suffered from guilt and self-blame because of her initial participation and pleasure in the forbidden sexual activity, and in both of her marriages disliked sex. Additionally, she viewed all men suspiciously as potential molesters.

Concern for the safety of her own children brought her into therapy. When her three children were young, she experienced panic attacks and migraines when her father and stepmother visited. In therapy, she connected these symptoms to her fear that her father might molest her children. She had, until this point, never spoken to anyone about her childhood trauma. I encouraged her to confront her father and warn him never to touch her children. She warned him that even a slight sexual gesture toward her children would result in her legally prosecuting him. Speaking out after a silence of three decades, she experienced total relief from her psychosomatic symptoms. It is interesting that the issue of the impact of the loss of the natural mother in infancy never became part of the manifest therapeutic dialogue.

STEPHANIE

Stephanie was raised on a large, prosperous dairy farm in Minnesota. Her parents, proper, proud, upstanding church-going people, worked hard. As the oldest of four children and the only girl, Stephanie did household chores before and after school and on weekends. She was never praised, was ignored, and led a life of sadness and despair.

At age 15, she entered into an "innocent" after-school relationship with a boy four years her senior. Her family disapproved because he was below their social class. Each day, he waited for her after school, and she defied her family, spending after-school time in his company. She looked forward to his praise, his touch, and his lightheartedness. Then, one afternoon in his apartment, he raped her. She stopped seeing him.

When she failed to get her menstrual period, she realized she had become pregnant, but kept silent until her seventh month of pregnancy. Incredibly, her parents had not noticed the change in her body, a strong commentary on the remoteness and absence of communication within the family. When Stephanie broke the news of her pregnancy to them, they locked her up at home, and quickly arranged for an adoption in the nearest big city, St. Paul. Stephanie gave birth to a baby girl but was never shown the baby. Her only contact was the sound of the baby's first cry, and then the footsteps whisking the baby away.

After she signed adoption papers, the door slammed shut on the incident. Her parents and other relatives never again mentioned the rape, the pregnancy, or the baby, but gave her dirty, sly glances, whispered in her presence, and shunned her. When she married at age 25, neither she nor her family told her husband of the baby. Later, after her divorce, she moved to St. Paul. After the divorce she dated but never formed a long-term relationship. She developed a haughty, unapproachable manner that, because of her great beauty, men found challenging, but only for a short time because they then tired of her aloofness. All of her energies went into her job as manager of an elegant men's store in St. Paul. She saved enough money to leave her family and move to Los Angeles, where she became a buyer in a fine men's store.

When she came to see me, at age 40, her presenting problem was her inability to form meaningful relationships with men, despite her intelligence and good looks.

Although her family situation accounted for many of her difficulties, the rape at 15, accentuated by the silence, shame, and scorn, were central to her personality and character. In therapy, for the first time in 25 years she spoke about the rape, the baby, and her loss.

The two main areas of therapy were mourning the baby and addressing the identity problems arising from the rape. Although Stephanie's trauma occurred in adolescence, it profoundly affected her adult relationships and self-image, as she was uncertain in her relationships with men, wary of being abused again. She no longer idealized her father but came to recognize his true allegiance to her brothers and his disdain of women. Her expectation that men would scorn and abuse her, as her boyfriend and father had done, had destroyed her ability to permit closeness.

As a 15-year-old girl struggling to form an identity in a family that defined her as a "whore," she looked for a way to preserve hope and meaning. Wanting to maintain her connection to her parents, she rejected the notion that something was wrong with them, and concluded that her badness and looseness were the reason for her parents' rejection. Thus, she retained a connection to her parents by maintaining a depreciated self-image.

THERAPY

Beth's and Stephanie's therapies addressed the primary impact of sexual molestation, the loss of trust in caregivers and people close to them. Therapy for abused patients must help in reestablishing trust in others. This is often difficult because patients fear that the therapist, if trusted, could abandon them and reawaken the painful past (Herman 1992). Sensitivity to this fear, along with empathy and support, played a crucial part in helping them regain trust. They were then able to direct their anger toward the perpetrators of the trauma and to regain their lost vitality.

REFERENCES

Bowlby, J. (1984). Violence in the family as a disorder of attachment and caregiving systems. *American Journal of Psychoanalysis* 44:9–27.

Herman, J. L. (1992). *Trauma and Recovery*. New York: Basic Books.

Piaget, J. (1962). *Play, Dreams and Imitation*. New York: W. W. Norton.

Van de Kolk, B. A. (1987). *Psychological Trauma*. Washington, DC: American Psychiatric Press.

12

The Psychodynamics of Child Abuse

Esther Fine, L.C.S.W.

The effect of physical abuse, of hatred, of seduction and rape on our children is a devastating one. It can lead to severe developmental arrest. Clearly what ensures survival during the vulnerable period of infancy, when a separate identity is just beginning to form, is the care of a mothering figure. Of course, no one in a mental health profession questions that early good parenting is a basic necessity for healthy psychological development, but what is good parenting? In our Western civilization, there is considerable stress on the need to control the child's impulsive behavior. As the child's spontaneous behavior becomes more and more unpredictable, some parents find it necessary to punish him or her, not only as a release for their own emotional tension but because they may be convinced that physical pun-

ishment is the best form of child rearing. The warning "spare the
rod and spoil the child" is a basic tenet in our society.

In this chapter, I present clinical material, drawn from my
psychotherapy practice, to exemplify the damaging effects of
parental brutality on children. The four children I describe were
all subjected to physical abuse in their very early years.

The first of these, Janie, was 9 years old when I began to see
her. She had developed a school phobia so severe that she had to
be carried kicking and screaming to school, pleading with her
parents not to leave her. Shortly afterward, the school authorities would notify her parents that she was ill in the nurse's office
and had to be taken home. Janie was obsessed with the idea that
her friends and her teachers disliked her and preferred others.
When her sister, 2 and a half years younger than herself, was
born, Janie developed a severe sleeping disturbance, remaining
awake 2 to 3 hours, crying and screaming. The parents felt that
Janie was tyrannizing them, and they beat her in desperation.
Once, the father became so enraged with her that he began to
strangle her. Treatment revealed that her school phobia related
to murderous fantasies involving her parents, and she had to
stay home from school lest they come true.

A second patient, Susan, was also brutally beaten at the ages of
1½ to 2½, primarily for the same reason—because she was
unable to fall asleep, and would cry and demand her parents'
attention. Her mother in particular was unable to tolerate these
demands, and beat her brutally. Susan was an adopted child. She
was referred for treatment by the school when she was 9 years
of age because she had been physically attacking other children
in the school. One time, she had used a weapon—a knife. The
authorities suspended her from school and threatened expulsion
unless she went into treatment.

Susan had made a strong tomboy identification. She walked
and talked in an exaggeratedly masculine way. It seemed to give
her a great sense of power. She had been known to be verbally
abusive to her teachers and, on one occasion, struck one. Her
fantasies, however, were rich with a central theme that somewhere her real mother existed and would love her, treat her
tenderly, and rescue her one day.

The third child I will call Denny, a 7-year-old boy, referred for treatment because he was extremely disruptive, hyperactive, and uncooperative in school. He refused to listen to the teacher, fought with the other children, and was unable to follow through with a task. The only time he would follow directions was when the teacher became very angry with him. He was expelled from one school and had just started another where he was again about to be asked to leave. This child had been physically abused during his toilet-training period. Both parents were furious with Denny because he resisted toilet training. The father would check him every morning and beat him in the head when he found that the child had wet or soiled. The mother, too, was abusive. The father continued beating Denny for his bed-wetting until the child was 5, at which time the bed-wetting stopped. Both parents had fathers who behaved toward them as they behaved with Denny. The father's father beat him severely and, on occasion, would actually pick him up and fling him against the wall.

The fourth child, Jonas, was 6 years of age. He presented a behavioral problem very similar to Denny's. He was provocative in school, fighting with the other children, sassing his teachers, until finally he was placed in a special class for disruptive children. He, too, showed signs of a serious learning difficulty. His parents were divorced, and Jonas was living with his mother at the time of referral. However, during his first couple of years, the father was the primary caretaker because the mother worked. He was a neglectful caretaker. At 13 months, Jonas fell down some stairs and suffered multiple fractures of the skull because the father had failed to watch him carefully. The father began to beat Jonas when the child was 15 months of age. The beatings primarily were related to Jonas's resistance to toilet training. Unlike Denny, he continued to be enuretic up until the time it was understood in his therapy.

These four clinical cases contain certain common denominators. All of the children had been physically abused in their earliest years. All had parents who had been abused as children. In their presenting symptoms, they all manifested severe problems in their school adjustment. Interestingly enough, their presenting symptoms related to marked difficulties in containing their own aggressive impulses. They identified with the aggressors and treated those who peopled their world, either in fantasy or in reality, the way they had been treated early in their lives. I noted also that these children all engaged in magical thinking, nothing unusual for latency and prelatency children. However, it seemed exaggerated in their cases. In a sense, all these children were attempting to master the problems related to their early physical abuse. Their pervasive use of magical thinking, or omnipotent thinking, can be considered a defensive maneuver to stave off their sense of helplessness and insignificance by creating an aura about themselves as special and all-powerful. Where this type of thinking becomes linked with destructive thoughts and feelings, it can create new monsters in the form of phobias, learning problems, and a multitude of interpersonal difficulties involving aggression, separation, and individuation. The provocative defiance some of these children displayed with teachers, parents, and peers could definitely be considered a form of mastery. They were irrationally beaten by their parents. When they can make it happen, they take some control.

Let us now consider some of the developmental issues involved when a child has been physically abused early in life. The major problem begins at a time when the I and the non-I begin to separate. This occurs around 3 months of age. Brandt F. Steele (1983), who has done extensive research in this area, paraphrases a typical parent in his study: "When I fed Timmy his first solid food at three weeks, he got hold of the spoon and messed the food around. I slapped his hand. He never reached for that spoon again." Steele points out that this response indicates that the infant experienced some kind of intrapsychic change concerned with early superego formation because it demonstrated control and suppression in the infant. The same suppressive child-rearing patterns are likely to be used in subsequent stages of the infant's development. Toilet training may begin as early as the fourth or sixth month of age and be accompanied by criticism, deprecation, and physical abuse, with high expectations for the child to develop other skills as well, such as crawling, walking, and talking. Clearly, such parents encourage a very early formation of a punitive superego. At the same time they arouse intense aggressive, hostile feelings in the child, with which the child must now deal. The child growing up under these circumstances can hardly have a normal oedipal phase, as this stage necessarily is hampered by the already preexisting, preoedipal conflicts and fixations. A little boy with unmet oral needs is too fearful of his mother's rejection or attack to form the appropriate oedipal ties. By the same token, the little girl can only turn to her father with an excessive need for him to supply the basic mothering she has lacked.

In adolescence, there is a tendency for the child to experience a restriction on his abilities to explore, observe, and think for himself. Moreover, the child's hostility is provoked when he is physically abused and, at the same time, he is forbidden to express his hostility overtly, producing an inner conflict of massive proportions and implications. In sum, the victim of brutal physical abuse is robbed of his identity and the ability to maintain authentic feelings.

Now let us examine the psychodynamics of the physically abusive parent. Leonard Shengold (1985) has borrowed the term *soul murder* to designate the cruel and bizarre child-rearing practices involving the physical abuse of children. How can we understand individuals who would inflict such brutality on their children? The literature is replete with the finding that child abusers were abused as children. The question can be raised, however, as to how these parents, these battering parents, differ from the disciplinarian who simply views punishment as the best way to achieve the aims of child rearing. A general finding is that such parents are extremely labile in their responses. They have a very low frustration tolerance, so that any tension in their psychic apparatus tends to throw their tenuous emotional stability off balance, and this is soon followed by a release of their hostile aggression. As they direct this aggression toward their own children, they often enact actively what they experienced passively as children: they can now identify with the aggressor. If the parent is not latently psychotic, he or she may behave normally between these battering attacks, and may even try to make up to the child for what he or she has done.

A special clinical condition, sometimes referred to as murderous obsessions, can be a derivative of postpartum depression. There are may women who become depressed after child-birth. In very severe postpartum depression, there is sometimes the danger of infanticide.

Sylvia Brody (1978) has done extensive research in mother–child interaction. She proposes that the tendency to hit or spank a child is deeply rooted in a defense against the fantasy of being beaten, and the act itself is both a loss of ego organization at the same time that there is an almost frantic attempt to reassert control. There is a wild effort to direct the child's aggression back onto the child.

What seems to be basic in the abuser's attitude toward infants is a conviction that children exist in order to satisfy parental needs. Moreover, these parents very often feel unloved and look forward to having a baby because that baby will love them. Should the baby be uncooperative and make parental caretaking difficult, the parent may feel disapproved of and unloved and respond with physical abuse as a justifiable reaction to the provocation. Very often, the abusive parent tends to see his child as a replica of himself as a bad child. It became very clear in my work with Denny's father that he viewed Denny, in a sense, as the bad part of himself, and had to punish his child the way his father had punished him.

There is a very strong narcissistic wound in these parents. They are exquisitely sensitive to any hint of lack of love or approval and to rejection of any kind. When these feelings of disapproval or rejection are aroused, they become a very important factor in triggering individual abusive acts.

It should be emphasized that abusive parents have a wide range of conflicts and character disorders as a function of the variations of their own developmental experience. These factors can be significant in determining which child is more likely to be attacked, when he is attacked, and for what purpose, and they interact closely with the developmental stages of the child. Rigidly obsessive-compulsive characters are more likely to attack their infants when they mess with their food, slobber, or vomit, and later are messy with regard to their excretory functions. In a later phase, such individuals will react when children leave their toys and clothes about. In order for the parent to maintain his own repression, he will aggressively attack the child who is stimulating his underlying conflict.

If a parent has not resolved his sibling rivalry, this can be a contributing factor to his need to abuse his child. The conflict is likely to relate to the need to be loved and nurtured and the feeling that one is not.

While my focus in this chapter has been on the physically abused child, it is not uncommon to find both sexual and physical abuse within a given family. It is also important to keep in mind that some forms of abuse are subtle and elude legal definition. Although repeatedly allowing the child to witness the primal scene is not considered an illegal act, it does have profoundly disturbing effects on the developing child. In my case presentation of Jonas, I mentioned that he had not resolved his enuretic problem until the later phases of therapy. Wetting his bed every night had become an embarrassment to him, and he wanted to work on the problem. Not surprisingly, we found that Jonas's enuretic problem had multideterminants. It was related to his underlying hostility and defiance, his exhibitionism, his underlying defenses against dependency needs, and last but not least his concept of sexuality, which clearly related to his repeated witnessing of the primal scene.

I would like to present a few examples from his clinical material. The following play sequence revealed the polymorphous perverse nature of his concept of sexuality and its possible connection with his bed-wetting. The Ken and Barbie dolls, together with their teenage daughter, Skipper, and their baby, constituted a family in his fantasy play. The baby was very unruly. He shit and pissed in Skipper's hair and then rushed over to nurse at Barbie's breast. When Barbie and Ken were in the bedroom together, the baby rushed in to suck Ken's penis and Barbie's pussy! These were Jonas's words. The baby was especially loving to Ken. I suggested that he was trying to keep them apart in this way, and Jonas agreed. When his hostility came out toward Barbie, I commented that the baby may have felt left out when Ken and Barbie were together, and maybe he felt that Barbie did not like him. Jonas agreed with this interpretation. However, in the material that followed, there were considerable references to Jonas's attempt to deny his dependency needs.

As he began to face and work through this problem, for the first time in his life he began to use transitional objects like teddy bears and stuffed animals, suggesting some relenting where those dependency needs were involved. He began to be dry occasionally at night for the first time. He hoped that he would be dry by the time he went to summer camp. I remarked that we would just have to figure out all the psychological reasons why he wet. "Here we go with all that psychological stuff again," he countered. I enlisted his help in understanding another boy who also wet at night, and Jonas's explanation was as follows: "Probably it was when he found out his mother was having sex and so he started wetting." I asked him if the boy thought he was having sex, too, by wetting. "Yeah, you got it," he told me. I responded that it was not urine that comes out when a grown man has sex. With great surprise, he came back with, "It's not?" He seemed genuinely surprised. When I described semen to him and told him how it carried the sperm, he said to me, "That is disgusting." I told him that now that he knew this, perhaps he could be dry at night, and he has been dry ever since. What Jonas was able to tell me was that his conception of sex when he repeatedly witnessed the primal scene was an infantile understanding of what transpired. And so we have an example of a child who was not illegally sexually abused, but obviously overstimulated sexually. This led to symptom formation, namely, his enuresis.

One very interesting research finding is that there is higher incidence of multiple personality disorder in children who have been abused than is found in the overall statistics relating to the multiple personality disorders. Bowman and his associates (1985) suggest that dissociation, the predominant mechanism utilized in multiple personalities, provides an effective way to cope with the strong affects that are evoked by abuse. This would apply not only to children who are physically abused, but also to children who have been sexually abused. Wilbur (1984), another researcher, suggests that a state of rage is produced in children when they are abused, and when they are told that the rage is unacceptable, this, in turn, leads to repression; however, the potential exists for explosions of feelings when the repression breaks down, which, in turn, leads to the emergence of an alternate personality.

In sum, child abuse has wide and pervasive detrimental effects on a child's psychological development. The focus in this paper has been on violence in the family. However, perhaps the prevention of violence in the family must also include a concerted, organized effort to change the basic societal idealization of the use of physical force, epitomized by such film media heroes like Rambo and Dirty Harry, and the knock-'em-dead characters in children's Nintendo games.

REFERENCES

Bowman, E. S., Blix, S., and Coons, P. M. (1985). Multiple personality in adolescence. *Journal of American Academy of Child Psychiatry* 24(11):109–114.

Brody, S., and Axelrod, S. (1978). *Mothers, Fathers, and Children—Explorations in the Formation of Character in the First Seven Years*. New York: International Universities Press.

Shengold, L. (1985). The effect of child abuse as seen in adults: George Orwell. *Psychoanalytic Quarterly* 54(1):20–45.

Steele, B. (1983). The effect of abuse and neglect on psychological development. In *Frontiers of Infant Psychiatry*, ed. J. Call, E. Galenson, and R. Tyson. New York: Basic Books.

Wilbur, C. B. (1984). Multiple personality in child abuse: an overview. *Psychiatric Clinics of North America* 7(1):3–11.

13

Patterns of Tragedy, Threads of Hope: A Young Man's Struggle to Heal the Wounds of Physical and Emotional Abuse

Bonnie S. Mark, Ph.D.

Tragedy, then, is an imitation of an action that is serious, complete, and of a certain magnitude . . . in the form of action, not of narrative; with incidents arousing pity and fear effecting the proper purgation of these emotions.

Poetics, Aristotle

I promise a tragic age: the highest art in saying Yes to life, tragedy will be reborn when humanity has weathered the consciousness of the hardest but most necessary wars without suffering from it.

Ecce Homo, Nietzsche

The fabric of our lives is largely woven out of the stories that we tell ourselves about ourselves. These narratives are sewn together with the threads of the experiences that make up the events of our existence. This chapter looks at a young man's attempt to uncover, discover, and recover from his childhood struggle in an abusive, dysfunctional family; it recounts the tragic patterns that structured his life and the threads of hope that he discovered through the therapeutic journey.

A central objective within the therapeutic process focused on a shift we worked toward in his perception of what a tragic life meant—that Peter's "life-as-tragedy" might be viewed in two radically different ways. The definition of tragedy by Aristotle quoted at the top of this chapter is the most famous and most widely accepted conception of the tragic. In short, Aristotle says that tragedy is defined by what human subjects do that makes them suffer. Aristotle's description of the tragic pattern is easily understood in the literature or drama where we watch the downfall of the tragic character due to some central, fatal flaw; Oedipus is an example.

Friedrich Nietzsche had a different perspective on tragedy. Nietzsche recognized that the human suffering basic to tragedy was also integral to human life. He argued that transcending the tragic in life can only be accomplished by an affirmation of the life force that lies behind it, the belief that "despite every phenomenal change, life is at bottom joyful and powerful" (*The Birth of Tragedy*, p. vii). Unlike Aristotle, who describes the tragic story as one that enables catharsis, a release or venting of the stored emotions engendered by the inevitability of the tragic in life to occur, Nietzsche actually demands that we embrace the tragic in life in order to overcome it. In Peter's case, we began the therapeutic journey by looking at the experiences in his life that made him see his life as tragic. As therapy progressed, he was able to illuminate, investigate, and reconstruct from his own experience the developmental derailments that resulted in what he stated as "going from tragedy to tragedy." The journey began to take us toward the path of the Nietzschean ideal. That journey continues.

From before he can remember, violence and anger characterized Peter's family environment. His parents' divorce when he was 5 years old came as a relief because it meant no longer having to bear witness to his father's anger, which often erupted into rage, violence, and physical abuse, primarily directed toward his mother and an older brother. The most vivid memory of these incidents occurred when his father, raging toward his mother, pushed her into a china cabinet. The panic and horror of seeing his mother bleed led Peter, who was 4 years old at the time, and his older siblings to run screaming in terror for their neighbor's assistance. The children were then chastised for making public the problem of abuse, which was the darkest secret of generally troubled family relations. The need for outside help was thus associated with vulnerability, embarrassment, and shame—a foreboding sense of humiliation that his family did not function like an ideal family, like the families he perceived that everyone else had.

The perceived dysfunctionality of the family was compensated for by the development of coping mechanisms that gave the illusion of an operating entity. There was a generally accepted collusion among all the members of the family to feign success and functionality. Peter became a "family survivor," a role facilitated by his mother. His role as survivor was determined by a desire to make it through the family chaos—not to be held back by the oppression, anger, violence, or fears that arose. Peter perceived his mother as a "martyr to the cause of the family," sacrificing her own pleasure for the well-being of the children. She never remarried, centering her existence around the role of the "worrying mother." An intense, positive relationship with his mother ensued as she began to grow stronger, seek therapy, and get out of the abusive relationship. His positive feelings, coupled with other negative, less available feelings, such as anger and guilt toward Mother, contributed to the vicissitudes of his transferential feelings, discussed later in the chapter.

An important coping mechanism that Peter developed early in life was his tendency to shut off emotions he experienced as intolerable: he learned to modulate his inner voice as a buffer to keep him from feeling pain. It also prevented him from developing insight into his feelings and desires. His emotional reality was perceived as toxic, and he was socialized early on to seal off his emotions lest they threaten to contaminate him. This was a lesson reinforced by his family and his friends.

He describes an early memory of sorrow and agony when fishing with some boys from the neighborhood. As the boys caught fish, they inserted little firecrackers into them to explode their intestines. Peter empathized with the fish, and the maliciousness of the children's actions caused him anxiety and distress. This resulted in his being ridiculed and called a sap. It was concomitant with this memory that Peter recalls shutting off his feelings by turning down the volume of his own inner voice.

He chose to be a loner, creating fantasy worlds that included play acting so elaborately conceptualized that it included dialogues with many characters—a situation Peter relished because he controlled all of the action and actors. Peter thus chose not to spend much time with other children or to join in their activities, which he considered beneath him. The space he created between himself and others became a protective barrier. Peter cultivated the external appearance necessary for conformity, but experientially he was isolated, so part of him set out to repair the wounds that childhood peer pressure and his mutilated family life had inflicted on him.

He overcompensated for what he saw as the failures of his family by his individual pursuit of success. He strove to fit the part of the "successful achiever" throughout his formative years. Peter realized his goals of excellence in both school and in sport. But neither activity was ever merely pursued for its intrinsic pleasure. Self-pressure for academic success resulted in his being awarded class valedictorian and accepted into a prestigious college; but his peers were jealous and judgmental, which resulted in his being aloof and exacerbated his sense of separation.

Peter was also extremely successful in his chosen sport, competitive swimming, but he never enjoyed competition for its own sake or for pleasure. Instead, he was animated by the internal pressure to "shave off" 2 or 3 seconds, to win in all four strokes. For Peter, winning in only three strokes was to have failed. Everything depended on results, and every goal he attained merely pushed the stakes higher. The tragedy was the impossibility of ever reaching contentment—the search for perfection that's never attained. In our work together, especially in the early sessions, much of Peter's anxiety was about doing therapy right—having the "right" thing to say. He tended to steer toward the cognitive sphere, an area he felt safe in due to his high intelligence and his gravitation toward conceptualizing, as opposed to allowing his inner feelings to come through. When interpreted, he acknowledged the safety of staying in "his head"—this was familiar, and he was on safe terrain.

The stigma of divorce in the midwestern community in which he was raised reinforced Peter's need to buffer his interactions in society from any connection with his toxic emotional world, which had developed as a response to the shame and secrecy that accompanied his father's violent and abusive behavior. The toxicity Peter identified with emotions resulted in a struggle to block out his feelings in order to avoid the depression that always loomed in the background. But whatever barriers he developed in order to protect himself from depression, the feelings eventually surfaced tainting the perfect picture he had constructed for the outside world and his ability to be satisfied.

Peter's experience in college and his subsequent studies in graduate school provided intellectual challenges and a freedom to flourish socially. However, graduate school was not Peter's choice, but rather his submission to the desires of his family. Here, he described himself as the tragic martyr, the archetype of the sacrificial victim that his family had forged to perfection. Once more his own passions—for Hollywood and film, acting and directing—were overridden. His own choices were overshadowed by his role within the family drama. This filled him with anger, resentment, and regret.

This regret and resentment became a dominant theme within our sessions. Peter spoke often of disliking this facet of himself, while paradoxically recognizing that his regret filled his emptiness. He was so intimately acquainted with a sense of regret that it was personified as a familiar bedfellow with whom he journeyed down the path of growing depression. The resentment and anger were key motifs that defined the contours of Peter's tragic persona. The fear of contamination, activated by anger, regret, and resentment, was the touchstone of Peter's general emotional disposition and was associated with a range of phenomena.

First, he feared becoming like his father, having no control over his anger and expressing it destructively. His father constantly reinscribed this fear by claiming that his grievous actions were "in the family blood," and that resistance was impossible because "you can't fight destiny." In our sessions, Peter continuously invoked the idea that the anger he felt was genetically binding and expressed fears that his "circuits were wired" very early in life. He felt that his father's lack of remorse for his violent behavior and his lack of responsibility for his actions could all be attributed to a genetic predisposition that Peter might well have inherited. This meant that the power of his tragic fate was absolute, that Peter would not have the *choice* to act out in any other way in the context of an intimate relationship. *Choice over the response to his feelings* was an element he felt was outside of his power.

Peter was disturbed at loathing his father. He felt that he should have pity, compassion, or sympathy for the father he considered a "disturbed and loathsome individual." He universalized his father's anger and rage and saw these as inherently male qualities that he despised. This connection between anger and "maleness" led Peter to a certain self-loathing, especially when his emotions drew him toward reacting in anger and violence. Exacerbating his self-punitive view of his "male anger" was the contrast of the idealized female—initially his mother, then his girlfriend—and extending to his female therapist.

Peter's experience of not being the victim of most of his father's abusive behavior resulted in a great deal of guilt over the fact that he escaped the anger and aggression his father directed toward his older brother and other family members. This guilt was compounded by Peter's love for his brother, who in many ways had become a father figure to him and his mother, whom Peter could not protect or help to protect herself.

Peter recalled dissatisfaction with his family from early childhood, and had the fantasy of an ideal family perpetuated by the facade of TV families and the external appearance of other "happy" families.

Due to the structure of Peter's perfectionist tendencies in school and sport, which translated into life and relationships, he was frustrated and dissatisfied with his performances, feeling that he could always do better "if only. . . ."

Finally, Peter's overarching feeling was that he was destined to live "a tragic life," a response so primitive that he cannot remember ever being without it. This tragedy was dominated by the scene of unrequited love—the constant replay of a drama where the child in the fantasy was never allowed a better life than that of his mother, who sacrificed everything for her kids. Peter once commented, "I seem to move from tragedy to tragedy," when recounting his relationships.

Peter described his emotional reality as a monster within—the "regret monster," who loathes himself, his feelings, and his behavior. When relating to others, especially those closest to him, the monster was bent on destroying what was wholesome and good in his life. Peter felt he could not escape the ogre of a father whose vicious rage had violently imprinted a pattern of behavior, interfering with his ability and that of his siblings to be in a mutually satisfying, communicative, fulfilling relationship. On an unconscious and at times conscious level, he was living out the tragedy he perceived his life was destined to be.

Peter acted out the tragedy that his father had prophetically declared, but instead of directing it outward, the attacks and beatings were directed toward himself or toward the people in his life who could provide him nourishment, support, and a mutually satisfying relationship. Peter described acting destructively toward the positive aspects of his life, which were never appreciated to their fullest until they were gone. He would then mourn the loss he had effected.

The clearest example of this psychic mechanism was enacted throughout the therapy, for paralleling the growing therapeutic relationship that was building was Peter's evolving relationship with his girlfriend of one and a half years. For the first phase of treatment, he felt that he was not ready for the commitment his girlfriend requested. Instead, he wanted to immerse himself in the "lifestyle" of Hollywood and the entertainment industry. Peter only realized the importance of the relationship once it was over—after it became clear that she had moved on because of his inability to involve himself in a committed, reciprocal relationship. Concomitant with her moving on, Peter felt devastated and began to feel intensely that she was all he ever wanted. She represented absolute goodness to him, the perfect manifestation of everything positive in the world—she was pure, unadulterated "female" goodness. She symbolized the possibility of his perfect future—the potential of escaping the tragic past and forging the ideal family he never had.

At the same time, Peter was filled with myriad self-deprecating feelings—anger at himself for not seeing clearly sooner, for not acting sooner, for being influenced by the "bozos whom [he] called friends," most of whom were not in successful relationships themselves. Peter loathed the abusive, hostile, and angry side of himself that pushed her away. This side, as described previously, was the "maleness" that his father's imprinting left—he was doomed to contaminate her with his destructive and angry tendencies. The times in the relationship in which Peter felt out of touch with his feelings, sensing moments of being out of control of his anger, were the most frightening for him. He described these moments in our sessions. His conflicting feelings and ambivalence within the relationship and the feelings of abandonment, loss, and inevitable tragedy facilitated his moving to a deeper level of insight.

Peter and his girlfriend grew apart after one and a half years, as they each attempted to try a separation; however, only when Peter learned that she had moved on did he begin to experience the deep loss. He relentlessly tried to reunite with her to no avail, and he was devastated by his inability to come to terms with the sense that he had destroyed his only hope for a pure, uncontaminated relationship. Peter expressed the sense of tragic fate that would be complete when she would inevitably marry someone else and have a child, which he said could have been theirs. For a few months, Peter was not in touch with his anger at her for moving on to a new relationship. Over time, he saw the anger existed and did not annihilate him, and that he could function despite the pain. Nevertheless, his greatest fear—that his father's fatal curse would perennially haunt him—had been realized. Peter struggled with how little control he had over his destiny, which he described in the terms of a struggle between "good and evil."

Peter suggested how ironic it was that he only found the voice to communicate his deepest feelings to himself and to her once he experienced losing the one "good thing" in his life. He abused himself for pushing her away, and only at that point found himself able to get in touch with his feelings—feelings about her and about the wall he had built shielding himself, her, and the therapist from the "danger" of his emotional world. In an eighteen-page letter that he wrote to her, whole regions of his emotional world that were in the dark came to light.

At that point, Peter began to be aware of changes that were occurring internally. He began to experience the loss, to sit in the sadness. He started to work through the fear of anger, the depression, and the black hole of numbness that immobilized him. He saw that over the years he had so completely shut down his feelings, lest the terror overwhelm him, that he could not experience the satisfaction of the relationship. That is, by building a wall between his feelings and his interaction with people in his everyday life, Peter lost access to the entire range of emotions—the positive emotions were sealed off with the feelings that frightened him. He began to discuss the buffers he had created to protect himself.

Throughout his young adult years, drug use offered temporary escape: he could conquer his feelings by numbing them until they came back full force and gradually took control of him. His attraction to illicit substances initiated a struggle with his healthier side that, time after time, said this would be the last time, yet inevitably he would relapse back into drug use. It was brought out in treatment that, in the past, Peter resorted to drugs in an attempt to push away responsibility for his own life and escape what he felt was a deep sense of melancholy about his life. Drugs depressed all his functioning, including his ability to resist more drugs, and his cognitive skills. In addition, the drugs masked his emotional pain.

Occasionally during our treatment, Peter would discuss "falling back" into recreational drug use and come into therapeutic sessions in a self-reproaching or confessional manner. He doubted that our work together could provide him with enough to fill up the emptiness and pain he experienced. These incidents would also serve as a test to find out if the therapist would tolerate him with all his "weaknesses." He suggested his "addictive personality" as a reason he was drawn to drugs, using this at times as an excuse and at other times as a motivator propelling him to say, "I must stop." We spoke about the therapy as offering him another way to work through the depression. The hope offered was that whereas in the past when he felt depressed, he could see no end to the depression, he now could be accompanied through those painful periods. While a part of him didn't trust that this was enough, over time his intermittent willingness to struggle with his emotional issues and the pain of losing the woman he loved led us further on his path toward a different perspective on his life.

As therapy progressed, he became more conscious of experiencing a range of emotional responses and feeling more secure with allowing those feelings to become a part of his persona. He began to see that his fear of feelings numbed him. The symptom of this repression contributed to his depression. Only through working through the suffering of his past and looking at the present pain of losing the relationship of his dreams (i.e., both on the level of the loss of his "real" girlfriend and the "idealized" image of her) did he finally allow himself to experience the sadness and misery and come to understand that he had survived those traumas.

At times during the treatment, Peter's relationship with his mother colored his process of working through his pain. As Peter's devastation and depression over the loss of his girlfriend grew, he "sat in the pain." Peter's solitude, introspection, writing, and sitting in the depression evoked concern and advice from his "worrying mom" that was strongly resisted by Peter. His "worrying mom" and his "worrying therapist" were caught in a transferential struggle between Peter's inability to move beyond a growing depression and his mother's role in attempting to get him to remain active and involved in his external activities. The therapeutic dyad recreated the relationship between Peter and his mother. The transference issues raised were cast in gender-specific terms, as well as along parental lines. Through a variety of suggestions, Peter made it clear that he did not want the therapist to play the role of his mother. When the therapist's inclinations led her to explore the feelings keeping Peter from moving forward, remaining busy, and working at transcending his depression, she experienced a wall, seemingly erected to protect Peter from the repetitive dimensions of the transference. He had both anger at Mom and "Mom-therapist" and concomitant guilt that he was irreparably "doing it wrong." It became important that the therapist keep in check her own tendencies to mother his emotional battles.

Key to this process was maintaining a focus on Peter's transference within the therapeutic relationship. Discussing the aspects of transference gave Peter the stepping-stone needed to look at his feelings in the moments in which they arose. Peter's history was one of difficulty sharing with anyone because it meant he would be vulnerable and could not avoid the feelings that came with an intimate connection. He described a certain comfort in being a loner because it meant he would not be violated and wouldn't have to risk being hurt by feelings when they were expressed. Examining the vicissitudes of the "mother-therapist" dimensions of the transference served as a breakthrough in getting Peter to the inner-subjective fields previously untravelled.

By allowing, even encouraging, Peter to be in his own affective experience, we could examine other areas that had previously gone unmentioned. For example, one year into treatment in the midst of his traumatic breakup, the therapist took a short vacation. Peter was not conscious of any specific feelings regarding the vacation, but in the following sessions he was disjointed, disoriented, and expressed that he was having difficulty focusing. As we struggled to interpret this response to the break, he was able to see the effect it had on him. Being in any way dependent or vulnerable within relationships was intolerable, and he could see that some issues within the therapeutic relationship mirrored his relationship with his girlfriend. Exploration of these feelings within the therapeutic dyad built a foundation of expression, communication, and sharing that enabled Peter to use these experiences as the base in working through his past and current relationships.

Reflecting on the curative factors of treatment, the relationship that Peter and the therapist built was a significant contributing factor to Peter's growth, self-awareness, and ability to express suppressed feelings. Surviving feelings of vulnerability through the acceptance of the multiple facets of his character—even the "messy" ones that came loaded with his own self-loathing and punitive superego—he went very deeply into the positive idealized transference, and concomitantly the therapist's affection for him grew. The tasks within the therapeutic dyad were first, to create safety and room for the expression of his transference idealization and fantasies, and second, to let him know that he was experienced positively by the therapist, and to explore his wish that he be seen that way. Thus Peter could recognize, trust, and communicate his feelings with a confidence that he carried forward into his world.

As the safety within the therapeutic relationship grew, strategies facilitating Peter's ability to identify the patterns that generated his emotional responses ensued. We identified his process as being twofold: (1) identifying feelings, and (2) expressing feelings. The identification process was blocked because all his feelings were lumped together and so solidly frozen off that accessing them was difficult. Peter began to distinguish his emotions, differentiating annoyance from anger and anger from rage. By distinguishing these three feelings as they arose, for the first time feelings become safer, less toxic. He could confront his fear of feeling any anger, which he identified directly with his father and intuited as necessarily destructive. He began to see that the insecurity of being angry and volatile was great enough so that it necessitated shutting off the emotions associated with all of his feelings, including those of pleasure.

The expression of feelings created fears of vulnerability and insecurity. He discussed the small child in him that so feared feelings because he could not control them. We looked at his pattern of communicating his emotions only when he had nothing left to lose. Expressing transferential feelings about the therapeutic dyad enabled him to feel more comfortable with the darkness and contamination he previously identified with his emotions. He began to say, "I see it [the feelings], now where do I go from here?" The therapist responded, "Into the tunnel, which you've described as dark and frightening, and where you haven't been able to go alone—now we can go in there together." He could acknowledge the significance of his attachment to the therapist as facilitating his experience of connectedness and of feeling truly understood and accompanied on his journey. Thus, his experience of being held and accompanied in the therapeutic dyad gave him a stepping-stone to look at the fabric of his emotional world and to access his feelings in the here and now.

The work of the therapy was now to facilitate Peter's weaving his way through the patterns he had begun to identify. He began to feel more comfortable with the sense of vulnerability that arose with his feelings. Twisting his way back into the tapestry of his past enabled Peter to begin to unravel the threads of his life and to begin to weave a new tapestry—to create a new pattern for his future that does not necessarily lead him from tragedy to tragedy. Peter still speaks of the tragic within the tapestry; however, the design has begun to include threads of hope that will heal his wounds.

PART V

Self-Inhibiting and Self-Destructive Behavior: Reexamining Mind, Body, and Psychosomatic Disorders

INTRODUCTION TO PART V

Many children and adolescents, unable to express their anger, internalize it, causing them either to be depressed, at times even to the point of feeling self-destructive, and/or to express their feelings through somatization. These children's emotional problems are often missed by parents and schools, who are more prone to respond to misconduct or behavioral problems, until the symptomatology of the internalizers has been exacerbated to the point they can no longer go undetected. Over the years the staff at the Reiss-Davis Child Study Center has found an increasing number of these internalizing children in its caseloads, as the Center has been making the community more aware of these "quiet" disorders.

Shifts in the role of the child in the family and the community as well as the role of the family in the life of the child often add unexpected stress to children and adolescents, causing them at times to deal with their anger and rage by choosing a course of self-destructive or self-inhibited behaviors. This section explores the deeper emotional issues that intersect to produce such symptoms.

Drawn from many years of work in Great Britain, Rita Lynn's "Beauty and the Beast: The Case of a Severely Eating-Disordered Adolescent" (Chapter 14) describes the psychoanalytic treatment of a severely eating-disordered, suicidal adolescent over a 4-year period in London, England. The significance of Lynn's chapter is its application of an object-relations perspective (Klein, Winnicott, Kahn) to the treatment of this disorder. Treatment issues include ritualistic and self-destructive behavior, magical thinking, and the uncovering of psychosexual issues previously unavailable to both the patient and the clinician.

In "Passion Play: A Psychoanalytic Approach to Mind–Body Issues" (Chapter 15), Shelley Alhanati discusses an unconscious fantasy of mind and body as a sexual couple and looks at how the lack of an adequate capacity to tolerate the primitive emotions stirred up by intense psychic passion can be expressed by setting up a sadomasochistic relationship with one's own body. Alhanati explores these issues through her descriptions of short vignettes of children, adolescents, and their parents, as well as relating these cases to contemporary theory.

In Chapter 16, "A Brief Psychoanalytically Informed Intervention: Tommy, a Traumatic Neurosis in a Five-Year-Old Boy," Carl Hoppe recounts the diagnosis and psychoanalytically oriented psychotherapy of a 5-and-a-half-year-old boy and his parents who have suffered from the impact of a series of family traumas centering on the effect of these factors on the young child's development and internalization of pain and anxiety. The case illustrates the role of short-term therapeutic interpretation and communication through the child's play to help him to express feelings that were unbearable.

14

Beauty and the Beast: The Case of a Severely Eating-Disordered Adolescent

Rita Lynn

This chapter presents the story of Cara, a beautiful girl of 19, who was admitted to my ward at the London Hospital in London, England. She came to break the habit of taking 60 laxatives every other day in an attempt to lose weight—in other words, she suffered from a serious eating disorder. At first it was not quite clear how serious. She joined the therapeutic community of the ward, attended large and small groups, and seemed to be cooperating with the aim of stopping the laxatives. But we soon discovered that she was leaving the ward whenever she got upset, especially with the staff. She seemed to withdraw more and more into herself, and became more difficult to reach.

The most striking thing about this truly beautiful girl (a young Monroe or Madonna) was her provocative clothing—transparent shirts and incredibly short miniskirts with zippers that opened upward. Her long, blonde hair was worn like the 1930s actress Veronica Lake, and completely covered her face so she could avoid eye contact at any time and did so constantly.

The young resident who had started working with her individually was leaving the hospital, and she was most insistent that I take this girl for analytic psychotherapy. Cara was very upset about the doctor leaving and was about to discharge herself from the hospital when she was offered individual sessions with me three times a week in the hospital, initially as an inpatient and then, eventually, as an outpatient on a once-a-week basis.

She agreed immediately, and much later I found out that a transference to me had already occurred, which was understandable, as I had conducted the large ward groups she attended every morning. In the early sessions, the family material that emerged was predictable. Cara was always the troublemaker—so much so that the family did not want her in the house anymore. Indeed, while she was in the hospital, her parents divorced and broke up the family. Subsequently, she had no home to go back to.

Cara was the second of four children. Her oldest brother, David, was a 21-year-old homosexual, very promiscuous, but at the start of her treatment in a stable relationship. Cara had an 18-year-old sister, Clara, who seemed to be doing well, good in school, extroverted, pretty, thin, but very private and and not the type to let things get her down. Her younger sister was a bright 10-year-old, who was nervous and unhappy, and had been stealing at school.

The climate at home had always been turbulent. Cara's father, 54, was a moody, introverted lawyer, often away on business and always a shadowy figure. Her mother, 47, worked as a nurse in a large teaching hospital. During her parents' frequent fights, Mother screamed and cried. With a breakdown of the marriage, Mother was in a relationship with a married doctor from her place of work. He had promised to leave his wife and child but had not done so.

Cara had fears throughout childhood and was always afraid to go to sleep, but did not go to Mother for reassurance, as she felt Mother had enough problems. She did poorly at school, and also stole when she was a child to gain attention and buy gifts for her mother and for her friends. She finally finished school and decided to become a nurse.

Cara went to nursing school at the London Hospital but decided she no longer wanted to become a nurse, and it was during this time that the eating disorder began. She also lost her room in the family home when she went to nursing school, and this was very significant to her. For two years she would not let anyone touch her or have any physical contact with her because she felt she was so ugly that she did not want anyone to see her figure—yet she dressed provocatively so that they might.

The taking of laxatives started because at 14 Cara discovered that it was a good way of losing weight. The patient began with 15 Senocot, at first once a week, but then, because she was "delighted with the results," she began to purge on Ex-Lax and then on 60 Maalox tablets every other day.

She took the laxatives at 8:00 P.M., would vomit at midnight, then would have diarrhea once every hour for 10 hours until she bled. This had been going on for 2 years. She was seen at first for outpatient medical treatment, and the professor had suggested she be seen as an inpatient in order to stop the laxatives and for psychotherapy.

She came onto the ward and seemed to settle well and to be happy to be there. She made friends with some of the patients and was provocative and manipulative with the staff members, especially the male nurses. I started seeing her in treatment 3 weeks after her arrival on the ward.

She was keen to see me, but would not look at me during the sessions, hiding behind her hair. Although she wanted to see me, she would not speak about herself, except to say that she would stop the laxatives. She said that she wanted to stop but that she wouldn't or couldn't tell me anything else. She gave a little family material, but very little, and I decided to wait with her and see what came up. The only time she would say anything was toward the very end of the sessions.

The sessions, however, were not empty—they were full of fury and destructiveness, as Cara would pound the arms of her chair so hard that eventually they came off, and would stick her fingernails in her hand as if distracting herself through pain (like during interrogation). Although I said very little except to acknowledge what I saw—that is, anger, fury, and so on with me and the hospital—she would speak with constant suppressed anger and tell me that I did not understand, that everything was hopeless, and that all she wanted was to kill herself.

From the beginning, these threats to her life had a strange quality—like a cryptic message that I had to read, and, of course, in the beginning I always got it wrong, whatever interpretation I made. It might have seemed hopeless, except she always came to sessions, and she was always on time and seemed eager to come in.

I eventually asked her how much of her was in the session. She said 2 percent. She explained that 2 percent was what brought her and made her stay—but that I had no idea about the other 98 percent. It was like she was trying to frighten me away, to protect me from destruction. Over the next 4 years she would occasionally report how much of her was with me, and it steadily increased, but before every break and holiday she would always tell me that this was the last time I would see her because she was going to kill herself. I would say, "Well, if you do, I won't see you, but if you don't, your appointment is at the same time, four o'clock." She would march out, but it gradually became clear that she needed me to say something to indicate continuity (I would be there for her) and choice (the choice was hers). As more of her family material emerged, it became clear that she functioned very much the same with the family as she did with me, furious, provoking, but needy as soon as they refused to accept her. She also started to talk about her eating behavior. I left the eating very much to one side, as I was sure it was just the latest in her efforts to show how needy and greedy she was. During a visit home from the hospital, she sliced her wrists and her neck and ran from the house, leaving Mother to follow her dripping blood down the street. Her parents did not visit her at the hospital, and although one family session was arranged, Cara treated it like a betrayal, and her parents were unable to speak to each other or to anyone else. Cara did not want any further family work, so it was postponed.

Very gradually, she began to talk about how she had many things she could not tell me, and then she started to bring fantasies and dreams. The dreams were extremely violent; she dreamed of being flayed alive, impaled, nailed to the floor, and other extremely violent images. After one of these dreams and reiterations of how I did not understand, I made the interpretation that there was nothing inside and no skin—only raw flesh. This made her very silent, but there was a great change—she began to tell me about her rituals, with many fears and hesitations. I made an interpretation that I was holding her, but that because she had no skin, I had to make myself into a spongelike form that could hold her without too much pressure. This also seemed to make sense to her, and she calmed down inside.

She began to tell me how she kept me alive by her rituals and by the laxatives, which allowed her some control of her feelings of despair. Very gradually, we were able to look at her ambivalent feelings toward me.

At this stage of her treatment, there was upheaval and reorganization at the hospital, and Cara grew a lot worse, increasing laxative abuse and other forms of self-abuse, like bashing her head against the bathtub. On the other hand, while still a patient on the ward, she started a job. This had been impossible previously, but now, although struggling, she went to work.

At first it was one day at a time, but she kept going, and she continued to see me twice a week. Her parents seemed to wash their hands of her. She was discharged from the ward, and as she had no home, she went to stay with her brother and his boyfriend. It was not satisfactory, but it was better than nothing, and gradually she began to search for an apartment for herself. However, she had enormous fears both of being with someone and of being alone. A few minutes at a time, she started to be alone with me, that is, alone in the presence of another in Winnicott's sense. There were moments when she relaxed with me. We continued looking at the rituals, and as they were revealed and she saw that I survived, she gradually became less afraid of talking about them. However, behind them were the further secrets of other dark things she did, which she said "would make [me] disgusted and would make [me] reject [her]." She would often say, "You hate—you must hate me now," but the fact that sessions continued finally convinced her that I did not, and that my lack of hate could be internalized as acceptance of herself, if not of her destructive behavior.

She said that she would give up the laxatives for me and did, then blamed me because it was too hard—the feelings were terrible. The anxiety and the shaking were awful. At this stage I took her into the hospital for 4 weeks to help her over this very raw and regressed period. She stayed for 3 weeks, working well, then burned herself badly with a cigarette and was consequently discharged, as the agreement with all patients was that they not damage themselves in the hospital but seek out a member of the staff and ask for help.

When she was leaving, she was totally distraught and was literally clawing herself, begging me to let her stay. I said no, she could not stay, but she could continue to see me as an outpatient. Then, quite spontaneously, as I said good-bye, drawing a firm boundary against her acting-out behavior, I took her clawing hands and gave her a brief cuddle. This spontaneous and, as I then thought, incorrect behavior on my part was a crucial turning point in her treatment. She calmed down and left the hospital, but a good object had been internalized.

After this watershed, work began to take on a more usual shape. She was able to look at what she brought, to accept interpretations, and to play just a little; that is, she was able to allow me to use a little humor in the sessions, and she also began to look and dress like me. The nurses on the ward would say, "Well, Rita, here comes your clone."

The only times she regressed and would go many steps back were around breaks and any other changes that implied that I might leave or move from the hospital. Finally, that inevitable time came, and when I told her I would be leaving the hospital, she said her heart stopped, even though I immediately went on to say that she could come and see me at my private office. She started to come to see me at my office, and then began the most exciting and productive work. Until then, treatment had all felt reparative developmentally—trying to fill the void and to grow some skin—but adult fantasies about how she wanted to live her life had not been present. It was like the present was the past—and finally we reached the present.

Enough structure existed internally for Cara to tell me what she had really wanted to do and be, before she took on the job of keeping the whole world alive and keeping alive in the world, a task that took all her time. Cara had wanted to study acting, and she began tentatively to audition. I can't tell you how wonderful this was for her. Even disappointments that would previously have reduced her to a heap of rubbish were borne stalwartly enough, and she survived.

A long time later I saw her give a tremendous performance in García Lorca's *Blood Wedding.* It was a great achievement. Let's look at Cara in terms of object relations theory.

BEAUTY

In the earliest months of a child's life, roughly the first 3, she is not able to integrate the mother into a whole separate person, but instead relates to a part of her, for example, her breast, her hand, her face. She also feels that these parts are extensions of her or her creations. Even when the mother begins to be perceived physically as a whole person, a combination of the loved part who feeds and the hated part who deprives and leaves one to cry, she is still two people, angel and devil, or fairy godmother and a witch. Moreover, the diffusion of the boundary between the self and the outside world is such that the two are not discriminated between, and the child feels she is the world—that she is omnipotent and omnipresent.

Even when some discrimination begins, it is so permeable and fluctuating that painful experiences are projected out and attributed to the outside world, thus keeping "bad" qualities outside and enabling the self to be experienced as positive and pleasurable. This stage, called the paranoid/schizoid position by Klein, (1937) is characterized by part object relationship, splitting, and projection, together with confusion over boundaries of the self.

Some of Cara's difficulties stem from this early stage, as neither father nor mother were able to provide the structure and limits within which Cara could develop sufficient inner control to cope with the outside world. She always experienced her mother as a split object, a bad object who rejected her because her demands for love and attention were too needy and extreme, and a good object, an idealized provider of all good things when she was a good girl and met Mother's needs. Cara always projected her hateful feelings into me when I was her therapist and then accused me of hating her. She was also very confused over her own boundaries, and often spoke about spilling out or of other people spilling into her. In Cara's family, Mother's and Father's problems began after the birth of the first child (a boy). It seems that mother was extremely closely involved with her first baby and that she found it difficult to tolerate any separation from her child, no matter how small. Father found it impossible to pull Mother back from her necessary regression to what Winnicott called her "primary maternal preoccupation," and felt neglected and deprived. The parents quarrelled. Cara, who was born only 18 months later, further separated Mother and Father. From her earliest memories Cara felt as if everything were somehow "her fault"; her parents' quarrels were because of her. She took on this role of scapegoat so wholeheartedly that the other children did not compete for it.

Winnicott (1975) describes the process of children taking parents' quarrels into themselves:

> The parents quarrel. He manages only by taking the whole experience into himself in order to master it. It can then be said that a fixed state of parents quarrelling is living inside him and a quantity of energy is henceforth directed towards the control of internalized bad relationships. Clinically, he becomes tired, or depressed or physically ill. At certain times the internalized bad relationship takes over and then the child behaves as if possessed by the quarrelling parents. We see him as compulsively aggressive, nasty, unreasonable, deluded.
>
> Alternatively, the child with introjected quarrelling parents periodically engineers quarrelling in the people round him, then using the real external badness as a projection of what was "bad" within. In the child's management of his inner world and in an attempt to preserve in it what is felt to be benign, there are moments when he feels that all would be well if a unit of malign influence could be eliminated.

Clinically, there appears a dramatization of ejection of badness, kicking, passing of flatus, spitting, etc., or we might add laxative abuse or manual evacuation. Alternatively, the child is accident prone, or there is a suicide attempt—with the aim to destroy the bad within the self; in the total fantasy of the suicide there is to be a survival, with the bad element destroyed. But survival may not occur. [pp. 208–209]

This follows the early three stages of ruthlessness and the era before purpose and before the integration of the personality. Winnicott explains earlier reasons for aggression in these terms:

1. In the healthy pattern, environment is constantly discovered and rediscovered because of motility. Here each experience within the framework of primary narcissism emphasized the fact that it is in the center that the new individual is developing and contact with the environment is *an experience* of the individual (in an undifferentiated Ego-Id state at first).

2. In the second pattern, the environment impinges on the baby and instead of a series of individual experiences there are a series of *reactions* to impingement. Here then develops a withdrawal to rest which alone allows individual existence.

3. In the third pattern, which is extreme, this is exaggerated to such a degree that there is not even a resting place for individual experience and the result is a failure in the primary narcissistic state to evolve an individual. The "individual" develops as an *extension of the shell* rather than of the core and as an extension of the impinging environment. The individual then exists by not being found. The true-self is hidden and what we have to deal with clinically is the complex false-self whose function is to keep this true-self hidden. [pp. 208–209]

The pain of recognizing that there is a desire to harm and destroy that which is most loved brings with it as a reward what Klein called (perhaps unfortunately) the depressive position. I prefer depressive anxiety or what Winnicott (1975), with his usual flair, calls "the stage of concern." This beginning of feelings of responsibility and desire to protect and help, the origin of the urge toward reparation, was in Cara grossly misapplied. Unfortunately, if Mother is depressed or if in reality there is conflict in the marriage, the child learns a way of reducing this conflict as her urge toward reparation. Because Cara felt it was her fault and because she could not see how to bring her parents together, she accidentally discovered that they stopped quarrelling together if they were united against her. She would then be naughty, and they would be united in punishing her. This relieved her anxiety but formed patterns of difficult behavior, for example, eating in her room or stealing at school in order to buy her mother and friends presents. When Cara was 1 year old, her mother had another baby, thus subjecting her to separation and then to the loss of her mother to a demanding, overly attached older brother in addition to a new baby. Cara never felt there was space for her, and she never got enough of her needs met—especially those early ones, of Mother mirroring and reflecting a sense of self-worth.

Cara picked up very early that everyone who looked after her was busy, preoccupied, had no time for her, and therefore that she was uninteresting. During therapy there were endless accusations: "You only see me because it is your job." Since she felt that it was her fault if anyone was depressed, angry, or hurtful, it was her job to try and keep them safe and well.

THE BEAST

As she grew older, this desire to keep bad from happening, at first from those she was closest to and finally to everybody, grew until she developed a complete and complex series of rituals pathetically designed to ward off evil, and in which she contained the whole world. The whole world would spill into her, and she felt everyone as if they were in her. Of course, it was her own destructive feelings she was controlling. This destructive Cara was referred to as Beastlike or Bestial.

If she did not perform these rituals and bad things happened, that is, some natural catastrophe or some accident occurred, she took on the responsibility for this and punished herself at first by deprivation and then by self-abuse. Only this relieved her feelings of guilt and responsibility. By the time I saw her, these rituals, which were amazingly secret, took up most of the time—

and the punishment took up the rest. The eating disorder started with trying to change her shape (she had an extremely feminine figure with big breasts and a tiny waist, and was tall and shapely) and deprive herself at the same time (killing two birds with one stone). But this was just the next step in an already established hierarchy of ritual. In order to protect this mammoth defense against her true self full of needy/greedy desire for holding, feeding, and unquestioned love, these rituals had to be protected with extreme secrecy, the breaking of which carried the ultimate punishment of death.

The first time she told me about the existence of the rituals, she had to whisper the words one by one with long intervals, wiping her hands brutally against her mouth as she did this and waiting for me to say some of the words for her. When I did not (because I could not), she would writhe around in her place and say, "You know, you know—why don't you just say it, to help me?"

Before this I had no access to these secrets, although I had plenty of evidence for their existence, as Cara would retreat behind her hair and in great conflict say, "I can't, I can't." Eventually and laboriously, we pieced together the rituals. She could not leave the room unless she touched all four walls in the correct order, the TV (because from the TV came most disaster stories), the telephone, and then a small decorative box she had had all her life. This was all following the laxatives, of course. If she saw a car on the street that was the color of any of the cars of any of the people she knew and cared about, she had to go back and start again in order to keep them safe. I had a green car at the time, and she later told me that if she saw a green car, she had to go back and do the ritual twice or three times to feel safe.

When we got to the later stages of being able to talk more freely about the rituals and they began to lose their magic power, it was this green car one that haunted her the longest. It seemed to be solved when I changed my car. The ritual never returned.

Winnicott says:

A principle might be enunciated, that in the false-self area of our analytic practice we find we make more headway by recognition

of the patient's non-existence than by a long-continued working
with the patient on the basis of ego-defense mechanisms; the
patient's "false-self" can collaborate indefinitely with the analyst,
in the analysis of defense, being so to speak on the analyst's side in
the game. This unrewarding work can only be cut short profitably
when the analyst can point to and specify an absence of some
essential feature: like "you have no mouth, you have not started to
exist yet. Physically you are a man, but you do not know from
experience anything about masculinity." [1960, p. 45]

These recognitions of important facts, made clear at the right
moment, pave the way for communication with the "true self."
A patient who has had much fertile analysis on the basis of a
"false self," cooperating vigorously with an analyst who
thought this was his whole self, said to me, "The only time I felt
hope was when you told me that you could see no hope, and you
continued with the analysis."

In Cara's case, without knowing why, I said one day, "You
have no skin, so everything spills in." I said this because while
she was speaking about her overwhelming despair and need to
be held, she was also saying she could not stand to be close
because it hurt too much. As she spoke, there came into my
mind an incident that happened when as a student I had worked
for the Westminster Society of Mentally Handicapped Children
in London. I was at a Christmas party for the parents and
children, and a mother arrived with a baby at the door. The baby
was handed to me to hold while her mother removed her coat.
When I took the baby, she started to cry, and as I looked at her
little face, where the tears ran down her face, her skin started to
crack and then bleed. I looked and saw that indeed she had no
skin, her skin was just like a thin layer of tissue paper. I
immediately tried to make myself into a sponge to hold her
without pressure of any kind, and her mother then took her
again. But I will never forget the experience of holding this
small, skinless person with a small, round, crying mouth of
distress. Because this came to me so clearly as Cara spoke, I said,
"You have no skin." This one small statement opened the door
to the secrets, tamed Cerberus at the gate, and gave me (and
more importantly, Cara) access to her true self.

After this she often referred to "growing some skin" and after a while to developing a slightly thicker skin so that eventually everything did not tumble into her and it did not hurt so much if someone touched her emotionally.

I also briefly want to look at the therapist as a transitional object. Winnicott (1969) talks about this sequence:

1. Subject relates to an object.
2. Object is in the process of being found instead of placed by the subject in the world.
3. Subject destroys object.
4. Object survives destruction.
5. Subject can use object.

"The object is always being destroyed, the destruction becomes the unconscious backdrop for love of a real object, that is, an object outside the area of the subject's omnipotent control. Here non-relating by the patient is no longer a negation of relating, but an attempt to move from object-relating to use of the analyst as an object" (p. xxi).

Winnicott's emphasis here is that in this area of psychic functioning, what is involved is essentially "the paradox and the acceptance of paradox. The analyst and the patient are part of a larger total process in the clinical setting, in which each is being 'created' and 'found' by the other. It is this mutuality and reciprocity that creates a new dialogic dynamism which is more than merely object-relating in the transference" (p. xxi).

Winnicott talks about his analysis of the adult 40-year-old woman who came to him after an unsuccessful analysis of 6 years and needed to have, from time to time, some kind of physical contact with him, either holding his hand or even one finger. But eventually, it came about that if he held her head in his hands and she rocked quite rapidly (like a heartbeat), this seemed to fit the bill. The experience was crucial to the therapy, and the violence that led up to it was only now seen to be a preparation and complex test of the analyst's capacity to meet the various communicating techniques of early infancy.

In Cara's treatment this major turning point came when she attempted destructive behavior on the ward, in a setting I arranged that allowed her to regress and offered a new chance for forward development (which was rendered impossible initially by environmental failure). She did not get enough holding—even in the hospital.

Winnicott says that a "person at the point of need to regress to dependence can never manage it on his own, or use it, unless someone can sense this need in him and reach out to meet it. . . . There are persons whose primary care-taking environment has been so difficult that what they need to tell happened when they had not the necessary ego-capacities to cope with or even to know it. They could only register it. Hence, the responsibility of the analyst to reach out, and read and meet their need" (p. xxi).

I offered Cara a short hospital stay to help her to stop (finally) using the laxatives and to stop the rituals. I really had to stick my neck out to get her admitted. My supervisor did not want her in again but finally agreed because I begged.

Cara knew that the rules of the ward prohibited acting out—talking endlessly, but no acting out. It was often a very disturbed ward, and my supervisor felt that these rules worked for him (and usually they did).

While in the hospital Cara did very well, but as the defenses against feelings were not being used, her initial fears of annihilation started to surface. They finally overwhelmed her one weekend, while I was not there. Instead of using the nurses to talk, she slashed her wrists and badly burned holes in her veins and on her chest. I realized that she had been doing this all along, whenever we approached her real self with all its needs unmet. The true self knew that all holding hurt unbearably, and that it was not acceptable or lovable or even capable of making someone love her with all her "stealing, hurting, and messing."

Winnicott (1969) says, "The environment must be tested and retested in its capacity to stand the aggression, to prevent or repair the destruction, to tolerate the nuisance, to recognize the positive element in the antisocial tendency, and to provide and preserve the object that is sought and found" (p. xxiii).

Like Masud Khan, I found this thinking very helpful at this trying time because it helped me to reevaluate what looked like resistance or negative therapeutic reaction in a positive light.

Masud Khan (1974) writes, "It is my clinical experience that we offer one thing to our patients, namely the space, time, and opportunity to say their hurt and deprivation in the idiom that they are capable of, and yet simultaneously a contrary demand, namely of compliance with the rigidly organized regime of our techniques to speak to us in a way vastly beyond their means and capacity."

I discharged Cara from the hospital as I was required to, but with no punitive affect. I finally understood. I just said that she had to leave the hospital. She had not expected this; she was used to anger from the caretaker, and I was truly not angry. I was finally aware that she had to show me, one more time, the degree of her hurt, need, and fear—the extremely painful wounds she had inflicted on herself were nothing in comparison to the feelings that threatened to overwhelm her.

Much later she said that moment during which I briefly held her was the turning point for her. The actual holding held her through the subsequent fears that came when she resisted ritual and did not execute punishment. I had no conceptual idea at that time—I wish I could say that I knew that this small moment would change everything, but no! I did, however, see and recognize the results. Quite soon after, we got into more secrets and much more anger at me and how useless I was. However, this destroying of me as an object felt different to her, and she did not check every time if she had destroyed me. Nor did she always apologize for her need to be loved. In Winnicott's book *The Piggle* (1977), a small girl felt she did not exist after the birth of her brother—she was always compulsively tidy, putting all the toys away at the end of each hour. As she learned that she did exist, she was finally able to leave all the toys in a mess on the floor. "[She] went off with her father, leaving me with the mess and the muddle. She showed growing confidence in my ability to tolerate muddle, dirt, inside things, and incontinence and madness" (p. 105).

At this stage the totally inaccessible sexual material began to emerge. It felt like early material. She thought that she was mutilated and had misshapen genitalia, and she forbade any mention of words such as *sex*, *vagina*, *sexual intercourse*. When any of these words came up in her talk, she would retreat behind her hair and say, "I can't, I can't, you know." I persisted in saying these words at least three times each session, in spite of her protests.

It was difficult. Finally, in despair, I introduced a book, an

American publication of a small pamphlet that had many different drawings of many women's clitorises and vaginas. The book was designed for frigid women, to acclimatize them to looking at themselves and exploring their bodies. I gave it to her and told her to keep it as long as she needed, that this book was just to give her some idea of how many different ways women varied in their anatomy and that there were infinite variations that were all normal and beautiful. She kept the book for a year but stopped forbidding the language. In fact, she started to be able to use language and humor in a different way and began to tease me occasionally. Play surfaced in our relationship. Winnicott's (1971) most famous quote is:

> Psychotherapy takes place in the overlap of two areas of playing, that of the patient and that of the therapist. Psychotherapy has to do with two people playing together. The corollary of this is that where playing is not possible then the work done by the therapist is directed towards bringing the patient from a state of not being able to play into a state of being able to play. Whatever I say about children playing really applies to adults as well, only the matter is more difficult to describe when the patients' material appears mainly in terms of verbal communication. I suggest that we must expect to find playing just as evident in the analysis of adults as it is in the case of your work with children. It manifests itself, for instance, in the choice of words, in the inflections of the voice, and indeed in the sense of humor [p. xxvii]

Now, why Beauty and the Beast? It occurred to me while talking to colleagues at Reiss-Davis that this beautiful girl was at first repulsed and afraid of parts of herself that had been split off in early development, but like Beauty in the story, as she lived with Beast, and got to know him, she gradually was able to love and finally wished to remain with him always and be at one with him. So Cara was finally able to accept her whole self, grow to love and accept and understand her Beast, and be at one.

REFERENCES

Khan, M. (1974). *The Privacy of the Self*. New York: International Universities Press.

Klein, M. (1937). *Love, Hate, and Reparation.* London. Hogarth.

Winnicott, D. W. (1960). Ego distortion in terms of true and false self. In *Collected Papers: Through Pediatrics to Psychoanalysis.* New York: Basic Books, 1975.

_____ (1969). The use of an object and relating through identification. In *Collected Papers: Through Pediatrics to Psychoanalysis.* New York: Basic Books, 1975.

_____ (1975). Aggression in Relation to Emotional Development. In *Through Pediatrics to Psycho-Analysis,* pp. 208–209. New York: Basic Books.

_____ (1977). *The Piggle: An Account of the Psychoanalytic Treatment of a Little Girl.* New York: International Universities Press.

15

Passion Play: A Psychoanalytic Approach to Mind–Body Issues

Shelley Alhanati, Ph.D.

Tell it to a wise person, or else keep silent,
Because the massmen will mock it right away.
I praise what is truly alive, what longs to be burned to death.
In the calm waters of the love nights, where you were begotten,
   where you have begotten,
A strange feeling comes over you when you see the silent candle
   burning
Now, you're no longer caught in the obsession with darkness,
And a desire for higher lovemaking sweeps you upward.
Distance does not make you falter.
Now, arriving in magic, flying, and, finally, insane for the light,
You are the butterfly and you are gone.
And so long as you haven't experienced this—

To die, and so to grow, you are only a troubled guest on the
    dark earth.

                                          "The Holy Longing," Goethe

I doubt if anyone who has seriously embarked on a path toward psychic growth with another human being can be a stranger to the sense of wonder and awe at the beauty of the soulful, passionate, intimate exchanges that occur regularly between the two people who come together in this way.

In this chapter, I will attempt to describe a set of phantasies in which the lack of an adequate experience of containment (Bion 1962) and exchange of psychic passion early on in life is expressed through the relationship that is set up with one's own body.

I do not refer here to psychosomatization, but rather to the attack on the perception of the body and to an unconscious object relationship that can be set up, using the body to express the need for passionate interplay with an external object.

Winnicott (1971) beautifully describes the mother–infant exchanges that form the building blocks for psychic passion.

A baby is held, and handled satisfactorily, and with this taken for granted, is presented with an object in such a way that the baby's legitimate experience of omnipotence is not violated. . . . The mother is in a "to and fro" between being that which the baby has a capacity to find and (alternatively) being herself waiting to be found. . . . The baby begins to enjoy experiences based on a "marriage" of the omnipotence of intrapsychic processes with the baby's control of the actual. . . . This is the precariousness of magic itself, magic that arises in intimacy, in a relationship that is being found to be reliable. [pp. 112]

The absence of this kind of fundamental experience can often engender intolerable feelings of pain and longing for it. When this occurs, the infant needs someone with whom to feel this unbearably painful feeling, who can process that feeling, think about it, digest it, make sense of it, and return it in a more tolerable form. This is what Bion (1961) termed *alpha function*. The form it can take may be a soothing gesture, a smile, a meal, a verbal explanation, a laugh, or even a meaningful silence.

Sometimes, when there is no one around who can contain the feelings or perform the needed alpha function, the infant attempts to use its own body in place of another person, as part of a common infantile phantasy that the body is another external object with whom the infant is having a relationship. In other words, there is the hope that the body, as another object, will be able to perform those functions. Since the attempt to use the body for these containing and alpha functions doesn't work, the infant is again left with the unbearable pain. In this state of longing, coupled with envy and jealousy, the infant often feels desperately bereft with no recourse but to protect itself by trying to convince itself that this is not really a longed-for state, but it is rather a hate state. The phantasy of mind and body as a passionate, creative couple breaks down and becomes a phantasy of a sadomasochistic couple. Creativity and love are now hated; destruction and sadism are longed for. This reversal is what Meltzer (1973) terms perversity.

> Perversion (that is, characterized by perversity of purpose) is a very apt term for the sexual states of mind engendered by the leadership, momentary or fixed, of this destructive part of the personality. Being overwhelmingly influenced by feelings and attitudes of envy towards goodness, generosity, creativity, harmony, and beauty of good objects: towards their relationships and the "idealized family" they produce; the destructiveness takes two forms. In the first instance it seeks to destroy these qualities. But that is really too easy to afford much sadistic pleasure. The great satisfaction is envious competition, which does not emulate, but deviates. Negativism, as a quality of impulse . . . is not satisfied to refuse: it must do the opposite. "Evil be thou my good!" is its motto, and under this aegis it wills to create a world which is the negative of everything in nature, in the realm of good objects. [p. 92]

Betty Joseph (1982), in her discussion of addiction to sado-masochism, states:

> My impression is that these patients as infants, because of their pathology, have not just turned away from frustrations or jealousies or envies into a withdrawn state, nor have they been able to

rage and yell at their objects. I think they have withdrawn into a secret world of violence, where part of the self has been turned against another part, parts of the body being identified with parts of the offending object, and that this violence has been highly sexualized, masturbatory in nature, and often physically expressed. [p. 311]

Klein (1931) posits the infantile phantasy that destruction imagined to have been inflicted on the mother's body has also occurred in the infant's own body. It has been my experience that when there has been a failure to establish a basic holding and/or containing relationship with the caregiver (Grotstein [1994] distinguishes holding as the background object function and containing as the foreground), fantasies of intrauterine life also often involve sadomasochistic kinds of exchanges. The fear of the mother having damaged the fetus or having retaliated for its existence can be particularly prominent when actual physical or genetic defects exist. Exceptional talents or gifts can also exacerbate the anxieties concerning retaliation.

Piontelli (1990), in her observations of fetuses through ultrasound, found that up to the age of 5, children's conscious and unconscious memories of their intrauterine experience conformed quite realistically to the actual experiences that she had observed. After 5 years of age, the actual facts were colored with additional fantasies and made meaning of in light of later experiences.

An adolescent boy with a severe learning disability would repeatedly reenact a situation in which he was in the womb (under my desk), banging and screaming—"Ow! Ow!" He would take objects in with him, remove one essential piece, and put them back together, incomplete. There were times when the violence in the room was so destructive that I had to stop the session early. After this happened a few times, he found a way to express how he experienced the limits of my capacity to contain his feelings. He began to play that he was a sadistic surgeon, cutting his patients (my dolls) up into bits and pieces, sawing off their arms and legs, and removing their spinal cords. When they would complain, he would hit them and scream, "Shut up! I love hurting people!" He would then pretend to commit suicide.

A young girl with a severe learning disability would come to session and try to push her head into mine in the hopes that she could fuse our brains together and thus transfer my mental capacity to her. She would make "shell bowls" (fusing my name with the container) out of clay and sort out "good" bits and pieces of clay into one bowl "for safekeeping," and "bad" bits and pieces of clay into another bowl "to get rid of them." In her play she created elaborate fantasies of the two of us being inside a dinosaur's body and exploring her internal organs, looking for pieces that were broken and fixing them.

In these children, fantasies of intrauterine life also often involve the idea of having body parts damaged or stolen by the mother.

A very bright woman with bipolar disorder and certain congenital abnormalities, with a very severe tendency toward self-mutilative and sadomasochistic behaviors, reported a phantasy that her body had been sadistically mutilated in utero. Severe emotional, physical, and sexual abuse exacerbated her fears, with the patient believing that her internal organs were still in danger of being stolen from her by her family as well as by me. Whenever she felt misunderstood by me, she would cut, burn, and whip herself. When she felt I could not feel her pain, she would turn to her body for this function. It seemed on the one hand that she was trying to use her body as a sort of voodoo doll, doing to it what she would like to have done to me; but when her body would experience the intense pain, she felt that it, unlike me, had understood her, and she would feel relieved.

A man whose mother nearly died during childbirth, and who was born with a host of neurological, endocrinological, and metabolic disturbances, had a fear of engaging in any kind of intense, passionate interchange with me, out of concern that it would kill me. As he began to trust me and allow this process to occur, a transferential situation was set up in which I was felt literally to be his thyroid gland as a result of the regulating effects (both emotional and physical) of the therapy.

I have found that when patients have been able to enter into a dialogue about the difficulties of maintaining a passionate relationship within the transference and between different parts of their own minds, the relationship to the body changes greatly.

For example, symptoms of severe bulimia which had persisted for over 10 years in one woman disappeared immediately once she entered treatment and began to verbalize her intense object hunger and its implications.

In treating and supervising cases in which there are strong somatic as well as intrapsychic components to a symptom (e.g., learning disabilities, manic depression, etc.), I have often noticed that patients' tremendous relief and pleasure in seeing their minds change and grow is at the same time accompanied by an increasing anxiety and confusion over the difference between unconscious phantasy and concrete, physical reality. That is, changing what was previously thought to be a physical defect simply through a discussion of emotional experience can be misconstrued as evidence that other physical defects (actual genetic defects) must have been caused by hostile attacks (from another object or the self) as had been feared and suspected all along. Doctors, parents, teachers, and others involved with the case also often fall into the trap of perpetuating the splitting and confusion of mind and body, with the therapist generally placed in the middle and being pressured to choose sides between seeing the problem as exclusively biological or exclusively psychological in origin. Obviously, the extent to which the mother's or the fetus's unconscious phantasies can be one of the epigenetic factors influencing genetic or fetal development is still unknown.

The fear these suspicions arouse underlies many of the resistances encountered in the treatment of such issues. Any discussion of emotional experience becomes persecutory because mental growth stimulates a parallel malignant growth in omnipotent fantasies and magical thinking (as opposed to the sense of magic and omnipotence that develops normally in relation to our subjective experiences and internal worlds when there has not been a failure in the interplay between the caregiver and the baby).

One adolescent girl, K., exhibited a sense of numbness and withdrawal so profound that it mimicked the symptoms of some form of neurological deficit or mild atypical subtype of autism. In session she would not or could not talk to me, would rock gently in her chair, and would sometimes bang her head against the wall. When I provided her with small plastic toy animals and Play-Doh, she stared at them for a very long time and then proceeded to bury all the animals in the Play-Doh until they were completely hidden. She would sometimes cover her head with a newspaper when in session and sometimes talked to an imaginary friend, laughing in an odd manner. She hated coming to see me and found it impossible to stay in the session for more than 5 minutes. One thing she did love was my clock. She would put it next to her ear and rock to its tick-tock. I commented once that maybe it sounded like the tick-tock of a heartbeat. She smiled, curled up in the fetal position, and listened to the clock for the rest of the session.

She did this frequently in subsequent sessions, finding my clock very soothing, but still completely uninterested in having anything to do with me. Slowly, in later sessions, she began to hit me on my arm. She was violent with me; she was violent with her family; and she was violent at school. She got involved with gangs, talked of wanting to become pregnant, and for a while, seemed to be getting worse. What started out as a constricted, withdrawn deadness was now developing into violence, grandiosity, and a blatant disregard for others. She began to see me as a bizarre object, "a hairy gorilla with a wig and no socks" and seemed to be identified with me. She enjoyed being cruel to me, and enjoyed tearing apart my office, gleefully shouting, "You are my maid; now you clean it up." She would say things like, "You and I have something in common. We're both ugly." Interpreting her sadism (or the "gang inside of her," as she came to call it) was very tricky, because, as Gooch (1990) cautions, the destructive part of the personality often deliberately misconstrues what is said, as if one's interpretations directed toward it were instead meant for the baby. The baby then feels as if it has been the object of a sadistic attack. Technically, it became extremely important to be able to identify the different parts of her self and stay focused specifically on the part being addressed at any given moment and how the other parts were reacting to it (e.g., when the baby was being attended to, the "gang" would feel threatened, and would use intimidation, humiliation, mockery, and so on to reinforce her allegiance to it). As this began to be talked about and worked through, her mental capacities, which previously had been quite restricted, began to emerge in a most fascinating way. She began to come alive, to interact, to think, to perceive, and to apperceive. At about the third year of treatment, she began to have a sense of gratitude. She began to see me more as a mommy, sister, baby, cousin. She began to feel the pain of not having had a mother, but even more than that, she began to feel more of a primary experience of loneliness. She entered into a profound dialogue with her loneliness, the quality of it began to shift from one of despair to one of responsibility for herself. She began to develop the capacity, for the most part, to remain connected to others and yet contain her violence, and she began to grow into an alive, intelligent, and passionate young woman. She began to write beautiful poetry, draw, compose music, and dance. She became quite interested in school, was placed in an advanced program, and began taking college courses; her interpersonal relationships improved quite a bit.

Winnicott (1971) has spelled out the importance of the mother's presence in surviving the infant's fantasied attacks on her as a basis for helping the infant to distinguish phantasy from reality. That is, if I kill you in phantasy but see that you still survive in reality, then I begin to learn the difference between internal and external reality.

If this process failed to take place with an external object for K., she may have attempted to set up this relationship with her own body. That is, she may have attempted to attack her own body and then look to see if it was still intact—to set up the conditions to distinguish internal physical states from internal psychic states in order to begin to develop a primitive soma-topsychic reality testing. This would leave her vulnerable to believing that all of the self-hateful phantasies were true in physical reality. References to being a monster, being retarded, having a piece missing or broken, being punished by God for sins, were not seen as fears, anxieties, projections, or symbols of emotional experience; they were seen as actual facts.

Bion (1957) extends Klein's concept of the paranoid-schizoid position in which there are phantasied sadistic attacks on the breast, and states that "identical attacks are directed against the apparatus of perception from the beginning of life. This part of his personality is cut up, split into minute fragments, and then, using projective identification, expelled from the personality,'' (p. 266).

Bion then goes on to describe the fate of the expelled fragments:

> In the patient's phantasy, the expelled particles of ego lead to an independent and uncontrolled existence outside the personality, but either containing or contained by external objects, where they excercise their functions as if the ordeal to which they have been subjected has served only to increase their number and to provoke their hostility to the psyche that ejected them. In consequence, the patient feels himself to be surrounded by bizarre objects. . . . Each particle is felt to consist of a real external object which is encapsulated in a piece of personality that has engulfed it. . . . The patient now moves, not in a world of dreams, but in a world of objects which are ordinarily the furniture of dreams. The patient strives to use real objects as ideas and is baffled when they obey the laws of natural science and not those of mental functioning. [p. 266]

Similarly, I think K.'s attacks left her feeling that her body was a hostile, bizarre object that surrounded her, and she was baffled when the "mind" of her body obeyed the laws of natural science and not those of mental functioning.

The capacity for psychic passion and creativity requires the ability to sustain intense emotional experiences, to attack one's objects respectfully, to have parts of the self die and be reborn, to stay focused on the passionate love and creative desires behind these feelings, to have the courage not to withdraw or tone down the intensity of the feelings for fear of the damage they might do or of the envy they might inspire, but also not to get sucked into an orgy of destruction for its own sake. In short, creative passion requires the ability to make full use of another object as well as the self without losing the sense of the sacredness of human intercourse. The desire to find the self and the object endures.

REFERENCES

Bion, W. R. (1957). Differentiation of the psychotic from the non-psychotic personalities. *International Journal of Psycho-Analysis* 38:266–275.

_____ (1961). A theory of thinking. *International Journal of Psycho-Analysis* 43:306–310.

_____ (1962). *Learning from Experience.* London: Heinemann.

Goethe, J. (1814). The holy longing. Trans. R. Bly. In *The Rag and Bone Shop of the Heart,* ed. R. Bly, J. Hillman, and M. Meade. New York: HarperCollins, 1992.

Gooch, J. (1990). Personal communication.

Grotstein, J. (1994). Personal communication.

Joseph, B. (1982). Addiction to near-death. *International Journal of Psycho-Analysis* 63:449–456.

Klein, M. (1931). A contribution to the theory of intellectual inhibition. In *The Writings of Melanie Klein,* vol. 1, pp. 236–247. London: Hogarth.

Meltzer, D. (1973). *Sexual States of Mind.* Perthshire: Clunie Press.

Piontelli, A. (1990). *From Fetus to Child.* New York: Routledge, Chapman, and Hall.

Winnicott, D. W. (1971). *Playing and Reality.* London: Tavistock/Routledge.

16

A Brief Psychoanalytically Informed Intervention: Tommy, a Traumatic Neurosis in a Five-Year-Old Boy[1]

Carl Hoppe, Ph.D.

This is a description of a brief therapy of a 5-year-old boy and his parents.[2] The work illustrates various aspects of child therapy such as the importance of taking a family history, the role of the initial assessment and diagnosis, the integration of parent conferences with child therapy, the role of play as communication, the child's use of toys, the role of therapeutic interpretation and reconstructions, and developmental considerations in the assessment of child pathology.

---

[1]Excerpted from a lecture given at Airport Marina Counseling Service, Los Angeles, 1993.

[2]For reasons of confidentiality, the names of the family members and the parents' occupations have been changed. Nevertheless, the pattern of the case is actually as it was.

The parents stopped the therapy after thirty visits and nine months of contact on the basis of their satisfaction with Tommy's social behavior at the school playground and at home, and good academic reports from his first-grade teacher. They also felt considerable financial uncertainty, because as artists they felt particularly vulnerable to the city's economic troubles. From a therapeutic point of view, this was a kind of initial diagnostic consultation and a trial of therapy rather than a complete psychotherapy. Nevertheless, it illustrates the pervasive impact family trauma can have on an infant's development.

THE REFERRAL AND THE FIRST INTERVIEW WITH THE PARENTS.

Although Tommy was only 5 years and 3 months old at the beginning of treatment, this was his family's second attempt to obtain therapy for him. They came on the advice of their preschool because Tommy was unhappy at this, his third preschool. He had been unhappy at this and earlier preschools because he was frequently the brunt of the children's sand fights or the one who was teased and tormented. When he spoke, he told bizarre stories, which the other children ignored or ridiculed. He spent a lot of his time in isolated daydreaming.

The director of Tommy's respected preschool who sought my consultation said, "This is a weird kid. There's something wrong with him. The family has tried therapy before, but it did not help." This kind of referral is of special concern: the symptoms describe a possible pervasive developmental disorder or psychotic functioning, and it is a second referral of a young child in an intact family. If a child has problems and there are also glaring problems within the home, that is, in a way, more sensible. To all appearances, however, this was a working, cooperative home atmosphere. Something was wrong with the picture.

ASSESSING THE FAMILY'S CAPACITY TO USE TREATMENT.

Initially, I met with Tommy's parents to take a developmental history and to determine their ability to cooperate with a treatment that I sensed might involve a prolonged diagnostic assessment period. Quickly, I got a sense from the parents that outside of their home was a troubled extended family. Tommy had frequent contact with his paternal grandparents, who visit the parents at least twice a week including, Mother added dryly, all day Saturday. The father said of Tommy's paternal grandmother, "She's not very supportive." Mother said of the paternal grandfather, a World War II veteran, "He talks a lot about dying in general, and then Tommy hears this. He's always ill. He's always talking about World War II and people getting killed."

Father's sister had provided baby-sitting for Tommy in the first year of his life when Father lost his job and Mother had to go to work. Father said, "She's weird, been married several times unsuccessfully." Father is a commercially successful artist who is supported on a stipend from his gallery, based on his previous year's gross sales of paintings.

There had also been traumas within the home. When Tommy was almost 2½ years old, his mother became pregnant. When Mother was 6 months pregnant and preparing Tommy for his sibling-to-be, she took Tommy with her to the obstetrician to see ultrasound pictures of the new baby, believing that her second trimester pregnancy was progressing well. But the ultrasound revealed that the fetus had died. Tommy was present with Mother at this sorrowful discovery, which necessitated a third trimester induced abortion. Father was there and was horrified. While Mother stayed overnight in the hospital, he came home and, he said, clung to Tommy all night. Thereafter Tommy asked ruminatively about death; Father tried to turn his questions aside. Although both parents were distraught, the death of the unborn child was not mourned. Instead, Mother became pregnant again as soon as she could, and at the time of referral Tommy had a sister 14 months old.

Thus, from the family history obtained in the first session there is reason to expect that Tommy might be preoccupied with death. What did Tommy make of that obstetrician's office and Mummy's dead inside baby?

There were other traumatic factors. When Tommy was 8 months old, he broke his clavicle, allegedly in a fall while learning to walk. He was asthmatic, and had already had to be rushed to the emergency room twice for acute attacks. I would learn from Tommy that having an asthma attack is like being hit with a chair. He had ear infections so severe that his eardrum had burst twice. At age 3 years and 10 months he had an adenoidectomy. He also had tubes placed in his ears.

I met with Tommy and was pleased to discover that he was bright and articulate. In terms of cognitive and motoric developmental stages, he was well developed, except for social behavior. However, his thinking was odd, as the referring preschool director and the parents had indicated. Tommy's verbatim response to card 4 of the Children's Apperception Test provides an example of his peculiar associations. This card is a picture of an anthropomorphized kangaroo wearing a bonnet and carrying a picnic basket. A little kangaroo is in the mother's pouch, and another kangaroo is by her side riding a tricycle. When asked to tell a story about this picture, most 5-year-olds either enumerate the various parts of the picture or tell a simple story of a picnic. Tommy said:

> If that little kangaroo touched her mother, then the tricycle would come alive and turn out to a house and the mother would be a chimney and the little one would be one of these leaves at the top. [I read the story back.] No. If this kangaroo is on here and touches the mother, the tricycle will come and be alive and turn out to his house and the mother will be his chimney and the little one will be, um, the poppa. [I said, hopefully, "The tricycle comes alive and it goes to the house?"] No, it turns out to the house. If it touched the mother, the mother will become the chimney.

There were many stories like this one.

INDICATIONS FOR TREATMENT

The parents had said, "Tommy is just different. He loses himself in thought." I was beginning to understand what they meant. The mother said, "Tommy has a very vivid imagination. He comes up with bizarre stories. I can follow them, but I can see where someone else might not be able to—for example, he'll say, 'Mom, I just saw an airplane shoot down a bird,' and he insists on it. And there was a bizarre story about a teacher at a previous nursery school who was naked, but didn't play rough with the children." The parents also said Tommy is overconcerned about death. As an example Mother said, "He'll say things such as his sister fell down the stairs and she's not going to live long." Tommy was unhappy at school and he himself could tell me about that directly in easily understandable phrases.

The parents seemed concerned about Tommy, and they were bringing him to a second try after a disappointing first try at therapy, which did not go at all well. I was also surprised to get this amount of information about a family in just 2 hours. There was a remarkable clarity of communication in the family about the history and the problem. I had made some interpretive statements to them that resulted in increased communications from the parents, and I also noticed that as I talked with Tommy and questioned him about his stories, I got more stories, not fewer stories. Tommy had good intellectual development. In addition, Tommy said he wanted to continue sessions with me.

However, there was the degree of confusion, Tommy's social difficulties, a history of possible abuse, and one failed treatment. Counterbalancing the confusion, I learned that he was fascinated with his paternal grandfather's war stories and other stories of war and death, and he had frequently been exposed to his grandmother's ruminations about dying. Perhaps that helps to explain the weird story about the airplane shooting down the bird. The parents said he loved his younger sister, but then I recalled the story that she'd fallen down the stairs and would not have long to live. This seeming contradiction points to the development of the structure of defensive reaction formation.

I presented the parents with the idea that we would continue to meet at least weekly with parent counseling separate from Tommy's sessions, which would be held with him alone. I conceived of this initially as being an extended assessment of what Tommy's and their responses to treatment might be. I thought it likely that this family would soon be referred to a clinic setting for extensive therapy of more than one session a week. However, they were not yet ready for such a recommendation, nor was I sure what might be helpful. Having discovered several potential traumas, the possibility of a childhood traumatic neurosis seemed likely in spite of the oddity of Tommy's vocalization, and his rejection by peers.

THE COURSE OF TREATMENT

At the first therapy session, Tommy separated easily from Mother, and he started exploring his drawer of toys. At first he said something about making cotton. He said to make cotton you put it in a machine that grinds it up, and it can grind up people's legs, too. I told him it was hard for him to forget about death and injury. He said, "Well, it wouldn't really grind up the legs, it would only cause a little bit of breaking of bones." I told him I knew a boy who had broken a bone a long time ago. He replied that he broke a bone when he was 3 and they showed him a picture of it. He said, "Your skeleton is white." He wanted to make a train with his Play-Doh. I interpreted this to mean that he was trying to understand something by linking together his thoughts. As he made the Play-Doh, he became very thoughtful. Then he went to find something among the toys with which to shape the Play-Doh, but he got distracted by a large toy truck, which was in open view near his drawer of toys.

He put all his toys in this truck, and said, "This is a real truck. It has real controls and a boy could drive, but he has to be careful not to crush his mommy's car." I then noticed that he had not put the father doll in, which was underneath a pad of drawing paper. He talked about wanting to be his mommy as he followed the mommy-car with the truck, and I remarked that there was no daddy. At this point he again disrupted the play sequence by saying he "wanted [his] mommy." He maneuvered his truck into the waiting room. It was now near the end of the hour. In the waiting room Mother told me that after he first met me, Tommy told her that I had lots of answers and that he needed to talk to me.

In his fourth session, 3 weeks later, he began again with the large toy truck. The truck was waiting for its load. He said,

"Sometimes the truck doesn't have a load." The trailer has to be connected to the truck somehow, he said, and sometimes the trailer deposits its load early in the middle of the road (illustrated by disconnecting the trailer from the truck in play). The failure of the truck to carry and the premature or early deliveries of Tommy's play brought to mind the idea of the fetal demise with Mother's ultrasound and what Tommy might be making of it, as well as of his own X rays. Attempting to stay within his metaphor (Ekstein 1973–1974), at first I talked about the truck making "deliveries" and about how the driver would be upset if the toys were lost in the middle of the delivery, and how the children would be disappointed and scared too. Tommy experimented with these affects, discarding some of them and owning up to others as he replayed the truck scenes. While he made several attempts to reconnect the truck and trailer, I interpreted that he was also deeply curious about the connection between people. He then shifted his activities to my desk and became fascinated with a pen.

He wanted to see the insides of the pen, and I again said that he was deeply concerned about the insides of things and the connections between his own ideas. He responded, "Oh, I know that. After all, we're all started as babies, even Dr. Hoppe was a baby once." I said I thought he was also very concerned about his mommy and daddy. He began playing with the stapler, which is, after all, an implement that puts things together. He wanted to see the inside of the "stampler." He wondered if the "stamples" got hurt when they got bent, and "stampled" several pages of his drawing pad. I interpreted this play to be his expressing concerns about the ideas of penetration and aggression, and he remained deeply concerned with his mother's insides and, possibly, the damage that could be done these by intrusive daddy-pens. He said he'd use that "stampler" to defend himself against a burglar by "stampling" the burglar's finger. Thus, he may have experienced my inexact interpretation as impinging, as a burglar might.

Father brought Tommy to the next session. In the consulting room Tommy began with a made-up word, which he insistently announced several times. I could not understand it at first, but I did say that it was important to Tommy that I consider this word seriously. Finally, I got the idea that he had eaten a yellow lollipop and thrown the paper into the trash. He was attempting to condense all these ideas into one neologism. He was very pleased with my understanding, and resumed playing old familiar themes. He became preoccupied with a detail on a toy car. "Know what that is? That's a gut ripper," he announced. He said the car could back into the truck (a symbol for mommy), and rip it up. There was also something about his own bodily emissions and their explosiveness, which suggested that he was considering infantile ideas of anal reproduction.

It was important to him to get the gutter, as he was now calling it, off of the car. Bad men would park the truck; it would be a bad truck; they'd take the gutter inside the truck and steal it. Once inside the truck the gutter would kill the men. I said that there was something daddylike about this car-with-gut ripper, and as Tommy talked about the gutter, he clutched his crotch as if to confirm the symbolic equation between this penetrating thing and his theories of sexuality. I remarked that the gutter went inside of people, and he said, "There's really no such thing." I said, "No, there is no such thing, but there is something familiar about it." Again he disrupted the play to go into the waiting room, to check on Father, this time. But thereafter he became preoccupied with the office equipment.

He put the truck up on the secretary's desk. As he rolled it around in the waiting area, he announced that he was "the management." And he had to "have a key," and he was going to "sharpen pencils." He jabbed a pencil into the lock on the desk and broke it off. I pointed out that there was something similar about the key, the pencil, the "stamples," the paper clip we used to extract the broken lead from the lock, and also a door stopper, which he had become preoccupied with. They all could go into something else. He was preoccupied with the locks for the rest of the hour. I related this important concern to a time when he had been concerned about Mommy's inside baby, which had not been born, and how sad and frightening that had been. It must have seemed that the doctor said nonsense and then Mommy cried and the baby went away. "You can be the management now," he replied as he opened up the "stampler" and observed, "Oh, there's more stamples in it than last week. It made babies."

These curiosities about babies and insides dominated the subsequent hours as well, for Tommy showed excellent memory for the contents of his sessions. He was often interested in the pencil sharpener, which he said "shrunk the pencil" or in how keys fit into locks. Over and again I showed him his preoccupation with the inside of things, and especially the inside where the babies are and what happens to them.

Later, in his ninth session, Tommy said he wanted to be a paleontologist. He got a small truck out of his own box of toys. He was satisfied with using the little truck from his own toy drawer instead of the big one, and it now carried people inside of it instead of the big truck. Although he was still interested in the inside of things, the "gut-ripper" play, the talk about killing people, and the thinly disguised interest in inside babies was now displaced onto dinosaurs. Thus, he seemed to have some additional layers of defense as he expressed the same kinds of concerns in a more sublimated form.

Sometimes he asked philosophical questions that I cannot exactly remember, such as, "What does life mean?" To these I responded, "I don't know, Tommy, let's talk about it." He was a much, much calmer child by this time. He tolerated and enjoyed the full consultation time with me without having to bolt to the waiting room.

Later that week I saw the parents for the eighth parent conference. Father was elated but at the same time quite anxious. Mother was calm. In the previous parent conferences we had discussed their problems with marital intimacy, their discordant role expectations, and their lack of mourning or even acknowledgment of the loss of a baby-to-be 2½ years earlier. They both spoke of this loss and what it meant to them. However, in this session Mother said that the father wanted to hear about Tommy. I noticed that she was talking about the father as though he were a child, unable to speak for himself. She said he was very concerned about Tommy, but before I could even respond to this, as if from out of nowhere, Father began to describe a film of Neil Armstrong landing on the moon.

In an excited, elated state of manic denial of underlying anxiety, Father talked at length about how the astronauts had landed a paper-thin craft, dressed only in underwear, guided by primitive computers, ignoring one warning signal after the next as they went. Not knowing if his breathing suit would work, Neil stepped onto the moon's surface believing he might sink into the dust never to return. But on the Moon's surface the astronauts talked to God and were transformed by the beauty they saw. Once home, they divorced their wives and became artists.

As Father spoke in this ecstatic, tangential fashion, I felt myself sinking. I thought, "What am I going to do with this strange tale?" However, I commented on his obvious excitement and guessed that this story must have personal meaning for him. He seemed pleased to have told his story, but slightly embarrassed by it. His wife looked entirely baffled and distressed. Struggling to relate Father's communication to the therapy process, I said:

> When you come to see me you don't know what is going to happen. It's like taking your boy into inner space. In the psychologist's office, you don't know if you're going to find out if he's a super-phrenic [Anthony and Cohler 1987] or a schizophrenic. The transforming moment in the astronauts' lives took a lot of work, years of preparation, and many people's efforts, and it worked. In the psychologist's office you hope for a transformation too. Although now Tommy is the focus, your own lives and your way of working with him must change. And like the men stepping on the moon, you don't know whether the boy will disintegrate into psychosis or whether he will become a creative or gifted person, or an ordinary boy.

The father looked at me wistfully and misty-eyed. In a pensive way he said, "I don't understand you. I don't know what you do. You kind of sprinkle fairy dust on us and we all get better. Even Ginny and I have gotten closer." Ginny gasped and blushed. He said, "Oh, I didn't mean anything by that. You're a very serious guy. It's just that I don't understand what you do; it just seems to work." Is it necessary to understand why interpretations or mourning relieve a person for that person to experience genuine relief? Do we have to understand how aspirin works to get relief? I told Father that to more fully understand, he would need many more consultations than we had had until now.

Everybody in the conference heaved a sigh of relief and began talking more specifically about what Tommy was doing, and about the parental relationship. Mother felt warmer toward Father. She noticed he no longer sought the weekend companionship of his parents as much as he formerly had. Together they felt that Tommy was doing well. As I had observed in my office, they also reported he was now playing more appropriately at home and at preschool. His peers now cooperated with him in play, and he enjoyed them.

They wanted to discontinue by the end of August or the beginning of Tommy's first-grade year. However, they accepted my recommendation to continue for a while to consolidate the gains we had made. I felt it would be several months before we would know whether to discontinue on the basis of having made adequate gains, or whether to continue as we were doing, or if it would be necessary to increase the frequency of Tommy's sessions. If Tommy maintained the gains made for some time, we could conclude that he was responding to reworking in therapy a traumatic situation, namely, the demise of the baby and his family's reaction to it.

By the beginning of October Tommy was dealing with oedipal themes. He was angry and jealous about Mommy and Daddy's date night; he denied that Mommy is Daddy's girlfriend. We talked about his fears of retaliation if Daddy knew what he was thinking and about date night. He voiced fantasies of being a daddy one day and what toys he would provide for his children, but regressed from this, saying, "Sister is the only hope to have children." Thereafter he reported, "I'm not scared of the dark anymore." These conversations, in the midst of lots of sloppy spilling of marking ink all over, indicated his defensive regression from the competitive wishes about Poppa to the earlier pleasures of smearing and messing. But the regressions were short-lived and contained within the therapy. School reports, playground reports, and home reports were satisfactory.

Although I thought it would be a good thing to see him longer, the parents were beginning to feel the financial pinch the artistic community felt first, of diminishing disposable income in the city. They felt they needed to protect themselves against the expense of psychotherapy and opted to discontinue, but to call me if they needed me again. I felt that this little boy had really consolidated his gains and that he was, in fact, going to be able to weather the first grade and subsequent challenges. In the middle of second grade, the parents called again to seek my opinion about having Tommy tested for a gifted track at school or moving him to a new teacher because they felt the current one did not hold his interest. I have not heard from the parents again. I can imagine that at some time, such as the resurgence of drives near puberty, further treatment will be needed. However, Tommy's life had improved dramatically for a significant period of time. The younger sister flourished; the boy flourished, managing things well; the marital relationship of the parents improved.

DISCUSSION

Tommy had numerous traumatic injuries and illnesses, but the event that shaped his odd behavior seemed to be his viewing with Mother the ultrasound of his sibling-to-be as Mother and her doctor discovered the death in utero of the 6-month-old fetus. All the doctor's remarks and everything the adults did and said at that anguishing and scary moment were but frightening gibberish to Tommy, whose personal reactions were overlooked by his distressed and horrified parents. His mother went to the hospital overnight, and the agonized father clung to Tommy "all night," communicating a further sense of imminent danger in what he intended to be loving protection and comfort.

Tommy's weird statements, which so alienated his playmates, were an echo of the original procedures and words that mystified and frightened him. He was not fully with the world of playmates, but was inwardly preoccupied with thoughts of dying or illness. After his reactions had been recognized and he began to express them in play, and, moreover, after his parents recognized their own grief, which had been obscured by a new pregnancy, Tommy's compulsion to make mysterious pronouncements dealing with odd transformations and death (as in the airplane-is-shooting-down-a-bird story) simply lost energy. He returned to present-time boyish concerns, which delighted his parents and his playmates. His initial transference was to "Mr. Science," one of the "doctors" or wise-parent figures who has answers, and he put me to the test with made-up words. But these were tests he was pleased to feel I passed. He felt related to even when I felt my interpretations to be wild guesses. In complementary countertransference to his as yet unrecognized traumatized state, I was terribly frightened for him, lest he die too in the sense of the temporary "death" of his rational processes and his being overwhelmed by psychotic processes.

In retrospect, his mother's insistence that she could understand him even when others did not might have been an indication that his weird stories and behaviors were not a psychosis but a reenactment of a mysterious and frightening event. His arranging for me to understand nearly impossible condensations, such as the neologistic eating-lollipop, throwing-wrapper-away word, also indicated his wish to be understood and his belief in the transference that this would happen. Prognostically, he may or may not have the groundwork for a future neurosis, but he has been freed from his dead unborn sibling.

REFERENCES

Anthony, E. J., and Cohler, B. J. (1987). *The Invulnerable Child*. New York: Guilford.

Ekstein, R. (1973–1974). *Seminars in Child Psychotherapy,* II. Reiss-Davis Child Study Center.

PART VI

Issues of Transference and Countertransference in Psychotherapy

INTRODUCTION TO PART VI

Any clinician working with children and adolescents will attest to the fact that the therapist must continually consider the patient–therapist relationship in terms of transferential and countertransferential issues in order to build an adequate treatment alliance and, equally important, in order to be able to maintain the treatment. At the Reiss-Davis Child Study Center these factors are regularly considered in our Postgraduate Fellowship Training Program, as the fellows and their supervisors analyze transference issues and explore possible countertransference issues stirred up by working therapeutically with children and adolescents. This "stirring up" of unresolved issues often leads therapists into their own therapy or analysis, making them even better equipped to deal with their patients.

In this section, these powerful dynamics are extensively addressed in a series of chapters that explore the evolution of transference and countertransference issues as the relationship between therapist and patient unfolds.

Chapter 17, "The Therapeutic Issues of Transference and Countertransference in the Play Therapy World," by Carol Francis, examines transference and countertransference during play therapy as an invaluable tool in aiding therapists to understand the world of children. This chapter introduces seven useful classifications of child transference with associated countertransference processes as they appear in play therapy. Case studies of four children illustrate each classification, making the techniques and dimensions of transference work with children come alive.

In Chapter 18, "Therapeutic Impasses: A View from the Theory of Self Psychology," Estelle and Morton Shane address the inevitability of therapeutic impasses and, through case description, offers the reader a lens to view how the reparation process can begin. Shane describes the treatment of a young woman who, after several years of analysis, experienced and recovered from a therapeutic impasse that propelled her into a pronounced and upsetting silence.

In "A Relational Perspective on What Is Healing in Therapy" (Chapter 19), Irene Pierce Stiver and Jean Baker Miller, founder of the Stone Center at Wellesley College, describe the "relational model," a specialized approach used at the Stone Center that looks at the communication and reciprocity that take place within the intersubjective space of the therapist–patient dyad, and apply it to case material.

17

The Therapeutic Issues of Transference and Countertransference in the Play Therapy World

Carol A. Francis, Psy.D.

Diligent work with insights gained from transference and countertransference produces profound changes in children during play therapy. This chapter clarifies how work with transference and countertransference during play therapy helps therapists move into the arena of each child's internal hidden or forgotten worlds. These processes also shed light on how each child perceives and relates to the external world. Without the use of these processes, structural change, deep exploration, and disclosure of unconscious or split-off material are less accessible. Discovery of unknown or denied patterns, resolution of reactions to traumata, resolution and reworking of developmental glitches or lags and other complicated personality states also remain less attainable to therapist and child alike.

The model presented in this chapter discusses seven classifications of transference and countertransference as they appear during play therapy. The discussion of these seven classifications is illustrated by four children and their work in play therapy. You will meet Sarah, a misbehaving 9-year-old desperately seeking love; Nate, an anxious and aggressive second grader; Scotty, a learning-disabled fifth grader; and Pedro, a highly sexualized 4-year-old. After studying classifications illustrated by these four cases, the play therapist will have a theoretically sound and pragmatically applicable understanding of transferential work with children to guide the therapy through many deep and evolving sessions.

CLASSIFICATIONS OF TRANSFERENCE

Table 17–1 outlines the various classifications or manifestations of transference that may become present within the therapeutic relationship. Any type of transference can be used by the child patient to *resist therapeutic process* or *resist change*. In contrast, any type of transference can also be used to *communicate* something to the therapist. Sometimes the transference is used simultaneously to resist and communicate to the therapist. In any case, recognizing both the presence of the transference and its purpose helps the therapist decode the child's material and promote change.

The seven classifications of transference discussed are actually seven different angles or perspectives from which to view the patient's transference reactions. Because a child may manifest more than one type of transference at a given moment, the therapist must choose which transferential issues most need to be interpreted at a given time. The therapist may attempt to address all of the transference reactions simultaneously or may determine that one of them has overriding significance and should be addressed first or solely. The following discussion of each classification of transference will help the therapist determine which transference response is dominant and which to address.

Classification 1: Transference as Positive and Negative

The first classification of transference is the patient's positive or negative reactions to the therapist. Love, idealization, appreciation, trust, compliance, and other positive reactions might be positive transference.[1] Hate, rebellion, fear, suspicion, anger, denigration, retaliation, power struggles, or avoidance might be manifestations of negative transference. Table 17–2 outlines how positive and negative transference can be used to resist or communicate in therapy and how countertransference might be used to detect these types of transference processes.

Sarah was a 9-year-old who had been molested twice before the age of 3 and had experienced sexual play with a teenage boy around age 4. She was especially femininely cute with large, hazel eyes, soft, waist-length hair, and delicate features, but she acted tough and rebellious, "like a boy" (described one teacher) at school and home. She would steal from other children and lie without apparent conscience. She would yell back at her teachers and guardian and scream her protests without restraint. She would deface school property with deliberate revengeful destructiveness.

Her legal guardian, the maternal grandmother, acted responsibly toward Sarah's needs. However, she was harsh and punitive. Grandmother rescued Sarah, at age 6, from a series of foster homes that proved unstructured and unsafe. Sarah had been 3½ when removed from her mother, who often unsuccessfully attempted to recover from substance abuse, legal entanglements, and reckless living arrangements.

Sarah responded to other adults who were harsh, distantly firm, or punitive in the same rebellious manner. However, she never displayed her anger, rebelliousness, or unruliness to those whom she generally considered gentle, reassuring, and emotion-

---

[1]Not all reactions of the patient toward the therapist are considered a product of transference. Many processes occur between the therapist and patient and transference is one among the many. However, throughout this presentation, reactions discussed are considered to be transference.

TABLE 17-1. Classifications of Transference

Classification of Transference	Transference as Resistance	Transference as Communication	Therapist's Reaction— Countertransference
Positive and negative	Positive and negative transference to stop therapeutic process	Positive and negative transference to reveal, explore, and rework	Positive and negative reactions to self and to patient
Repetition of real events, relationships, and patterns	Repetitions that prevent working through or moving forward	Repetitions that reveal, explore, and rework past events, relationships, and patterns	Awareness of being perceived as someone associated to patient's experience; awareness of being involved in repetition of events
Developmental issues and processes	Fixation at or regression to a stage of development that prevents progress	Developmental processes, issues, relationships revealed to assist exploration and reworking of such issues	Complementary and concordant reactions that resemble the actual/perceived or wished-for parental reactions or childhood experiences

Pathological features (personality disorders, mood disorders, etc.)	Maintenance of pathological features as ego-syntonic or defensive in nature, resulting in resistance to change	Manifestation of pathological features for purpose of revealing, exploring, and reworking	Specific countertransferential responses typically associated with profile of the specific pathology
Emotional processes or states	Specific emotional responses that are aimed at maintaining psychological status quo or making change difficult	Emotional responses that facilitate the revelation, exploration, and reworking of issues	Empathic resonance with emotional responses or defensive reaction against emotions expressed by patient
Impulse processes	Impulsive processes that work against change or respond in a distressed fashion to change	Impulsive process as reflective or part of developmental processes, thus supportive of or motivating change	Resonance with impulsive processes or defensive responses to impulses manifested by patient
Existential quests (love and belonging, meaningfulness and destiny, death, disillusionment, disappointment)	Fear or hesitation to confront issues associated with the specific existential issue	Motivation by existential quest to confront, explore, and resolve issues	Therapist's personal existential phase, goals, values, etc., will be triggered, revisited, challenged, reconfigured

TABLE 17-2. Positive and Negative Transference

Classification	Resistance	Communication	Countertransference (examples)	Case Examples
Positive Transference Appreciation, trust, idealization, compliance	Positive reactions to therapist used to avoid issues	Positive reactions to therapist reflect actual or wished-for experiences or relationships	Possible feelings of overconfidence, being idealized, feeling superior, erotic or love reactions	Sarah's compliance and persistent sweetness as transference from idealized image of abandoning mother
Negative Transference Hate, rebellion, power struggles, suspicion, devaluing	Negative reactions to therapist used to avoid issues	Negative reactions to therapist that reflect actual or dreaded experiences or relationships	Possible sense of devaluation, self-doubt, anger at or power struggle with patient	Nate's yelling and screaming protesting coming to therapy

ally giving toward her. Her transference reactions would follow these patterns.

Sarah never displayed any negative reactions or behavioral complications with me. Accordingly, I felt at ease being gentle, emotionally responsive, and warm toward her even when firm limits were needed. In fact, Sarah was surprisingly loving, unrestrained in her gestures of affection, and eager to observe all rules—stated or unstated. She tested limits but responded quickly and easily without engaging in the extreme power struggles or protests she manifested elsewhere. She played creatively, mutually, and gently at all times. Sarah would not steal from me and would choose to refuse politely to answer a question rather than have to lie.

Sarah actively pursued my favor. Transferentially, she seemed to view me with the same idealistic and loving images she had of her mother, whom she had not seen for 6 years. Therapy was to be a world of perfection and love, and she would not let anyone, including herself, or anything violate the sacred relationship.

I considered over many sessions whether such positive transference was predominately defensive in purpose or communicative in nature. Was Sarah sabotaging therapy so that no exploration of her angry, unruly, or rebellious side could occur by being defensively and artificially good? Or was she reconstructing a fantasized or actual loving bond with her mother? If Sarah was defensively using positive transference to resist the therapeutic work, I would need to interpret actions, play, words, or conversations as attempts to hide "the bad, angry Sarah from the therapist" or avoid "the aggressive, demanding Sarah, who often wanted to hurt or retaliate," for example.

If, on the other hand, Sarah's positive transference predominately communicated need, wish, and actual or fantasized memories, my responses would need to focus on the nature of the carefully protected and blissful world and relationship that Sarah created and maintained tenaciously in therapy the way she wished she could have been able to do with her own mother. After many months of decoding, exploring, and testing, I confirmed that the positive transference was predominantly communicative and constructive in nature, even though the defensive aspects of the positive transference would likely need to be addressed much later in therapy.

Session after session was spent with Sarah applying play makeup to my face with me reciprocating. These hours were intimate and playful but rarely accompanied by deep revelations or profound psychological discoveries. The time felt rich and moving, but I worried that positive moments shared were preventing the negative internal processes from being resolved. However, it later became obvious as therapy progressed through different stages, that this makeup play was a vitally significant mirroring transference of the most idealistic and positive nature, and was an absolutely necessary experience for Sarah, who basically lived deprived of warm, intimate, untroubled relationships. Through her transference and behaviors Sarah created and maintained a relationship. In this relationship she could be enjoyed and treated with gentle mirroring from a transferentially idealized individual (therapist) who was also realistically engaged in Sarah's need for warmth and liking (Kohut 1971, 1984).

As Freud described as early as 1895, and later clarified with considerable caution, therapists have reactions to patients that often arise from unresolved or unconscious personal issues. Such countertransference interferes with therapeutic work, and the conscientious therapist must appropriately and aggressively resolve potential hindrances for the welfare of the patient's progress (Freud 1915, Langs 1973). Countertransference subsequently is also viewed as a useful tool whereby the therapist can detect subtle, complicated, or unusual processes emanating from the patient by way of transference, projective identification, or intersubjective processes (Hedges 1992). At any given moment, therapists need to examine countertransference responses as potentially personal and interfering reactions or as potentially enlightening and informative hints (see also Heimann 1949, Racker 1972, Searles 1965).

Countertransference as a tool can decode positive transference that is either communicative and constructive or resistant and defensive in nature (Greenson 1979). Positive transference that is communicative and constructive, for instance, often will trigger sincerely warm, affectionate, and bonding affect. At these times fluid empathic responses are stimulated by the patient, and the therapist may often respond with spontaneous feelings of warmth toward the patient. Positive transference that is resistant or defensive in nature can be detected by the therapist's countertransferential feelings of being manipulated by, artificially valued by, or politely kept at a distance from the patient.

Countertransference reflecting the therapist's unresolved issues distorts the patient's messages. When patients express positive transference, therapists sometimes feel awkward being valued or loved, or become grandiose because of deep wishes to be admired. Similarly, if negative transference is present, a therapist may be immobilized by fear of anger, conflict, or devaluation or may become defensively combative. Also sometimes therapists wrongly overemphasize a patient's positive transference to avoid the inevitable eruption of negative transferences, and vice versa.

Nate, in contrast to Sarah, epitomized negative transference. He hated me, calling me "stupid" and therapy a "boring waste of time." He screamed, cried, and hung on to his mother's legs, refusing to enter the play room. Once "dragged" or "coerced" into the play therapy room by his mother and sometimes by me, he would scream as if being horribly tortured or would frenetically begin throwing himself or objects against the walls, furnishings, and me in angry, aggressive outbursts.

He had begun therapy at age 7 because his teachers, peers, and parents found him to be excessively aggressive, stubbornly oppositional, compulsively perfectionistic, and highly anxious. These negative responses would be a part of his transference as well as my countertransference. At first Nate determined that if he was compliant and cooperative during the sessions, he would soon not have to come to therapy. This is a prime example of positive behavior as an expression of negative transference. During this pseudo-positive phase, he demonstrated that he would not and seemingly could not attach words to any of his feelings, positive or negative. When he eventually realized that this was not freeing him of the awful shame and dread of therapy, he began to spend the hour before therapy and the first 15 minutes of therapy intensely resisting coming by kicking, screaming, refusing to move, and wrestling with his mother. Therapy sessions during this phase were dominated by screaming through the walls for his mother to take him home and physically attacking me and the room to the point where a 10-second physical restraint became necessary. He also would attempt to escape out the door or windows during this phase. I attempted to attach words to all the behaviors with the intent of eventually helping Nate describe how he felt instead of using actions.

After a few months Nate began to yell his hatred for me with clear but primitive language, until one day he screamed, "You are so stupid, you can't even help!" to which I screamed back, "You want me to help you with all that's angry and upset inside, but I'm too weak and foolish!" This type of dialogue continued for the remainder of the session, and then at the end I explained, "I am here to help you; I want you to learn to talk about how you feel; show me, tell me; I'm here to help."

The week following this session was calmer at home. More significant, Nate's mother seized an opportunity to help him put his anger into words as the therapist had instructed her to do. She told me in his presence during the next session, "He says he becomes filled with red inside when kids won't play with him at school, and that makes him want to hit them. I told him he was angry and showed him one way to be angry without having to hit." He protested coming into this session as well, but for the first time, he began to use symbolic play of soldiers filled with "red anger" fighting a mean, awful lady, only to end up dead in the "grave of anger." During the next session the "lady" became the "Queen of Anger," and the soldiers became the soldiers of truth fighting for the "God of Truth," which was Nate's identity in the play. If the soldiers landed on the Queen of Anger's platform, they were converted to "soldiers of anger who would lie and hurt others without knowing what they were doing." Eventually, all the soldiers died in the grave of anger, leaving the God of Truth undefended and having to fight for himself. The God of Truth temporarily killed the Queen of Anger, who later would be resurrected and joined by the "King, Prince, and Princess of Anger." The God of Truth, now soldierless, would be outnumbered but would "kill the Queen of Anger and the King, Prince, and Princess in the next session."

The description of this and subsequent sessions would illustrate how negative transference to me and the therapeutic endeavor was an inevitable and essential part of Nate's work in therapy. Initially, his negative transference was used to resist all therapeutic interventions or changes. Eventually, however, it became a clear communication of the depth and pain of his own struggle with negative processes, which had not found an effective outlet and containment in his daily relationships. He developed a linguistic and symbolic expression of his emotions, starting with anger, and eventually portrayed helplessness, shame, and anxiety.

Negative transference is never pleasant to encounter but is always essential to recognize and often the core representation of central issues for a patient (Klein 1927, 1928, 1955). Countertransferentially, negative transference might result in reactions of fear of retaliation, power struggles, counterattacks, anger, defensiveness, self-denigration, despair, helplessness, or avoidance. Effective work with negative transference will often depend on how therapists deal with negative processes from others and from inside themselves; nothing can replace thorough self- or professional analysis and supervision when negative transference is first encountered (Greenson 1979, Langs 1973, Searles 1965).

Countertransference may detect when negative transference is defensive when the therapist feels despair, helplessness, powerlessness, avoidance, fear, or the urge to senselessly counterattack. Negative transference used as a communication might be detected by more active reactions of counteranger or empathy for the pain behind the anger. Negative transference easily entangles many therapists into power struggles or urges to retaliate as well as into self-deprecating or powerless reactions (Francis 1991).

Unfortunately, negative transference often subverts therapists, especially if negative material feels personally threatening or if it seems to be a large threat to the therapeutic alliance. As a consequence, therapists often feel tempted to ignore the negative material or to overemphasize the positive material. Little progress, however, can be made in therapy if a significant quantity of the transference relationship, negative or positive, is avoided. Interpretive interventions when negative transference is present often result in reactions of openness, relief, therapeutic movement, or renewed therapeutic alliance. Dealing with the negative transference effectively can never be replaced by avoiding the negative or emphasizing the positive.

Classification 2: Transference and Repetition

Transference as a repetition or replication of past events, past relationships, or established patterns constitutes the second classification of transference. Actually, by our definition, all transference is a repetition or replication of events, relationships, or patterns (Fenichel 1945, Freud 1912). However, transference as repetition is discussed here as a distinct classification because sometimes the patient specifically needs to recognize that what is occurring in therapy is repetition and replication (Fenichel 1945, Freud 1914, Lacan 1981). Table 17–3 outlines how transference as repetition can be used to resist or communicate in therapy and how countertransference can be used to detect this type of transference.

Patients reenact their extratherapeutic life in a number of ways. In one instance, a child might begin treating the therapist the way he or she treats other individuals. As a consequence, the therapist gains an understanding about what it is like to be on the receiving end of the child's behavior. Countertransferential reactions to this type of transference process is considered *complementary* because the therapist's response is complementary to the patient's behavior (Racker 1972).

Transference as repetition experienced through complementary countertransference can be resolved in two ways: (1) repeated description of the patterns and repetition so they can be consciously perceived and eventually avoided, and (2) a therapeutic reparative relationship wherein the cycle of repetition is reenacted initially between the therapist and patient but is eventually stopped because the therapist recognizes the pat-

TABLE 17-3. Transference as Repetition

Classifications	Resistance	Communication	Countertransference (examples)	Case Examples
Repetition Transference as reenactment of real past events, relationships, or established patterns, perceptions, or processes	Repetition of past events, relationships, patterns that inhibit therapeutic alliance or therapeutic progress	Repetition that reveals to patient and therapist information about past events, relationships, patterns, etc.; aimed at healing or altering past issues	Complementary, concordant countertransferential reactions	Nate: Repetition of pattern that resists therapy but reveals pattern. Therapist: complementary reaction: mother to child.
				Nate: Repetition that reveals relationship. Therapist: concordant reaction: feeling inferior, similar to Nate.

tern, avoids participating in it, and provides healthier interactions. Since repetition compulsion, as expressed through transference, is often present because the individual has never been able to recognize and correct the processes inherent in the repetition, therapy becomes helpful in dealing with transference of repetition by both describing and altering the process within the therapeutic relationship.

To illustrate, Nate repeated his angry, oppositional behavior with all adults and children. Predictably, he would repeat this behavior with me. I had to be able to decode the nature of these repeated encounters and explain it to Nate, and to develop a healthier interaction with him over his anger and opposition. This occurred quite naturally when Nate's anger and opposition began to produce the same helpless and timid reactions in me as it did in his mother. When the complementary countertransference was detected and examined, it revealed that Nate was repeating this significant relationship because he wanted eventually to make his mother competent to endure and manage his anger, which she had not been able to do thus far.

Nate also wanted to learn to endure and manage his anger without being destructive, but had never met an adult who could be exposed to the intensity of his anger and yet be able to endure, manage, and remain present—not aloof and controlling as other adults had been. Once I recognized this process, I was able to become bolder but not controlling; be empathic to the anger but not inclined to cater unwisely to his angry demands; openly discuss the anger, without needing to pretend or coerce him out of it; be the direct object of his anger without feeling or manifesting any fear that his anger was big enough to permanently damage. These were the various reactions he needed from his mother. Therefore, during the course of therapy, I also attempted to help his mother and father resolve personal issues and modify responses that would break the cycle.

Alternatively, patients can create a *concordant* countertransferential reaction in their therapist by treating the therapist the way others treated them in the past or in a manner that will make the therapist feel exactly how they feel. Nate's brother was 7 years older and very competitive, as was Nate's father. Both his brother and his father would play competitive games with Nate and then gloat over winning. This contributed to his perception of being "stupid" and a "loser." During the second phase of therapy, which lasted for about 6 months, Nate would play competitive games with me. Whenever he lost, he would lie about the loss or begin to cheat in order to change the inevitable loss into an artificial win. After such "wins" he would spend a few minutes telling me how stupid I was and how I could not win at anything. When he won, he also would gloat about his victory and belittle me for being so stupid.

Countertransferentially, this repetition created concordant responses in me such as inferiority, defensiveness, the urge to gloat over my victories, or to argue with and to demean Nate for losing. Such concordant countertransference provided a wealth of information about Nate's internal reactions and identity. I employed the information gained from the concordant countertransference by (1) describing feelings Nate experienced that he also created in me, (2) playing the role of the loser and describing feelings and reactions in that role as Nate fascinatedly watched and interacted, (3) choosing alternative responses that broke the repeated patterns Nate experienced with his brother and father such as fully and sincerely rejoicing with Nate when he won (Example: "Wow, Nate you won. That feels terrific doesn't it!") or recognizing how he felt when he lost without being demeaning, condescending, or patronizing (Example: "Gee, you hate it when you lose, don't you, because it feels so rotten inside.")

In summary, repetitive playing and actions are common in play therapy and provide the therapist with multiple opportunities to experience, decode, and work with the repetitive processes that entangle the child. Through complementary and concordant countertransference, the messages of the repetitive play and associated transference repetitions can be discerned and the information applied to various interventions in the play therapy arena.

Classification 3: Transference and Developmental Issues

Transference may also arise out of the child's developmental issues or processes. Therefore, a detailed understanding of various developmental models and associated issues that characterize each stage is necessary to detect which developmental process is being expressed in the transference. Working with children in particular demands that the therapist have a clear grasp of many models of development, since developmental processes are present to even a greater and more immediate degree than with adults. Sigmund Freud (Hall 1954), Anna Freud (1937), Erik Erikson (1963), Margaret Mahler (1968), Melanie Klein (1921, 1928, 1984b,d), D. W. Winnicott (1965a,b, 1971), Daniel Stern (1984) and other theorists provide valuable information concerning how developmental issues become portrayed through transference.

Table 17–4 outlines how transference that pertains to developmental issues can be used to resist or communicate in therapy and how countertransference can be used to detect this type of transference.

Inevitably, developmental issues symbolically and literally affect the drama in play therapy. Transference associated with these developmental issues can cast therapists into the role of parents or other significant individuals who perhaps failed to manage the developmental issues in the past or present. The child's transference may also cast the therapist into the child's role when the child has failed to settle developmental issues due to anxiety, confusion, or poor coping skills. Complementary countertransference, as described earlier, will likely be experienced in the first instance, and concordant countertransference will be evident in the second.

Often parents bring children to therapy when a current developmental task is proving too difficult or unnerving to manage at home. For example, adolescent sexuality or adolescent self-assertion, toddlerhood toilet training and power struggles, or sibling responses to a newborn represent a few developmental issues parents typically find uncomfortable to resolve. Consequently, parents view the therapist as a substitute who will address the associated developmental hurdles with their child. The transference–countertransference generally becomes complementary in nature in these situations.

In other cases, past developmental tasks may have been poorly addressed and not resolved positively. As a consequence,

TABLE 17-4. Transference and Developmental Issues

Classification	Resistance	Communication	Countertransference (examples)	Case Examples
Developmental Issues or Processes	Fixation at or regression to a developmental phase utilized to avoid dealing with other developmental issues or therapeutic process	Developmental issues or processes expressed through the transference process May reveal patient's level of development, issues pertaining to a developmental phase or issue, or attempt to resolve issues pertaining to a developmental issue	Complementary: therapist resonates with imagined, experienced, or hoped-for mother, father, etc. while the patient remains the "child" in the specific developmental phase Concordant: therapist resonates with patient as "child" during the associated developmental phase	Nate's transference associated to Freudian anal stages (retentive and expulsive)

subsequent development becomes compromised by previously missing, distorted, or incomplete developmental processes. Chronic immature behavior, regression to or fixations at a developmental phase, frequent reenactment of behaviors characteristic of an earlier phase, as well as current developmental tasks handicapped by failures at previous phases may be manifested. Typically in these situations, the developmental task of the past could not be managed well by the parents due to parental fear, unfamiliarity, unresolved conflicts and anxieties, or situational preoccupations such as divorce, traumas, other births, careers, and so on. The therapist in these situations often becomes the surrogate parent who must more ably discover, address, untangle, and more completely resolve the previous developmental issues. The therapist–child relationship in these situations, too, is typically characterized by complementary transference–countertransference dynamics.

Aspects of Nate's treatment were characterized by unresolved developmental issues. Apparently, the mother's conscientious, compulsive, harried, and anxious responses during toddler toilet training became a breeding ground for multiple developmental complications. While the complications were evident at the time of toilet training, they became intolerable to parents and teachers when Nate entered elementary school. These complications developed into behavioral, personality, and social handicaps during the first 2 years of school.

Predictably, these difficulties at home and at school extended from developmental issues classically associated with the anal phase of development. According to the developmental schema of Sigmund Freud and subsequent theorists, this stage of development is the arena for issues of control, self-assertion, messiness or neatness, perfectionistic qualities, and pathological traits of obsessive-compulsive disorders. Control issues, power struggles, temper tantrums, compulsive and repetitive actions during art projects or academic tasks were evident in Nate at home and at school. Nate also manifested perfectionistic, tedious behaviors alternating with moments of extreme sloppiness that sabotaged successes. Throughout therapy, similar behaviors were manifested, and frequently transference became a central avenue for expressing and working through the anal developmental processes.

One session symbolized Nate's developmental issues associated to anal expulsive and retentive traits. As described, Nate had actively been "killing" the members of the "Family of Anger." He began this particular session with the same activity, but this time his killing was controlled, hesitant, and meticulous. Transferentially, I was then perceived as too controlling and interfering. I experienced this transference in a complementary countertransferential manner by feeling and acting unusually controlling and critical. This controlling and interfering transference was a blending of his mother's and father's reactions to his anger and self-assertion.

During the first half of this session, he frequently would stop the play to reorganize his "soldiers" and resume the play with an unannounced explosive attack on the Queen of Anger. Finally, the Queen died; Nate apparently was tired of her unrelenting ability to be resurrected and decreed her death without any true signs of battle but with a definite and controlling proclamation. He made it clear that I was not to argue about his proclamation, even though no clear battle had been won between his soldiers and the Queen of Anger.

Urgently, he needed to use the bathroom. We rushed out of the room to the restroom and soon thereafter ran back into the therapy room. Suddenly, the entire room was under siege. Legos were thrown up in the air with abandon such that the carpet, chairs, and couches were covered with sprinkles of his "riches." He was now, I told him, the "richest man in the world who could recklessly throw all his money [Legos], that is, his spoils [metaphor for 'poop'], around and keep all the world in a shambles as a consequence."

With the Legos entirely dispersed, he focused on the new washable watercolor paints. He wanted all the colors to ooze from their containers onto his eager hands. At first he was controlled and careful with the messy paints. But after his first drawing, which he later clearly rejected, he insisted that his hands be filled again with the gooey, thick liquid now called "poop paint." Four colors were combined, creating a dark brown, thick slime, which he squished together sensuously and gleefully between his hands. He triumphantly splashed the poop paint on the next paper, splattering everything within range with "diarrhea poop paint." This activity continued for 5 minutes until he insisted on using the bathroom to clean his hands. He cleaned the mess from his hands and showed no signs of the usual anxiety about "soiling" his clothes. His favorite painting looked like toilet water filled with loose bowels, swirled and thick. He had never wished to show his mother his productions after therapy until this day, displaying the painting with the pride and glee typical of children who produce feces for admiration and pride.

Notably, during the month after this session, all his teachers and his mother began to remark on how much less controlling, perfectionistic, and feisty he acted. Nate was also freer, lighter, more spontaneous and emotionally connected to me. His competitive play was not cruel, deceptive, or anxious as in past games. Something about the pleasure of being able to explosively produce something in which he could take great pride released some compulsive anxiety.

Classification 4: Transference and Pathological Profile (Diagnosis)

Transference reactions specific to diagnostic psychopathological categories are as apparent in work with children as with adults. For example, a patient diagnosed as suffering from some form of paranoia will eventually manifest transference reactions of mistrust, suspicion, and fear. Patients suffering from depression will eventually perceive therapists transferentially as helpless and depleted.

As therapists recognize the patterns and dynamics relevant to the diagnosis of a child, they can anticipate the transference patterns that will become evident within the therapeutic relationship. Therapists may also recognize certain countertransferential reactions, which may usually be considered indicative of specific diagnoses. Thorough understanding of a diagnosis facilitates the therapist's capacity to recognize, explore, and work through various transferential processes (Blanck and Blanck 1979, Fenichel 1945, Francis 1985, Anna Freud 1965, Horner 1982, Klein 1984a,b,c,d).

Table 17–5 outlines transference and countertransference reactions associated to disorder often diagnosed during childhood.

The child's transference perceptions associated to a diagnostic profile will reflect several factors. First, the child's transference may coincide with how the child perceives others responding to the disorder. Of course, the child's perception may be accurate or may be distorted. Therefore, the dynamics of the transference may accurately represent the responses others give the child or may only represent what the child distortedly fears or believes are their responses.

Sarah (diagnosis of Oppositional Disorder, secondary to Posttraumatic Stress Disorder) believed that I would stop seeing her if she became any sort of discipline problem during therapy. Her transference reaction was based on real events—three times in the past legal guardians disposed of her because she was too oppositional. Sarah also distortedly believed that being a "bad kid" intrinsically implied that she could only be accepted by bad people, and since I was categorized as good, she would never be genuinely accepted by me. Both of these transference reactions hindered progress in therapy and yet were central to many issues Sarah faced in everyday life; as a consequence, resolving and clarifying these issues required regular attention to the transference.

The second factor reflected in a child's transference is the manner in which it relates to patterns and dynamics of each diagnostic profile. As stated above, if a patient is paranoid, the transference will reflect the patterns and dynamics of paranoia. If a child is diagnosed with some type of anxiety disorder, transference will reflect patterns associated to the child's anxiety. Endings of sessions and vacations, for example, will trigger transference reactions in a child with Separation Anxiety. Sarah's diagnostic profile of Oppositional Disorder would be associated with transference patterns of power struggles, obe-

TABLE 17-5. Childhood Diagnoses and Transference

Diagnosis or Pathology	Typical Transference	Typical Countertransference
Learning disabilities	Anticipation of judgmental attitude Anticipation of inferiority/superiority dynamics Anticipation of rejection	Urges to patronize Urges to judge, compete, or demean Urges to subtly disrespect Responses similar to parents' (complementary) Feeling incompetent (concordant)
Anxiety diagnoses	Separation/abandonment Demanding of immediate comfort, perfectionism, or resolution	Reactions of urgency as if emergency present Urges to minimize (i.e., ridicule patient or use of compensatory defenses against anxiety in therapeutic process) or exaggerate (unrealistic identification with anxiety)
Eating disorders	Therapist as sufficient/insufficient Confusion of need vs. desires regarding therapist Urges to incorporate or purge therapist	Reactions of fear or dislike when feeling incorporated Reactions to overindulgences, overdemandingness, self-denial Reactions to confusion of needs vs. desires Reactions like patient's parents (complementary) or like the patient (concordant)
Disorders associated with psychosomatic processes	Child's perception of therapist as medical doctor as a form of transference	Inclination to address issues medically without due regard for complexity of psychological contribution to physical problems

dience–punishment dilemmas, and control issues. Diagnosis does not dictate transference but accurate diagnosis can help therapists anticipate the nature and pattern of transference.

Countertransference reactions may parallel the behaviors of those who have responded to the child's pathological patterns. This complementary form of countertransference helps the therapist understand the systemic patterns that have likely developed in the family in association with the child's pathology. When the child is the identified patient (that is, the individual in the family who personifies the pathology that is actually the pathological pattern of the entire family), complementary countertransference provides considerable information about the entire family system. For example, Sarah's Oppositional Disorder may actually mirror the power struggles and control issues apparent between her mother and her grandmother.

Countertransference that resembles the child's reaction to the pathology is defined as concordant countertransference. Under these circumstances, the therapist will begin to react to the child's pathology in the same way the child reacts overtly or covertly. For example, Nate hated to lose at any game because it stirred intense feelings of stupidity and failure. He would treat me as if I was stupid and would pretend that I was the only one who ever lost. I felt inferior, defensive, and compensatorily driven to prove I could win at the games. I was reacting concordantly, resonating with Nate's reactions to his fear of failing, his source of compulsive anxieties.

As illustrated in the next case description about Scotty, the therapist's task with transference work associated with a child's diagnosis includes the following.

1. Define and describe the nature of the diagnostic patterns that have affected the adjustment of the child to the world and the world to the child.
2. Examine potential primary or secondary causes of the child's pathological patterns as manifested through transference reactions and attempt to resolve patterns unnecessarily adopted.

3. Recognize and describe how behaviors, self-perceptions and interpersonal patterns have been directly and indirectly influenced by the pathological patterns as detected by transference and other tools.
4. Develop patterns of responses that do not recapitulate harmful responses to the pathology of the child.
5. Recognize and describe anxiety and disorientation experienced by the child when the therapist responds in unfamiliar ways and when the child is attempting to provoke familiar responses.
6. Maintain responses that are congruent with defined patterns of health despite the provocations of the child's pathological behaviors.

Scotty manifested clear signs of expressive language skills deficiencies. Officially, however, these deficiencies were not diagnosed as learning disabilities until late in the fourth grade, thanks to a conscientious teacher. Unfortunately, Scotty's self-perceptions became organized around the strong conviction of being "stupid," which had developed during the first 5 years of school. Peers would ridicule him regularly, and he began to believe that such ridicule was appropriate. Adults often would react out of pity and frequently would insensitively patronize him, or they would discount or ignore him.

Since Scotty believed that he was stupid, he developed a pattern of "stupid" behaviors that became problematic themselves. His self-esteem was low. He isolated himself from others. He refused to pursue learning activities that otherwise were of considerable interest to him because he was certain that he would be too stupid to understand the information. He also created a fantasy world wherein he was the "all-wise, all-knowing wizard of good" and also the cunning, cruel "underworld magician of evil." He created this world in which he would express his above-average intelligence even though he was certain that he was retarded.

He transferentially expected me to react with ridicule, as did his father and most male peers. At other times, he expected pity and infantilizing responses, which his mother and two older sisters unnecessarily lavished on him. When I did not act in accord with these transference expectations, he reacted with various behaviors intended to provoke such responses. For example, he became excessively immature and silly to convince me that he was indeed stupid, and became even more anxious when I did not respond to him with the familiar ridicule or pity. But following this period of anxiety and confusion, Scotty began to express the creative and intelligent sides of his personality, which he had hidden within his complex fantasy world. As I interacted with this side of Scotty, the previous self-perceptions gradually began to conform to the reality of his intelligence and the handicap of his disability.

Classification 5: Transference and Emotional States

Sometimes emotional states such as love, anger, sadness, or fear become the primary focus of transference responses. In these situations the emotion itself, and not the cause or object of the emotion, is the most important element to be addressed. For example, if Nate has an explosive temper and expresses anger toward the therapist, the quality and experience of the anger might be more appropriately described or explored at that moment instead of its potential cause. In these circumstances the therapist might describe, "When you feel anger it becomes very big and powerful inside you, sometimes scaring you or scaring off others."

Sarah never wanted to let adults know that having possessions confiscated as a means of discipline bothered her. She would pretend to have no desires or attachments to objects so that adults would be less likely to take them away as a means of punishment. In reality, she was deeply troubled by losing items. It duplicated many losses of significant persons, transitional objects, and other objects that gave her a rare but necessary feeling of ownership and control. She needed to feel that she could permanently possess some things without fear of losing them. This emotional need to be attached securely entered into many aspects of the play therapy. For example, she possessed her own toys, which no one else used, in the play therapy room, and she daily set aside these objects with ceremonious deliberation in a locked container.

I also became a real and transferential object that was a key focus of her emotional need to attach. However, her need to be attached and to possess something was not always associated to a particular object or person; instead it existed as an entity in itself that needed to be described, recognized, satisfied, and accepted. She needed to feel that she could love and keep whatever was selected as the object of her attachment, or else she would not allow herself to love anything or anyone. In cases such as this, the emotion expressed in the transference must be the focus of interpretations, not the transference relationship associated with the emotion.

Table 17–6 illustrates how three emotions can be associated with transference as a form of resistance or communication. Countertransferential reactions to these three emotions are also shown.

Classification 6: Transference and Impulses

Urges, drives, cravings, or impulses present themselves transferentially in primitive fantasies, spontaneous gestures, or hidden but intense behaviors directed toward and away from the therapist. Patients will sexually, hungrily, destructively, and aggressively pursue therapists according to the developmental stage and needs associated with their impulses. Whether a therapist accepts the basic premises of theories by Sigmund Freud (1914), Karl Abraham (1924), and Melanie Klein (1921, 1928) or not, these theorists' writings about impulses and the therapeutic manner of handling drives when they appear transferentially are instructive (see also Hall 1954). Freud, for instance, acknowledged the impulses associated with somatic regions such as the oral cavity, anal muscles, and genital organs that affect development of the self and relationships. Abraham and Klein explored how destructive or creative urges somatically and psychologically affect aspects of relationships and self-perception. Each theorist explored sadistic and incorporative processes intrinsic to all impulses. Understanding these types of patients' transferential responses and being able to explore and describe their various dimensions will increase the

TABLE 17-6. Emotions and Transference

Classification	Resistance	Communication	Countertransference
Hate (irritation, frustration, anger)	Hate used to alienate, ward off, estrange, disarm, disempower therapist from performing therapy	Hate conveyed to create an opportunity to have anger present, explored, experienced, worked through, or integrated	Resonance with hateful emotions as they function as resistance to therapy, as destructive processes, as powerful personal feelings within the patient and shared between patient and therapist
Love (warmth, closeness, peace, joy, safety, desire)	Love used to disarm, seduce, undermine, avoid confrontation or negative material	Love conveyed in order to allow such emotion to be revealed, explored, understood, and integrated	Love resulting in being or feeling seduced, disarmed, kept from performing therapeutic tasks because of apparent positive emotions; resonance with love as communication of patient's reaction to feelings of love
Fear (mistrust, anxiety, worry, apprehension)	Fear used to rationalize need to avoid material or changes	Fear conveyed in order to be revealed, explored, understood, resolved, or integrated	Fear producing urge to avoid or prematurely soothe; fear empathically felt, with urge to contain, understand, and soothe in timely manner

therapist's comfort level and facility with such inevitable material.

As the reader may have already ascertained, Nate's anger had a basic aggressive nature to it that was impulsive and nonemotional. He grappled with aggressive impulses that were anally sadistic. In other children, oral impulses that are sadistic or incorporative may be the basis of eating disorders. Genitally driven impulses, sadistic or erotic, are also seen in children in early and latent stages of development.

Pedro, for instance, was a 5-year-old nonverbal child who manifested raw sexual impulses throughout the first phase of therapy. During many sessions he would climb on top of my desk and jump down and tumble on the ground, making guttural animal-like sounds as he landed. Initially, I interpreted this repeated action as either discharge of aggressive impulses or as triumphant gestures of controlling and conquering some unseen force. But, following more than a month of sessions wherein this activity was repeated around twenty times during each session, Pedro began to play with two dolls. The male doll would leap on top of the female doll with the same energy and sounds repeatedly. Eventually, undressing the dolls accompanied this gesture. His gesture, energy, and sounds were clearly sexualized. His first complete sentences concerned his intent to have sex with me. Thereafter, the transference relationship, established on the basis of these sexual impulses, became the focus of his communications. I would have been remiss to focus on his need or desire for me as an object; clearly, his basic sexualized impulse was the focus, not me.

Table 17–7 illustrates how two types of impulses might be transferentially expressed to either resist or communicate in therapy. Common countertransferential reactions are also presented.

Classification 7: Transference and Existential Issues

Abraham Maslow (1968), Rollo May (1969), and Irvin Yalom (1980) have outlined how therapeutic issues are associated with existential issues patients face. Existential issues about love,

TABLE 17-7. Transference and Impulses

Classification	Resistance	Communication	Countertransference	Case Examples
Impulses (drives, urges)	Impulses aimed to inhibit or alarm therapist in order to stop therapeutic interventions or change	Impulses expressed in order to be revealed, examined, and understood by patient or shared in a reparative relationship	Defensive responses (avoidance, denial, minimization, intellectualization); urges to act on or react to impulses	
Examples: Sexual	Sexual urges, drives, and gestures aimed at undermining therapist	Sexual urges associated with desire to connect, self-express, or resolve issues around sexual urges	Denial, disregard of sexual impulses; sexual arousal; moralizing; inappropriate acting out of sexual responses	Pedro
Destructive	Destructive urges, drives, and gestures aimed at alarming or undermining therapist so that therapist cannot continue effective therapy	Destructive urges associated to unresolved issues, unintegrated rage, or distorted expression of aggression for purposes of expression, exploration, integration or repair	Fear, defensive avoidance, or minimization; counterattacks	Nate

belonging, meaningfulness, destiny, death, or disillusionment can be expressed philosophically and inquisitively by patients in the transference. Religious issues about God, life after death, truth, morality, spirituality, and so on may also preoccupy patients in an existential manner. Those suffering profound illnesses must face questions about mortality, fairness, surviving, and dying. Political, judicial, and societal concerns can also be existential concerns for patients.

When existential issues are expressed in terms of the transference relationship, the therapist may become aware of being treated as if the child patient believes the therapist is in complete agreement with the beliefs or values presented or in complete or partial disagreement with the position of the patient. These transference reactions based on assumptions and projection can distort or impede therapeutic progress or result in issues remaining unexplored. Therefore, the therapist must recognize, describe, and explore existential issues that become transferentially revealed in order to avoid stalemates in therapy and to allow communication of all aspects of the patient's personality to enter into the therapeutic arena.

Like adults, children face existential dilemmas regularly. Traumatic events such as parental divorce or death, child abuse, natural disasters, and chronic or fatal diseases often create existential confusion in children (Francis 1984, Francis and Thrasher-Maync 1991). Such confusion may be manifested in terms of issues of *responsibility* (blame, guilt, innocence, causation), issues of *fairness* ("If I'm good, why do disasters happen to me?" "Why me?" "Since the world is fair, I must be bad, because bad things don't happen to good people"), and issues about *control and influence* (fatalism or pessimism giving way to passivity; withdrawal or compensatory gestures, such as excessive attempts to control).

Religious beliefs associated with death, life after death, punishment, the nature of God (kind, aloof, fair), guilt, and control or influence believed to be attained through prayer or faith can also become concerns for children. Moral development and issues about right versus wrong, good versus bad frequently enter into the therapeutic process.

Common transference reactions associated with existential

concerns of children include the following. First, the child patient might view the therapist as a guru or possessor of truth through idealistic transference. Idealizing the therapist thus may be an attempt to reduce anxieties of not knowing answers to existentially overwhelming questions. It may also express an existential need to belong or be safe by erecting the therapist as the all-knowing guide. Second, the child may view the therapist as a threat to needed or strongly held existential beliefs that help the child cope with difficult circumstances. For instance, the abused child may feel a strong need to view the abusing parent as being loving and justified in inflicting cruelty. It may be more existentially important to the child at that time to believe that the parent is loving than to acknowledge the reality of the abuse. Third, a child may view the therapist as unable to sympathize with the dilemmas being experienced because the therapist may too quickly answer, advise, explain, or ignore the child's situation. In this case, the therapist's eagerness to resolve existential issues by these interventions will contribute to the transferential processes of not being understood. Fourth, a child may view the therapist as biased for or against a particular existential solution; the transference based on this view would be one of resistance or avoidance. Fifth, a child may view a therapist as too powerless to deal with anxieties and confusions associated with a particular existential dilemma, as might be the parents.

Sarah faced issues about good and bad, right and wrong on a daily basis. Her mother praised her for stealing money, drinking beer, and smoking cigarettes before Sarah was 3. This behavior was considered good, charming, and admirable. Her other guardians considered these behaviors loathsome. Sarah was greatly confused for many years about who was correct and what truly comprised "goodness." She needed the love of her mother and her grandmother, but each adult required opposing behavior. Her existential need to belong could not be reconciled with her existential confusion about good and bad. Not surprisingly, Sarah brought her existential plight into the therapeutic relationship and alternated her transference reactions associated with her mother with transference reactions associated with her grandmother.

Therapists typically grapple with three countertransferential responses to existential issues. They may feel obliged to alter a child's "damaging" existential position by way of examples, lectures, persuasion, or education. This type of response usually inhibits the child from exploring the reasons or bases for the existential belief as well as the impact of an existential belief on the remainder of the child's life. With Sarah, I could have erroneously described what is socially "good" behavior. If I had done so, Sarah might have jeopardized her ability to impartially address her need to be loved by her mother and to love her mother (who endorsed "bad," unacceptable behavior).

A therapist may also feel inclined to deal with existential dilemmas or belief systems as if they were not therapeutically relevant. Religious beliefs, for example, have far-reaching impact on a person's life. If they cannot be part of the therapeutic exploration, then aspects of life so affected remain untouchable.

Finally, the existential quandary of all patients often parallels the therapist's quests, since everyone faces similar existential questions. When the quests are similar, the therapist may become hampered countertransferentially by personal uncertainties, personal crises, or dogmatically held beliefs. Too often, therapists feel obliged to provide answers, clarifications or guidance when, in actuality, the existential issue may best be acknowledged as an unresolvable conflict. The dissonance and anxiety about unresolved questions must be tolerated by the therapist as the patient confronts the issues and recognizes the inevitability of anxiety. For instance, children with chronic illnesses often must face their mortality before adults can tolerate facing it.

Table 17–8 reviews how existential issues can be used to resist or to communicate in therapy. Countertransferential reactions common to existential issues are listed as well.

SUMMARY OF TRANSFERENCE
CLASSIFICATIONS

At any point during a therapeutic session, children will express transference reactions that likely will fall within one or

TABLE 17-8. Transference and Existential Issues

Classification	Resistance	Communication	Countertransference
Existential Issue	Existential positions attributed to the therapist that aim to view the therapist as inept, wrong, or too different to be able to help	Existential positions attributed to the therapist that aim to help the patient reveal, explore, and understand personal issues in therapy	Urge to agree or disagree
Religion, death, love and belonging; destiny; illness; disillusionment			Urge to educate and change or improve patient's existential position
			Urge to avoid socially tabooed subjects

more of these seven classifications. Listening with the classifications in mind can facilitate the therapist in evaluating verbal and nonverbal transferential material, dynamics, issues, and countertransferential reactions. After evaluation occurs, interventions of silence or words can be wisely framed that will assist the patient's understanding and subsequent growth.

REFERENCES

Abraham, K. (1924). A short study of the development of the libido. *Selected Papers on Psycho-Analysis.* New York: Hogarth.

Bird, B. (1972). Notes on transference: universal phenomenon and hardest part of analysis. *Classics in Psycho-Analytic Technique.* New York: Jason Aronson, 1981.

Blanck, G., and Blanck, R. (1979). *Ego Psychology 2: Psychoanalytic Developmental Psychology.* New York: Columbia University Press.

Breuer, J., and Freud, S. (1985). Studies on hysteria. *Standard Edition* 2.

Erikson, E. H. (1963). *Childhood and Society*, 2nd ed. New York: W. W. Norton.

Fenichel, O. 1945. *Psychoanalytic Theory of Neurosis.* New York: W. W. Norton.

Francis, C. A. (1984). *Your Child and Divorce.* Fallbrook, CA: Child Focus.

_____ (1985). Theory and treatment of schizoid anxiety. *Dissertation Abstracts International.* Rosemead School of Psychology, Biola University, La Mirada, CA.

_____ (1991). *Power-struggles within the therapeutic relationship.* Unpublished manuscript.

Francis, C. A., and Thrasher-Maync, R. (1991). *Helping Children Cope with Traumatic Events.* Fallbrook, CA: Child Focus.

Freud, A. (1937). *The Ego and the Mechanisms of Defence.* New York: International Universities Press.

_____ (1965). *The Writings of Anna Freud,* vol. 6, *Normality and Pathology in Childhood: Assessments of Development.*

Madison, CT: International Universities Press.

Freud, S. (1905). On psychotherapy. *Standard Edition* 7:125–245.

_____ (1912). The dynamics of transference. *Standard Edition* 14:111–140.

_____ (1914). Remembering, repeating, and working through. *Standard Edition* 12:145–156.

_____ (1915). Observations on transference love. *Standard Edition* 12:156–172.

Fromm, E. (1967). *Man for Himself*, 4th ed. New York: Fawcett.

Gill, M. M. (1979). The analysis of the transference. In *Classics in Psycho-Analytic Technique.* New York: Jason Aronson, 1981.

Greenacre, P. (1954). The role of transference. In *Classics in Psycho-Analytic Technique,* ed. M. M. Gill. New York: Jason Aronson, 1981.

Greenson, R. R. (1979). *The Technique and Practice of Psychoanalysis,* vol. 1. New York: International Universities Press.

Hall, C. S. (1954). *A Primer of Freudian Psychology.* New York: Mentor.

Hedges, L. E. (1992). *Interpreting the Countertransference.* Northvale, NJ: Jason Aronson.

Heimann, P. (1949). On countertransference. In *Classics in Psycho-Analytic Technique,* ed. M. M. Gill. New York: Jason Aronson, 1981.

Horner, A. J. (1982). *Object Relations and the Developing Ego in Therapy.* New York: Jason Aronson.

Klein, M. (1921). The development of a child. In *The Writings of Melanie Klein,* vol. 1, *Love, Guilt, and Reparation and Other Works, 1921–1945.* New York: The Free Press, 1984.

_____ (1923). Early analysis. In *The Writings of Melanie Klein,* vol. 1, *Love, Guilt, and Reparation and Other Works, 1921–1945.* New York: The Free Press, 1984.

_____ (1926). The psychological principles of early analysis. In *The Writings of Melanie Klein,* vol. 1, *Love, Guilt, and Reparation and Other Works, 1921–1945.* New York: The Free Press.

_____ (1927). Symposium on child-analysis. In *The Writings of Melanie Klein,* vol. 1, *Love, Guilt, and Reparation and Other Works, 1921–1945.* New York: The Free Press, 1984.

_____ (1928). Early stages of Oedipus conflict. In *The Writings of Melanie Klein,* vol. 1, *Love, Guilt, and Reparation and Other Works, 1921–1945.* New York: The Free Press, 1984.

_____ (1952). The origins of transference. In *The Writings of Melanie Klein,* vol. 3, *Envy and Gratitude and Other Works, 1946–1963.* New York: The Free Press, 1984.

_____ (1955). The psycho-analytic play technique: its history and significance. In *The Writings of Melanie Klein,* vol. 3, *Envy and Gratitude and Other Works, 1946–1963.* New York: The Free Press, 1984.

_____ (1984a). *The Writings of Melanie Klein,* vol. 1, *Love, Guilt, and Reparation and Other Works, 1921–1945.* New York: The Free Press.

_____ (1984b). *The Writings of Melanie Klein,* vol. 2, *The Psycho-Analysis of Children.* New York: The Free Press.

_____ (1984c). *The Writings of Melanie Klein,* vol. 3, *Envy and Gratitude and Other Works, 1946–1963.* New York: The Free Press.

_____ (1984d). *The Writings of Melanie Klein,* vol. 4, *Narrative of Child Analysis.* New York: The Free Press.

Kohut, H. (1971). *The Analysis of the Self.* New York: International Universities Press.

_____ (1984). *How Does Analysis Cure?* Chicago: University of Chicago Press.

Lacan, J. 1981. *Fundamental Concepts of Psychoanalysis.* New York: W. W. Norton.

Langs, R. (1973). *The Technique of Psychoanalytic Psychotherapy, vols. 1 and 2.* New York: Jason Aronson.

_____ ed. (1981). In *Classics in Psycho-Analytic Technique.* New York: Jason Aronson.

Little, M. (1951). Counter-transference and the patient's response to it. In *Classics in Psycho-Analytic Technique.* New York: Jason Aronson, 1981.

Mahler, M., Pine, F., and Bergman, A. (1975). *The Psychological Birth of the Human Infant: Symbiosis and Individuation.* New York: Basic Books.

Maslow, A. H. (1968). *Toward a Psychology of Being,* 2nd ed. New York: Van Nostrand.

May, R. (1969). *Love and Will,* 4th ed. New York: W. W. Norton.

Racker, H. (1972). The meanings and uses of countertransference. In *Classics in Psycho-Analytic Technique*. New York: Jason Aronson, 1981.

Searles, H. (1965). *Collected Papers on Schizophrenia and Related Subjects*. New York: International Universities Press.

Stern, D. N. (1984). *The Interpersonal World of the Infant: A View from Psychoanalysis and Developmental Psychology*. New York: Basic Books.

Winnicott, D. W. (1965a). *The Family and Individual Development*. London: Tavistock.

_____ (1965b). *The Maturational Processes and the Facilitating Environment*. New York: International Universities Press.

_____ (1971). *Playing and Reality*. London: Tavistock.

Yalom, I. D. (1980). *Existential Psychotherapy*. New York: Basic Books.

18

A Self Psychological View of Therapeutic Impasses

Estelle Shane, Ph.D.
Morton Shane, M.D.

A therapeutic impasse occurs whenever one or both of the parties involved persists in failing to meet important needs or urgent wishes of the other. Inherent in the theoretical perspective presented in this chapter are a number of assumptions. The first is that therapy is a two-person process, an exquisitely interwoven, interactive, dialogical system, within which each person influences the other. This can be understood in the familiar terms Stolorow and colleagues (1987) have articulated from an intersubjective perspective; the continuous intersection of two mutually influencing subjectivities, or, alternatively, from the interpersonal context of Harry Stack Sullivan (1953), Louis Sander (1983), and Daniel Stern (1985); or, yet again, from the social constructivist view of the mutually constructed transference experience promoted by Irwin Hoffman (1992, 1994) and Donnel Stern (1992); or, finally, from the growth-in-connection perspective of the Stone Center (Jordan et al. 1991). This approach is in contradistinction to a one-person view of therapy, which features a patient objectively perceived by the observer-analyst who is functioning as a catalyst to evoke internal urges, drives, and transferences displaced or projected from the past life of the patient, and which does not conceive the therapist as an interactive, co-constructive part of the process.

The second assumption informing my theoretical perspective on the therapeutic impasse is that human beings exist, grow, and develop only within an interpersonal matrix embedded in the cultural surround. This understanding comes to us both from infant research and from evolutionary and biological studies of the brain and of the development of consciousness, self-awareness, and language. This latter perspective is exemplified in the work of Gerald Edelman (1992), and emphasizes the social embeddedness of all of man's ostensibly singular, independent mental attributes. Thus, even if we take a one-person view of therapy, as is inherent in the self–selfobject relationship concept of Kohut (1984) and of much of self psychology, the *interpersonal* aspect of the dyad is accounted for by the very composition of the self as being constituted by its selfobjects (Goldberg 1992), even though the focus in treatment is principally and uniformly on the intrapsychic, one-person experience of the patient. For example, the view of countertransference in self psychology is the counterpart to transference in self psychology, wherein the patient either serves, or fails to serve, the one-person selfobject needs of the analyst.

The third assumption inherent in my view of therapeutic impasse is that given the inevitable two-person nature of the enterprise, the impasse, too, is best understood in terms of the contributions of both patient and analyst. Nevertheless, ultimately, responsibility for recognizing, understanding, and ameliorating that impasse lies principally with the analyst.

It is a commonplace to view the impasse as inevitable in the therapeutic relationship, and, in fact, the impasse is as old as psychoanalysis itself. It begins with Breuer and his patient Anna O. (Breuer and Freud 1895), who fantasied giving birth to

Breuer's baby, which so frightened her unwilling analyst that he withdrew, depriving her of sustenance and care. Thus, each experienced the other as failing to meet urgent needs and wishes. The same had been true with Freud and his patient Dora (1905). Dora's need to be understood in her own right, and to not have imposed on her an agenda first conceived of by Dora's father and then by Freud himself, was not met by Freud. Concomitantly, Dora did not meet Freud's wish for a dedicated, compliant patient willing to do the analysis on his terms. Later Freud was able to acknowledge his inability at the time to fully fathom Dora's response to him as mainly transference, and in the end he made something very useful both from Breuer's earlier failure and his own later one, namely, the concepts of countertransference and transference. Thus, not only the experience of therapeutic impasse but also the notion of learning from and benefiting from our failures began with psychoanalysis itself. What we have come to appreciate in more current times is the fact that both transference and countertransference are mutually constructed, an idea not inherent in Freud's original formulations.

We have also come to understand that the therapeutic impasse exists on a spectrum, or continuum. On one end are impasses that are irreversible, despite all efforts, and that constitute failures in treatment—Breuer's Anna O., a failure disguised as a success, and Freud's Dora, a failure acknowledged as such. On the other end of the spectrum are impasses most easily reversed, perceived of as inevitable outgrowths of the therapeutic process itself. In fact, Kohut's view is that such impasses, which he called empathic failures, are not only unavoidable but are necessary for therapeutic benefit, that is, for structural change and developmental progression. I imagine that most impasses are of this more easily reversible variety. In a therapy going well, they often constitute the bread and butter of interpretive work. Finally, in the middle zone along the impasse continuum lie those disruptions that are somewhat more difficult to resolve, encompassing greater risk and uncertainty. Often we don't know until, or if and when they are resolved, where they fit on the impasse spectrum.

But I believe that across the entire continuum, the impasse is always mutually derived, born of wishes and needs unmet, and is mainly the responsibility of the therapist to handle. What I mean by this is that were we functioning optimally, we would catch these impasses early and resolve them quickly. And while I agree with contributors who speak to the benefits that attain for both therapist and patient in terms of what they learn about themselves and each other in the process, I don't agree with the view promulgated by Kohut and others that this is the *only* way in which the patient can build structure and enhance development. We know from infant observation, and specifically from the work of Beebe and Lachmann (1988), that the infant learns via a number of self experiences. One of these self experiences is the one emphasized by Kohut of disruption and repair, or optimal frustration and transmuting internalization, a concept based on, perhaps left over from, his own classical training, but certainly valid and often observable in the therapeutic situation.

However, there are at least three other ways in which infant researchers have observed that the infant learns and develops. One is through the frustration/gratification cycle first identified by Freud as the basis for all learning, that is, the infant's experience of intense, libidinal, bodily desires and their ultimate gratification. Another is based on the heightened, affectively charged "magic" moments put forward by Fred Pine (1988), based on his reformulation of Mahler's symbiotic phase of development. The least dramatic but most predominant, and probably the most effective experience for optimal normal growth and development, is the almost continuous background stream of affective resonance, responsiveness, and attunement that exists between the individual and his or her surround when the individual is in a state of alert and untroubled activity.

Thus, while Kohut promotes the disruption–restoration cycle as being the most effective in producing therapeutic change, it would seem that it is not the only way, and in fact, we might discover that it is not even the best way. It may turn out that our day-to-day moments of affect attunement and resonance with our patients are the most beneficial to them for accomplishing the work of therapy. That is, it may be that patients do not learn best in moments of heightened negative or dysphoric affect, even when that heightened affect has been reduced by the sense of having been understood, and the person restored to a cohesive state. Perhaps our patients learn best when they are in an ongoing state of calm, feeling unguarded, open, and curious about new experience. This is the view put forward by Lichtenberg and colleagues (1992), who contend that the patient is most accessible to interpretation when she or he is in a self state organized by the exploratory-assertive motivational system. All of this has implications for our views about the importance of the impasse in therapeutic progress. It may be that a therapy that is going well, and that is characterized by an intense involvement between therapist and patient, does not always have to be punctuated by the empathic disruption of a therapeutic impasse for progress to be observed. Affective turmoil is certainly important in therapy, but it need not reach the heights of an impasse to be beneficial. While in my experience few therapies exist with no memorable impasses, I know they do exist.

I would like at this point to illustrate my theoretical position on the therapeutic impasse—namely, that it derives from the experience of unmet needs and wishes—with clinical examples on both sides of the spectrum I have identified.

I'll begin with an example that highlights a self psychological theoretical perspective, the experience of empathic disruption and repair. It involves a 22-year-old woman, Kathy K.[1], in analysis for several years and having formed a relationship with me that can best be characterized as an archaic selfobject transference with mirroring features; that is, her particular response to me was to elevate the experience of our being together to a central importance in her life, to bask in my presence, and to express her deep satisfaction at being so closely and exclusively attended to, feeling for the first time in her life that her needs were not frustrated. For my own part, I came to experience with Kathy, whose mother had committed suicide while she was still in college and whose father had died suddenly just two months after our work together began, a deeply felt concern for and commitment to her well-being, so that her sense that I was there for her was met by my own sense that I

---

[1]Vignettes from this patient's analysis have been described in other papers (e.g., Shane and Shane 1993, and Shane and Shane, In press).

should be and wanted to be there for her, and, perhaps, a hidden wish to be appreciated for it. Separations from me were always difficult for Kathy. Early in treatment, they were preceded by her protests that if I really understood her, I could only leave her if I wished to cause her to suffer. It was through these complaints, preceding and following interruptions, that Kathy came to understand that my leaving her without her protesting bitterly would make her feel as if she didn't exist at all; that is, the protest itself, the longer and more vehement the better, defined her very selfhood for the first time. She could never argue wholeheartedly with her mother, who would respond when Kathy had dared to do so with a "silent treatment" lasting for days and making Kathy feel as if an essential essence were destroyed. But, as angry, as accusative, and as vituperative as Kathy would become at these times, her protests never became disruptions between us. I felt neither greatly threatened nor put off by her anger, which I saw mainly as a necessary developmental expression, and she in her turn was able to take in and benefit from what I could offer her by way of understanding and explanation.

After several years of analysis and right before a vacation of mine, our ongoing working relationship was disrupted. Kathy, who had by this point acquired a better ability to tolerate my absences, had been describing how she hoped, once I returned, to get over several troublesome symptoms through, it seemed to me, a kind of osmosis, by just being passively in my presence. I found myself mildly irritated by her confidence that things would just happen without her work and my specific involvement, as if my activities as a distinct person didn't count. I ordinarily accepted this characteristic in Kathy, but for whatever reason and, actually, without my realizing it, I found it difficult to tolerate at that moment. In response, I disagreed with her breezy prediction, asserting in a tone that probably conveyed disapproval and undoubtedly was poorly attuned to Kathy's own optimistic mood, that I believed it would take additional work, and on both our parts, to understand and resolve these issues.

Kathy made no immediate answer to my comment, but after my return from vacation, she found she was unable to talk to me at all for several sessions, a most unusual situation, and qualifying as a therapeutic impasse of uncertain proportion. I was puzzled at first, as was she, and then she disclosed that she had experienced my last absence as the most intolerable to date. We were able to piece together what had happened between us prior to my leaving, that my remark was taken by her as a criticism, leading her to feel misunderstood, and then internally disrupted. She remembered in retrospect feeling that my misunderstanding her was an unbearable thought that she had needed to suppress until the moment the interchange was aired between us. I explained that she must have felt it was inconceivable that I could be so out of touch with her, and she realized that she could not afford to confront this possibility, that she needed me too much. I connected this to the times when she was small when her much loved father was forced to leave town on business, and her depressed and ordinarily distant mother would attempt to interact with her the way her father had, to replace him, but her mother was incapable of being with Kathy for long without becoming critical of her and then removing herself in anger from Kathy's presence. My irritated comment concerning the need for us to work harder must have been reminiscent of her mother's way with her, making her feel as if she were once again being humiliated by criticism, and once again having her needs dismissed.

I told her then that when I had left on vacation this time, it was for her not only like her father leaving her, as was usual when I went away, but this time like her mother was as well, retreating from her in apparent disgust. Talking about the incident and what it recalled for her was helpful, not only in retrieving the past but also in relaxing the tension that had grown up between us in this therapeutic impasse, allowing Kathy to feel once again the helpful effects of a background selfobject presence. Thus, the disruption was consequent to my not meeting Kathy's need for continued acceptance and for affirmation of the progress we had made, as well as the potential for future improvement. This patient was especially vulnerable to having attention withdrawn from her, and experienced such withdrawal as a confirmation of her worthlessness. For my part, Kathy had, for whatever reason, strained me beyond my ability to tolerate her just taking me and the process and progress for granted; it seemed I needed something from her at this time, some recognition of my importance to her as a person and as an analyst, and not just as a function. I also wanted some assurance for my own purposes that the analysis would not go on indefinitely. Behind my apparently reasonable statement, then, was an impatience with the slow pace of our work and an irritation with Kathy's contentment to keep it that way. I was able to recognize my own defense from childhood of growing up in a hurry in order to cope with the vulnerability inherent in dependence on inconstant caretakers, and my own envious resentment that Kathy had no such anxiety in relation to me. These are, I should emphasize, retrospective introspections, a self-analytic insight not available to me when I made my spontaneous comment to her before the vacation

I consider this experience a typical example of disruption and repair, wherein, following its resolution, therapeutic and developmental progress ensued in both Kathy and myself (Shane 1980). What Kathy understood was the extent to which she had to deny experiences that challenged her sense that I was unfailingly available to meet her needs. The experience also revived in the transference and thereby clarified what it was like for her when she was left with her depressed, withdrawn, critical mother. Kohut postulates that such instances of empathic rupture and repair lead to transmuting internalizations of capacities in the patient not previously present, that this is how, in his words, analysis cures. In this case, the experience of being let down by me, and then, with my analytic help, reconstituting her self-integration strengthened Kathy's resilience, making such inevitable future disruptions in her connection with me more easily sustainable. As for me, I learned once more about my need to be acknowledged as a valuable person in my own right, despite my theoretical understanding of the importance of allowing Kathy the space she required to express to the fullest her selfobject longings.

In this instance, the disruption and repair rests on the more benign side of the spectrum. It was rather easily interpreted and understood, and what I came to know about my own contribution was not shared with Kathy. I saw no need to do so. I want to make the point, however, that where impasses are of a more malignant variety, as in the case to follow, self-disclosure to some extent may be important to the eventual clarification and resolution of the impasse. I will present such a clinical illustration in which an impasse occurred in a previously well-functioning therapy. The disruption was not resolved, despite significant, but ultimately inadequate, efforts by both therapist and patient, leaving each feeling defeated, angry, and helpless.

The patient, Jessica S., is an attractive woman in her late twenties who suffered from intense and unremitting depression following the deaths of her mother, father, and only sister in a plane crash several years before she entered into analytic treatment with Dr. R. The family had been close and of great importance to her, and Jessica had been relatively symptom free before the loss. She was married to a brilliant and successful, somewhat emotionally distant, attorney who, though clearly kind and loving to her, and apparently adequate for her needs before the loss, was unable to provide the additional support she required during her bereavement. Jessica S. had no children, and one reason for entering analysis when she did was her concern that she would be incapable of being sufficiently available to justify starting a family of her own, which desire, she feared, was partly motivated by the wish to replace the family she had lost. Moreover, her depression seemed to her to be endless and unremitting, and had been unresponsive to medication.

The psychiatrist with whom she entered treatment was in his middle thirties and had been divorced for several years. Although depressed himself over the failure of his marriage, he was nevertheless very helpful to Jessica and the analysis went well. As Jessica felt better, she began to comment upon the works of art in Dr. R.'s office, which included not only fine paintings but, in particular, fine examples of photographic art. She talked about how she especially admired some of the photographs. She noted that those works were unsigned and wondered if he might have been the artist. Dr. R. admitted that not only were the works she most admired his own, but also that at one time he had wanted to become a professional photographer. It was then that Jessica spoke of her own longings to be an artist and, in fact, began to talk about her own efforts at photography. The bond was thus strengthened between them, with his encouraging her to do more with this interest as a way of coming out of her depression and further expanding herself. The analysis continued, and about six months later Dr. R. said to her, in response to her talking about her photographic efforts, that she should bring in some of her work, explaining that he would not comment on the quality, promising to say nothing of that, but rather he would focus on the content, to see what they together could learn about important themes in her life as displayed in her art. But when Dr. R. actually viewed Jessica's work, he was overwhelmed by her talent and, breaking their agreement, couldn't help but tell her how impressed he was by her obvious capacity. Thus began Jessica's career in photography, which, in fact, has been a sustaining force for her to the present. Her gratitude was very real, but Jessica also realized, and later could tell me, that it seemed to her that she was required to perform successfully in order to please Dr. R.

What followed was an intensification of the relationship, steady progress, and then, inexplicably, an impasse. The impasse was characterized by conflicts between them. What Jessica later reported to me was that when she would begin to speak of what was on her mind, he would take some exception to what she said, and they would get into an argument. For example, they would find themselves in contention about the rate of her progress, he insisting that she was doing well, and she still uncertain whether she could risk having a child. It seemed to her that he had lost his clear ability to listen to her without reacting defensively. He admitted to her that he found himself overly involved with the issues she would raise, and that he couldn't seem to maintain a steady analytic stance in relation to her. But no matter how they attempted to understand what had happened and continued to happen between them, somehow it couldn't be resolved. Finally, Jessica spoke her mind. She said, with much fear and hesitation, that she felt she might be in love with him, and, even more difficult to say, that he might be in love with her, and that these feelings between them might be interfering with their therapeutic relationship because they weren't being talked about. Dr. R.'s response was immediate and vigorous: he disagreed entirely, he said. By her account, Dr.

R. proceeded to give a rather long speech, which included his insistence that he had worked out any such feelings in self-analysis previously, and that there was no chance he could ever fall in love with a patient, any patient. Jessica was understandably upset and disappointed by him and by his response. She noted to me afterward that he didn't even stop to consider the possibility, and that, to her, was a dead giveaway of at least some unconscious discomfort in relation to her. Moreover, she felt he was angry with her for even suggesting the idea, and this despite the fact that she was supposed to expose all her thoughts and feelings to him.

Following this disruption, both patient and analyst attempted to regroup, to repair the rift between them. Dr. R. even sought help through consultation with a senior analyst, and then reported back to Jessica that perhaps, on further consideration, he *was* attracted to her, possibly through some resonance with their shared artistic interest, but that he didn't believe he was in love with her, or that what feelings he did have for her would interfere with the analysis. So they continued, but despite all their efforts, he would again become testy about small matters, even argumentative, and would then apologize and agree he was acting inappropriately, only to repeat the performance. Jessica finally felt she had no choice but to leave him and to seek another therapist.

What can be said about this unfortunate turn in an analysis that had seemed to be going so well? It appears that Dr. R. had established a kind of extraanalytic mentorship with Jessica, whose career blossomed under his tutelage, but that this seeming sidebar issue had infused their whole relationship, destabilizing his own more comfortable analytic stance, and for whatever reason, he was not able to negotiate a self-righting maneuver. Once she had gained the courage to confront him with what she understood to be the source of their difficulty, and he proved to be unavailable for an open consideration of it, she lost a measure of trust in him. She was mollified by the fact that he was willing to seek consultation, but felt that he was again less than open with her about what he might have discovered about his own feelings. Above all, she felt that somehow their relationship had shifted, and he was no longer there consistently to serve her needs and to help her sort out her feelings. He had come to require something from her, and all of what was entailed in that was never clear to her. Did he require her to be a success? Did he require her to continue to look to him for guidance in her burgeoning career? Was he envious of her commercial success in a field he had once entertained for himself?

Her view was, along with any of this, that he was made uncomfortable by his romantic feelings for her, which she might have been able to work through with him had he had the courage to be honest with her. Above all, she felt disappointed in his inability to face with her and, perhaps, within himself, whatever feelings he had about her. She wondered what she could continue to learn from a person who could not be open, honest, and authentic within himself. Of course, we have only Jessica's subjective perspective on this matter, but the experience from her perspective has left her feeling disillusioned and vulnerable, not so sure she dares to be open with me. Her depression and sense of loss have returned. Recently she ran into Dr. R. on the street. He clearly saw her, but turned away, apparently to avoid acknowledging her presence. Again, this is Jessica's perspective, but in any case this incident reveals the degree to which there remain unresolved, and, presumably, unresolvable, tensions between them. I don't know how Dr. R. feels about this experience, but I know that Jessica was damaged by it, and particularly damaged by the fact that the impasse could not be overcome and to some degree remains a permanent wound.

I don't wish to leave the impression that we are incapable of righting the impasses that occur. On the contrary, impasses, more often than not, are correctable and ultimately valuable. At the same time, I do want to stress that analysis is a risky business, involving as it does strong feelings in both participants, and depending as it does on our always fallible human capacities. When it goes well, it can be lifesaving, but when it goes badly, it can really hurt, and hurt both parties.

REFERENCES

Beebe, B., and Lachmann, F. (1988). Mother–infant mutual influences and precursors of psychic structure. *Progress in Self Psychology* 3:3–26.

Breuer, J., and Freud, S. (1895). Studies on hysteria. *Standard Edition*, 1. London: Hozarth.

Edelman, G. (1992). *Bright Air, Brilliant Fire: On the Matter of Mind*. New York: Basic Books.

Freud, S. (1905). Fragment of an analysis of a case of hysteria. *Standard Edition* 7:1–122.

Goldberg, A. (1992). *The Prisonhouse of Psychoanalysis*. Chicago: University of Chicago Press.

Hoffman, I. (1992). Some practical implications of a social-constructivist view of the psychoanalytic situation. *Psychoanalytic Dialog* 2:287–304.

_____ (1994). The dialectic in the analytic situation. *Psychoanalytic Quarterly* 187–218.

Jordan, J., Kaplan, A., Miller, J., et al. (1991). *Women's Growth in Connection: Writings from the Stone Center*. New York: Guilford.

Kohut, H. (1984). *How Does Analysis Cure?* Chicago: University of Chicago Press.

Lichtenberg, J., Lachmann, F., and Fosshage, J. (1993). *Self and Motivational Systems*. Hillsdale, NJ: Analytic Press.

Pine, F. (1988). Motivation, personality organization, and the four psychologies of psychoanalysis. *Journal of American Psychoanalysis* 37:31–64.

Sander, L. (1983). Polarity, paradox, and the organizing process in development. In *Frontiers of Infant Psychiatry*, ed. J. Call, E. Galenson, and R. Tyson, pp. 315–327. New York: Basic Books.

Shane E., and Shane, M. (1993). Sex, gender, and sexualization. *Progress in Self Psychology* 9:61–74.

_____ (In press). In pursuit of the optimal. In *Progress in Self Psychology*. New York: Guilford.

_____ (In press). Varieties of love in the transference: essays in response to Theodore Jacobs. *Psychoanalytic Inquiry*.

Shane, M. (1980). Countertransference and the developmental orientation and approach. *Psychoanalysis and Contemporary Thought*, 3:195–212.

Stern, D. B. (1992). Response to I. Z. Hoffman. *Psychoanalytic Dialog*, 2:331–364.

Stern, D. N. (1985). *The Interpersonal World of the Infant*. New York: Basic Books.

Stolorow, R. D., Brandchaft, B., and Atwood, G. E. (1987). *Psychoanalytic Treatment: An Intersubjective Approach.* Hillsdale, NJ: Analytic Press.

Sullivan, H. (1953). *The Interpersonal Theory of Psychiatry.* New York: W. W. Norton.

19

A Relational Perspective on What Is Healing in Therapy

Irene Pierce Stiver, Ph.D.
Jean Baker Miller, M.D.

In studying women's lives at the Stone Center, Wellesley College, we, along with the group working with Gilligan (1982, 1990), have found that an inner sense of connection to others is a central organizing feature in female development. In this chapter, we will explore the implications of this perspective for healing in the psychotherapeutic treatment of children, adolescents, and adults.

It is interesting to note that in the history of psychotherapy there have been voices introducing a more relational component into psychotherapeutic approaches, such as Sullivan (1953), Fairbairn (1952), Rogers (1951), and others. However, the field in general has always resisted placing them in the center of interest.

Again, more recently over the last 5 to 10 years, there has been a resurgence of attention to therapy as a relational process, for example, in the work of Modell (1984), Gill (1983), and Havens (1986). In particular, a growing recognition of new levels of meaning of countertransference has led to a greater focus on the interactional dynamics between therapist and patient (Tansey and Burke 1989, and others). We know Kohut's contributions initially encountered resistance from the analytic establishment but have, over the years, gained a large following. In self psychology there has been a more recent shift from the one-directional "self–other" empathic conceptualization to a somewhat greater emphasis on two-way process in the therapeutic encounter (e.g., Wolf 1983). The works of Stolorow and his colleagues (1987) best illustrate this trend. It is worth noting, however, that even in writings more attentive to relational dynamics, the language and the use of highly intellectualized concepts convey an attitude of objectification of all persons involved and a movement away from the powerful affective meanings of the ideas presented.

A number of papers from the Stone Center on the relational approach have contributed to understanding therapeutic process in a new way. For example, Kaplan (1984), Jordan (1991), Stiver (1990c), and Surrey (1987) have written about mutual empathy, mutual empowerment, and disclosure in the therapeutic encounter. From the work of Gilligan and her colleagues, a paper by Steiner-Adair (1991) offers an innovative reframing of therapy and especially countertransference. In a paper on "Connections, Disconnections, and Violations," one of us (Miller 1988) focused on relational or, more accurately, "nonrelational" settings in a family that lead to significant disconnections in all the people involved. More particularly, the child growing up in such settings experiences a deep sense of isolation and self-blame. Under these conditions, a significant paradox emerges that is central to understanding relational development and, analogously, to understanding the therapeutic framework and process.

A PARADOX

As Surrey (1984) has proposed, we see the underlying processes of psychological growth as mutual empathy and mutual empowerment. Trying to spell out mutual empowerment more concretely, we've described it as composed of at least five beneficial components. These are increased sense of zest or well-being that comes with feeling connected to others, the motivation and ability to act right in the relationship as well as beyond it, increased knowledge about oneself and the other person(s), increased sense of self-worth, and a desire for more connection beyond this particular one (Miller 1986).

We would define the goal of therapy *precisely* as mutual empowerment that includes these five elements. Not only are they goals in the sense of the endpoint of therapy, they are the features that occur at many steps along the way whenever patient and therapist engage in a growing connection. Of course, we don't attain them at every moment, but we can keep trying for them.

However, therapist and patient have to struggle with the forces within them that stand in the way of creating mutual empathy and mutual empowerment. We all grapple with these forces. They follow from experiences in childhood or in later life that occur whenever a relationship has been hurtful, disappointing, dangerous, or violating—that is, disconnecting and not mutually empathic or mutually empowering. When this happens, we experience a reversal of these five "good things." It is not a simple reversal, however, but a compound and confusing mixture: we feel a decreased sense of vitality and well-being because of feeling less connected and more alone in the face of a difficult experience. Along with it, we feel an inability to act, but, more than that, a sense that acting out of our own feelings will lead to destructive consequences. We have less knowledge about ourselves and others, that is, more confusion and also a diminished sense of worth. As a result, we turn away from others and toward isolation.

Most important, when this kind of disconnection or violation occurs, a person tends to feel the problem is all in her, especially, but not only, if she is a child. This perception occurs precisely *because* of the disconnection—because she cannot deal with what is happening in true engagement with the other people involved. The problem is "between them," in the relationship. If, however, the other person(s) is not engaging with it, the child or adult begins to feel not just alone with the problem, but that the problem is all *in her*. She *has* the problem. (Incidentally, by contrast with other processes, for example, projective identification, this process is much more common and important. If we were to use similar terminology, we might call this phenomenon something like "introjective relational identification," that is, the individual taking into herself the problem that is relational—or that, in large part, originates in the other person, if the other person is an abuser or even unresponsive to what is going on in the relationship. This process occurs especially when one person has more power to determine what can happen in the relationship.)

In the face of repeated experiences of disconnection, we believe people yearn even more for relationships to help with the confused mixture of painful feelings. However, we also become so afraid of engaging with others about our significant experience that we keep important parts of ourselves out of relationship, that is, we develop techniques for staying out of connection. Again, we all do this to varying degrees. Several people have recently described, in nice detail, the specific steps in this process, for example, Stiver in alcoholic, incest-, and Holocaust-survivor families (1990b), and Steiner-Adair (1991) and Mirkin (1990) in anorexic and bulemic adolescents and their families.

Thus, we see psychological problems centered in this fundamental paradox that in our deep desire to make connection, we keep large parts of ourselves out of connection. Precisely in the face of so needing connection, we develop a repertoire of methods that we believe we must maintain that then keep us out of real engagement. As we have described elsewhere, some people may present a picture of seeming connection, for example, as they play out a role, such as that of the good child, parent, or caretaker; yet this very role serves to keep them out of true engagement about what matters for them (Stiver 1990b, Miller 1988). The central issue is the power of the often unseen desperate reaching for connection, hoping others will perceive and respond to this yearning while simultaneously continuing the techniques for staying out of connection. This is the paradox that patient and therapist face as they undertake therapy.

Here we want to note that Gilligan (1990c) in her work on

adolescent girls arrived at almost exactly the same statement. She has beautiful data to indicate that at adolescence girls begin to keep large parts of themselves out of connection in order to try to stay in connection in the only ways available in this culture.

Another way to put this main point is to say that being in connection means to be emotionally accessible. And this means to be vulnerable. First of all, to express our own perceptions and feelings always places us in a vulnerable position, opening ourselves to the responses of others to "what is really me." To do that, we really do need other people who can relate to the feelings or who can bear them with us, as contrasted to not engaging, withdrawing, punishing, or violating us—that is, disconnecting in various ways. When the latter occurs regularly, the child learns that allowing herself to be vulnerable is too dangerous. Here, as Jordan (1989) has described it, shame enters, and with it the terrible feelings of loss of empathic possibility.

Another result is that a person is forced to lose the full possibility of representing herself and developing knowledge about her experience—of developing authenticity. If we don't have people who can emotionally resonate and respond, we have to start to focus, instead, on methods of not putting forward our perceptions and feelings. We start down a path away from knowledge of ourselves and away from a sense of authenticity.

THE ESSENTIAL STEP

With this brief recap of the background, let us start by saying we think the essential step toward change or healing in therapy occurs when the therapist can feel with the patient; that is, when the therapist is moved by the patient and the patient is then moved by feeling the therapist feeling with her. This is mutual empathy in its therapy form, an idea many people find perplexing. That is, as the therapist really "gets with" the patient's experience, something happens—first of all in the therapist; she is changed. If the patient can feel this happening, feel the therapist move in this way, something very important occurs. It means that she, the patient, has had an impact on the therapist by just her feelings and thoughts or, since there is not a good word in the language, her "feeling-thoughts."

This experience can be very new and very hard for a person to believe, but if she can begin to believe it she will be moved. A person can feel another person truly with her about something that matters and that she felt, until now, that no one could engage with. For the child, this may be the first experience of this nature. Therapist and patient are then both in this movement together; they are both "moving in relationship." The therapist, as well as the patient, has the experience of being opened up. They have moved toward the kind of joining that is mutual empathy. At such times, the patient is moved by the therapist's empathy with her and the therapist's genuine involvement in the relationship. Each time a person has this experience in therapy, she further mobilizes her empathic capacities.

To explain this central point of change or healing in therapy, we need to go back to describe the overall movement or flow of therapy. To do that, let us say that we believe all relationships in life, from infancy through adulthood, even the most optimal relationships, probably proceed through periods of connection to disconnection and to new connection. This would be true inevitably because each person is different from every other and from the family group or other groupings of people. At times this engagement will flow relatively smoothly; at other times one or another person will feel not heard, not understood, not responded to, not valued, diminished, hurt, angry, and numbers of other untoward reactions. If, however, both (or all of the people, if we are talking about larger groupings) are able to continue to represent at least some of their thoughts and feelings, and if both can continue to try to be with, or to hear and respond to the other's experience, they can proceed on to a new connection. When this process occurs, it is not going back to some old connection; instead, each person and the relationship inevitably move to a new level, to more than they and the relationship were before.

Of course, this growth to a new level doesn't go on at every minute of life, nor always at the same rate for all the people involved. Children, for example, often grow at a faster rate. Incidentally, they always force adults to confront the need to grow and expand. Their more "original" and sometimes urgent expressions of feelings and needs always face us with the challenge of moving out of our old patterns, our old strategies for disconnection if we are to engage with them as they put forward their experience.

We see therapy, too, as a process of moving repeatedly into disconnection and then new connection. Indeed, therapy could be described as a special place designed to work on disconnections (that's why it can be so hard) and to learn to move in relationship through to new connection (that's why it can be so fulfilling and enlarging for all people involved). It seems fair to say that therapy, by definition any therapy of any theoretical orientation, should be a process of the person bringing more and more of herself into relationship with another person (or persons, for example, in the case of group therapy). As therapy proceeds, this means the patient bringing in more of her feelings and thoughts, those parts of herself she believed she could not possibly bring into relationship because it felt as if it would be absolutely devastating.

We want to repeat and emphasize this point: in the face of the threat of disconnection, something different can happen, something new can happen. A person can discover that by being more herself and bringing in more of her own experience and feelings, the other person can be moved, the other person can feel more and can feel more with her; that is, she can be more connected to another person. Again, this is the wonderful essence of therapy.

EMPATHY WITH BOTH PARTS OF THE PARADOX

Movement into more connection also leads into the hard parts of therapy. Therapy is now threatening the person's strategies for staying out of connection. As the person begins to shift away from these strategies, she moves toward a greater sense of her longing for more authentic connection, for true relationship. This longing, however, makes a person feel very vulnerable; it is a frightening place to be.

(Perhaps we should clarify this point. For example, we know that women often talk about wanting relationships and close relationships, but we are saying that, in therapy, the frightening aspect is longing for an *authentic* relationship based on the fuller truth of the woman's experience.)

Here, we want to elaborate on the strategies of disconnection, especially, to emphasize their great importance—they are not simply defenses that the therapist hopes to get rid of as soon as possible. Probably the greatest fears in therapy arise from the fear of giving up these strategies. While the original terrible things that happen to a person can lead to horrible fears, it is now the possibility of relinquishing these strategies that seems so utterly terrifying. This is so because they seem so essential for psychic survival. To be without them feels as if it would put a person into a most dangerous and exposed position without the only means she's been able to construct for managing at all. It can feel as if a person is being pressured in therapy to give up the ways of feeling and acting that promise some protection, some power, some strength. This is, of course, in contrast with more mutual relationships in which a person's feelings and thoughts are the source of strength and impact. Other people should resonate with them and respond to them because "they're there," they matter. A person shouldn't need these extra means of protection or power, but we have all developed them to varying degrees because we have not developed optimally mutual relationships.

We also want to emphasize the point that these strategies were ways of staying out of connection because the only relationships available were in some fundamental ways disconnecting and violating, and, indeed, current relationships may be too. In many instances, a person's relationships were deeply destructive. There was good reason to develop these strategies. Often the strategies can be ways of not capitulating, as it were, of holding out in these destructive relationships. Thus, they have a kind of authenticity. They can be life-saving or mind-saving methods that people have developed under great duress. Often a person is saying to the therapist, in effect, "No I won't engage with you because that means to me that I have to do what you want, and I won't do that," or, "I won't go along with or capitulate to your demands or to reality as you seem to define it."

Here, Carol Gilligan and her co-workers have illuminated how all girls have to face the basically destructive forms of relationships imposed on them in their development and especially at adolescence. If these relationships violate girls' very being, then there is great validity in the girls' developing what Gilligan calls resistance, what we call strategies, for not going along with these relationships. Such strategies, then, are to be deeply respected.

A woman with multiple personalities dramatically illustrated the authenticity contained in these strategies. Her main personality was very likable and compliant; one of the other personalities was an adolescent boy who was very angry, threw things, wouldn't contract for safety, and made life difficult for everybody. This personality expressed anger and noncompliance. It was very important that the therapist feel empathic with this part of this woman as the only expression, so far, of the outrage of the violation she had experienced.

Thinking about these strategies for staying out of connection in this way can make a big difference in our whole attitude. We can feel a new kind of respect and honoring, sometimes admiration, for some of the strategies women have developed, even as we believe they are making problems for themselves and for the therapist. Most important, this attitude can help us stay empathic with both sides of the basic paradox, that is, empathic with the side that is militating toward staying out of connection as well as the side that is longing for connection.

In saying this, we want to emphasize again that it is not just a question of the therapist understanding the strategies but of really being able to "get with" the feeling of them that makes the difference, that makes the therapy move. The therapist's deep respect for the strategies is very important because the strategies are usually the parts of therapy that make the most trouble, the parts in which people can seem most off-putting or angry-making or numbers of other things. They are the parts that lead therapists to label people manipulative, narcissistic, entitled, and the like, the kind of labeling that moves the therapist further out of connection and does a great deal of harm. (Incidentally, this approach is not to be confused with the paradoxical interventions used by some family therapists—that is something different.)

AN ILLUSTRATION

A period in treatment with a young woman, whom we'll call Ruth, may help to illustrate these points. Ruth came to therapy with several issues. She was very competent at work, but she had some problems there. She had a number of physical symptoms. Ruth had a very rapid, articulate, clever, witty way of talking, often using ridicule and contempt for the many people she criticized. I (J.B.M.) often felt put off and ineffectual and also critical of this contemptuous approach, particularly so when I felt this attack turned on me, though it wasn't directly yet. However, I didn't believe it would be helpful to be critical. As a result, I used a strategy for staying out of connection that I find ready at hand, which was to be more silent. However, I did think I was sensitive to Ruth's strategies, and I felt that I was able to be empathic at least some of the time.

Ruth had described her parents as loving, often involved with the children, doing fun things at times. However, it was becoming more apparent that her father was probably a heavy, consistent drinker, a fact that she had never fully recognized. She remembered her mother also as there for her sometimes, but it was becoming clearer that there were important times when her mother was psychologically "not there." She was beginning to put this together and to recognize that her mother was probably depressed and preoccupied with attending to her father. She was talking about what it would mean to raise questions about her father's drinking and realized that it felt, even now, like an absolute impossibility in her family. No one would tolerate it; in fact, they would turn on her and attack her. Then Ruth remembered a specific time in childhood when she was ill and really wanted her mother, and her mother was not there. She spoke of being able to feel that longing and of feeling terribly alone, frightened, and especially humiliated to think of feeling this desire and feeling it unresponded to. Ruth's whole manner of talking revealed the importance of this experience. She spoke haltingly, without any of her cleverness and wit; and as she talked of her longing and her humiliation, she spoke with much pain. I was very moved and felt that we were really progressing.

At the next session, Ruth seemed totally back to her old style; there was none of the moving emotion of the prior session. I felt pushed away and less connected. But she brought a dream. There was a terrible explosion in a house. Ruth knew a child was in the house; she was struggling through it to reach the child. She had the sense that other people were around. She managed to reach the child, who was lying unconscious. Now, however, no one else seemed to be there.

We discussed the dream and talked about the feeling that an explosion would have occurred in her family if she talked about what was going on, as she saw it. Also, we talked about her feeling that she would be badly hurt if she stated her own experience and there would be no one there to be with her. Perhaps she had learned to become unconscious, to not know the trouble in her family and what was affecting her. She herself, however, was trying to search for the hurt child and trying to attend to her. I raised the possibility that the dream might also portray Ruth's fear that I, too, would not be there when she needed me, or if she attended to her own experience, thoughts, and feelings. Ruth discussed all this but without much feeling; the strategies were back.

The session was quite dull by comparison with the very moving prior session. However, I felt that Ruth's creating, remembering, and bringing in the dream conveyed the other side of the paradox and represented her attempt to stay connected. Simultaneously, the explosion image taught us both how terrifying it felt to move away from her strategies. Also, she was perhaps beginning to feel that I could be with her when she talked about the feelings that really mattered to her, but she probably just couldn't proceed without having a chance to recognize more fully how terrifying it was and without making more certain that I knew that. She also needed to know that I could withstand her feelings, feelings she had to assume must have been so unacceptable and terrible that her family couldn't be with her in them.

Within a short time, Ruth returned to her growing recognition of her own experience in relationships. However, the pattern of following a period of moving connection with a period of clever, nonfeeling conversation repeated many more times in various forms. At these times, I had to deal with the disappointment I felt when I thought we were moving along and then found Ruth back to her old style. I would feel immobilized and without impact as well as shut out and not connected. But both Ruth and I were able to keep finding the ways to forge a new connection.

However, I mainly wanted to highlight Ruth's dream because it so nicely illuminated the paradox and helped us both to really "get with" her strategies for staying out of connection, even as the dream itself was a way of moving toward connection. The picture of the hurt child helped me to experience with Ruth those terrifying feelings of being so hurt with no one there to respond. In a way, this is one of those dreams that is everywoman's dream or, indeed, everyone's dream. I suspect that as I was moved more, Ruth was moved more and began to be more convinced that I could be with her. I think this helped me drop more of my strategy of being silent with her. This process made it possible to move to new connections even as we moved out of connection repeatedly.

BUILDING CONNECTIONS

A more accurate way to state all of this is to say that as we moved into new connections, the relationship between us was enlarged and empowered. We now had more resources, more energy, action, knowledge, sense of value, and sense of connection in the relationship, that is, as was suggested in the beginning of this chapter, the five components of any mutually empathic and mutually empowering connection. These aspects of the relationship were there for both of us. It was not a question of giving or getting for one or the other, or of being gratified or not gratified in the usual meaning of those terms.

At the times when a person moves into more connection based on her more real representation of her experience, she simultaneously makes a change in her inner experience. She comes to feel in greater connection with her own experience and to feel a right to that experience; she grows in authenticity and in "self-empathy," as Jordan (1991) has described it. Also, she and the people with whom she involves herself feel a greater sense of her "being there," of her presence in the relationship.

As we said at the beginning, we believe that the moments of therapist and patient moving into greater connection are the levers of change in therapy. We all know that we can make all the interpretations in the world and nothing changes. Many theorists have said that the affective level has to be added and that dissociated or repressed material has to be brought in and integrated. We are adding that the more basic step is the therapist feeling *moved* and more connected. When this shift toward greater authentic connection occurs, it means the therapist has expanded. Each patient will call for the therapist to stretch in certain dimensions.

Now we want to make clear we are not talking about a quest for an ecstatic experience or emotional high, nor are we talking about some attempt to generate a "feel-good" experience. We are talking about the therapist participating in the relationship in a way that will lead to mutual empathy and mutual empowerment. This means that if therapist and patient participate in this way, they will inevitably become more connected. We don't see how it could be otherwise. We also want to make clear that bringing in the emotional component does not mean that the thinking component goes out. We believe that the whole dichotomy between thinking and feeling is a false one and, incidentally, a gender-specific one.

Therapy consists of the often difficult, painstaking attempts to move from disconnection to new connection. It requires from the therapist a deep knowledge of psychological development, a knowledge of the experiences of disconnection and violation and their accompanying emotions and sequelae. It requires training and work with supervisors and peers on how a therapist can learn to "move in relationship" and to facilitate the difficult steps away from strategies of disconnection, through the terrible fears of vulnerability, and on to new connections.

Through this movement the patient can come to understand what has happened to her, both the disconnections that have occurred but, more important, how they felt to her and, specifically, the awfulness of these experiences in their particularity for her. She can also understand her very specific strategies for staying out of connection. All of these or parts of them may have been dissociated, repressed or out of awareness to varying degrees. This might be called insight or self-understanding, but we believe it cannot occur, that the patient cannot feel safe to enter the realms of pain and terror without feeling a movement toward connection in the therapist—the connection brought about by mutual empathy. Simultaneously, these experiences of enhanced connection lead to the growth of something we might call the "relational self." That is, as we said at the beginning, we see the process and goal of development as the increasing ability to participate in mutually empathic and mutually empowering connections. These connections then lead to a strong and more empowered individual who, in turn, can participate more fully in more enlarging connections and so on in a cycle of growth.

All therapists have talked about relationships in that they've talked about the therapeutic relationship. However, often in therapy, as in life, the relationship has been seen as a means to another end, such as individual development. We view it as the means and the end or, as Jordan (1991) has put it, "the key to the process of therapy not just the backdrop" (p. 284). We suspect that good therapists of many schools of thought do something like this, at least in part. However, they have not described their work in terms of building connection. We believe it helpful to continue to study therapy in this way.

In conclusion, let us say that this perspective creates a whole new attitude that we bring to the therapeutic encounter with children, adolescents, and adults, and to an understanding of what it is to struggle with problems in life. It moves away from objectifying, hierarchical, pejorative ways of describing people and leads us to appreciate how everybody comes into a relationship carrying this relational paradox in some form. The only difference between patient and therapist is that it is the therapist's job to facilitate the movement for change to more connection. We believe that the focus on connection and disconnection speaks to the central core of the human condition, the core that has remained obscure and out of focus in many psychodynamic theories because of an underlying preoccupation, not usually made explicit, with individual gratification and power. Once we examine more accurately the lives of all people, we think inevitably we find ourselves moving away from that preoccupation and toward a recognition of the necessity of human connection and the sources and consequences of disconnection.

REFERENCES

Fairbairn, W. R. D. (1952). *An object relations theory of personality*. New York: Basic Books.

Freud, S. (1910). The future prospects of psychoanalytic therapy. *Standard Edition* 11:139–152.

Fromm-Reichman, F. (1950). *Principles of Intensive Psychotherapy*. Chicago: University of Chicago Press.

Gill, M. (1983). *Analysis of Transference*, vol. 1. New York: International Universities Press.

Gilligan, C. (1982). *In a Different Voice*. Cambridge, MA: Harvard University Press.

_____ (1990). Joining the resistance: psychology, politics, girls, and women. *Michigan Quarterly Review* 29:501–536.

Gilligan, C., Lyons, N., and Hammer, T. (1990). *Making Connections*. Cambridge, MA: Harvard University Press.

Havens, L. (1986). *Making Contact*. Cambridge, MA: Harvard University Press.

Jordan, J. (1989). Relational development: therapeutic implications of empathy and shame. *Work in Progress*, no. 29. Wellesley, MA: Stone Center Working Paper Series.

_____ (1991). Empathy, mutuality, and therapeutic change: clinical implications of a relational model. In *Women's Growth in Connection*, ed. J. Jordan, A. Kaplan, J. B. Miller, et al. New York: Guilford.

Kaplan, A. (1984). The "self-in-relation": implications for depression. *Work in Progress*, no. 14. Wellesley, MA: Stone Center Working Paper Series.

Miller, J. B. (1986). What do we mean by relationships? *Work in Progress* 22. Wellesley, MA: Stone Center Working Paper Series.

_____ (1988). Connections, disconnections, and violations. *Work in Progress*, no. 30. Wellesley, MA: Stone Center Working Paper Series.

Mirkin, M. (1990). Eating disorders: a feminist family therapy perspective. In *The Social and Political Contexts of Family Therapy*, ed. M. Mirkin. Boston, MA: Allyn and Bacon.

Modell, A. H. (1984). *Psychoanalysis in a New Context*. New York: International Universities Press.

Rogers, C. R. (1951). *Client Centered Therapy: Its Current Practice, Implications, and Theory*. Boston: Houghton Mifflin.

Steiner-Adair, C. (1991). New maps of development, new models of therapy: the psychology of women and treatment of eating disorders. In *Psychodynamic Treatment of Anorexia Nervosa and Bulimia*, ed. C. Johnson. New York: Guilford.

Stiver, I. (1990a). Dysfunctional families and wounded relationships, part 1. *Work in Progress*, no. 41. Wellesley, MA: Stone Center Working Paper Series.

_____ (1990b). Dysfunctional families and wounded relationships, Part II. *Work in Progress*, No.41. Wellesley, MA: Stone Center Working Paper Series.

_____ (1990c). *Movement in therapy*. Paper delivered at the Annual Meeting of the American Psychological Association.

Stolorow, R. D., Brandchaft, B., and Atwood, G. E. (1987). *Psychoanalytic Treatment: An Intersubjective Approach*. Hillsdale, NJ: Analytic.

Sullivan, H. S. (1953). *The Interpersonal Theory of Psychiatry*. New York: W. W. Norton.

Surrey, J. (1984). The self-in-relation: a theory of women's development. *Work in Progress* 14. Wellesley, MA: Stone Center Working Paper Series.

_____ (1987). Relationships and empowerment. *Work in Progress*, no. 30. Wellesley, MA: Stone Center Working Paper Series.

_____ (1991). Some conceptions and reconceptions of a relational approach. *Work in Progress*, no. 49. Wellesley, MA: Stone Center Working Paper Series.

Tansey, M. J., and Burke, W. F. (1989). *Understanding Counter-*

transference: From Projective Identification to Empathy. Hillsdale, NJ: Analytic.

Wolf, E. S. (1983). Countertransference in disorders of the self. In *Countertransference*, ed. L. Epstein and A. H. Feiner. Northvale, NJ: Jason Aronson.

PART VII

The Use of Fairy Tales and Metaphors in Psychotherapy

INTRODUCTION TO PART VII

Much of the therapeutic work done with children explores their fantasy life through play therapy. Narratives and other fabricated stories often find their way into the therapy room. One important tool to help the therapist communicate about and, at times, interpret deeper intrapsychic material to a child patient is through the use of metaphor. At Reiss-Davis this technique is taught to the fellows as part of their play therapy course and is encouraged in their supervision, so that they can more effectively enter into the psychic life of their patients. The Center has also been fortunate to have had two experts in the field of metaphor, especially as it expresses itself in fairy tales, Rudolf Ekstein and Bruno Bettelheim. It is, therefore, not surprising that this section focuses solely on metaphor and fairy tales.

The two chapters in this section consider the realm of fantasy: the child's narrative through fairy tales and the domain of the fairy tale. Through the child's story we can get a glimpse of the relations between conscious and unconscious processes in the inner world of the child. In Chapter 20, "What the Tales in Fairy Tales Tell Us," Joan Lang examines the impact of myths, legends, fairy tales, and fables as important sources of information about the shaping of the feminine psyche. Looking at recurrent themes presented by female patients, Lang emphasizes that we cannot escape our metaphors and myths, that they are influenced by unconscious processes, and that they shape our theories, our perceptions of data, and the questions we formulate. Her article suggests that studying these issues in the treatment of women helps us to formulate and implement greater comprehension of the nature of the feminine psyche.

Rudolf and Jean Ekstein argue in Chapter 21, "Children's and Adolescents' Own Fairy Tales and Their Treatment Implications," that analysts realized very early that mythology and folklore—the fairy tale or the private fantasy of a patient—are immensely important in understanding the mind of the person who seeks help. The authors look at aspects of fairy tales written by children, the first by an 8-year-old boy, followed by that of an adolescent girl. This chapter illustrates how the invention of a story or the additions and deletions to a traditional fairy tale enable the therapist to come nearer to his or her goal of understanding the child. Finally, excerpts of other fairy tales generated by children are also explored. These focus on the manifest content to further examine the latent drives and desires evident in fairy tales.

20

What the Tales in Fairy Tales Tell Us

Joan A. Lang, M.D.

THE MEANING OF *CULTURAL MYTHS*

The thesis I will advance here begins with the premise that myths are neither misconceptions nor absolute universal truths. Rather, I propose that we understand cultural myths as representations of part of a people's effort to capture, in story form, some aspects of their most critical existential puzzles and conflicts, as well as their efforts to understand and resolve these conflicts. In some ways, myths are to cultures what dreams are to individuals; in other ways, they are instruments of cultural transmission—the socializing tools of cultures. I shall return to these analogies and their implications later.

Mythic themes can be expressed culturally in a variety of forms. Myths, legends, fairy tales, and fables, the traditional forms of myth, are augmented by modern story forms of American culture, such as the Horatio Alger story and tales of science fiction superheroes. These can be as rich in mythic themes and symbols (and serve the same "cultural function") as classical myths and fairy tales.

My own interest in cultural myths is rooted in my belief in their importance as sources of information about the shaping of the feminine psyche. Presumably, such myths can tell us just as much about the formation of the male psyche (and perhaps the lesbian, gay, and androgynous psyche as well); however, those questions will not be addressed in this chapter. I come to this topic as neither a mythologist nor a social scientist, but as a psychoanalyst, a woman, and a mother of two daughters. I list these personal facts in relevant order: the recurrent themes presented by my female child, adolescent, and adult patients in their painful struggles to understand and realize themselves first led me to an interest in this topic; in turn, I was forced to reexamine my own struggles of this type. Finally, I have been motivated by my concern that my daughters have as fair a chance at self-fulfillment as can be achieved in our society.

I offer this personal data because I believe it is an important part of the context within which ideas must be evaluated. Moreover, it is crucial to realize that any serious attempt to explain the nature of human existence becomes, in itself, equivalent to yet another cultural myth. All of our concepts, however "scientific," are constructs of consciousness. As such, all have a cultural history, and all have been influenced by the unconscious processes of those who have invented and used them. We cannot escape our metaphors and myths: they shape not only our theories but our perceptions of data, what we choose to regard as data, and even the questions we find important to ask in the first place. This implicit mythic structure can be destructive or enriching; in any case, it must at least be recognized. Otherwise, we risk confusing myth with fact, and treating metaphors as proven truths. The grave misuses of the metaphors of Darwin, translated into social Darwinism, and those of Freud, whose myth of penis envy has been well analyzed by others,[1]

---

[1]See Bruno Bettelheim's *Symbolic Wounds* (1954) for an example of the ways

illustrate this danger.

Thus, when I use the word *myth*, I am not referring to a specific literary form but rather to themes or symbols, in any narrative, that transcend the concrete to express something felt to be essential and enduring; themes or symbols invested with, or evocative of, a belief about this essential nature; or themes or symbols experienced as explanatory of observable phenomena.

With all this in mind, we must now ask what special relevance the study of cultural myths can have for an understanding of the formation and nature of the feminine psyche and the treatment of female patients. In response to this question, let us return to my analogies of the nature of myths: myths as dreams and myths as socializing tools.

MYTHS AS DREAMS

Dream is the personalized myth, myth is the depersonalized dream; both myth and dream are symbolic in the same general way of the dynamics of the psyche. But in the dream the forms are quirked by the peculiar troubles of the dreamer, whereas in myth the problems and solutions shown are directly valid for all mankind. [Campbell 1968, p. 19]

This eloquent description of myths as dreams can be found in Joseph Campbell's book, *The Hero with a Thousand Faces.* I take issue only with his use of the word *valid*. Campbell believes that what he calls the "timeless vision" of mythic (and/or dream) symbols and themes can be trusted, that myths have some intrinsically validating cosmic source. In contrast, I contend that a belief about the existence of such a cosmic source is in itself a myth, as defined here. As a belief, Campbell's timeless vision can be thought about, and his arguments for it responded to, but it cannot be taken for granted. We must ask: Without assuming cosmic validation, what are myths?

---

in which Freudian theory distorted "scientific" observations of behavior. See also William Irwin Thompson's exposition of scientific mythologizing in *The Time Falling Bodies Take to Light: Mythology, Sexuality, and the Origins of Culture* (1981).

I maintain that myths are the culturally refined distillations of a culture's "collective dreams" (Campbell 1968, p. 256). They possess some of the advantages, when it comes to determining what is "true," that a jury has over a defendant, or that history has over rumor. On the other hand, they possess some of the disadvantages of the product of a committee (or a mob). That is, myths represent what is collectively believed (or hoped, or feared) about human existence, its problems, and its salvations. Unavoidably, human belief systems are shaped by the psyches of "believers," with all of their fallibility and irrationality. (This must be granted, even if one accepts the existence of a cosmic source, because of the distortion introduced by human filters; limitations, agendas, and "noise." As Campbell asserts: "There is no final system for the interpretation of myths. The various judgements depend upon the viewpoint of the judges. Mythology, like everything else, is amenable to the obsessions and requirements of the individual, the race, the age" (p. 382).

MYTHS AS SOCIALIZING TOOLS

This brings us to my second analogy: myths as tools for socialization and for the transmission of culture. This viewpoint has been forcefully argued by such feminist writers as Simone de Beauvoir, Andrea Dworkin, Mary Daly, and Rosemary Ruether. They contend that myths essentially function to brainwash people (men, races, but especially women), to socialize them into culturally defined, stereotypic roles. For example, Dworkin writes:

When one enters the world of fairy tale one seeks with difficulty for the actual place where legend and history part. One wants to locate the precise moment when fiction penetrates into the psyche as reality, and history begins to mirror it. Or vice versa. Women live in fairy tale as magical figures, as beauty, danger, innocence, malice, and greed. In the personae of the fairy tale—the wicked witch, the beautiful princess, the heroic prince—we find what the culture would have us know about who we are.

The point is that we have not formed that ancient world—it has formed us. We ingested it as children whole, had its values and consciousness imprinted on our minds as cultural absolutes long before we were in fact men and women. We have taken the fairy tales of childhood with us into maturity, chewed but still lying in the stomach, as real identity. [1974, pp. 32–33]

Ruether (1975) equates mythopoetic symbols with ideologies (she includes religions and psychology in this category), and holds that they are the absolutely essential "cultural superstructure for a system of male domination which is socioeconomic and systemic in character. These ideologies try to make the social structure look 'natural,' inevitable, and divinely given" (pp. xiv), thus providing "symbolic rationalization" of a cultural definition of reality.

I take issue with the notion that "we have not formed that ancient world." Have women not participated? Did all of human culture really arise from something totally "not us"? Like Campbell's "timeless vision" or cosmic source, such a claim lies in the realms of personal belief and myth.

MYTHS ABOUT MYTHS

As we look at the writings of Campbell and other mythologists, and those of Dworkin and other feminists, we notice a very interesting dichotomy. Essentially, we can discern two competing *myths about myths*, which I will call the *visionary myth about myths* and the *feminist myth about myths*.

In the visionary myth about myths, Man, the Hero, is perpetually engaged in a titanic struggle. He must resist the obstacles placed in his path by a hostile or mundane reality (or by human frailty) that threaten to drag him down and distract him from his Quest. He must remain true to his search for the vision. In this struggle, myth is "the living inspiration . . . the secret opening through which the inexhaustible energies of the cosmos pour into human cultural manifestations [Campbell 1968, p. 31] . . . to supply the symbols that carry the human spirit forward" (p. 11).

In the feminist myth about myths, Woman, the true Heroine, has been enslaved by the Villain, Man, who has succeeded in imprisoning and degrading her with the assistance of the institutions of Culture and the tools of Myth, and with their Authority he robs her of her spirit. It is her true Quest to dispel these myths, break free of her bonds, and realize her destiny as a Heroine. Only if she succeeds in doing so is there any hope of rescuing society from its mad, doomed course toward total self-destruction, and of restoring humankind to a state of harmony with itself and with nature.

Must we really choose between these views? Are there alternatives? Is there some resolution, some transcendence that acknowledges the truth within each?

There are certainly alternative schools of interpretation: for example, the Jungian approach to myth via the concepts of *collective unconscious* and *archetypes* (Hillman 1972, Neumann 1963), the purely psychoanalytic analyses (Heuscher 1974), Thompson's (1981) notion that there are different levels of understanding and appreciation of myth that correspond to different "ages" of civilization, and so on.

I propose that all of these interpretations have hold of a piece of the elephant,[2] and could add something to our grasp of the overall truth. By the same token, as Thompson points out, "one man's [or woman's] noise is another's information," and we may be able to learn as much by noting what data scholars throw out or cannot perceive as by considering what they believe to be key. I maintain that we need *not* commit ourselves to any one school of thought, or deny that approaching myth with different questions in mind could yield different kinds of knowledge. In my effort to elucidate the formation of the feminine psyche, I will use here the tools of psychoanalysis to approach myths like dreams, that is, for what they may reveal about our unconscious symbolizations and images of the female. In this, I will pay allegiance to both of the opposing myths about myths outlined

---

[2]My philosopher husband points out, however, that to accept the terms of my thesis is to deny the existence of any "elephant" at all: there *is* no objectively definable "reality," only our efforts to organize our perceptions and experience into useful and meaningful patterns.

earlier. I will assume that mythic themes and symbols are products of the human psyche, but I will also assume that psyche is formed by culture, in the manner of Dworkin's "fiction penetrat[ing] the psyche as reality" (1974, pp. 32–33).

I have chosen two myths to consider in some detail, but before I turn to them, let me address one obvious objection: that as there are thousands of myths from which one might choose, no limited sample can provide a valid base for generalization. While humility and caution are always appropriate constraints to generalization, there is yet another myth about myths hidden in this objection that we must expose.

Bettelheim dismisses the concerns of feminists about sexual stereotyping in fairy tales with the following two claims:

> Fairy tales do not render such one-sided pictures. Even when a girl is depicted as turning inward in her struggle to become herself, and a boy as aggressively dealing with the external world, these two *together* symbolize the two ways in which one has to gain selfhood . . . In this sense the male and female heroes are again projections into different figures of two (artificially) separate aspects of one and the same process which *everybody* has to undergo in growing up. While some literal-minded parents do not realize it, children know that, whatever the sex of the hero, the story pertains to their own problems. [1976, pp. 226–227]

And

> Since there are thousands of fairy tales, one may safely guess that there are probably equal numbers where the courage and determination of females rescue males, and vice versa. This is as it should be since fairy tales reveal important truths about life. [p. 227]

In contrast to Bettelheim's "safe guess," consider the efforts of Ethel Johnston Phelps, who sifted literally thousands of fairy and folk tales in a search for tales of clever, resourceful heroines, using sources from around the world. In two volumes (*The Maid of the North*, 1975, and *Tatterhood and Other Tales*, 1978), she was able to present only forty-six tales, out of the thousands recorded, that demonstrate this kind of heroine. Not surprisingly, Phelps concludes that such heroines are rare.

Relevant here, too, are studies analyzing children's texts and literature for their presentation of images of boys, girls, men, and women. The results are uniformly dismaying: a typical analysis reveals boys outnumbering girls as protagonists by 881 to 344, with girl protagonists usually engaged in more passive, homemaking activities. Nearly all mothers are found in the kitchen (Belotti 1976).

The point made by this type of study is that the attribution of roles and qualities to boys and to girls is not random and cannot be disregarded as "artificially separated aspects of one and the same process," nor as incidental details. In fact, it is just those gender-descriptive aspects of popular myth that are the most relentlessly stereotypic. Thus, children *accurately* perceive that such details are intended to be part of the message conveyed by the tales. As Dworkin (1974) says, "They delineate the roles, interactions, and values which are available to us" (pp. 34–35).

Thus, I am forced to conclude that mythologists may be no freer of androcentric bias than was Freud. Questions of sexist bias in myths, and of the origins, meanings, and effects of such bias do not interest them much; they simply cannot "see" the data that are so compelling to feminists. This is not to say that their belief in the irrelevance of gender among mythic heroes is absolutely foolish. It might well be that, all other things being equal, a free and equal identification of boys and girls with any and all of the heroes and heroines would indeed occur, as I think it did in my own little girls. But increasingly, as children grow up in our society, all things do *not* remain equal for girls and boys, and it is unrealistic to expect that children will continue to think and act as though the "data" conveyed in fairy tales had nothing to do with other gender-stereotyped cultural messages.[3]

WOMEN IN MYTHS AND FAIRY TALES

The overwhelming majority of myths and fairy tales that our culture presents to us and our children, and the social realities

---

[3]See also the works of Erik Erikson on identity and the ego's roots in social organization and R. Stoller's research on gender identity, which demonstrates the power of parental myth.

they reflect, offer a consistent split of roles along gender lines. The good heroine is beautiful, innocent, passive, and waiting—for rescue and for a life lived happily ever after with the hero, the prince. Here we include Snow White, Sleeping Beauty, Rapunzel, Lois Lane, and countless others. Alternative leading roles for women are limited: she can be a temptress or a witch—in either case, wicked and deserving of a bad end—or she can play a supportive role as a fairy godmother or kindly grandmother type, but in these she is almost always old and never sexual.

The details of "living happily ever after" usually remain vague, and what is said defies reality with its depressing incidence of divorce, rape and abuse, depression and mental illness, discrimination in the workplace, and so on. We avoid confronting such unpleasant realities by perpetuating such mythic notions as Adam's rib; woman is, man does; a man's home is his castle; a woman's place is in the home; Mom and apple pie; woman, the peacemaker; and many others. As de Beauvoir (1974) has observed, "The contrary facts of experience are impotent against the myth" (p. 286).

A crucial point in all of this has often escaped feminists who analyze sex discrimination solely in terms of power, politics, law, economics, and history: the need to explain the collusion of women in their own subjugation. Powerful sources of resistance to change in the prevailing male-dominance system often arise from within the woman herself (witness Phyllis Schlafly and others). Even female analysts (Helene Deutsch, Marie Bonaparte, and others) have concluded that attributes described in fairy tales (e.g., passivity, masochism, narcissism, dependency) are integral parts of the female psyche. Alternative explanations relying on learning-theory models assume that "liberation" from male-dominance mentalities will be achieved by reeducation and new role models; other explanations seek to eliminate one or another source of fears on intellectual objections. Unfortunately, matters turn out not to be so simple. The interactions by which conflicts embedded deep in the human psyche work to shape our cultural institutions and myths, and by which the culture in turn works to shape the individual psyche, are much more complex than existing models have so far explained.

Some years ago, a patient of mine discovered, in a particularly

vivid and poignant way, the extent to which she had unconsciously internalized a culturally determined view of the value
of women. A successful female surgeon who had assumed total
responsibility for managing her home and children—an arrangement regarded as "natural" by her busy lawyer husband—
rejected my interpretations of her deep unconscious resentment
of this family arrangement, and was impatient with my interpretations of her unconscious devaluation of herself as a woman.
But one morning she came to my office pale and shaken. She had
worked all night in the operating room trying to save a baby, but
the child had died, and it fell to her to tell the parents. As she
walked out, collecting herself for the painful task, she found
herself thinking, "Thank God it wasn't a son!"

Let us now consider two specific myths: the Cinderella myth
and the cultural mythology surrounding ten centuries of Chinese footbinding.

I will not recount the story of Cinderella, which is by all
accounts the best known and best loved of all fairy tales
(Bettelheim 1976, p. 236). It has existed for centuries in various
versions from different countries (some folklorists record as
many as 700). Analysis of this myth reveals many levels and
kinds of meaning. Remembering that the answers found are
likely to depend heavily on the questions asked, we should not
be surprised that Bettelheim, a male psychoanalyst, discovers
themes of sibling rivalry and wish fulfillment, as well as deeper
levels of unconscious association to complex material (including
some that we will consider later); feminists (e.g., Kolbenschlag,
Dworkin), on the other hand, find a moral fable about sex-role
stereotyping and female socialization. Remembering, too, that
one approach does not necessarily invalidate the other, let us
assume that Bettelheim offers valuable insights into psychological and personal levels of meaning that the tale can evoke in a
child's conscious and unconscious mind. Given this, however, it
becomes all the more important, in light of our interest in the
formation of the feminine psyche, to see also that which eludes
him.

Bettelheim writes:

The discrimination which females suffer when compared with
males is an age-old story now being challenged. It would be

strange if this discrimination did not also create jealousy and envy between sisters and brothers within the family. . . . Each sex is jealous of what the other has which it lacks, much though either sex may like and be proud of what belongs to it—be it status, social role, or sexual organs.[1976, p. 266]

But having gone this far, he is then motivated to search the Cinderella myth for manifestations of sexual rivalry as though they are deeply hidden, specifically for covert allusions in the tale to "castration anxiety," since he is convinced that only such associations can possibly explain the story's wide appeal. Not too surprisingly, he finds the expected allusions. (His path to them, however, seems so convoluted that I will not detail it here.) The question of whether interpreting the story's themes in terms of this psychological theory does or does not illuminate it is not central to the main line of my argument, in any case. I wish to focus, instead, on one aspect of the story that captures Bettelheim's attention and becomes crucially woven into the castration anxiety theme: an incident, in almost all versions of the story, in which the stepsisters mutilate their feet to make them fit the tiny slipper. If this gory episode was absent from the Disney-ized versions of your childhood, here is the relevant portion from the complete *Grimm's Fairy Tales* (1944):

The eldest went with the shoe into her room and wanted to try it on, and her mother stood by. But she could not get her big toe into it, and the shoe was too small for her. Then her mother gave her a knife and said: "Cut the toe off; when you are Queen you will have no more need to go on foot." The maiden cut the toe off, forced the foot into the shoe, swallowed the pain, and went out to the King's son. Then he took her on his horse as his bride and rode away with her. . . . Then he looked at her foot and saw how the blood was trickling from it. He turned his horse round and took the false bride home again, and said she was not the true one, and that the other sister was to put the shoe on. Then this one went into her chamber and got her toes safely into the shoe, but her heel was too large. So her mother gave her a knife and said: "Cut a bit off your heel; when you are Queen you will have no more need to go on foot." The maiden cut a bit off her heel, forced her foot into the shoe, swallowed the pain, and went out to the King's son. He took her on his horse as his bride, and rode away with her. . . . He looked down at her foot and saw the blood was running out of her shoe, and how it had stained her white stocking quite red. Then he turned his horse and took the false bride home again. [pp. 126–127]

Bettelheim (1976), who sees this as "a detail of such extraordinary crudeness and cruelty," and tells us that "self-mutilations are rare in fairy tale," decides that the only explanation is "that it *must* have been *invented* for some specific, though probably unconscious reason" (pp. 267–268, emphasis mine).

Thus can mythologizing distort "scientific" explanation. For as I shall presently show, there is another, far less convoluted possible explanation. And it is one that most probably was within Bettelheim's ken, for he has earlier told us (as matter of passing, historical note) that the Cinderella story has "facets which point to an Eastern, if not necessarily Chinese, origin," and has even commented that "the modern hearer does not connect sexual attractiveness and beauty . . . with smallness of the foot, as the ancient Chinese did, in accordance with their practice of binding women's feet" (pp. 267–268).

An alternative explanation of the "crude details" of the mutilation can be found in the historical practice of Chinese women of having their feet crippled and mutilated for precisely the reason the fairy tale depicts: to make themselves desirable to a man and to obtain a good marriage. These bound feet did, in fact, bleed. The girls were, in fact, urged—usually even forced—by their mothers. They were, in fact, thus rendered unable ever "to go on foot": the feet, reduced to 3 or 4 inches long (the ideal "Golden Lotus" was 3 inches), were not very functional. Consider this account of a young Chinese girl's experience:

My feet felt on fire and I couldn't sleep; Mother struck me for crying. On the following days I tried to hide but was forced to walk on my feet. Mother hit me on my hands and feet for resisting. Beatings and curses were my lot for covertly loosening the wrappings. The feet were washed and rebound after three or four days, with alum added. After several months, all toes but the big one were pressed against the inner surface. Whenever I ate fish or freshly killed meat, my feet would swell, and the pus would drip. Mother criticized me for placing pressure on the heel in walking, saying that my feet would never assume a pretty shape. Mother would remove the bindings and wipe the blood and pus which dripped from my feet. She told me that only with the removal of the flesh could my feet become slender. If I mistakenly punctured a sore, the blood gushed like a stream. My somewhat fleshy big toes were bound with small pieces of cloth and forced upwards, to assume a new moon shape.[4]

In contrast to the brutal reality of footbinding, however, an elaborate sexual and romantic mythology surrounded the practice, involving shoes, body movements, and sexual play. The mythology rationalized, romanticized, and sanctified the painful crippling of women. And it did so most effectively. It was internalized. Mothers did it to their daughters. Women did it to each other. Women who had natural, unbound feet were ashamed.

From our distance of time and space, we can penetrate the mythology of Chinese footbinding to its true horror. But what of the reality that has been "prettied up" in our version of the Cinderella myth? Cinderella's feet are naturally tiny. Is this not a parable for the internalization of constrictions into the feminine psyche, constrictions that are cruel in their own way, when stripped of their mythology? No one has to do it to Cinderella: she willingly accepts her abasement, she is proud of this definition of her "beauty" and worth, and she relies on her expectation of rescue through a man and marriage.

The essential meaning of this fairy tale was well understood and conveyed in a cartoon I saw some years ago that depicted Cinderella and her fairy godmother, with the beautiful castle visible on a mountaintop in the distance. The caption showed Cinderella saying to her godmother, "Thanks very much, but would you mind terribly sending me to law school instead?"

WOMEN'S PSYCHE

How are we to understand this phenomenon of women's participation in and internalization of their own subjugation?

---

[4]For the rest of the harrowing, first-person account of this brutal practice, see Dworkin (1974), pp. 99–101), who is quoting part of an interview with a Chinese woman in 1934, from Levy's *Chinese Footbinding: The History of a Curious Erotic Custom* (1966). Note that to this male scholar, this horrible mutilation is "curious" and "erotic"!

Specifically, for those of us who look to psychoanalysis for tools of insight, how are we to attempt to answer two basic questions?

1. How can we understand the psychodynamics that generate such cultural myths about women? Answering this will involve asking subsidiary questions such as: What needs does such mythology serve? What problems does it solve? What dangers does it seem to avert? Since we are talking about cultures in which men have had the power, the most fundamental question might be: What *male* needs does it serve? This leads to our second basic question.

2. Why did, and do, women consent? To say "she had no choice; she was forced," does not tell the whole story, for it does not explain women's collaboration. To return to Chinese footbinding, what happened to transform feisty, vigorous Chinese girls who at first resisted and rebelled into mothers who insisted, enforced, and participated actively? Remember that we are *not* talking here about a few "trustee"-type betrayers, but about "normal" women. We are talking about processes that transformed personality—about identity and psychic structure, conscious and unconscious.

As to the first question, regarding the psychodynamic origins of cultural myths about women, much has been written in recent years about the possible meanings and psychic origins of the male need to control and subjugate women. Vital as that body of thought is, I cannot undertake to summarize all of it here.[8] Suffice it to say that in works dealing with this idea, the notion that women's second-class citizenship is the natural order of things has been somewhat undermined by examination of such factors as male envy of women and his need to define her as "the other." I do not mean to say that this is finished business or common knowledge—much research remains to be

_____

[8]See, for example, such works as de Beauvoir's (1974) *The Second Sex*; Kate Millett's (1970) *Sexual Politics*; and Bettelheim's (1954) *Symbolic Wounds*. Refer also to Greenson's (1968) paper, "Disidentifying from mother: its special importance for the boy."

done—but I wish to focus here on the second, less asked question: What of the feminine psyche? It is in answering this question that I believe the tools of psychoanalysis, put to proper use, can be indispensable in our quest for understanding.

If we can learn to *listen* to—to hear and to wonder about—our patients' psychic material, without needing to force this material into a procrustean bed of preformed theoretical expectations (like castration anxiety), we cannot help but progress toward answers to the basic question about the feminine psyche and its interaction with cultural myths (see, for example, Bettelheim's [1954] description of the progression in his thinking about questions of male psychic development). If we approach the tools of psychoanalysis with unfettered curiosity and honesty, they can provide us unique access to the psychic raw material—ever present and potentially available—in our own experience and in our own conscious. And if we employ the concepts and tools of psychoanalysis tentatively, in the positive spirit of myth making, they can be critical in forming our analysis of the psychosocial realm—what Kohut (1980) has called "the ambiguous never-never land between endopsychic reality and social reality" (p. 495). That is, the precepts of psychoanalysis can help us investigate the roots of the psyche not only in its intrapsychic conflict with instincts, but also in its emergence from the matrix of relationships to and struggles with parents, and, importantly, in its interaction with the possibilities and limits defined and sanctioned by the culture.

The most basic tools of psychoanalysis, still indispensable, were provided by Freud, who drew our attention to several quite crucial aspects of human development:

1. Much of what we feel and do is the product not only of our conscious intentions and our rational responses to external forces, but of psychological forces such as wishes, hopes, needs, fears, and conflicts between these that operate unconsciously. (I differ from Freud here in that I do not think of biological drives as being the most determinant of these forces.)

2. The process of growing up human requires the development of psychic structures capable of thinking about, symbolizing, communicating, and mediating our con-

scious and unconscious mental processes. (Whether one conceptualizes these psychic structures as id, ego, superego; internalized object relations; invariant organizing principles; or in terms of other categories is a separate question.)

3. The prolonged period of infancy and childhood during which humans are dependent on adults ensures that social interactions will crucially determine the nature and contents of these psychic structures.

4. Such psychic structures, though difficult to change once formed, *can* be altered in adults (fortunately for us all, as individuals and as a species), but not usually by willpower or education alone, since much of what needs to be changed is unconscious and not directly accessible.

Much of what Freud described (such as the Oedipus complex or castration anxiety) must be seen in the context of the culture and the social conditions in which he lived. Thus, his clinical observations, as well as his metaphors and myths, were rooted in the patriarchal social organization, the pervasive sexual repression, and the dominant capitalist economy that prevailed in late nineteenth- and early twentieth-century Austria. Freud took for granted these aspects of social organization, which impinge greatly on the psychosocial interactions he described. Thus, he could not even consider the question of how differently a phenomenon such as penis envy might develop if some of the crucial social realities—such as the actual social advantages possessed by the penis possessors and the disadvantages of vagina possessors—were to change.

It has fallen to later theorists to challenge Freud's assumptions, and this has taken place. But do we need to throw Freud's "baby" out with its "bathwater"? The basic tools Freud provided for understanding the psychosocial dynamics of human development seem to me useful indeed. And subsequent developments in psychoanalytic theory similarly provide effective tools in our efforts to decipher male–female arrangements in our culture, and in our attempt to devise means to bring about changes in these arrangements.

Dorothy Dinnerstein (1976), in her powerful book *The Mermaid and the Minotaur*, uses insight and conceptual tools from the works of Freud, Norman Brown, and Melanie Klein. She argues compellingly that our prevailing male-dominant, female-subordinate gender arrangements represent a collective effort to resolve, in an uneasy equilibrium (or a kind of pseudosolution corresponding to an individual's neurotic symptom), some fundamental psychological tensions that lie at the heart of the human condition. We attempt to avoid a genuine confrontation of our terrible feelings of vulnerability, loneliness, and dread of dying by means of our gender definitions and arrangements. The central pillar of this "collective neurosis" of unresolved ambivalence that we thus create is the societal arrangement ensuring that we all spend a prolonged period of infancy in the direct care, almost exclusively, of women (mothers or substitute females). Dinnerstein analyzes the complex and powerful psychological repercussions of this crucial social arrangement and its implications for our cultural mythologies and institutions. Perhaps, most important, she argues that we must come to appreciate the extent to which our family and child-rearing institutions distort our psyches and produce individuals whose inner tensions led them, in turn, to perpetuate distorted and distorting cultural myths. Any efforts toward sexual liberation and social reforms that do not address these core psychological functions cannot succeed.

In *Toward a New Psychology of Women* (1976), Jean Baker Miller uses the tools of psychoanalysis to focus more specifically on the female psyche. Her starting point is the clinical material of her patients; her conceptual tools include especially those of the object-relations school of psychoanalysis. Like Dinnerstein, she believes that our gender arrangements are the result of a cultural pseudosolution to our existential human dilemmas: it is possible to avoid coming to terms with such painful issues as sexuality, mortality, and aggression in ourselves if we can instead split them off and disavow them. Yet we also recognize that we cannot—and do not even unambivalently desire to—do without the experiences related to such crucial aspects of our human nature. The effect of the pseudosolution is a projection of the unmanageable parts from ourselves onto others, and yet a retention of those others close by and under as much control as possible. Thus, men try to turn women into the carriers of all that is "carnal," while men become the carriers for that which is aggressive. Both genders lose, but both also win something, and a failure to appreciate and address our investment in this aspect of the "deal" is likely to doom any efforts to change it.

THE PSYCHOLOGY OF THE SELF

I would now like to turn to some aspects of a more recent development in psychoanalysis, the psychology of the self, as it has been elaborated by the late Heinz Kohut and his colleagues. As I will try to demonstrate, the conceptual tools offered by this theory are especially useful in our efforts to understand the relationships between cultural myths and the female psyche.

Let me first sketch very briefly the broad outlines of Kohut's theory. He considers the "self" of a human individual to possess a developmental line of its own, which includes but transcends in importance the development of such aspects of the self as its sexuality, its aggression, and even its object relationships ("aspects" that have, of course, been the central foci of drive theory and object-relations theory). This self is organized around two basic psychological functions: healthy self-assertiveness (healthy "grandiosity" or "exhibitionism") and the capacity for healthy admiration ("idealization"). In a mentally healthy adult, then,

> a core self—the "nuclear self"—is established. This structure is the basis for our sense of being an independent center of initiative and perception, integrated with our most central ambitions and ideals and with our experience that our body and mind form a unit in space and a continuum in time. This cohesive and enduring psychic configuration, in connection with a correlated set of talents and skills that it attracts to itself or that develops in response to the demands of the ambitions and ideals of the nuclear self, forms the central sector of the personality. [Kohut 1977, pp. 93–94]

Healthy development of the child's self requires that the environment provide certain features, function as a milieu of "average expectable empathic responsiveness" (pp. 252–253). Basically, this milieu depends on the availability and effectiveness of the child's important others, who provide "selfobject functions" for the child's developing self. The terms *selfobject* and *selfobject functions* are of special importance both to Kohut's overall theory and to our particular purposes here. The selfobject can be any person (or sometimes an inanimate object, such as music) that is providing functions that keep an individual's self intact and in reasonable psychic equilibrium.

During development, two kind of selfobjects (and selfobject functions) are of crucial importance: the "mirroring" and the "idealized" selfobjects. The mirroring selfobject reflects affirmation and acceptance of the self, its attributes, and its achievements back to the child. Such mirroring is vital if development is to progress normally from archaic forms of grandiosity to their adult analogues: healthy ambitions. The idealized selfobject provides a powerful, admired figure whom the child can identify with and emulate. This relationship between the child and the idealized selfobject is essential for evolution of that pole of the adult self that is organized around its ideals and values.

To understand the implications of the psychology of the self for the formation of the feminine psyche, we must consider two aspects:

1. "Mirroring" and "accepting idealization" are strictly defined in self psychological theory as *functions* that ought not be confused or conflated with specific others. This is an important distinction, helping us escape (for example) from our uncritical reference to "the mother" when thinking about influences on early development. Still, in the actual life of an individual self, these functions must be supplied by real people. Thus, the shape and contents of the developing self are vulnerable to powerful influence via the specifics of which qualities are mirrored (and which are not) and which attributes are presented as appropriate for idealization (and which are not).

2. If selfobject functions are withheld, or are delivered under distorted conditions, the impact on the developing self is grave, including the production of areas of conflict

and ignorance, but more profoundly a deficit in psychic structure. The "possible self" does not unfold; instead, there is exclusion from the consolidating self of some of its original potentials, and the distortion and derailing of the whole course of development (Kohut 1977, pp. 177–183, Lang 1984).

The first of these aspects is addressed to a degree in self psychology by Kohut's concept of "transmuting internalizations." Under optimal conditions, where trauma and disappointment at the hands of needed others are not overwhelming, the specifics of various selfobject experiences with these real people are "homogenized out." What the child absorbs and metabolizes into the self are *functions* (of soothing, admiring, etc.), shorn of their personalized aspects, which can now be performed by the self for itself, or recognized and sought from others who merit trust. This formulation assumes that the child can separate the "signal" from the "noise"—perceiving as the signal the functional aspects of *how* others respond, while discarding as unessential the specific content of the interaction. In an ideal world, such an assumption might be valid. But what of a real world where the following conditions prevail?

1. The baby's growing capacities are mirrored, or not, depending on how those capacities fit some consciously or unconsciously predetermined and arbitrary rules and categories, many of which are gender determined, rather than in ways that are freely responsive to all of the child's capabilities and natural attributes.
2. Many of the attributes presented to the child as (a) worthy of admiration and (b) possible eventually to attain are similarly rigidly classified by gender.
3. The "cultural myths" that pervade the child's milieu so stereotype the conscious and unconscious expectations of *all* potential providers of selfobject functions that they can hardly be experienced as idiosyncratic "noise."

I suggest that as long as the above conditions hold, Kohut's conceptualizations of the development of the self point us directly toward a more careful understanding of the role played by such psychosocial factors as cultural myths in the formation of the individual (male or female) psyche via the directly distorting influences of gender-based stereotypic restrictions on the mirroring and idealizing processes. In theory, there is no reason why men and women cannot fulfill both mirroring and idealizing functions equally for boys and girls (or at least fulfill these functions in ways strictly determined by gender alone). In practice, under our current gender-based child-care arrangements, this outcome is highly unlikely. Instead, girls are taught to be "good girls," and socially prescribed masculine and feminine identities are woven into the very core of the developing selves of boys and girls. All too often, a young girl thus learns that certain masculine-assigned potentials of her self are to be disavowed and excluded (made "not me"); at the same time, she discovers that those feminine-assigned potentials left to her are devalued by society. (A similar self-constricting process occurs, of course, in a boy who learns that his feminine-assigned attributes must be disavowed.) In a private conversation, I once asked Joseph Campbell what he really thought little girls could learn from our traditional heroic myths. Shockingly (to me, at least), this hero of mine answered flippantly: "Perhaps, their place!"

It seems to me inevitable that under such conditions the "expectable" empathic milieu that Kohut describes as essential for the healthy development of a child's self will likely be strained, distorted, and badly impaired. It would also seem to follow that an obvious and necessary change for the better, following directly from Kohut's formulation about the development of the self, would be exactly that recommended by feminist writers who arrived at their conclusions from a different direction: the equal sharing of parenting by men and women, and their freely empathic responsiveness to the emerging selves of their children, boys and girls, unconstrained by cultural myths defining masculinity and femininity.

REFERENCES

Bachofen, J. J. (1967). *Myth, Religion and Mother Right*. Bollingen Series 84. Princeton: Princeton University Press.

Belotti, E. G. (1976). *What Are Little Girls Made of? The Roots of Feminine Stereotypes*. New York: Schocken.

Bettelheim, B. (1954). *Symbolic Wounds: Puberty Rites and the Envious Male*. Glencoe, IL: The Free Press.

_____ (1976). *The Uses of Enchantment: The Importance and Meaning of Fairy Tales*. New York: Knopf.

Campbell, J. (1968). *The Hero with a Thousand Faces*, 2nd ed. Bollingen Series 17. Princeton: Princeton University Press.

Capra, F. (1982). *The Turning Point: Science, Society, and the Rising Culture*. New York: Simon and Schuster.

Chodorow, N. (1978). *The Reproduction of Mothering: Psychoanalysis and the Sociology of Gender*. Berkeley and Los Angeles: University of California Press.

Daly, M. (1978). *Gyn/Ecology: The Metaethics of Radical Feminism*. Boston: Beacon.

De Beauvoir, S. (1953). *The Second Sex*. New York: Random House, 1974.

Dinnerstein, D. (1976). *The Mermaid and the Minotaur*. New York: Random House.

Dworkin, A. (1974). *Woman Hating*. New York: Dutton.

Greenson, R. (1968). Disidentifying from mother: its special importance for the boy. *International Journal of Psycho-Analysis* 49:370–374.

Grimm's Fairy Tales (1944). New York: Pantheon, 1972.

Heuscher, J. E. (1974). *A Psychiatric Study of Myths and Fairy Tales: Their Origin, Meaning, and Usefulness*. Springfield, IL: Thomas.

Hillman, J. (1972). Part three: on psychological femininity. In *The Myth of Analysis*. New York: Harper Colophon.

Kohut, H. (1971). *The Analysis of the Self*. New York: International Universities Press.

_____ (1977). *The Restoration of the Self*. New York: International Universities Press.

_____ (1978). *The Search for the Self*, vol. 1, ed. P. Ornstein. New York: International Universities Press.

_____ (1978). *The Search for the Self*, vol. 2, ed. P. Ornstein. New York: International Universities Press.

_____ (1980). Selected problems in self psychological theory. In *The Search for the Self,* vol. 4, ed. P. Ornstein, pp. 489–523.

Madison, CT: International Universities Press.

_____ (1984). In *How Does Analysis Cure?*, ed. A. Goldberg, and P. E. Stepansky. Chicago: University of Chicago Press.

Kolbenschlag, M. (1979). *Kiss Sleeping Beauty Goodbye: Breaking the Spell of Feminine Myths and Models*. Garden City, NY: Doubleday.

Lang, J. A. (1984). Notes toward a psychology of the feminine self. In *Kohut's Legacy: Contributions to Self Psychology*, ed. P. E. Stepansky and A. Goldberg. Hillsdale, NJ: Analytic Press.

_____ (1990). Self psychology and the understanding and treatment of women. *Review of Psychiatry* 9:384–402. Washington, DC: American Psychiatric Press.

Luthi, M. (1970). *Once Upon a Time: On the Nature of Fairy Tales*. New York: Ungar.

Miller, J.B. (1971). Psychological consequences of sexual inequality. *American Journal of Orthopsychiatry*. 41:767–775.

_____ (1976). *Toward a New Psychology of Women*. Boston: Beacon.

Millett, K. (1970). *Sexual Politics*. New York: Avon.

Neumann, E. (1963). *The Great Mother: An Analysis of the Archetype*. Bollingen Series, 47. Princeton University Press.

Phelps, E. J., ed. (1975). *The Maid of the North: Feminist Folk Tales from Around the World*. New York: Seabury.

_____ (1978). *Tatterhood and Other Tales: Stories of Magic and Adventure*. New York: Feminist Press.

Rich, A. (1976). *Of Woman Born: Motherhood as Experience and Institution*. New York: W. W. Norton.

Ruether, R., (1975). *New Woman, New Earth: Sexist Ideologies and Human Liberation*. New York: Seabury.

Stoller, R. (1968). *Sex and Gender*, vol. 1. New York: Science House.

_____ (1975). *Sex and Gender*, vol. 2. London: International Psychoanalytic Library.

Stoller, R., and Herdt, G. H. (1982). The development of masculinity: a cross-cultural contribution. *Journal of the American Psychoanalytic Association* 30 (1): 29–58.

Thompson, W. I. (1981). *The Time Falling Bodies Take to Light: Mythology, Sexuality, and the Origins of Culture*. New York: St. Martin's.

Von Franz, M. L. (1979). *Problems of the Feminine in Fairy Tales*. Irving, TX: Spring.

Yolen, J. (1981). *Sleeping Ugly*. NY: Coward, McCann, and Geoghegan.

Zipes, J. (1986). *Don't Bet on the Prince: Contemporary Feminist Fairy Tales in North America and England*. NY: Methuen.

21

Children's and Adolescents' Own Fairy Tales and Their Treatment Implications[1]

Rudolf Ekstein, Ph.D.
with
Jean Ekstein, M.S.

When addressing readers or an audience on a topic concerning fairy tales, I think of myself in a warm atmosphere, near a fireside with but ten or fifteen friends to share it. But then, would I want to be a child listening to others' stories, or would I prefer to be the storyteller? I am unsure which position I would take: teacher, parent, or imagine myself back into childhood. Those who tell fairy tales and speak of myths must believe them and must be able to identify with those who listen and become themselves children. If they were children listening to parents, teachers, or educators, they would need to be able to identify

---

[1]The edited version of an address given at the UCLA symposium on "Images, Myths, and Fairy Tales: Timeless Therapeutic Tools" on October 18, 1981, in Los Angeles, California.

with them. In that process of identification and counteridentification there is a mutual process of attempting to teach and trying to learn. Children who tell us fairy tales teach us something—beyond and behind every fairy tale there is a psychological truth (Ekstein 1974). Those of us who teach children through fairy tales, mythology, and children's literature have something to say beyond the manifest content.

But we must keep in mind that fairy tales and mythology are not only cautionary tales (Sharpe 1952) that try to create morality; they are also magical and wondrous and try to instill faith and do something positive and gratifying for us. Perhaps the reader may try to take both positions. Let us imagine for a moment that a child speaks to us and speaks indirectly through these stories invented by and about himself. At other times you might take the position of the child who listens to an older person.

When I was a young boy in Austria, there was no radio or television; the adults of my world told me fairy tales and would also read them to me. The best fairy tales, of course, were those they did not read, but knew by heart. That's the way it was in old days. We listened to folklore that was not yet published, told by mothers and grandmothers from generation to generation until the Brothers Grimm and others collected them for preservation for the future. The old traditions were then superseded by the new traditions. Oral tradition gives way slowly to written tradition.

I listened to the fairy tales, and when my own children were young, they listened to the fairy tales I would tell them. At that time I was a newcomer to this country and had not yet acquired the English translations of the stories that gave me enchantment and happiness and magic as a little boy. I would take the German editions I had brought with me and would translate them, word for word, into English. When I read Grimm to my daughter, I was often fearful because some of these tales seemed to be cruel and full of sadism, and I was tempted to change them or leave some parts out. I could see that she might become anxious. But she would say, "Don't do that, don't do that. Don't change it. Repeat it. Tell me just exactly the way it is in the book. I'm not really scared. I want to hear the story just the way it goes." And

I learned a great deal while reading to her and remembered myself as a little boy listening to those very same fairy tales. The difference was, having become a father and an analyst, I was the one to be somewhat anxious about anxiety. I didn't see the positive part of it as did those who read the fairy tales to me; they were not anxious as they told me the old tales. In the mind of the child, it is the relationship between the conscious, the preconscious, and the unconscious; it is the total inner world.

Later, I found that the old traditions and fairy tales were in danger of being lost. It would be television now, a Disney movie or something that reminds one of mass transportation rather than a walk through the *Wienerwald*, the forest of Vienna. What a pleasure it was to learn that at universities, institutes, and other places of learning there was a possibility of getting adults together, psychologists, psychiatrists, teachers, and social workers, to restore the tradition and see that fairy tales will not be an endangered species, that they are to remain a part of children's culture.

Now, the reader may be puzzled and wonder that there is that turnabout when children begin to tell us their own tales. Allow me to throw light on the problem by means of a comparison. There is a holiday around October or November in Austria and other Catholic countries: All Souls' Day, *Allerheiligen*. In earlier years, all the families would go to the cemeteries, bringing flowers, candles, and gifts of all kinds to the graves in order to restore unity and continuity among themselves and the generation that had passed before them. Often it seemed that they were only carried by love, as if to say, "We do not care to accept the loss, we want to be near you when we come to your grave." But it became clear, as Sterba (1948) once wrote, that it was not only love that drove them to the cemeteries on that day, but also fear, unconscious fear, that the ancestors might return and be angry and demand revenge. Perhaps they were not loved enough, were permitted to die, enough was not done in order to ensure their happiness, and many sins were committed before. The Catholic ritual, meant in part as an act of love, was also the struggle against loss and remembrance, at least once during the year, and gave reassurance through the giving of flowers and gifts that the living deserved to be loved. By their visits and gifts they said, "Stay there and don't frighten us, we don't want to have skeletons come out of the grave."

But in Vienna, the story about All Souls' Day is told to children by the adult world. They tell us what it means to go to the grave; that we must love those who have left us and that we shouldn't be angry with them. We do for the dead what should also be done for the living.

In this country, I found that there was no All Souls' Day, and it was some time before I realized that we do something here that is exactly the same, albeit in reverse. Here, life is devoted more to the future than the past. Therefore, rather than All Souls' Day, we have Halloween. It is another form of All Souls' Day, but the children come not to the graves, but to the doors of the living. And they say to us, "Trick or treat." In essence, the question is: Do you love me? "Then you will give me a treat." Do you not love me? "Then it will be tricks." We are just as our ancestors were. We are ambivalent; sometimes we love and sometimes we hate. As they go around they masquerade, and often they masquerade as if they were dangerous and angry adults who have enormous power. It is the first time that they play with future identities before Erikson's (1968) *Adolescent Search for Identity*. As children, they begin to search for identity but masquerade in an identity of the wicked witch, the devil, Superman, and so on in order to frighten us into submission so that we should love them. The ambivalent relationship between different generations is expressed in both countries. In Europe, it is told to the children by their parents or the spiritual leaders. It is meant to maintain tradition. In this country, we often use the tradition in order to forget the past and to prepare for the future. We speak of a future that should be different for our children, and in Europe they speak about a past that one should honor. And this struggle between the value of the future and the value of the past is expressed in the comparison of these two festivities.

One can easily identify with both positions. We go to the graves in order to remember those who loved us once, toward whom we had and may still have ambivalent feelings, and who may have had ambivalent feelings toward us. On the other hand, often we can identify as well with the young people who come to our door, and we want to tell them that we love them but sometimes get sick and tired of their pranks. And since we don't want tricks, we want to give them treats. Or, we refuse them the treat because we feel that the trick was too dangerous or was not welcome.

This is a country, as I learned on my arrival, where one goes west in order to create a completely different life; we often give up the connection with those who were part of the past. At the same time, we constantly return to the past because we do have and need a tradition. I recall when we Americans celebrated the Bicentennial, how proud we were of our emerging history. Perhaps Europeans hold on to too much of their history and prepare too little for the future. This is a struggle between tradition and change carried out on all continents, everywhere.

So the notion that one should listen to the children's stories— what comes out of the mouths of babes—is important. As we grow older as parents, we change with our children. It is not only that we educate them, lead them to a higher level (*educare*, to lead out), but it is also that we are being educated. It is in that sense that parents go through the life cycle of parenting, as children go through the life cycle of childhood, adolescence, and early adulthood, learning from each other, often carried by struggle or by love. But hate or anger often carry us as well as anxiety. In any case, through these stories we try to restore continuity. I feel one of the greatest dangers this country faces, and has faced for quite some time, is that we have too many discontinuities in our lives, too many relationships between parents and children, between different generations broken by discontinuities. More than thirty percent of our children live in one-parent homes.

Fairy tales require us to want children to listen to our stories; but they also require us to listen to children's stories as well. Therapists have known this for quite some time. When patients come to us, we frequently use the word *regression*. They say to us, "I am helpless, I need help, listen to my story." Of course, they are eager to get our interpretation and counsel. But first, they come and say to us, "Can you listen to me, can you understand me, can you help me to see what I mean when I talk to you?" It is for this reason that analysts realized very early that mythology and folklore, the fairy tale or the private fantasy of a patient, are immensely important in order to understand the mind of the person who seeks help.

Two illustrations from my own work convey how the invention of a fairy tale, or the edited version of a fairy tale, enables the therapist to come nearer to his or her goal of understanding the patient and communicating that understanding in order to help the patient overcome his or her symptoms and restore adaptive options.

The first illustration is of an 8-year-old boy who came to me full of anger and hate against his mother. He felt persecuted because she constantly protected his younger sister and blamed him. He could not get along with her; Mother and he could not quite communicate with each other, and Father did not know how to intervene. Often the father wanted to protect the child, and at times he tried to protect the marriage. During the first therapy hour the child tried to build a house. I recalled the exciting scenes about which Erikson (1940) wrote; the exciting things about this house were missing.

It was a beautiful house with a beautiful layout (one of the expensive homes one can buy in Brentwood, California), but at first there were no people in it. There was not even a bedroom for the parents. The only room that was perfect was the kitchen, and there was an overwhelming amount of food. There was also a room for the maid who took care of the boy, but that room was outside of the house, as if she didn't belong. She, too, had a lot of food; otherwise, there was nothing. When I wondered about the people, he said children would be in it, but he never quite got around to locating the parents and the story was broken off. Erikson tells us that at the moment the topic becomes too dangerous, the information is discontinued, the play interrupted. But this child could not really give up the wish to communicate, and now began to communicate on a different level.

Thus, he said he wanted to write a television show with me. He would be the hero; he would be Superboy. I wondered what my task would be, and he said that I could annotate the script that he would write. (What a beautiful metaphor for the task of an analyst who annotates the stories that are written by the child patient.) The story was quite simple: Superboy, like Superman, is somewhere up in space and has enormous power. He gets a communication that there is tragedy on Earth and he must come to the rescue. As he comes down to rescue the people who need his help (I hadn't yet found out what the trouble was, whom he needed to rescue: his sister, whom he sometimes hated; his father, who was on his side; the maid; or perhaps the mother), he lands on Mount Saint Helens just at the moment of a volcanic eruption (even Superboy could not always project where he would land). Once there was a ten-year Trojan War, and this time there stood the little boy, surrounded by fire and earthquake. Would he be destroyed or would he save himself? I tried to annotate, and, as it usually goes with therapists, I tried to annotate too much. I was premature when I spoke about the danger of the fire; why did the mountain have a woman's name, and did the mountain (woman) hate the child? Would he be destroyed or would he help himself? Perhaps Superboy and the mountain had some way to speak to each other. Then came the boy's "Shut up, I don't want to play any longer."

The second illustration, an adolescent girl whom I treated many years ago and described in the literature (Ekstein 1966), occasionally used fairy tales. This psychotic girl wanted to tell me a story. First, she came into the consulting room and said, "How do you like my new dress?" I thought instantly that we had gone away from delusions and hallucinations and that finally I was able to see the whole situation in a more hysterical transference perspective. "Oh, that's a lovely dress. Did you just get it?" She said, "Well, it's all right, but Snow White has a much more beautiful dress." I said, "Oh, no" (first mistake), "your dress is more beautiful than Snow White's." She said, "How come? Impossible." I said, "Because your dress is real and the dress of Snow White is but magic" (second mistake). I don't need to comment on the nature of the response. At that moment, I thought the reality of the adult world was more important than the fantasy life of this sick and extremely disturbed girl. I did not want to get into her world, but I invited her into my world as if a dress, as described by the Brothers Grimm, could possibly be less beautiful than a dress you can buy at the May Company. She said, "Oh, no. Snow White's dress is much more beautiful because when her mother killed her with poison, with the apple, she was put into a coffin by the seven dwarfs and there she was in the coffin. And she was so beautiful that the little men could not let go of her. And they had her in a glass coffin and were sitting around her and were longing to hear Snow White's fairy tales because she also used to be a storyteller whenever the little men came home from work. And there they sat, and she did not move. But suddenly there came a prince, and when he saw her, that beautiful maiden, he opened the glass coffin and he kissed me on my mouth and took me on his white charger and off we went to the castle."

I had lost her again to her private delusional world because I was unwilling to see that for her the world of Snow White, the private world with the poisoning mother and the fantasy lover, was more important than my belief in boring, normal reality. I don't usually do that, but when we work with very sick people and are caught in a countertransference stance, we are so eager to win this battle of love and get the patient on our side, we don't realize we must be on their side first and identify with them if we are ever to reach them. Such patients can only identify with us after we identify with them.

Another time the same patient said, "I want to tell you a story, but I changed it. I have a better story. It is the story of Cinderella. Cinderella learned that her stepmother and her stepsisters would go to the prince's ball, and so she wanted to go along too. And she asked her stepmother and the stepsisters whether she could go along. They said, 'Of course, come along, we would love to have you join us.' And she went to the ball and she danced with the prince all the time. She didn't need to listen to the order that at midnight she must go home, she should not overstep the time limit. She would not need to go home but went on dancing. And as she went on dancing, the prince told her he wanted to marry her. She said she would, but first she would have to ask her stepmother and her stepsisters and the king. And they went to all of them and all of them said 'yes.' "

Of course, I was eager to listen to that new Cinderella and see what would emerge in this patient's mind as she was trying to move toward an aspect of adolescence that tries to search for new adult identity and intimacy. She went on: "Well, all said 'yes' and next day they would marry. The prince heard that the next day they would marry and he said, 'In that case we can sleep together today.' And she said, 'Oh, no. We don't sleep before the wedding, only after the wedding.' But he urged her and urged her and she finally said, 'If my stepmother and stepsisters give their consent.' All said 'yes.' So they went into the best room, and as she fell asleep, she had a terrible nightmare. She dreamt that a monster was after her and was going to jump on her. [And all the traditional interpretations came to my mind.] She screamed and screamed for help and woke the prince up, but the prince didn't know what to do. He called for the doctor [and I always suspected the doctor of having a Viennese accent]. The doctor came and said, 'No wedding, the wedding is off, the night is off, she needs to recover. Give her an opportunity, and we'll see whether she gets better.' As she woke up, she said it was her birthday. My birthday. And the prince brought her a huge cake and that made her well. She sat up and ate the cake.''

The reader can see that the patient's way of changing Cinderella, instead of moving forward to a place where sexual intimacy was possible, moved backward toward an older kind of intimacy, namely, the intimacy of being fed. These were two case examples of children in treatment.

Now we will introduce the material of children in a schoolroom telling stories to and for their teacher when required. The teacher gave the children the task of writing big lies: "Try and invent the biggest lie that you can." Later, the task was to be to invent fairy tales. These children, in a classroom of fifth graders between 9 and 10 years old, are in an integrated classroom. There is one white child who is an Egyptian, Asians, Hispanics, and black children. For the first task, one Hispanic child, Glenda, writes:

I live in a mousehole down in some book. I go to school at 3:00 A.M. My teacher is a gorilla and I can't understand her. That's why I skipped from first to college. I fly everywhere from England to Hawaii, from Asia to Florida, and it takes two minutes. And I made Magic Mountain in one second. I will live for 2,000 years and I am still living.

It's an interesting way of trying to create, out of helplessness —the helplessness in the schoolroom, where the teacher is seen as a dangerous person, a gorilla—a world in which there is omnipotence for her. Helplessness, omni-impotence, is turned into omnipotency: I can do all, I am extremely powerful, and she suddenly acquires magic. But indirectly, she tells the teacher that the ordinary demands of school life cannot quite be met. I can only do it if I feel myself omnipotent. Magic helps me to give up the sense of worthlessness and helps me to overcome.

A boy from the Philippines writes:

I ate my breakfast in Saturn; I ate my lunch in Jupiter; I ate my dinner in the moon. I can run 50 miles per second. I am born in a star. The moon is made of Swiss cheese and I have a hundred legs. My coat is made of gold; I am one million years old; I ate a mouse for a snack.

It is as if, at the end, suddenly he becomes smaller again and sees his true size.

A black child:

The principal eats flesh. Miss Ekstein is a big wart. I have a '97 Corvette. Mr. Hill is a queer. Dolly Parton has a small breast. Kareem Abdul Jabbar is short. I killed the United States twice. Ronald Reagan ate his momma.

We can feel humor, but also we realize that in the mind there is a jungle of unrest where the ethnic problem makes us feel we want a world in which America is not simply a melting pot. I would much rather think like the Canadians about it, and think that America would become a mosaic where they are united perhaps by one language and by one government but where none give up their culture and heritage, the mother tongue.

The reader can see that behind every lie there is truth. The truth is that these children live in a world of rage. Those who share their world are also enraged. How can the teacher make use of these truths as she reads between the lines?

Another black child, a girl:

I live in a mouse hole. I ate a nail. I drank black paint. Ten balloons made me float up in the sky. I got married when I was 12. I am a cheerleader for the football team. I ate a whale. I am dirty rich. I ate a thousand jelly beans. I read a hundred books in one minute. My mother is Diana Ross.

A Hispanic child:

I hate horses, unicorns, and puppies. I love eating fish. I hate doing spelling. President Reagan is so cute. I hate chewing gum. I love watching cartoons. I live in a flea. I have the stupidest sister in the world. I hate Miss Ekstein. I hate having pets in my house. I murdered 400 people. I love my neighbor. I hate girls. I swam in the middle of the Pacific Ocean. I don't know how to swim. I hate teachers. I live in Arizona. I hate Miss Ekstein.

The relationship of these children to parents, government, community, and to their teacher becomes clear. We get a vivid picture of the problem the teacher has in getting together with such children and in turning that marginal adjustment into a possibility for learning, change, and education.

The fairy tales follow in a vein much more complicated than the first task. One child who speaks English and Spanish writes:

Once upon a time I was walking in the woods. I found a silver rock. I caught it and it was very soft. When I rubbed it, something strange happened. I was suddenly on another world where everything was made of plastic. There were flowers on the sides and a river in the middle. The ground was all grass and the sky was red and yellow. Then I liked the flowers that were there so much that I cut one. Then I felt that the flower was made of plastic. Then I walked and walked. I was very scared. Then a voice told me, "You cut one of my flowers. You should have to die."

(Instantly we think of *Beauty and the Beast*.)

Then I said, "I'm sorry." And he said, "Well, I'll just not let you go to your world." And I said, "But what am I going to eat and sleep? I'm not going to play with my friends and not go to school to learn." Then he said, "You'll have all that. But what does school mean?" Then I explained and told him that school was a place where we go to learn math and spelling. Then he said, "What is math and spelling?" Then I explained what math and spelling was and I started to cry because I'll never see my family again.

One wonders whether she describes relationships to parents. Does she describe parents who really do not endorse education, who have doubts about the school?

Then I remembered about the rock and there in my hands was the rock. Then I asked the man, "Where are you? Where are you?" Then he answered, "What do you want?" Then I said, "What's your name?" Then he said, "My name is the Great Creature." Then I said, "Please let me go." And he said, "No, never." He said it so angrily that I threw the silver rock because I got very scared. Then he went away and the rock talked to me and told me, "Tell me a wish and it will come true." Then I said, "Who are you?"

One can see all the doubt in the relationship. She wants to find out who makes these promises and who threatens.

"Don't ask me who I am, just tell me a wish of yours and it will come true."

You see the struggle? One says, you have to find out about me if you want magic wishes. The other says, you do not know my identity.

Then the Great Creature asked me, "Who are you talking to?" And I said, "No, I am not talking to nobody." Then he went away and I said to the rock, "Are you hearing me?" And the rock said, "Yes." Then I told the rock I wish I could go to Earth to my family. And suddenly I was at home. Then I told my family about it.

It's an interesting encounter, like a dream where you do not quite know whether she describes parental figures, the relationship to school, the tension she has as she moves back and forth between the school that will teach and the home that means security. She tries to find out about a new life and finds the flower, as she slowly moves toward preadolescence, moves into puberty. On the one hand, she knows too much, wants to know less. On the other hand, she wants to know everything and has someone who says to her, "You are not allowed to find out. It is as if her own taboo says to her, the things you want to know about adulthood you should not find out when you want to restore the unity with the family. Enlightenment is dangerous. She says, "But I want to go to school, I want to be enlightened." Then she uses magic, because her struggle between enlightenment and the wish for an infantile adjustment, the wish for home, succeeds. Think about *Beauty and the Beast* and about Dorothy in *The Wizard of Oz*.

Here is another story, from a Hispanic girl who had a poor relationship with her critical mother, a good relationship with her father, and who tries very hard to please the teacher.

> Once upon a time there was a little girl named Lupita [her own name]. She was very poor. She lived with her father and two brothers. She lived in the woods. Once me and my little brother went for a walk.

Hansel and Gretel come to mind.

> We went past the woods. It was getting dark but we did not know what way to go home. We wanted to go home but we did not know the way home. Then it became very dark and I began to cry. My little brother said to me, "Don't cry. We will get home." In the morning we tried to get home but we could not find the way home. So we walked and walked but we could not find our way home. But one day we saw something shine. I saw something. It was a ring. I said to my little brother, "Come here." So he came running. He said, "What is it?" "I found a ring." He said, "Good. Then we can sell it and then we can eat."

He was more realistic and practical than the little girl, because little girls do different things with rings.

> I said, "Yes, but who can we sell it to?" "I don't know." So we began to walk and saw an old man and we said, "Do you want to buy this ring?" The old man said, "I will trade this lamp." So we gave the ring to the old man and he gave us the lamp. One day I

was scrubbing the lamp and I saw a big man come out of it. I was very scared.

And now, of course, we instantly think of the genie in the bottle.

The man said, "You may wish any time." So I said, "I wish to go home." And so I was very happy to see my mother and my father and my big brother. We were all happy. We said we had a lot of food, a big house with a swimming pool and we lived happily ever after.

The poor child goes, as it were, in the woods, moves away from the home, plays with the idea that a new life is coming, that she can grow up fast. But as she tries to emancipate herself and separate herself from the home, anxiety mounts and she wants to be a little girl again.

The material is unlimited. During my career as an educator and in my earlier years, I collected autobiographies of young people, adolescents, many of them in the psychoanalytic literature. Among these stories is the one of a 14-year-old boy I happened to know well. I found his story, written in German, saved among my papers and translated it into English. It loses something in the translation, but here it is:

Perspective of a Gas Lantern

Do you know that gas lantern that stands in the middle of a crooked lane and throws its dim light on the uneven cobblestones during the night? Surely you know it. You might object and say that many such gas lanterns exist in many a crooked alley. But my observations are meant for all of them. Now, this gas lantern stands here opposite a small food store. On its right, about 10 meters away, is a small, plain shop for coal and firewood. And on its left side is a large horse stable. All other buildings are monstrous, grey apartment buildings, *Zinskasernen,* hardly worth mentioning. Always, day after day, year after year, *my* gas lantern sees this environment and cannot remember ever having seen anything else. It doesn't know how long it has lived, how it came here. But then, what else are we to expect? It's simply a gas lantern.

I would imagine that the boy loved the gas lantern and projected his own thoughts into it. He didn't know how long the gas lantern was there, what its past was, and, of course, I could not help but see that the lantern that gives light, and that stands there at the corner where he lives, was a kind of transitional object, stood for a parent because there was light. The gas lantern sort of watched out for him, something that was very important to him, an object around which he could weave his own fantasies. Robert Waelder (1933) spoke about the nature of play, which weaves fantasies around external objects. That gas lantern might have been the substitute for a mother; it was perhaps also at times the reliable and protecting father. The story goes on:

> Nevertheless, in spite of this, it knows many other things and, could it but speak to us, it could tell us a great deal. Unfortunately, it cannot speak but only feel. The other day, as I stood under its gloomy light, I felt all of that, as if the gas lantern had whispered it all into my ear. And now I want to relate to you these thoughts of a gas lantern.

Rather, these were the thoughts the little boy had projected onto the gas lantern in order to say something about his inner world, disguised in such a way that the teacher at the high school should measure him by his capacity to tell a story, not use the story in order to really understand him.

> In its ostensibly monotonous life, it has experienced many things. For the observer though, it seems that the lantern sleeps all day and that only the man in the white smock who comes in the evening, when darkness breaks in, wakes it up and brings it to life.

(These lanterns couldn't be turned on mechanically; someone came in the evening to turn them on and in the morning to turn them off.) This is as it is in the life of a child who goes to bed in the evening and is awakened in the morning, just the opposite from the gas lantern's routine.

> In reality it was always awake, the gas lantern, and thought constantly. It saw the lives of generations hurry along and pass

away. It saw little boys and girls shoot marbles at its feet and drive loops.

And how well I can see that little boy playing in that street.

It saw poor proletarian schoolchildren with their school satchels hurry to school. It saw hollow-cheeked darlings who visited the lantern from time to time, crawling up its iron body, and saw them grow taller and taller.

And now I realize, of course, knowing that little boy, that he became a person who had a social conscience. He could not think anymore just about marble shooting and climbing the gas lantern. He saw hungry children, and as he saw them, he could not help but identify with them.

The lantern saw how the young people met each other in the evening in the glimmer of its light and how they spent happy hours there. The lantern also saw a great deal of sadness. It could recall how lines of women and undernourished children stood in front of the small food market and coal shop and how one of them broke down and died, killed by hunger and cold.

His remembrance of the First World War.

It listened to the crying of the hungry and sick people. Oh, yes, don't you remember how out of pain for many years that lamp was not even lighted? There came again better days, and life proceeded once more on its normal course, its own life cycle. But even then the lantern saw a great deal of sadness. Many of the beloved ones grew old and grey, and finally they were carried to the graveyard as they passed away. Instead, there came many little children, which the lantern began to love. That went on until a great change came into the gas lantern's life, which it could not explain to itself until this very day. Its quiet neighbor, the old shaky house, was torn down, and a big and beautiful one was put in its place; the stables were restored, but instead of horses, there came out of the stables black, smoking monsters, automobiles.

All that the lantern couldn't grasp, but things got even more confusing. One day some men came with a ladder and began to work on the gas lantern. It believed it was going to get a new filament, a new mantle, but something entirely different happened. When the evening came it shined much more fully, and instead of a filament or mantle it had a lightbulb. All that made it feel very good. It did not miss its old, grouchy head but preferred the new, brilliant one. But one thing saddened it.

The children no longer came. Often, it sees the children marching by in groups, singing happily. But they don't want to play any longer in the street. Endlessly does the electric lamp look down at all that's new and unaccustomed. But, actually, as parents should, it likes it better when the children of which it was so fond jubilantly sing a song for the it.

"With us strides the modern time. . . ."
"*Mit uns zieht die neue Zeit. . . .*"
And they go singing,
"When we stride side by side,
And when we sing the songs of old,
We feel we must succeed.
With us strides the new time,
With us marches modern times."

Of course, the reader will realize this 14-year-old boy was now in the midst of adolescence, had joined the youth movement full of hope.

As a young man he came to America, and one day when he had become a father, a little 7-year-old girl continued the tradition of making up fairy tales. She was to write about Thanksgiving as we celebrated that holiday. She wrote:

There were some good men and women in England, but the king did not let them pray as they wanted to. They could not be free. The soldiers wanted to kill them or put them into prison, so they escaped and went to Holland. In Holland, they were free but they could not talk English and that made them unhappy. Therefore, they left and they came straight to Topeka and lived there happily ever after.

The history of the Puritans and her father's immigration merged into one. I think by now you must have guessed who the young man is and who the coauthor of that young, now older, man is, and why I had to say she and I wrote this chapter together. We still believe in magic; we know fairy tales will not disappear, and our hope is America, soon to be again a place for children who are loved and who are our future.

REFERENCES

Ekstein, R. (1966). *Children of Time and Space, of Action and Impulse.* New York: Appleton-Century-Crofts.

———— (1974). Clinical considerations concerning the expansion of language space from the autistic to the interpersonal. *Reiss-Davis Clinic Bulletin* 11:125–135.

Ekstein, R., and Friedman, S. W. (1983). The function of acting out, play action and play acting in the psychotherapeutic process. In *The Psychiatric Treatment of Adolescents,* ed. A. H. Esman, pp. 143–199.

Erikson, E. H. (1940). Studies in the interpretation of play. *Genetic Psychology Monographs* 22: 557–671.

———— (1968). *Identity, Youth and Crisis.* New York: Norton.

Sterba, R. (1948). On Hallowe'en. *American Imago* 5:213–224.

Waelder, R. (1933). The psychoanalytic theory of play. *Psychoanalytic Quarterly* 2:208–224.

A Dialogue between Two Giants in the Field of Child Mental Health

INTRODUCTION TO PART VIII

In this final chapter of Volume 1 of the *Handbook,* the reader is privy to the musings of two internationally known child analysts in this excerpt of a conversation that occurred between Rudolf Ekstein, the former director of the Psychosis Project at Reiss-Davis and Bruno Bettelheim, a former senior psychoanalytic supervisor and instructor at Reiss-Davis. This conversation focuses on the linking of past and present psychoanalytic theory. The discussion explores the genesis of the psychoanalytic method and traces its migration to the American stage, which has served as fertile soil for redefining psychodynamic processes. It is a rare glimpse into the minds of two giants in the field of child mental health.

22

A Tribute to Meaning: A Conversation between Bruno Bettelheim and Rudolf Ekstein

For the final years of Bruno Bettelheim's life, he was a consultant in Los Angeles at the Reiss-Davis Child Study Center, and through his weekly staff seminars provided insight, direction, and hope. Bruno Bettelheim was caught between two worlds. Born in Austria in 1903, he matured in the rich intellectual environment of Vienna. In the world of artists like Gustav Klimt, Egon Schiele, and Oskar Kokoschka, and writers like Arthur Schnitzler, Bettelheim participated in an efflorescence of thought centered on describing and accounting for the inward experience of modern individuals. He was trained in the original circle of adherents to Freud, all of whom were exploring the internal world of neurotics and hysterics, and applying their interpretations to a general theory of consciousness that was radically new. Their notion that the world was overdetermined by structures within consciousness that were beyond the total control of individuals was shocking to the Victorian bourgeois "enlightened" hegemony in Europe. Beginning in 1933, the loose threads on the borders of this European tapestry pulled apart. Four years later Bettelheim found himself in a Nazi concentration camp. He was redeemed from certain death through the personal intervention of Eleanor Roosevelt. Forced to come to the United States in 1939, after spending 2 years facing the horrors of the concentration camp, Bettelheim always maintained a critical distance from the American culture that had rescued him.

He found American culture superficial—fixated on a surface of material demands and expectations. America understood only eros—desire, sex, immediate gratification—symbolized by the predominant images of half-starved, half-naked nubile women that decorate the American advertising landscape. Thanatos—the death drive, the instinctive drive at mastery and perfection without recognition of the limits of human dignity—was repressed by a modern nation that had no connection with the deep wounds of European history. Like a pubescent boy, America wanted only to affirm its invincibility.

Bettelheim insistently probed the questions of human identity—Who am I? and What can I do with my life?—in a variety of written works beginning with his influential study *Individual and Mass Behaviour in Extreme Situations* (1943). His first work in the United States was deeply immersed in the psychological implications of living in a world where Auschwitz had become a reality. Bettelheim is best known for his work with severely disturbed children at his Orthogenic School in Chicago. He applied his findings to the relationship between the parent and child in the modern family situation. *Love Is Not Enough* (1950) explores the nature of parental authority derived from work at the Orthogenic School and forges a series of principles on the study and education of "normal" children. His most famous work, *The Uses of Enchantment* (1976), discusses the psychosocial significance of fairy tales by arguing that they are repositories of universal human dilemmas. Again and again in his books and interviews, Bettelheim urges that we must continue to understand human consciousness as necessarily caught between antagonistic forces—id and superego, eros and thanatos, past memories and present possibilities. In a sense, Bettelheim's existential experience of being caught in the death throes of European civilization and being thrust violently into the dithyrambic convulsions of modern American culture was the dilemma that permeated his life work. On January 10, 1990, several weeks before he died, Bettelheim met with his countryman and close friend for almost 40 years, Rudolf Ekstein. The taped meeting has been excerpted by Dr. Scott May, a Los Angeles psychotherapist.

IN WHICH LANGUAGE SHALL I SPEAK TO YOU?

Ekstein: I would often come to the University of Chicago's Orthogenic School, a residential treatment institution for severely disturbed children, where Bettelheim worked. I had been in his private home with his family, I had been in his office, but at some point I realized that I had never been allowed inside the hospital. I always saw the children outside.

There is an interesting door at the Orthogenic School. Nobody can get in from the outside. The guests are welcome in the office, but they cannot get into the hospital. This door operates in such a way that it cannot be locked from inside. If the children want to run away, they can run away. They are not in a prison.

Suddenly, it became clear to me. Bruno once went into an organization where he could get in from outside, but he couldn't get out. I speak here about concentration camps.

And when he came to America, Bruno thought, "I will now create a world where these sick children will not be destroyed by outside trauma." The parents had to trust that he would help these children and give them a safe haven.

Bruno turned these children's trauma around, which is perhaps the greatest contribution he made to psychoanalysis and psychology.

Bettelheim: What I tried to do in my work was to use all of what I learned from Freud, and from Anna Freud, about human dignity and respect for the human being, even the mentally deranged ones.

I felt very strongly that all strange behavior must have good reasons in the eyes of the person who behaves with it. I believe, with Freud, that a man's improvement comes through understanding.

E: I sometimes ask myself what love is. I feel loved if I am understood. And I love another person if I understand them.

B: Yes, but love is not enough. Authority is also important. When I say that love is not enough, I mean that love can be very selfish, very self-centered; it can make demands. Empathy and understanding are most important. Love will then come all by itself.

E: Whenever I teach in Salzburg, I find a poster in the waiting room where patients sit, which says in German, "Tell me, in which language shall I speak to you?"

In which language do I speak to someone who is a Catholic, an orthodox Jew, a revolutionary, a businessman?

It is the patient who determines what he wants to talk about and how he wants to talk about it. And if I can lift myself into his language, it will dictate in which way I must speak in order to be understood.

In the old days, in the Austrian monarchy, we announced that German was the "first language." The other languages—Serbian Croatic, Czech, Hungarian—did not count.

B: And that was the undoing of the monarchy.

E: They should have said, "If you want to go to Prague, speak Czech." This lack of understanding, of empathy, heralded the breakdown of the monarchy. If all of us insist on having our own private language, it may very well mean the breakdown of psychoanalysis as well.

THE BIRTH OF CULTURE

B: Vienna's intellectual culture at the turn of the century had a great deal to do with the decline of the Austrian monarchy.

After the battle of Königgrätz in 1866, which Austria lost to Prussia, Berlin became the new capital of the German Reich. Though in the period that preceded Königgrätz was externally directed and politically active; there followed in Austria a period of internalization, a withdrawal into the psyche. This movement produced writers like Arthur Schnitzler, whom Freud named his alter ego because he wrote novels and plays full of psychological insight—ideas that Freud had worked out with great difficulty through work with his patients. Schnitzler was a doctor by training but gave up medicine to write literature.

This concentration on the inner, hidden world of man could also be seen in the art of Gustav Klimt, Egon Schiele, and Oskar Kokoschka. This movement attempted to deflate the importance of the external, and its participants did not only see themselves merely as healers but as people who could renew a world and lead it out of the Middle Ages.

B: Psychoanalysis was seen by its practitioners to be much broader than just working with individual psyches: more than anything, it was seen as a humanistic movement.

In the beginning, Freud was looking for justification or corroboration of his theories in the field of art and literature. Some of his germinal papers, such as his papers on Leonardo da Vinci, Michelangelo, and Dostoyevsky were efforts to show the application of psychoanalysis to other artistic and intellectual fields.

Though Freud had a certain skepticism about the effectiveness of psychoanalytic therapy, he never had any doubt that psychoanalysis would lead to a deeper understanding of the human psyche and human intellectual life.

FREUD, AMERICA, AND THE DENIAL OF DEATH

E: I wonder sometimes what people in America do with their free time, whether they are psychiatrists, social workers, psychologists, or analysts. In America, it is as if the computer is more important than a book that is 400 years old.

Bruno often phones me and asks, "What are you doing right now?" It's sort of a humorous encounter between us. He will say, "If you live long enough, in order to catch up with me, you must write four more books." And I respond, "I already sent one manuscript away, so now it is only three books." And he replies, "Yes, but I also sent one away. It's still four."

We write and we engage in intense intellectual exercise not merely because we are old men. We have always been occupied in this manner.

In Vienna, I studied linguistics and psychology on the side. And today on my desk there are a number of Freud's letters which he wrote to someone between 1910 and 1936. I am now reading these letters to see if I can translate them into English. I want to find out what happened between 1910 and 1936 in the mind of Freud as reflected in these letters.

In some ways, this endeavor has no pragmatic value. But there will be some Bruno Bettelheims who will read my work when I am finished.

We never gave up this kind of intense interest, which is a part of the Viennese culture and, of course, part of Freud's legacy.

In 1909, Freud came to America, but he was very disappointed. He thought it was a superficial society, much too interested in external success—bigger buildings, more money. If one looks at the America of today, was he right or was he wrong?

B: Though psychoanalysis has many adherents in America, I don't know the degree to which it really benefits psychoanalysis as an intellectual discipline. In America, there is a desire to better oneself, to improve oneself, rather than to understand oneself. Understanding might be disappointing, depressing even. But Freud was interested in understanding the inner world of man.

Freud feared that psychoanalysis in the U.S. would be superficially accepted without really being understood. And some of his fears have turned out to be valid. Psychology in the United States is pragmatic and experimental, but not introspective.

The American critic and fiction writer Lionel Trilling certainly understood psychoanalysis very deeply. He, too, was very critical of the superficial way in which he believed that, particularly, the liberal element in the United States accepted psychoanalysis without really accepting, for example, the death tendency, which is so very important in Freud's thought. To achieve a dynamic system one needs two opposing forces: the libido, or life drive, on the one hand, and the death tendency on the other.

Death is something that is denied in American culture. People don't die, they "pass on," or they "depart." They don't die. Yet, it is death, in many ways, which gives life its deepest meaning.

Freud was preoccupied with death all his life. The omnipresence of our mortality was part of the Viennese culture. In the middle of life we were surrounded by death: the crown prince, for example, committed suicide after he committed murder right after sex. This close connection between death and sex was proscribed in the culture of Vienna.

American culture, on the other hand, is much more vital, much more interested in life.

E: In Vienna, there is a holiday called All Souls' Day. On that day, the Viennese go to the graves of their loved ones and bring them flowers and other gifts.

We have no All Souls' Day in America. We have the reverse: Halloween. In Austria, the living go to the dead and try to appease them. In America, young people disguised as witches, devils, or skeletons come knocking on doors to ask for gifts.

The Austrians say, "Honor the dead." But America says, "We are the living, and we ask you old people for something." One culture goes to the grave to give and another goes to the house to ask for something.

I remember one of the first phrases I learned when I arrived in America at the end of 1938: "Go west, young man."

We go west and west, like adolescents, still leaving the original home. Yet, there comes a point where we cannot go west anymore, and we must settle. When we finally come to the point where we say we are settled, we can then begin to wonder, "Who am I? What can I do with my life?" This question of identity was no problem for Bruno and me in Vienna. We knew who we were. We always knew who we were. Even in the days when we were seen as dirty Jews.

Today, many people in America in psychiatric, psychological circles say that psychoanalysis is outmoded. It is not outmoded. It is something for which this culture is not yet ready, in spite of the fact that the big cities are full of analysts who have a lot of patients. In order to make psychoanalysis into a cultural influence, we have to get America to the point where we don't just admire the invading generals who take over little islands. America must become a nation in the way we sometimes referred to Vienna: a culture of poets and thinkers.

THE ETERNAL BATTLE BETWEEN EROS AND THANATOS

B: Each fairy tale speaks a common language, not necessarily of childhood, but of imagination and of basic human problems. In fairy tales, the hero or heroine feels rejected, misunderstood, or considers himself a dummy. These are universal human problems. We are all afraid we are dummies. We are all afraid we are not loved and are not lovable. This is an anxiety that is so universal that practically all fairy tales, in one way or another, address themselves to this problem. Whether it is Cinderella, who is misunderstood and mistreated, or Hansel and Gretel, who get lost in the forest and meet a child-eating witch, they all deal with universal anxieties.

E: I recently saw the movie *The Little Mermaid* and was deeply impressed by it because it follows Hans Christian Andersen—except at the end.

The ending of *The Little Mermaid* goes like this: She gets the prince, and she can talk, and she has no fish body. In Hans Christian Andersen, however, the mermaid must go back under the sea, and the prince must give her up forever. They cannot be with each other. Hans Christian Andersen's story ends in sadness. It is as if the underworld wins.

The Disney version changes it around because it must have a happy ending. Those of us who come from Europe believe one cannot understand life if one is tied to a happy ending.

Europeans know there is a terrible struggle between eros and thanatos. The idea that there must always be a happy ending belongs to the American culture. On the one hand, I envy the Americans for their youthful optimism, but on the other hand, I know it is self-deception.

B: I hope that people will think much more seriously about the destructive tendencies in man: where they come from, what can be done about them, how we can master them—so that, to quote Freud, in the eternal battle between eros and thanatos, eros will win out, at least for the time being. However, in the end thanatos always wins out. If we take this seriously, life will become much more meaningful to us.

Credits

The editors gratefully acknowledge permission to reprint the following:

"One Way to Build a Clinically Relevant Baby," by D. N. Stern, in *Infant Mental Health Journal,* vol. 15 (1), pp. 9–25. Copyright © 1991 by the Michigan Association of Mental Health. Used by permission.

Excerpts from "Ego Distortion in Terms of True and False Self," "The Use of an Object and Relating through Identification," and "Aggression in Relation to Emotional Development," by D. W. Winnicott, in *Collected Papers: From Pediatrics through Psychoanalysis.* Copyright © 1975 by Hogarth Press and Basic Books. Used by permission of Hogarth Press, Basic Books, and The Winnicott Trust.

Excerpts from "Differentiation of the Psychotic from the Non-Psychotic Personalities," by W. Bion, in *International Journal of Psycho-Analysis,* vol. 38, pp. 266–275. Copyright © 1957 by the Institute of Psycho-Analysis. Used by permission of the Institute of Psycho-Analysis.

Excerpts from *Women Hating,* by A. Dworkin. Copyright © 1974 by Andrea Dworkin. Used by permission of Dutton Signet, a Division of Penguin Books USA Inc.

Subject Index